MEL EISMAN

DESIGN TO COST

NEW DIMENSIONS IN ENGINEERING

Editor
RODNEY D. STEWART

JACK V. MICHAELS, PE, CVS
WILLIAM P. WOOD, CVS

Design to Cost

DESIGN TO COST

JACK V. MICHAELS, PE, CVS
WILLIAM P. WOOD, CVS

WILEY

A Wiley-Interscience Publication

JOHN WILEY & SONS

New York • Chichester • Brisbane • Toronto • Singapore

Library of Congress Cataloging in Publication Data:

Michaels, Jack V.
    Design to cost / Jack V. Michaels, William P. Wood.
        p.   cm.

    "A Wiley-Interscience publication."
    Includes bibliographies and index.

    ISBN 0-471-60900-5
    1. Costs, Industrial.   2. Cost control.   3. Engineering design.
I. Michaels, Jack V., 1920-   . II. Wood, William P., 1927-   . III. Title.
TS167.M53   1989
658.1'552—dc19   88-31936
                                                                 CIP

Printed in the United States of America

10 9 8 7 6 5 4 3 2 1

To Esther Michaels and Verna Wood

CONTENTS

FOREWORD

This is the first in a series of books entitled *New Dimensions in Engineering,* a series to be published during forthcoming years by John Wiley & Sons, Inc. to recognize, document, and instruct in important emerging engineering disciplines that have resulted from large, multidisciplinary, high-technology projects, processes, products, and services. It is fitting that this first book address the subject of design-to-cost because it sets the tone for books to follow on a wide range of engineering disciplines, including logistics, the new quality technology, induced reliability, system safety, maintainability, automated configuration engineering, testing, distributed simulation, advanced decision systems and fractals in engineering, and computer-aided engineering in an era of shrinking budgets and increasing costs. Designing to cost encompasses the emerging practice of achieving capabilities based on available funds rather than vice versa. This practice will pervade the new engineering dimensions.

Messrs. Michaels and Wood have done an excellent job of capturing the fundamentals of planning, designing, and carrying out activities or producing outputs within given financial constraints. They have folded into this book all the necessary tools, techniques, and information needed to successfully set and adhere to cost goals. They show how the disciplines of value engineering, cost estimating, and cost control are used to establish realistic cost goals and then to carry out projects without exceeding these preestablished targets. They touch on management methods, procurement techniques, and engineering approaches required to live within a budget, and they describe how to set basic requirements and specifications based on available resources. Most importantly, they provide true-to-life examples of projects and services that have become affordable through the application of systematic methodologies, and they give examples of tools and methods structured specifically to perform the design-to-cost task.

We predict that this new dimension in engineering practice will grow and expand in future years as more is learned about it and that engineering professionals will find themselves increasingly engaged in the use of design-to-cost principles. As you read and apply these principles, born of an age where increasingly complex and demanding engineering projects abound, you will find new avenues for fruitful utilization of scarce resources and will be able to bring your company, firm, or project into new realms of profitability. Careful adherence to the suggestions of this book are vital links to achieving engineering excellence at reasonable cost. We commend this text to you as a classic in a difficult but important engineering dimension.

RODNEY D. STEWART

Series Editor

PREFACE

In the broadest context, design to cost is a tool used to enhance the afford-ability of products, systems, or services over their useful lifetime or, in short, their life cycle. The concept of life-cycle cost, which encompasses the acquisition, operation, and support of products or systems, is often associ-ated with the military and then is envisioned in terms of millions or even billions of dollars expended over the useful life of a weapon system.

Life-cycle cost is, in fact, the dominant economic factor in all walks of life. Life-cycle cost is the ultimate measure of affordability because it is what users pay in the aggregate for the function they desire from the product, system, or service they purchase. If life-cycle cost is equal to or less than its functional worth to the user and is within the user's ability to pay, then the item is affordable in the economic sense.

The formal practice of design to cost as a multidisciplinary effort has its roots in the broad production base of the military–industry complex. World Wars I and II were won by highly motivated and well-trained troops sup-ported by this production base and by an abundance of supplies. Cost was secondary to victory with survival of a nation at stake.

Subsequent changes in priorities and restrictive budgets led to intense competition in the military marketplace and spawned a cost-sensitive culture in both government and industry with an intense interest in design to cost. The original version of this book covered the practices developed over many years by a major aerospace contractor.

The private sector of the economy has come to realize, under similar economic pressure, that competitiveness with excellence is essential to both survival and growth. Ensuring affordable quality and making design con-verge on cost rather than allowing cost to converge on design is the essence of design to cost.

The need persists for affordability in the defense establishment, and much of this book's original emphasis has been retained. It has been adapted, however, to serve the needs of a broad spectrum of industrial and commer-cial ventures that are relying increasingly on high technology and facing ever-increasing competition from abroad as well as at home.

  This book can also serve as a textbook for a highly motivational course at both the graduate or undergraduate level. The subject matter is reinforced with case studies and exercises drawn from real-life experiences in design to cost. The book can thus be used profitably by students with a wide range of interests, by coalescing their previous learning experiences into the multidisciplinary approach essential to affordability known as design to cost.

Jack V. Michaels
William P. Wood

Orlando, Florida
May 1989

ACKNOWLEDGMENTS

This book is the beneficiary of the pioneering effort of many colleagues, whom the authors recognize for their contributions to the state of the art and thank for their encouragement, guidance, and suggestions regarding this work. The authors are particularly grateful to the Martin Marietta Corporation for so graciously providing the extensive source material used in the book.

J.V.M.
W.P.W.

1
INTRODUCTION

The United States is treading in new economic waters. Its share of the world market has dwindled from about 40 percent to less than 20 percent in a matter of three decades. It is conceivable that the nation might enter still another phase where it could be dependent on offshore sources for defense hardware because of the shrinking defense budget and the high cost of doing business with American companies.

By the year 2000, major high-technology enterprise will be dominated by those organizations that understand affordability and practice design to cost. Keys to success in the new marketplace will be technical supremacy, business acumen, integrity, and affordability, all of which add up to competitiveness with excellence.

The essence of design to cost, the subject of this book, is making design converge on cost instead of allowing cost to converge on design. Design to cost is a management concept that mandates cost success in terms of producing products or systems at costs deemed to be affordable from the perspective of customers. This is similar to mission success from the perspective of the military and its suppliers.

In design to cost, cost is elevated to the same level of concern as performance and schedule, from the moment the new product or service is conceived through its useful lifetime. Realistic cost goals are established from early trades with performance and schedule, but not at the expense of the basic function the product or service is to provide, and never at the expense of quality.

Early attempts at design to cost were limited to building systems within specific targets for the recurring cost of hardware. This is now considered as only one of the elements of design to cost and is referred to as "design to unit production cost" (DTUPC). These attempts were characterized by many iterations of redesign until unit cost goals were realized. Extensive nonrecurring expenditures were justified in terms of securing a competitive edge by contractors and of reducing recurring out-year expenditures on hardware procurement by customers.

1

In addition, there was not too much concern expressed in earlier days for ownership cost, which is primarily in the domain of the user. It is now recognized universally that ownership cost consumes the largest portion of the overall life-cycle cost, and ownership cost goals, usually expressed in terms of "design to operation and support cost" (DTOSC), appear as frequently as DTUPC goals. Taken together, R & D cost, DTUPC and DTOSC constitute "design to life-cycle cost" or (DTLCC). The terms DTLCC and "design to cost" are synonymous.

Design to cost is now concerned with all elements of cost from the conceptual phase until the retirement of a product, system, or service and attempts to strike the optimal balance of acquisition cost and ownership cost. The key message of this book is "do the job right the first time, and continue to do it right," so that the ultimate in economy may be realized. This message is addressed to designers, business people, workers, managers, producers, and customers.

1.1 COMPETITIVENESS WITH EXCELLENCE

The inability of the United States to compete in the international marketplace has, in recent years, been the subject of much serious thought and discussion. Numerous articles and forums have been devoted to the subject, all with the central theme that for the United States to regain its dominant position as world leader, it must regain its lost productivity, attention to quality, and competitiveness (1).

Proffered solutions are generally global in nature because of the dimensions of the problem. Included are revisions in federal tax policy to stimulate investment in technology, changes in national priorities to reduce the budget deficit, and assistance to debtor nations to increase worldwide demand.

There have been, however, more specific suggestions for improving productivity through means such as increased worker involvement in manufacturing innovation and decision-making, and increased emphasis on product and process technology, generally in the context of reaping the benefits of innovations such as automation and the just-in-time (JIT) strategies.

Several manufacturing approaches have emerged in concert with these suggestions notably flexible manufacturing and manufacturing resources planning. In the aggregate, the benefits sought from the various approaches are the essence of competitiveness with excellence. Competitiveness with excellence is also a product of design to cost. However, design to cost goes the one step further by considering product functionality and affordability from the consumer's perspective of need and priority.

Affordability is the characteristic of a product with a selling price that is no greater than its functional worth and that is within the customer's ability to pay. Functional worth is the lowest cost means for providing the basic function required of the product. As a simplistic example, the functional worth of the requirement to hang a picture on a wall is the cost of a nail plus the labor to do the work.

Design to cost also examines the issue of affordability, that is, the ability to pay from the consumer's perspective of the relative priorities of other related and unrelated needs. The classic example is the early Ford motor car whose basic function was to provide all-weather, personal transportation; this was a relatively high priority, as indicated by the extant number of horses and carriages. The horse and carriage established a threshold for the worth of the basic function over its life cycle, which, considering the marketing success enjoyed by the horseless carriage, was obviously not exceeded by Ford.

1.2 CUSTOMER'S PERSPECTIVE

There is a tendency in many organizations in both the public and private sectors to be more concerned with initial investment rather than overall life-cycle cost, especially when large expenditures are involved. However, wise buyers generally recognize that the true ownership cost consists of the cost elements of the production and deployment phase and of the operation and support phase as shown in Figure 1.1.

In the illustration, cost of government furnished equipment and administration are added to hardware cost for what is called "flyaway cost." Although the expression "flyaway cost" is suggestive of the U.S. Air Force, it originated in the U.S. Army; alternative expressions with the same meaning are "rollaway cost" and "sailaway cost."

To flyaway cost is added the cost of initial spare parts and training materiel for what is called "weapon system cost." Procurement cost includes the aforementioned and also the cost of spare parts provisioning for the operation and support phase of the program. Figure 1.2 shows an alternative way to view life-cycle-cost composition that emphasizes the hardware and procurement relationships.

Life-cycle cost is essentially the sum of program peculiar research-and-development (R&D) cost, procurement cost, and operating and support cost. Depending on the complexity of the product or system and the maintenance philosophy observed, operation and support can equal or be as much as three times the procurement cost. The maintenance philosophy can range from one of "discard at failure" to repair at the organizational level, intermediate depot or main depot.

High-technology products in the private sector tend to observe the philosophy of repair at intermediate depot (service facility), with operation and support cost over the useful product lifetime being equal to about twice the purchase price. In addition, there is an interesting parallel with the military in the private sector.

Under the "wooden round" concept in the military domain, live rounds

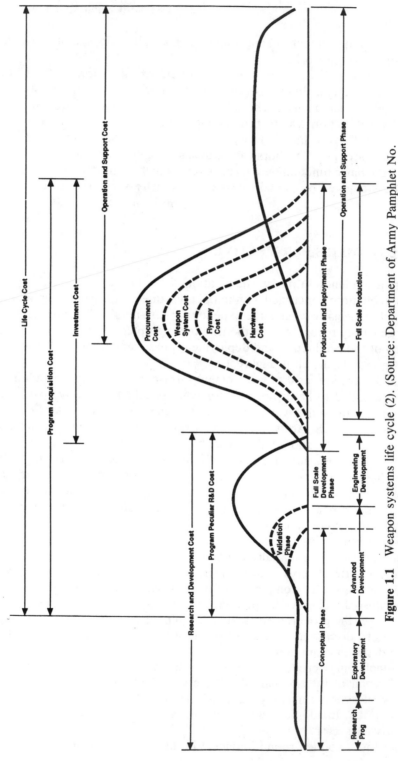

Figure 1.1 Weapon systems life cycle (2). (Source: Department of Army Pamphlet No. 11-3, *Investment Cost Guide for Army Materiel Systems*, 1976.)

4

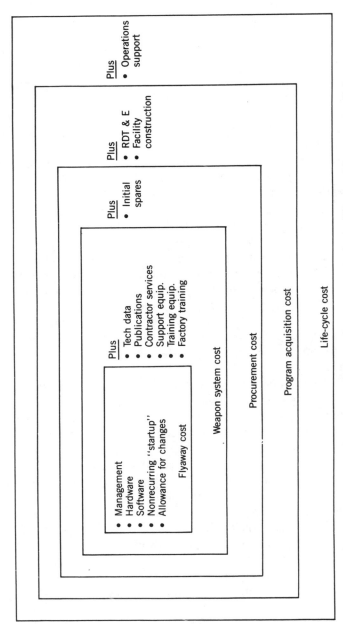

Figure 1.2 Life-cycle-cost composition (3). (Source: Defense Systems Management College, *System Engineering Management Guide*, 1982.)

of smart ammunition are stored in containers that also serve as the launch platforms. Consequently, there is zero maintenance on weapon systems from the time of delivery to the time of release. The operational strategy for wooden rounds, depending on their cost, is either to replace them periodically or to fire a predetermined number as a sample to measure the health of the remainder.

The wooden round concept prevails to some extent in the private sector with moderately priced products utilizing solid-state devices and other sealed components. Generally, it is more cost-effective to replace than repair these products. A key life-cycle cost driver in such cases is the manufacturer's warranty.

There are other important parallels to high-technology enterprises in the private sector, such as how to orient R&D to support long-term organizational goals and how to trade development and production costs to optimize profitability to the producer and affordability to the customer.

Producers are customers with regard to their suppliers, who, in turn, are customers to someone else. The customer influences price in a free marketplace. Thus, the customer's perspective on affordability and functionality pervades this book, and the theme "why design to cost" is addressed in the context of the trades customers make between initial investment at one end of the spectrum and ownership cost at the other.

The terms "customer" and "consumer" may be synonymous in the private sector, but there is sufficient difference in the public sector to warrant some consideration. There are many instances in government where the customer is not the consumer.

In the U.S. Department of Defense, for example, one military service may be designated the executive agency for developing a product or system that will be funded in part and used by other military services. The choice of executive agency is usually based on the technical capability of some command or laboratory within the particular military service.

There are obvious motivational differences. The executive agency is more interested in near-term investment, whereas the user agency is more interested in functionality and long-term operation and support cost.

Frequently, product and production decisions are biased at the low end of cost for political and financial expediency in the near term rather than based on overall performance and cost. A three-way adversarial relationship often develops between the executive agency, the user, and the contractor, inevitably causing schedule and funding problems.

A frequent result is that the user's requirements are compromised, and the user emerges from this relationship with a dim view of the producer's commitment to excellence and affordability. To some degree, this situation exists at the local government level, especially where federal assistance prevails.

This attitude is shared in the private sector, where strategies such as extended warranties are sometimes viewed as compensation for poor design and workmanship. The salient difference, however, is that the private sector is not constrained by public law or defense policy to buy at least 50 percent "American" and has demonstrated its willingness to go abroad for high-technology products.

There has been a significant trend in this direction over the past decade. This has tended to discourage U.S. manufacturers from practicing design to cost and affordability at home and to induce them to join the buying public and look overseas for the means of competition.

1.3   NATURE OF DESIGN TO COST

Design to cost can be described as a step-by-step process that is both deliberate and iterative. The essence of design to cost is captured by Figures 1.3 and 1.4, which illustrate the continuum of analytical studies and trades needed first to bound the limits of acceptable cost, schedule, and performance and then to ensure the goodness of functionality with affordability as programs progress through development, production, and delivery of end products.

The steps depicted in Figure 1.3 are concerned primarily with issues of functionality and producibility and those in Figure 1.4, with issues of functional worth and affordability. It should not be assumed, however, that

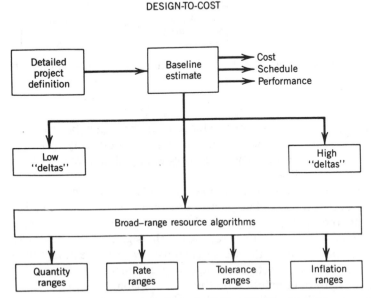

Figure 1.3   Issues of functionality and producibility (4). (Reprinted by permission of Mobile Data Services.)

DESIGN-TO-COST

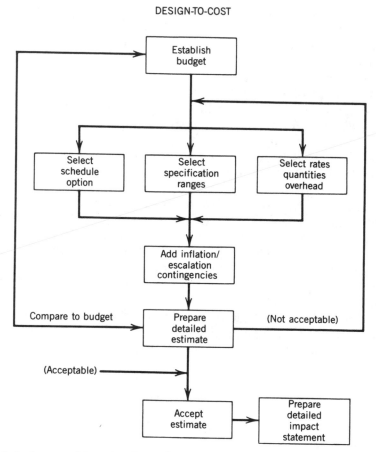

Figure 1.4 Issues of functional worth and affordability (5). (Reprinted by permission of Mobile Data Services.)

either group of steps takes precedence over the other, but rather that they should be performed on an interactive basis. Functionality should always be weighed against affordability, and affordability should always be judged in terms of functionality.

There should be no question about the additional front-end cost brought about by design to cost. The pursuit of alternative designs can add about 20 percent to the cost of design. Design to cost is a deliberate management commitment to invest in the present for the significantly greater reward of the future. Design to cost is the single most levered investment in profitability through affordability that management can make. However, it takes the utmost strength of conviction on the part of management to embrace design to cost and to adjust the way of doing business to its dictates.

Fundamentally, design to cost should be undertaken only with the conviction at all levels in the organization that it not only is here to stay but also will enjoy continued management interest and support. Above all, there should be the universal belief that it will inevitably lead to cost success. Furthermore, design to cost should be undertaken only under a system of unwavering control of configurations, responsibilities, and actions to ensure an unerring audit trail of cost experiences and the means for rewarding cost performance.

Design to cost is also called "iterative" because it is a closed-loop process performed over the life of the program starting with the up-front analysis that is so essential to establishing meaningful cost goals. The process is steadfast in its interactive approach to the tasks at hand with changing emphasis only as a function of maturation of the program.

Design to cost impacts every established practice in the classical way of doing business. The whole nature of product and process design is oriented toward an approach of pursuing alternatives with cost as the constant argument. Design is made to converge on cost rather than vice versa; only in this way can cost success become a primary measure of both organizational and personal performance.

1.4 DESIGN-TO-COST PLAN

The design-to-cost plan is the core document of design-to-cost programs. In the arena of government contracting, requests for proposal (RFP) for all major acquisitions, and many of smaller financial magnitude, should require the submittal of a design-to-cost plan as part of the contractor's proposal or shortly after contract award. The absence of such a plan in proposals is deemed as being unresponsive to the requirements for the solicitation. The inadequacy of such plans is viewed as a lack of fiscal conservatism on the part of offerors.

From the customer's perspective, therefore, the purpose of the design-to-cost plan is twofold. First, it serves in the process of source evaluation and selection. The design-to-cost plan is a statement by the prospective contractor of how design-to-cost goals would be established (absent initial goals from the customer) and the steps that would be taken to prosecute these goals and to ensure the affordability of the end product. Proposal evaluation criteria provided with RFPs place high scores on the credibility of such goals (if they are requested by the RFP to be submitted with the proposal) and the offeror's approach and commitment to affordability. Second, the design-to-cost plan serves as a management tool for use by both the customer and the contractor who is awarded the work. In this regard, the plan is placed under configuration control so that it cannot be unilaterally altered.

The plan is expected to provide complete insight into the contractor's design-to-cost organization and the delegation of responsibility, authority, and accountability. The plan is also expected to provide time-phased details on cost trade studies and other elements of up-front analysis that are vital to effective design to cost. The plan is further expected to illuminate the maintenance of audit trails starting with the allocation of cost goals to specific individuals and the subsequent tracking, reporting, and review processes.

It would appear that each component of the Department of Defense (DoD) has its own concept of how the design-to-cost plan should be organized, however, the agreement on the overall content of the plan is just about universal. There is a contract data requirements list (CDRL) accompanying the RFP. The CDRL specifies when the design-to-cost plan should be submitted initially, when it should be updated, and the distribution list and number of copies required.

The CDRL is used consistently throughout the DoD and is prepared on a form called "DD Form 1423." However, the requirements for the design-to-cost plan are spelled out on data item descriptions (DID) that vary from service to service and agency to agency. However, the DIDs are identified by code number on the appropriate DD Forms 1423 in the CDRL and thus can be accessed.

The subject matter of these DIDs is a small-scale distillation of the contents of this book. Among the rationale for the way this book is organized is the desire to facilitate the preparation of responses to the requirements of RFPs, including the requirement for a design-to-cost plan.

1.5 ORGANIZATION OF THE BOOK

Contemporary literature abounds with excellent guidance on manufacturing advances, JIT strategies, and interactive management as well as the art of cost estimating (6–8). The book devotes considerable detail to those precepts and practices that are the added dimensions of effective design to cost but within the framework of the overall design and production process so that the forest is not obscured by the trees.

Chapter 2, on getting started in design to cost, builds on the theme of management commitment to affordability as the road to profitability and details the up-front analysis needed to optimize both the affordability and profitability of the company's products. The chapter provides the step-by-step procedure that leads to setting design-to-cost goals. Although the emphasis is on the public sector, a clear parallel is drawn to industrial and commercial ventures relative to customer requirements, priorities, and budgets. The concept of making design converge on cost instead of the reverse emerges from Chapter 2 as the basic tenet of design to cost.

The objective of up-front analysis is to establish meaningful cost goals, optimize approaches, and quantify the risk inherent in their prosecution. Chapter 3 defines activities, organizational roles, and individual responsibilities for realizing these goals and mitigating risks. The need for clear enunciation of responsibility, authority, and accountability, particularly at multidisciplinary interfaces, is emphasized. Special insight is provided in specification practices, configuration and data management, schedule control, reviews, technical performance measurement, and work measurement as they apply to design to cost. Guidelines for establishing audit trails and for controlling schedules are given.

Chapters 4 considers new technology from the viewpoint of design to cost and then presents an arsenal of low-cost design practices that should be employed. The concepts of product simplification and work simplification are explored as the key elements in product uniformity and producibility. Castings and power supplies receive special emphasis because they appear in virtually all high-technology items as well as consumer products produced, and because power supplies inevitably seem to become both schedule and cost drivers. The concept of production readiness is also included in Chapter 4 because it is a natural evolution of the design process.

Chapter 5 provides similar insight into various business strategies that are supportive of low-cost production without sacrificing functionality and quality. Some emphasis is again placed on the public sector in terms of strategy for fostering competition and cost reduction such as the practices of best and final offers and industrial modernization incentives. The applicability of such strategies to industrial and commercial ventures is clarified, particularly the cost advantage of multiple sourcing and JIT procurement are illuminated. In addition, scheduling strategies, capacity planning, and inventory strategies conducive to reduced cost are addressed along with the subject of personnel motivation.

Facility in cost estimating is essential for deriving meaningful cost goals and assessing alternate designs, production processes, and business strategies. Chapter 6 not only addresses cost estimating techniques in the context of design to life-cycle cost and of design to initial acquisition support cost but also presents a philosophy for design to cost that is explored in the context of could-cost, should-cost, would-cost, and functional worth of systems, products or services. Confidence factors in cost estimates and the use of statistical techniques in estimating confidence are discussed along with the formulation used for the time value of money. Elements of cost control are included in Chapter 6 with some emphasis on the use of price indexes in making cost predictions.

Having reached this juncture, the question is now: "Where do we go from here?". The preceding chapters have described the tools for competitiveness with excellence in the marketplace. Like most tools, facility comes with practice. Many people have tried design to cost with varying degrees of success. Following a summary of its contents, each chapter provides a number of case studies and exercises based on these attempts.

Chapter 7 summarizes the book in terms of the dictates of design to cost and bounds these dictates with lessons to be learned from a program that was a notable failure and one that is enjoying notable success. The reader i urged to remember history and benefit from the experience of others, or condemned to relive it. Toward the end of benefiting from the experience of others, Chapter 7 provides an objectival summary of the book with some observations on the problems encountered in transition from development to production.

The language of design to cost contains terms, acronyms, and abbreviations with specific meanings regarding the subject. Their definitions are given in the text and repeated in Appendixes 1 and 2 for the reader's convenience. Appendix 3 lists a large number of requirements documents for readers interested in government contracting.

These readers will find interesting the discussion of the government's emphasis on design to cost by program phases, particularly the recent initiatives called "acquisition simplification" and "could-cost." These hold the promise of substantial reduction in the cost of weapon systems acquisition and ownership. In addition, Appendix 3 contains the text of a recent circular by the President's Office of Management and Budget in an attempt to promulgate the use of value engineering throughout the federal government. It will be interesting to see what kind of cost savings can be attributed to this circular over the next 10 years.

As stated earlier, Chapters 2 through 6 contain a copious quantity of case studies and exercises that are intended to amplify key points in the respective chapter and allow the reader to relate personal viewpoints to the events that are unfolded. A number of the exercises require a numerical solution, and these solutions are given in Appendix 4.

REFERENCES

1. "Can America Compete," *Business Week,* April 20, 1987.
2. Department of Army Pamphlet No. 11–3, *Investment Cost Guide for Army Materiel Systems,* 1976.
3. Defense Systems Management College, *System Engineering Management Guide,* 1982.
4–5. ALS, *Design to Cost,* Mobile Data Services, Huntsville, AL, 1988.
6. Robert H. Hayes and Steven C. Wheelright, *Restoring Our Competitive Edge, Competing through Manufacturing,* John Wiley & Sons, 1984.
7. Thomas G. Gunn, *Manufacturing for Competitive Advantage: Becoming a World Class Manufacturer,* Ballinger Publishing Company, 1987.
8. Rodney D. Stewart and Richard M. Wyska, *Cost Estimator's Reference Manual,* John Wiley & Sons, 1987.

2
GETTING STARTED

To paraphrase Confucius: "The longest and shortest trips both start with the first step." What it takes to be successful in any undertaking is to get started properly. Getting started properly in design to cost requires fundamental commitments on the part of management that result in certain overt actions taking place at the appropriate times.

Foremost is the need to dispel the notion that quality and affordability are mutually exclusive. This notion is a reflection of the long-standing approach to quality in high technology, particularly in the aerospace and defense industries, that involved numerous iterations of test, analyze, and fix. This is the first subject discussed in this chapter from the viewpoint that quality can be affordable.

A commitment to affordable quality on the part of management is necessary and can be facilitated by understanding that quality control need not be a significant cost driver. The point is also made that the marriage of affordable quality and value analysis (discussed in a subsequent section of this chapter) produces a synergistic union of affordability and quality by tailoring functionality to the needs of the user.

This commitment to affordable quality is the first of many overt actions stemming from the series of management decisions needed to ensure the success of the design-to-cost undertaking. The next section presents these decisions in the framework of the management decision profile needed to support design to cost.

The remainder of the chapter addresses the activities that management needs to support with proper emphasis to ensure product affordability and the producer's competitive posture. These activities are both the bases for economically and technically sound management decision-making and th cornerstones for successful design-to-cost programs. The order in whi they are presented, starting with the system engineering process, is es tially the order in which they should be undertaken. The amount of detail provided is sufficient to get started properly.

The system engineering process is the fabric from which successful design to cost is woven. Hence, the next section is concerned with affordability analysis as one of the stepping-stones in the path toward establishing realistic cost targets or goals. Key to the analysis is the concept of affordability. An attempt is made to impart a basic understanding of its meaning as background to the discussion of the analytical processes involved.

The first of the analytical processes addressed is cost-effectiveness analysis. Extensive details are provided on the methodology that has provided favorable results in high-technology applications. This is followed by some insight into Pareto analysis of cost drivers. Pareto analysis separates the vital few concerns from the trivial many and allows for more efficient utilization of resources.

The next section addresses the accommodation of new technology so as to minimize capital investment and to maximize return on investment. Application guidelines and some insight into how to schedule the acquisition of new technology are presented. The section also elucidates some of the promises of "Manufacturing Resources Planning II" (MRP II) and some of the requirements for its implementation.

This is followed by the section on value analysis, which is viewed as one of the effective disciplines for cost saving and, as stated earlier in this section, can provide synergistic results when applied in conjunction with affordable quality. Both value engineering techniques and the clauses encountered in government contracting are covered.

The next section is concerned with risk management, which is needed to ensure that the fruits of design-to-cost labors are not consumed by unforeseen problems. That section also discusses the importance of maintaining the right perspective on the effects of risk items and the methodology of assessing risk and estimating the potential costs in the event that risks materialize.

At this juncture, it is appropriate to introduce the subject of setting design-to-cost goals. The importance of understanding the scope of the program of interest and of paralleling the scope by the trade study process is stressed. The need to allocate goals to individuals rather than organizational entities is underscored.

Management's perception of business opportunities and return on investment provides the framework for up-front analysis that culminates in cost goals that should optimize affordability and profitability. Cost goals may be challenging, but they should be achievable given supportive and timely management decisions and the proper priority.

Following the summary of its contents, the chapter concludes with a number of case studies and exercises that are intended to amplify key points e chapter. The exercises allow the readers to relate their experiences iewpoints to the events that are unfolded in the case studies.

2.1 AFFORDABLE QUALITY

Philip B. Crosby, in his classic work, *Quality is Free,* claims that quality can be managed so that it becomes the mechanism for additional business profit. In effect what he is saying is that the "cost of quality," which is the cost of not doing work correctly the first time but repeating the work a second or even a third time, can consume 15 to 20 percent of every sale dollar. It is possible to eliminate rework, scrap, and redo and leave only the true cost of quality that can be as little as 2.5 percent of the sale dollar (1).

This section examines the bases for the foregoing hypothesis. It is appropriate to do so, however, within the context of the emphasis placed on quality by the Department of Defense (DoD) insofar as working for the DoD epitomizes high technology.

Table 2.1 gives the recent pronouncement by President Ronald Reagen's Secretary of Defense Frank Carlucci regarding the posture of the DoD on quality. Note the association of the word "quality" with the words "productivity," "competition," and "cost". Note also the shift in emphasis from relying on inspection to designing and building quality into the process and product.

TABLE 2.1 DoD Posture on Quality

Quality is absolutely vital to our defense and requires a commitment to continuous improvement by all defense personnel

A quality and productivity oriented defense industry with its underlying industrial base is the key to our ability to maintain a superior level of readiness

Sustained DoD wide emphasis and concern with respect to high quality and productivity must be an integral part of our daily activities

Quality improvement is a key to productivity improvement and must be pursued with the necessary resources to produce tangible benefits

Technology, which is one of our greatest assets, must be widely used to improve continuously the quality of defense systems, equipments, and services

Emphasis must change from relying on inspection to designing and building quality into the process and product

Quality must be a key element in competition

Acquisition strategies must include requirements for continuous improvement of quality and reduced ownership cost

Managers and personnel at all levels must take responsibility for the quality of their efforts

Competent, dedicated employees make the greatest contribution to quality and productivity and must be recognized and rewarded accordingly

Quality concepts must be ingrained throughout every organization with the proper training at each level, starting with top management

Principles of quality improvement must involve all personnel and products, including the generation of products on paper and data form

Source: Secretary of Defense Frank Carlucci, 1988.

TABLE 2.2 Quality Management Maturity Grid (2)

Measurement Categories	Stage I: Uncertainty	Stage II: Awakening	Stage III: Enlightenment	Stage IV: Wisdom	Stage V: Certainty
Management understanding and attitude	No comprehension of quality as a management tool; tend to blame quality department for "quality problems"	Recognizing that quality management may be of value but not willing to provide money or time to make it all happen	While going through quality improvement program, learn more about quality management; becoming supportive and helpful	Participating; understand absolutes of quality management; recognize their personal role in continuing emphasis	Consider quality management an essential part of company system
Quality organization status	Quality is hidden in manufacturing or engineering departments; inspection probably not part of organization; emphasis on appraisal and sorting	A stronger quality leader is appointed, but main emphasis is still on appraisal and moving the product; still part of manufacturing or other	Quality department reports to top management, all appraisal is incorporated and manager has role in management of company	Quality manager is an officer of company; effective status reporting and preventive action; involved with consumer affairs and special assignments	Quality manager on board of directors; prevention is main concern; quality is a thought leader
Problem handling	Problems are fought as they occur; no	Teams are set up to attack major problems	Corrective action communication	Problems are identified early in their	Except in the most unusual cases,

	resolution; inadequate definition; much yelling and accusations	lems; long-range solutions are not solicited	established; problems are faced openly and resolved in an orderly way	development; all functions are open to suggestion and improvement	problems are prevented
Cost of quality as percent of sales	Reported: unknown Actual: 20%	Reported: 3% Actual: 18%	Reported: 8% Actual: 12%	Reported: 6.5% Actual: 8%	Reported: 2.5% Actual: 2.5%
Quality improvement actions	No organized activities; no understanding of such activities	Trying obvious "motivational" short-range efforts	Implementation of the 14-step program with thorough understanding and establishment of each step	Continuing the 14-step program and starting; make certain	Quality improvement is a normal and continued activity
Summation of company quality posture	"We don't know why we have problems with quality"	"Is it absolutely necessary to always have problems with quality?"	"Through management commitment and quality improvement we are identifying and resolving our problems"	"Defect prevention is a routine part of our operation"	"We know why we do not have problems with quality"

Reprinted from Philip B. Crosby, *Quality Is Free*, 1979, McGraw-Hill, by permission of McGraw-Hill Book Company.

The DoD posture, in particular that quality concepts must be ingrained throughout every organization with proper training at each level starting with top management, is also the thrust of quality management maturity grid given in Table 2.2. The grid relates the five stages of management maturity to the six key measurement categories including the cost of quality as a percentage of sales.

A candid assessment by management of its own quality maturity should be among the initial steps in getting started properly in design to cost. Reference 1 provides detailed guidance on making the transition from the stage of uncertainty through awakening, enlightenment, and wisdom to the stage of certainty with the reward of the cost of quality being reduced from 20 to 2.5 percent.

In itself, the reward of increasing profit by 17.5 percent with essentially the same business base is well worth the effort. Of course, some of the additional savings could be used to reduce selling prices for competitive advantage. There is, however, a union to be had with value analysis (see Section 2.8) that will provide cost savings that can only be described as synergistic.

It is natural for designers to be performance oriented; their primary goal is to design a functional end item. This focus on performance, combined with schedule urgencies, often leads to neglect of cost. Emphasizing quality alone ignores those areas where economies can be made without sacrificing essential functionality.

However, cost reduction alone accents thrift to the exclusion of other factors such as the discernment of essential functionality. Value analysis is a more powerful and totally different approach, providing a disciplined and logical approach to reducing unnecessary product costs without sacrificing functional worth and quality. Value analysis follows a prescribed progression, a job plan that is an essential and mandatory element of the process and, when applied with the leverage of full management support, has produced savings of up to 30 percent of the total cost of complex products.

The next overt management action following the commitment to affordable quality is the concomitant commitment to the practice of value analysis, which is also called "value engineering." Employee perception of management interest from the initial onset of programs is the most effective means for ensuring the success of value engineering as well as the quality program.

2.2 MANAGEMENT DECISION PROFILE

In the contracting domain, the term "management" is meant to comprise customer management and the producer counterpart, whereas in entrepreneurial undertakings the management burden is solely the producer's. Decisions made by management early in a program, as well as those not made, ...ain the life-cycle cost of products or systems. An optimum profile of management decisions is an essential element in design to cost with the goal of optimizing affordability and profitability.

It is axiomatic that the more cost-conscious effort applied upfront in a program, the greater the return on investment to the producer as well as affordability to the consumer in terms of life-cycle cost. Life-cycle cost is defined as the acquisition cost of products or systems plus the cost for their operation and support.

The window of opportunity for optimizing affordability and profitability shrinks exponentially as programs mature. The term "program" connotes, from the consumer's viewpoint, an undertaking to acquire a new product, system, or service. From the producer's viewpoint, it is an organized effort to develop, manufacture, market, and support new products, systems, and services as they enter the marketplace and are used by consumers.

Figure 2.1 illustrates management's diminishing window of opportunity to affect significant saving in life-cycle cost with relatively small investment of capital or other resources. The relationships in the illustration are exponential. Typically, 40 to 70 percent of the life-cycle cost of high-technology products or systems have been ordained by the end of the conceptual phase. Opportunities for life-cycle-cost saving decrease rapidly beyond that point.

Life-cycle cost and saving opportunity are depicted as ranges of values or bands. The width of the bands reflects uncertainty in discerning and address-

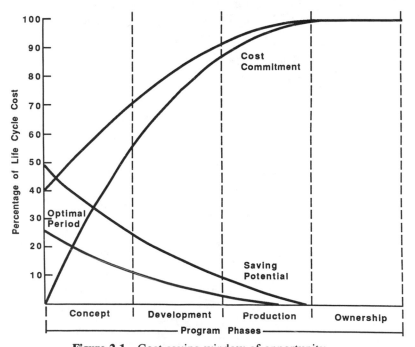

Figure 2.1 Cost saving window of opportunity.

ing cost drivers. The bands narrow as programs mature into the ownership phase.

As shown in Figure 2.1, there exists an "optimal period" when timely management action could probably save at least 20 percent of life-cycle cost. The probability is predicated on the proper upfront investment in product and process design by the producer, balanced by the ensuing product demand by the consumer.

Management is faced by a continuum of decisions that are needed to effect this balance in the most cost-effective manner possible. The decision flow in Table 2.3 should be viewed as an iterative process of management decisions that remains constant in purpose and only changes in emphasis as programs mature.

The sequence of management decisions is essentially as shown in Table 2.3. Finalization of process decisions awaits finalization of product decisions; finalization of program decisions awaits the finalization of both product and process decisions. The interactions between these decisions usually require a substantial amount of judgment and simultaneity of action.

Certain things are inevitable, however, unless management literally intervenes, and does so from the onset of the program. Left to their own resources, engineering will design future products in substantially the same way as it designed previous products, and manufacturing will continue to design tooling and build as it always has.

Management should never direct specific product and process design approaches. Management should, however, make it perfectly clear from the

TABLE 2.3   Continuum of Decisions

> *Product Decisions*
> System architecture
> Piece parts technology
> Materials selection
> Packaging
> Cost goals
> *Process Decisions*
> Make or buy
> Manufacturing processes
> Tooling philosophy
> Quality assurance philosophy
> Facilitization
> Cost goals
> *Program Decisions*
> Procurement strategy
> Support philosophy
> Warranty
> Product improvement
> Cost and schedule control

start that approaches that violate cost goal are unacceptable and will be rejected, and that performance in this regard will be rewarded commensurately. In essence, management should direct what is to be done, and not how it is to be done.

The view held by the Department of Defense (DoD) on the time-phasing of decisions affecting life-cycle cost is shown in Figure 2.2 and is more pessimistic, or perhaps, more realistic regarding what goes on in high-technology enterprises. The reported perception of the DoD is that 70 percent of weapon system life-cycle cost is ordained by the end of the concept phase, at which time an approved system definition is in hand.

This view underscores the need for decisive management commitment to design to cost within the aforementioned window of opportunity. The concurrent commitment to value engineering can be equally rewarding. As stated in Section 2.8.3, the contractor's share of value engineering savings can be as much as 50 percent.

Table 2.4 summarizes decision milestones used by the DoD as gates for transitioning from one program phase to the next. Although the emphasis is military, the decision criteria and resultant actions provide good role models for all high-technology endeavors in their various program phases.

Decision processes are far more formalized in the DoD, in its components and in its contractors, than are those encountered in the private sector. They are similar, however, in that they are a continuum of decisions whose interactions frequently require a significant amount of simultaneity. A typical example is planning for spare parts provisioning before first articles of production are tested and accepted.

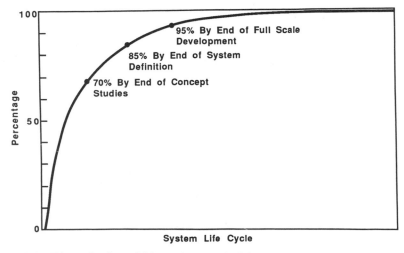

Figure 2.2   Time-phasing of life-cycle-cost decisions (3). (Reprinted by permission of the Martin Marietta Corporation.)

TABLE 2.4 Weapon System Decision Milestones (4)

Program initiation
    Decision criteria
        Mission element needs and priorities
        Affordability limits
    Resultant actions
        Define alternative systems
        Develop life-cycle cost estimates for alternatives
Demonstration and validation
    Decision criteria
        Alternatives life-cycle cost estimates
        Alternatives operational effectiveness
        Alternatives schedules
    Resultant actions
        Demonstrate alternatives hardware
        Refine alternatives life-cycle cost estimates
        Identify specific requirements that impact life-cycle cost
Full-scale engineering development
    Decision criteria
        Selected alternative
        Selected design-to-cost goal
        Affordability decision
        Tentative decision to produce and deploy
    Resultant actions
        Develop prototype
        Trade processes within system
        Refine life-cycle cost estimate
Production and deployment
    Decision criteria
        Refined life-cycle cost estimate
        Firm decision to produce and deploy
    Resultant actions
        Produce system
        Deploy system

Source: Department of Defense Instruction No. 5000.2, *Major System Acquisition Procedure*, 1985).

2.2.1 Conceptual Phase

The term "conceptual phase" is somewhat synonymous with preproposal and proposal phases in the exploratory and advanced development contracting domain. In other business enterprises, it is synonymous with market and product exploration. Conceptual phase decision highlights are given in Table 2.5.

The purpose of the management decisions and attendant actions in the ncept phase is to ensure that the up-front analysis leads to product and cess decisions that optimize affordabilty and profitabilty; to elevate cost

TABLE 2.5 Conceptual Phase Decision Highlights
_____

Functionality and affordability limits established
Product and process concepts selected
Product support approach defined
Design-to-cost organization created
Audit trails instituted
_____

to at least the same level, if not to a higher level of concern as performance and schedule; to allocate cost goals to specific individuals; and to institute audit trails, reporting media, and systems for accountability and recognition.

It is equally important that product planning evolve in the context of the long-range strategy for the organization as a whole. For example, decisions to acquire new technology should be supportive of the overall organizational goals rather than merely those of a particular product line.

The long-range strategy must flow through the organization in unequivocal statements of policy and procedures. Specific roles, responsibilities, and practices should be spelled out for the various functional disciplines as management mandates.

Before entering the development phase, management must address each production decision that may influence affordability and profitabilty and must come to grips with the investment of resources, payback period, and return on investment (ROI). Furthermore, management must understand the implication of the product support commitment throughout the ownership phase.

Regarding ownership, the issue of warranties in the private sector and reliability improvement warranties in the public sector, which can add 2 to 10 percent of the basic product cost to the consumer, should also be resolved before the development phase of the program is entered. Such issues are resolved with reliability and maintainability trades, and these parameters must be part of the development baseline.

2.2.2 Development Phase

The initial responsibility of management is to ensure that the long-range process of capitalization and facilitization are under way properly. Beyond that, management must ensure that make-or-buy decisions and production planning are not only supportive of the planning for production phase and subsequent ownership phase but also compatible with initial product and production decisions, and with product support in the ownership phase. Development phase decision highlights are given in Table 2.6.

The paramount management responsibility in the development phase is to ensure that design converges on the cost goals rather than allow cost to converge on design during development. This means that essential functionality becomes the design objective, and that design efficiency must be m

TABLE 2.6   Development Phase Decision Highlights

Capitalization and facilitization approved
Make-or-buy decisions effected
Manufacturing and quality control approaches established
Design-to-cost goals allocated
Performance incentives implemented

mized with modern tools such as computer-aided design (CAD) to the extent warranted by the scope of the program.

This also means that the audit trails and systems of accountability and reward initiated in the concept phase should be continued with full management emphasis and support. Commitment and involvement of the entire organization are essential in design to cost.

Problem solutions that violate cost goals should not be tolerated unless essential functionality and quality are in jeopardy, and then they should be challenged with the same rigor that led to the initial product and process decisions. The ambience of cost goal preeminence should emanate from management through the entire organization.

Well before the completion of development, management should mandate the approach to quality control. From the perspective of design to cost, the issue is statistical quality control versus intensive inspection, rework, and scrap that can consume as much as 15 to 20 percent of unit production price.

The recommended approach is statistical quality control, provided it is accompanied by the concerted effort to achieve product uniformity as described in Section 4.7. This is the essence of the "new quality" that is being practiced successfully by the Japanese and a number of progressive American concerns (5).

2.2.3   Production Phase

Prior to the production phase, management should ensure that production efficiency has been maximized using such modern tools as computer-integrated manufacturing to the extent warranted by the scope of the program. Cost and schedule controls and an integrated management and factory information system should also be in effect. Production phase decision highlights are given in Table 2.7.

TABLE 2.7   Production Phase Decision Highlights

Production efficiency maximized
Suppliers integrated in operations
Cost and schedule controls established
Product support organization created

Regarding reliability or product improvement actions, the management policy should be to accommodate these as block changes. The cost of such changes, as well as other requirement changes, must be separated from other costs and charged to specially created work-breakdown-structure (WBS) elements. These costs must be traceable to their root causes and auditable.

The production phase is the final training ground and staging arena for the ownership phase of the program. Although the process must start in the development phase, it is here that spare-parts provisioning is implemented, service aids are produced, and service personnel are trained.

2.2.4 Ownership Phase

Many factors contribute to success in the marketplace, some of which are given in Table 2.8. The factors relating to functionality and affordability are crucial to initial success, but the customer's perception of the company's business integrity is essential for remaining and prospering in the marketplace.

TABLE 2.8 Keys to Success in the Marketplace

Technical supremacy and recognized technical leadership
Product quality and perceived customer support
Affordability and competitive posture
Business integrity

Business integrity, that is, simply a matter of keeping promises, is perhaps the most important factor of all. The pattern of integrity that should prevail over the life of the program becomes the predominant discriminator during the ownership phase.

Long before entering the ownership phase, management should ensure that facilities, spare parts, technical data, and people are in place to train users and to fulfill warranty and service commitments timely and fairly. The product support organization is responsible for customer training and service and the logistics related thereto. Done properly, product support contributes to the profitability of the venture, engenders customer loyalty and ensures continued success in the marketplace.

2.3 SYSTEM ENGINEERING PROCESS

System engineering is the application of scientific and engineering efforts to (1) transform an operational need into a description of system performance parameters and a system configuration through the iterative process of definition, synthesis, analysis, design, test and evaluation; (2) integrate related technical parameters and ensure compatibility of all physical, functional, and program interfaces in a manner that optimizes the total system definition and design; and (3) integrate reliability, maintainability, safety, survivability, human factors, and other such factors into the total engineering effort to meet cost, schedule, and technical performance objectives (6).

In simple terms, the system engineering process is the time-oriented application of system engineering over the life cycle of systems or products. The system engineering process is a balance of both a technical process and a management process with the balance changing as systems or products mature. The technical aspects are more predominant during the formulative and development phases and are overtaken by the management aspects in the production and deployment phases.

Table 2.9 lists the various activities constituting the system engineering process as functions of given system acquisition phases. As stated in the

TABLE 2.9   System Engineering Process Activities

Activity	Section
Mission Feasibility and Concept Formulation	
Technology advancement	2.6
Mission feasibility and utility analysis	2.2.1, 2.3, 2.4
Life-cycle cost assessment	2.3, 2.5
Concept Exploration	
Performance requirements analysis	2.5
Requirements definition and specification	2.5, 3.6, 3.7, 3.9
Requirements allocation	2.5, 2.10, 3.7
Operational trades	2.5, 3.4
Functional trades	2.5, 2.10, 3.4
Technology and risk assessment	2.6, 2.9
Interface definition	2.5, 3.6
Logistic supportability	2.5
Functional baseline development	2.5, 3.6, 3.7
Life-cycle cost assessment	2.5, 3.6
System requirements review	2.5, 3.6, 3.7, 3.9
Demonstration and Validation	
Allocated baseline definition	3.2, 3.6
Element specifications	3.6
Performance, cost, and schedule refinement	3.10
Logistic supportability validation	3.2
Interface specifications	3.6
System integration planning	3.2, 3.3
Configuration management definition	3.6, 3.7
Risk management planning	2.9.1
Test and evaluation planning	3.2
Production capability assessment	4.9
System engineering management plan (SEMP)	2.3, 3.2, 3.3
System design review	3.9, 4.9

TABLE 2.9 *(Continued)*

Activity	Section
Full-Scale Development	
SEMP implementation	2.3, 3.2
Documentation update	3.7
Configuration management	3.6, 3.7
Human-factors and training planning	3.3
Integrated logistic support (ILS) planning	2.3, 3.2
Preliminary design review	3.7, 3.9
Critical design review	3.7, 3.9
Functional configuration audit	3.7, 3.9
Product baseline development	3.6, 3.7, 4.9
Production and Deployment	
Production engineering	2.7, 4.9
Production readiness review	3.7, 3.9, 4.9
Physical configuration audit	3.7, 3.9, 4.9
ILS implementation	6.2
Technical data package preparation	3.7
Change management	3.3, 3.7
Life-extension planning	3.1
Operation and support	6.2

beginning of this chapter, the system engineering process is the fabric from which successful design to cost is woven. The activities comprising the system engineering process are listed in Table 2.9 as functions of program phases. The table identifies the section in the book wherein the influences of these activities on design-to-cost goals are discussed in some detail.

The following summary of decisions during the system engineering process in the DoD is offered as the counterpart to the discussion of the contractor's management decision profile in the previous section. The discussion is now from the perspective of the customer.

The objective of concept exploration is to define and select system concepts for further development in order to meet new or unfulfilled military requirements. The concept exploration is initiated on the approval by the Secretary of Defense (SECDEF) of a program objective memorandum (POM) from one of the components of the DoD. The POM includes the justification of a major system new start (JMSNS). The approval by SECDEF is in the form of a program decision memorandum (PDM) and is contingent on the particular component of the DoD having sufficient funding reserve to complete the concept exploration. One of the gates for transitioning from concept exploration is provided in a system requirements review (SRR). Life-cycle cost is a major issue at the SRR.

The output of the demonstration and validation phase should include performance specifications that satisfy the requirements of the functional baseline. The culmination of this phase includes a system design review (SDR) that serves as one of the gates for transitioning to full-scale development. Life-cycle cost is again an issue at the SDR.

A decision-coordinating paper (DCP) and an integrated program summary (IPS) are prepared by the program office for review by the system acquisition review council (SARC), or if the proposed system is sufficiently large by the defense system acquisition review council (DSARC). If requirements are satisfied, the SARC or DSARC forwards the ratified DCP and IPS to SECDEF as the bases for approving full-scale development.

The objective of the full-scale development phase is to ensure that detail design has been completed, major problems have been resolved, achievement of performance requirements has been proved by testing, and the system or product design is producible. A preliminary design review (PDR) is conducted before the start of detail design and provides the authentication of development specifications. A critical design review (CDR) is conducted before the design is released for production. Life-cycle cost continues as an issue at PDR and CDR.

A functional configuration audit (FCA) is performed on each design to ensure that performance requirements have been satisfied before final acceptance of the development effort. A production readiness review (PRR) is usually held at the end of the full-scale development phase to verify that the system or product is ready to proceed into production.

The objective of the production and deployment phase is to produce and deliver an effective supportable system or product at an optimal cost. The first segment starts with low-rate production of relatively small lot sizes and gradually increases to full-rate production as changes resulting from initial operational trials and from hard tooling (i.e., full-rate tooling) are incorporated. Usually the first production article produced by hard tooling is subjected to a physical configuration audit (PCA) to verify that the as-built article conforms to the detailed product specification.

2.4 AFFORDABILITY ANALYSIS

Affordability analysis establishes the functional worth of the product and its relative priority from the consumer's perspective. It provides a yardstick for allocating limited budget resources to the various needs of the consumer. To the producer, affordability is both the yardstick for allocating the producer's limited budget resources and the measure of affordability for systems and products responding to consumer needs.

Conceptually, affordability is an individualistic issue from both the personal and business points of view. The allocation of resources is really based on individual perception of the relative urgency of needs and not on some global definition. This concept of affordability is the first subject addressed in this section. This is followed by the discussion of federal budget and monetary concepts.

These budget and monetary concepts and their status exert considerable influence on affordability in government contracting. One should understand the role these concepts play in the system acquisition process before attempting the analytical methodology that concludes the discussion of affordability in this section.

2.4.1 Concept of Affordability

Numerous definitions have been attempted for the term "affordability"; a typical one is: *Affordability is the characteristic of a product with a selling price that approaches its functional worth and is within the customer's ability to pay.*

In actuality, there is no one, single definition suiting all situations. For example, the basic business of the airline industry is to transport passengers and freight. Aircraft are essential in performing the basic function of the industry.

Consider a fledgling airline. All its resources must be dedicated to acquiring and maintaining at least a single aircraft. For such an airline, therefore, affordability would be defined as all the resources and credit needed to keep one machine flying, and would be a simple matter of reacting to an obvious priority.

World War II is the classical example of reacting to an obvious priority. The need for weapons clearly outweighed the need for consumer goods. The issue was survival rather than affordability. When the urgency is so clear, determination of priorities is simple.

Unfortunately, most decisions in business or personal life are not so simple. Household budgets always include such staples as food, shelter, and clothing; however, other perceived needs often cause budget excesses. Because of personal disposition, the affordability of items fulfilling these needs is too often gaged in terms of credit card and mortgage limits. In large measure, this situation prevails in business and industry.

"Murky" seems to be the most apt description of the frequent scenario wherein the distinction between priorities becomes blurred. In fact, it is almost impossible to maintain a set of well-defined priorities when proponents of competing systems or products are at work, unless a clear-cut set of criteria for screening potential candidates has been established, and unless these criteria are applied uniformly and consistently from a vantage point of absolute authority. This is one of the major reasons for the active role of the SECDEF in approving systems for acquisition as described in Section 2.3.

The SECDEF is responsible for the overall defense budget, which encompasses the budgetary requests of the military departments and of the other components of the DoD. Table 2.10 summarizes congressional action on defense budgets for fiscal years 1981 to 1987. By act of Congress, the definition of affordability for the DoD is thus proclaimed in Table 2.10.

Note from Table 2.10 that with the exception of 1981, approved fundi has been less than requested and was approximately 10 percent less in 1

TABLE 2.10   Congressional Action on Defense Budgets, $ Billions (7)

Fiscal Year	Requested	Approved	Difference
1981	180.7	182.4	+1.7
1982	225.3	218.7	−7.6
1983	263.0	245.2	−17.2
1984	280.5	265.2	−15.3
1985	313.4	294.7	−18.7
1986	322.2	289.1	−33.1
1987	320.3	289.7	−30.6

and 1987. In these situations, the SECDEF had to reapply the aforementioned screening criteria in order to allocate the reduction in funding among the individual requestors and to adjudicate attendant appeals. The annual occurrence of this event underscores the need to understand the federal budget and monetary concepts in order to plan properly in design-to-cost programs.

2.4.2   Federal Budget and Monetary Concepts

Under the unified budget concept, all federal monies are included in one comprehensive budget. These monies comprise both federal and trust funds. It should be noted that social security is now off-budget and, by law, excluded from coverage of the congressional budget resolutions.

All receipts of the federal government, with a few exceptions, are deposited to the credit of the U.S. Treasury. Under the Constitution, no money may be withdrawn from the Treasury unless appropriated by the Congress. Financial accounts of federal departments and agencies are maintained on the same basis as the unified budget.

The federal government including the DoD uses four different monetary concepts: budget authority, obligation, cost incurrence, and outlay.

1. BUDGET AUTHORITY

Budget authority is the authority to enter into transactions in the name of the federal government that ultimately cause funds to be expended from the U.S. Treasury. Budget authority is what the President requests from Congress each year in the budget, and what the Congress creates by the appropriation process. Budget authority is not money in the usual sense. As noted in the previous paragraph, it is the authority to commit a certain amount of public funds and is analogous to possessing a credit card with a certain credit limit.

2. OBLIGATION

An obligation is the actual transaction entered in the name of the federal government, and it is usually a contract or a purchase order. An obligation is analogous to using the aforementioned credit card up to the credit limit. The concept of obligation is important because of the limited lifetime of budget authority, which in the DoD appropriation ranges from 1 to 5 years. In essence, obligation continues the lifetime of the budget authority over the duration of transacted obligation.

3. COST INCURRENCE

Funding for research, development, test, and evaluation is budgeted annually only for the amount needed to finance the work actually performed during each fiscal year. Funding for production and for production-related work is incremented in what is called a "program year." A program year can encompass one or more fiscal years. Actions by either government entities or their prime contractors that create liabilities, such as ordering parts and material, constitute cost incurrence.

4. OUTLAY

Outlay is the physical disbursement of funds from the U.S. Treasury. The concept of outlay is significant from two points of view. First, the rate of outlay can be used to monitor progress on a particular program. Second, and more importantly, outlay is the monetary measure of the size of the federal budget deficit and is at the center of political controversy. The recent congressional action on direct outlay control (i.e., Gramm, Rudman and Hollings Act) is in response to the deficit.

2.4.3 Methodology

Three basic factors are used in determining affordability: program priority, availability of budget resources, and program cost. Affordability analysis deals with all three factors to reconcile available resources with essential needs. Details on the process follow.

1. PROGRAM PRIORITY

Appetites always seem to exceed financial resources, thus raising the issue of affordability. One factor that determines affordability is the relative priority of the programs competing for the same resources. In an environment where there are more programs than funding, the programs must somehow be ranked according to importance so limited resources may be properly allocated. In the DoD, certain programs are essential because of the urgency and severity of the threat against which they are to be deployed. Their high priority makes them affordable. For such programs, considerations such as balanced budgets have little bearing on whether the program should be pursued. The pertinent issue is how to best minimize their cost without degrading their ability to carry out the essential elements of their mission (see Section 2.5). Similar situations exist in other areas of the publisector such as public safety, health and welfare, environmental protection, and transportation. Funding is often a matter of political expediency and, in the short term, there is frequently no clear correlation between essential needs and funding. Although the correlation may become more apparent in the long run, funding instability along the way is counterproductive in design-to-cost programs. The correlation is somewhat clearer in the private sector. Individual expenditures are direct functions of perceived needs albeit not always essential. The arguments for business funding are based on individual perceptions of profit and growth relative to inherent risks.

2. RESOURCE AVAILABILITY

Ability to forecast out-year budget resources is essential in addressing affordability. For the most part, the database for such forecasts exists in the public domain. Notable sources include the U.S. Department of Commerce, the Federal Reserve System, the Office of Management and Budget in the Executive Branch of the federal government, the General Accounting Office of Congress and, of course, Congress itself. For example, the *Statistical Abstract of the United States,* published annually by the Bureau of the Census of the U.S. Department of Commerce, is an excellent compendium of economic history for many aspects of forecasting. Figure 2.3 illustrates the use of regression analysis to project through the year 2000 the share of the Gross National Product (GNP) in manufacturing electric and electronic equipment from data for 1976 to 1985. An introduction to regression analysis (i.e., curve fitting) is given in Section 6.6.2. In addition, the *U.S. Industrial Outlook,* published annually by the U.S. Department of Commerce, predicts

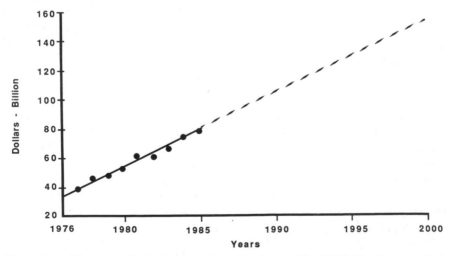

Figure 2.3   Electric and electronic equipment share of the GNP (8). (Source: U.S. Bureau of the Census, *Statistical Abstract of the United States,* 1987.)

**TABLE 2.11   Projected Distribution of the DoD
Fiscal Year 2000 Production Expenditures (9)**

Class of Cost	Percentage
Aircraft	30
Ships	15
Missiles	15
Strategic defense initiative	10
Communication–electronics	10
Tanks	5
Spacecraft	5
Munitions	5
Other	5

Adapted by permission of the Martin Marietta Corporation.

future prospects for over 350 manufacturing and services industries. The contents of the document are organized in accordance with standard industrial codes (SICs) to facilitate correlation with other sources of data. Forecasts of federal expenditures can be reinforced with additional data from congressional hearings and budget authorizations. For example, the projected distribution in Table 2.11 of the Department of Defense production expenditures for fiscal year 2000 can be replicated with readily available data for most other departments and agencies.

3. PROGRAM COST

Because of the importance of program cost in the determination of affordability, it is imperative that estimating be realistic, and that the cost of essential functions be distinguished from the cost of all others. The issue of aesthetic value should not be ignored, however, but rather considered from the perspective of the customer. The concern for program cost should encompass the cost of contemplated production facilities and processes as well as the products to be produced, in essence, nonrecurring and recurring costs. Chapters 4 and 5 are devoted to the elements of design and to the business strategy for low-cost production. However, these considerations have meaning only after the functional worth of the proposed product or system has been established and viewed in the light of the consumer ability or willingness to pay. This is the purpose of cost-effectiveness analysis, which is the subject of the next section.

2.5   COST-EFFECTIVENESS ANALYSIS

The cost and complexity of today's high-technology products are such that consumers cannot afford to buy those that prove to be ineffective or to costly to operate and maintain. Therefore, analytical studies are performed, usually by the system engineering organization under the guidance of the marketing organization, to assist management in selecting or developing products or systems. The process is called "cost–operation-effectiveness analysis" (COEA) or simply "cost-effectiveness analysis."

Cost-effectiveness analysis is concerned with the combination of resource-use and attained effectiveness. Resource-use represents the expenditure of money, manpower, material, and time for the development, operation, and support of a system. Effectiveness is a measure of the system's ability to accomplish its mission objectives. The terms "system" and "mission" have their roots in their military origin but are now used in a generic sense to describe any product or group of products in an intended application.

2.5.1 Methodology

The step-by-step procedure is intended to ensure that nothing is overlooked in assessing concepts and can be equally valuable in both the public and the private sectors when complex, high-technology products or systems are contemplated. The general approach for cost-effectiveness analysis consists of the steps shown in Figure 2.4.

Note the feedback loop in Figure 2.4, which ensures that mission objectives and intended use are redefined if they do not fit within the boundaries of available resources and operational constraints. The methodology, which is described below, should be adapted to the nature and scope of the program.

1. DEFINE MISSION OBJECTIVE AND INTENDED USE

Cost-effectiveness analysis is conducted in an orderly flow from the mission level to the system and component levels, although the system is optimized at the component level by trading performance and cost within the limiting envelope of functionality and reliability. For example, a military mission might be air defense. The objective would be stated, therefore, as "Suppress air attack against certain targets." The requirements would specify the class of threats, environmental conditions, and the probabilistic aspects of the mission such as percentage of threats defeated and response time distribution. The system would be optimized by trades among the surveillance and countermeasure components of the air defense system.

2. IDENTIFY RESOURCES AND CONSTRAINTS

Resources are those items available to accomplish a task or program and include technology, commodities, facilities, time, money, and personnel. Resource requirements are inherent in both the statement and priority of a mission or a task and constitute limits on resources. For example, the task to

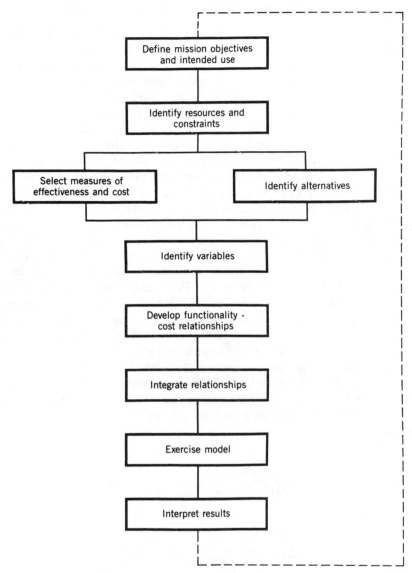

Figure 2.4 Cost-effectiveness analysis flow (10). (Adapted by permission of the Martin Marietta Corporation.)

implement a system for collision avoidance in commercial aviation defines the needed technology, commodities, facilities, and personnel. The urgency of the task defines timing, but this is usually tempered by funding constraints. The commercial nature of the task defines airline revenue as the source of money and constrains the amount available.

3. SELECT MEASURES OF EFFECTIVENESS AND COST

The optimization process involves essentially the achievement of a combination of resource use and attained effectiveness that is best by some set of criteria. To render the optimization process feasible, criteria must be developed that are expressed in precise, quantifiable terms. These criteria are developed in recognition of the stated program objectives and those limitations inherent in the available resources. The quantitative measures of cost are also expressed in terms of time, manpower, and other resources. For example, one measure of effectiveness in highway design is vehicular capacity per unit time. Associated measures of cost include highway patrol and maintenance requirements as functions of vehicular capacity per unit time. The form that measures take is related to decision criteria for the particular product or system. Some typical measures for a weapon system are given in Table 2.12. The approach is adaptable to the private sector. Note that each measure of effectiveness (MoE) is quantifiable. For example, reliability can be expressed in terms of so many hours for mean time between failures (MTBF) and maintainability in terms of so many minutes for mean time to repair (MTTR). Simple measures of effectiveness and cost are recommended provided they are applied consistently. For example, the comparative measures of electricity versus gas in heating a foundry furnace should be cost per millions of Btu (mBtu). Consider electricity with an energy content of 3413 Btu, or 0.003414 mBtu, per kilowatt-hour (kWhr) and a cost of $0.10/kWhr, and gas with an energy content of 95,500 Btu, or 0.0955 mBtu, per gallon and a cost of $1.00/gallon. The heat-conversion efficiencies of electricity and gas are 0.85 and 0.75, respectively. The following calculations show that gas has more than a twofold cost-effectiveness advantage over electricity.

Electricity

$$\frac{\$0.10/kWhr}{(0.003413 \text{ mBtu/kWhr})(.95)} = \$30.84$$

Gas

$$\frac{(\$1.00/gallon)}{(0.0955 \text{ mBtu/gallon})(.75)} = \$13.96$$

TABLE 2.12   Some Measures of Effectiveness for Weapon Systems

Availability	Survivability	Capability	Resources
Reliability	Nuclear	Range	Commodities
Maintainability	Environmental stress	Accuracy	Facilities
All-weather performance	Energy countermeasures	Penetrability	Personnel
Threat response time		Lethality	
		Duty cycle	

4. IDENTIFY ALTERNATIVES

The ability to optimize a system depends on the availability of alternate means of meeting the requirements as illustrated in the previous example. Alternatives include the means, approaches, or techniques that can be employed to meet mission requirements within the constraint of cost. The task of identifying alternatives consists basically of examining the mission requirements together with the proposed basic system concept and listing all possible alternative means of meeting the requirements. The alternatives thus listed should then be screened against available resources to ensure that they are, in fact, feasible. Continuing the highway example cited earlier, alternatives for increasing vehicular capacity could include alternate routes, multilane roadways, and multilevel roadways. If it evolved that right-of-way acquisitions were the cost driver, multilevel roadways could be the candidate alternative.

5. IDENTIFY VARIABLES

"Variables" are defined as parameters used to define the various aspects of the mission and that, when varied, impact the effective accomplishment of program objectives. Stated another way, changes in the variables cause changes in resource requirements to maintain a certain level of performance. In the statistical sense, these parameters are independent variables and resource requirements are the dependent variables. This step consists of identifying those independent variables that drive dependent variables in each selected alternative. In the highway example, vehicular capacity, speed, and weather are the independent variables that drive the dependent variables of construction time and money, operation, and maintenance costs. It is necessary to bound these independent variables in the way they will occur in operations. For example, reliability should be bound by minimum and maximum values of MTBF and maintainability by minimum and maximum values of MTTR.

6. DERIVE FUNCTIONALITY–COST RELATIONSHIPS

This step in the process relates cost to the various levels of functionality in the contemplated alternatives. In essence, cost behaves as positive exponential functions of performance, power, complexity, reliability, weight, and density. Consider the detection subsystem in the previously cited example of an aircraft collision-avoidance system. The key performance parameters are probability of detecting and locating an oncoming aircraft with given radar cross section, detection distance, and system reliability.

These parameters not only drive equipment complexity, but do so interactively. Figure 2.5 shows a typical interaction of probability of detection and detection range on equipment complexity expressed in terms of the number of components for the detection subsystem portion of the aircraft collisic avoidance system. Note that a probability of detection of .95, detection from a distance of 4 kilometers (km), requires about 20 components, whereas doubling the distance to 8 km increases the required number to about 65. Assume the requirement for .95 probability of detection at a distance of 8 km for the discussion that follows. Figures 2.5 to 2.9 can be used to select preliminary design-to-cost goals. The word "preliminary" is stressed because many other factors should be considered before final design-to-cost goals can be pronounced (see Section 6.4). The procedure to use is as follows:

Establish Design Complexity   Reference is again made to Figure 2.5. Probability of detection and distance are the independent variables. A vertical line is drawn from the 8-km point on the abscissa to where it intercepts the probability of detection curve of .95. A horizontal line is drawn from this point to where it intercepts the ordinate at about 65 components.

Establish Component Reliability   Figure 2.6 shows the interaction of equipment complexity, in terms of the number of components, and of the required system reliability on the inherent reliability of the components used in the system. In this figure, the number of components and the required system reliability are the independent variables and the dependent variable is the required component reliability. For a required system reliability of .95 with 65 components, the required component reliability would be about .999.

Estimate Development Cost   Figure 2.7 shows the interaction of equipment density and component reliability on development cost. The range of development cost in the illustration is typical for such undertakings and can vary as much as threefold as function of density (weight of components per unit volume). Density is a commonly used measure of equipment complexity because it accounts both for weight and volume. This is particularly valuable where both volumetric density and power density coincide. In structural applications, a similar relationship for weight as a function of the number of components often suffices. Equipment density and component reliability are the independent variables in Figure 2.7; the dependent variable is development cost. Assuming the volume of the detection subsystem to be about 0.5 cubic foot (ft^3), the 65 component in this volume would constitute medium density. Medium density and a required component reliability of 0.999 yield a development cost of about $600 million in Figure 2.7.

Estimate Production Cost   Figure 2.8 introduces a new parameter, production quantity, and shows the interaction of production quantity and component reliability on production cost. The greater the required reliability, the greater are expenditures on inspection and test. Again, the range of total production costs is typical for such undertakings. The independent variables in Figure 2.8 are production quantity and component reliability; the dependent variable is production cost. Assuming a quantity of 1000 detection subsystems is to be produced, the total production cost would be about $0.1

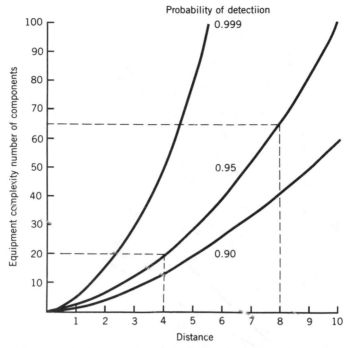

Figure 2.5 Complexity as a function of detection probability and distance.

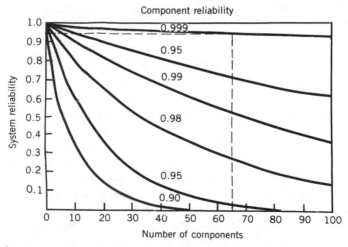

Figure 2.6 Component reliability as a function of system reliability and number of components.

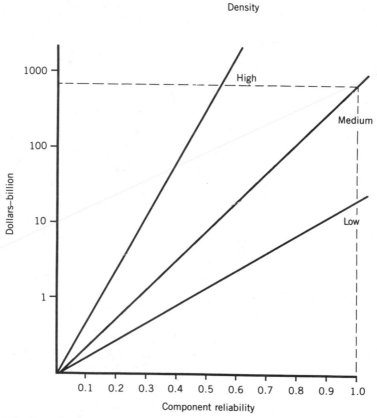

Figure 2.7 Development cost as a function of equipment density and component reliability.

billion, for a per-unit cost of about $10,000 and appears reasonable for the intended application.

   Estimate Operation and Support Cost   Figure 2.9 shows the interaction of component reliability and production quantity on operation and support (O&S) cost. The slope of the curves is established by component reliability. The lower the reliability, the greater will be the expenditure on maintenance. Scalar values on the ordinate of Figure 2.9 are established by the quantity produced. Larger quantities allow greater economy of scale in spare parts provisioning and more sophisticated maintenance facilities for reduced O&S cost. The independent variables are the quantity of deployed detection subsystems and component reliability; the dependent variable is O&S cost. For 1000 units deployed and a component reliability of 0.999, the O&S cost over the lifetime of the detection subsystem (say, 10 years) would be about $1.2 billion. Interestingly the O&S cost of $1.2 billion is about 63 percent of the

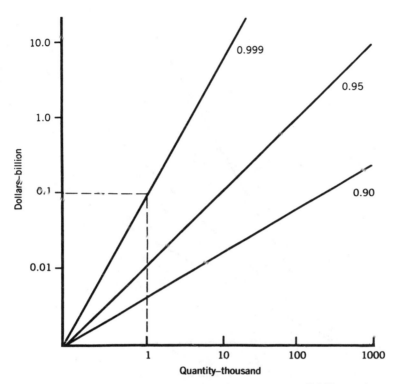

Figure 2.8 Production cost as a function of component reliability and quantity.

preliminary estimate of the life-cycle cost compiled below. This percentage is typical for equipment in such intended applications.

Compile Life-Cycle Cost The foregoing estimates are repeated below and serve as the preliminary design-to-cost goal for the detection subsystem in a quantity of 1000:

Development:	$600 million
Production:	$100 million
Operation and support:	$1.2 billion

7. INTEGRATE RELATIONSHIPS

This step integrates functionality–cost relationships into an overall measure for evaluating alternatives. Life-cycle cost is the preferred measure. Figure 2.10 shows how these relationships are typically displayed. Th

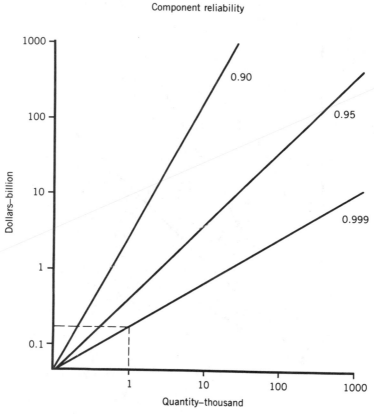

Figure 2.9 Operation-and-support cost as a function of quantity and component reliability.

achievable mean time between failure at lowest life-cycle cost is indicated by the vertical line drawn from the low point of the curve for reliability investment plus maintenance cost. Improving reliability reduces the amount of maintenance over the useful life of the system, and the objective is to find the optimum balance of investing in improved reliability during development and of reduced maintenance cost in operation so that life-cycle cost is a minimum. This balance is achieved at the intersection of the two curves in Figure 2.10. The illustration provides a grasp of life-cycle-cost sensitivity to reliability with a fixed set of values for probability of detection, detection distance, and production quantity. Similar curves would be prepared for discrete increments of the aforementioned independent or driving variables over their parametric ranges. One reliability issue that should be addressed is the use of mature parts versus the product of new technology such as military standard (MIL STD) carbon composition resistors instead of solid-

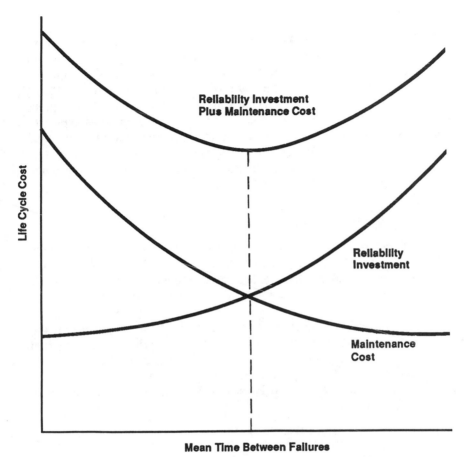

Figure 2.10   Life-cycle cost as a function of reliability and maintenance.

state resistor arrays. In any case, part selection should consider not only the interaction of unit production cost and maintenance cost but also the cost of eventual obsolescence.

8. EXERCISE MODEL

The cost-effectiveness model is exercised for each of the various alternatives under consideration. In the previous example, detection with radar, infrared, or carbon dioxide laser would probably be considered because of all-weather requirements. Again, the same measures of effectiveness and cost are used with each alternative along with the same parametric ranges of independent or driving variables. It should be remembered that these are varied one at a time with the others held constant.

9. INTERPRET RESULTS

It should be recognized that cost-effectiveness models are not exact replicas of the "real world" and should not be used blindly. The case study in Section 2.12.7 points out the importance of anticipating that something yet unknown will happen. However, the interpretation of results may be difficult if too many assumptions and qualifying statements are needed to complete the models. Nonetheless, these statements should be presented as explicitly as possible so that they can be verified in detail as time unfolds. This final step in the methodology is management's domain. This underscores the fact that managers, not analysts, make decisions. Analysts should only provide the bases for decisions.

2.5.2 Pareto Analysis of Cost Drivers

The issue of cost drivers revealed by the completed cost-effectiveness analysis is a major concern of management. The question is how to best concentrate program resources on their resolution. Techniques based on Pareto's principle can be used to reveal the point of diminishing returns in attacking cost drivers.

The principle, which was evolved by economist Vilfredo Pareto (1848–1923), can be used to isolate the vital few problems from the trivial many that obscure priorities (11). Its use is demonstrated with an application to the critical procurement list of a typical aerospace program.

The first step is to prepare the Pareto analysis worksheet as shown in

TABLE 2.13 Pareto Analysis Worksheet (12)

Rank	Item Cost ($)	Cumulative Cost ($)	Percentage of Total Cumulative Cost
1	30,000	30,000	10.9
2	30,000	60,000	21.7
3	29,000	89,000	32.2
4	29,000	118,000	42.8
5	28,000	146,000	52.9
6	28,000	174,000	63.0
7	27,000	201,000	72.8
8	13,000	214,000	77.5
9	11,000	225,000	81.5
10	10,000	235,000	85.1
11	10,000	245,000	88.8
12	10,000	255,000	92.4
13	9,000	264,000	95.7
14	6,000	270,000	97.8
15	6,000	276,000	100.0

Adapted by permission of the Martin Marietta Corporation.

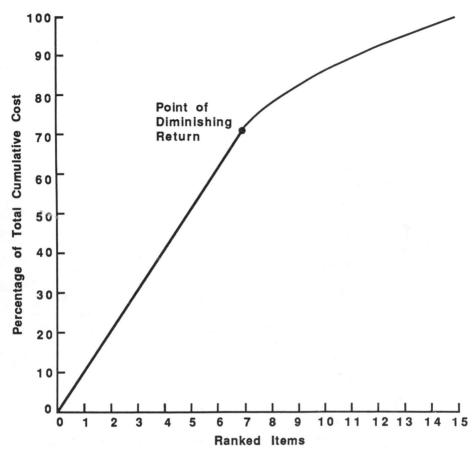

Figure 2.11   Pareto plot (15). (Adapted by permission of the Martin Marietta Corporation.)

Table 2.13. The items are ranked in descending order of cost, and cumulative cost and percentage of cumulative cost are calculated for each line item. From Table 2.13 it can be seen that the point of diminishing return (PoDR) occurs after item 7, where the step change in percent of cumulative cost decreases from about 19 and more to about 5 and less. The conclusion that the first seven items are the logical candidates for concerted effort is reinforced by the Pareto plot shown in Figure 2.11.

2.6 NEW TECHNOLOGY

Appropriate use of new technology can further optimize profitability to the producer and affordability to the consumer. Proper planning and scheduling are crucial to successful application of new technology.

TABLE 2.14   Principles for Developing New Technology (16)

> Encourage specialty houses to sponsor development
> Pursue limited partnerships with specialty houses for R&D programs
> Use combined resources of the organization to underwrite development
> Guide customers on technical and cost issues in future solicitations
> Coordinate long-range strategic planning and technology investment

Reprinted by permission of the Martin Marietta Corporation.

New technology should be examined as part of cost-effectiveness analysis for help in satisfying requirements within affordability limits and should be approached from the viewpoint of both product and process design. Much data exist in the public domain; key sources are the *National Technical Information Service* of the U.S. Department of Commerce and the *Technical Applications Bulletins* of Oak Ridge National Laboratory (13, 14).

Development programs involve new technology to a great degree, raising the issue of how to predict production cost. The problem is exacerbated in total package procurement because of the finality of the upfront funding commitment required both by the customer and by the contractor. As shown by the C-5a aircraft episode, it typically does not work and should not be emulated by commercial enterprises.

2.6.1   Application Guidelines

Technology issues resolve into (1) how much the development will cost, (2) how producible the resulting design will be, and (3) how much tooling will cost. Answers to these issues can be given only on an abstract or relative basis in most cases; however, observance of certain principles can produce the lowest possible cost solutions. Tables 2.14 and 2.15 list a number of principles for developing and applying technology that can mitigate cost and reduce risk with its inherent cost.

TABLE 2.15   Principles for Applying New Technology (17)

Use the same producibility checklists and yardsticks for new technology as for
  existing approaches
Do not apply traditional allowances and factors to new technology
Use modern analytical technologies for design factors based on statistical relation-
  ships
Close-couple manufacturing technology to design technology
Conduct risk–cost analysis relating the risk probability to corrective-action cost
Above all, do not be overwhelmed by new technology, and use common sense in
  program planning.

Reprinted by permission of the Martin Marietta Corporation.

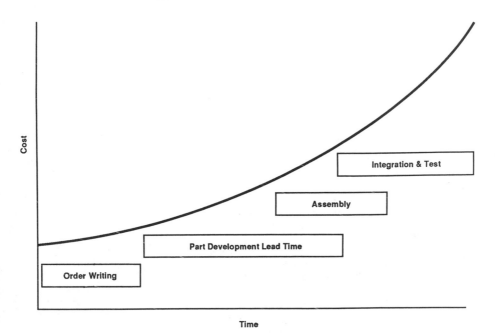

Figure 2.12   Risk–cost of concurrency in procurement.

2.6.2   Technology Scheduling

Time is money; therefore, if a new product can be made to reach the market in 3 instead of 5 years, development cost will be reduced by 24 months of labor expenditure. However, the accelerated schedule presents risk when development and production are overlapped as a result of the lead time for new-technology realization.

Figure 2.12 illustrates the cost consequences of the risk in concurrent development and production in the area of procurement. The exponential shape of the curve is a measure of how the risk exposure increases with time. Were there no technical risk and only increased cost incurrence were present, the relation would be depicted by a straight line in the illustration. A technique for quantifying risk–cost in dollars is discussed in Section 2.9.3.

The logical approach to technology scheduling is to develop and apply technology as part of the long-range planning strategy for the organization. Basing decisions only on near-term opportunities is counterproductive to long-term competitiveness and growth.

2.7   MANUFACTURING RESOURCES PLANNING II

The Roman numeral II in the title is intended to herald the advent of the paperless factory of the future. From an operations point of view, the two-fold objective of Manufacturing Resources Planning II (MRP II) is to (1)

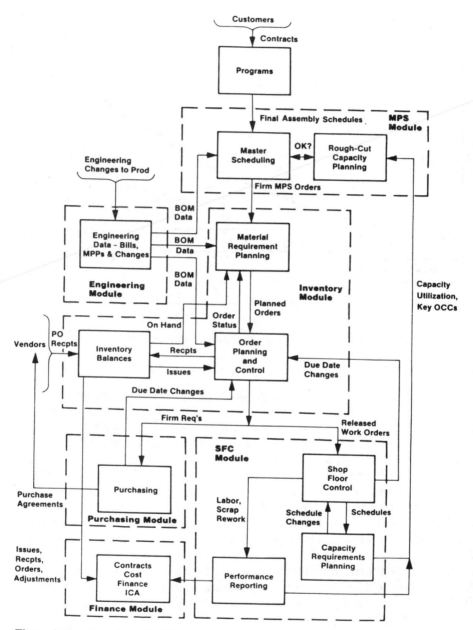

Figure 2.13 Manufacturing Resources Planning II concept (20). (Reprinted by permission of the Martin Marietta Corporation.)

enhance the management information system to the point where management can intervene before causes of problems even take root and (2) render each manufacturing operation a center of excellence for its particular expertise in terms of affordability and capability.

The promise of MRP II for U.S. industry is documented in contemporary literature along with the reasons for hesitancy on the part of U.S. industry to move forth in that direction (18, 19). Although it is not cited, perhaps some of this hesitancy is due to the very overwhelming nature of the implementation concepts themselves.

Figure 2.13 shows the conceptual configuration for a MRP II system that is just in the requirements definition stage. The breadth and depth, however, can be envisioned from the number of modules and their numerous interfaces.

The names of these components in the descending order shown in the illustration are as follows: "Master Production Scheduling (MPS) Module," "Engineering Module," "Inventory Module," "Purchasing Module," "Shop Floor Control (SFC) Module," and "Finance Module." Abbreviations used in the figure are defined in Appendix 2.

It is also easy to envision the amount of skilled resources that would be needed to be diverted from other jobs in order to implement MRP II. This is a difficult decision for management to make, and often the approach has been to make no decision at all.

The best guidelines for the decision to implement MRP II are the size of the production operations and the number of personnel already involved in the kind of functions shown in Figure 2.13. If, indeed, many of these functions are already being performed but on an independent, uncorrelated basis, then MRP II not only is feasible but will ultimately afford economy in the number of people who are presently on board.

2.8 VALUE ANALYSIS

It is natural for designers to be performance-oriented; their primary goal is to design a functional end item. This focus on performance, combined with schedule urgencies, often leads to neglect of cost.

However, cost reduction alone accents thrift to the exclusion of other factors. Value analysis is a more powerful and totally different approach, providing a disciplined and logical approach to reducing unnecessary product costs without sacrificing functional worth and quality. Value analysis follows a prescribed progression: a job plan that is an essential and mandatory element of the process (21).

2.8.1 Job Plan

The value analysis job plan governs the organization of investigations through their implementation. The basic tenet of value analysis is: "No job is too small for a job plan."

1. ORGANIZATION

The team "approach" is the most effective way to implement value analysis, and the expertise and experience of the team should encompass the design, cost, and production aspects of the products under study. Team members should be reasonably skilled in human relations. The job entails questioning, challenging, and criticizing others' ideas in order to induce constructive changes. Tact, honesty, empathy, cooperation, and diplomacy go far in developing a positive, enthusiastic attitude for value analysis and lead to its eventual success.

2. SELECTION

Candidate study projects should be weighed against the benefits to be derived from the resources expended. The relative priority of study projects should be based on the urgency of need and the cost-saving potential. Table 2.16 provides a basis for examining current or proposed designs and processes and for selecting study candidates. The case study in Section 2.12.3 is an excellent example of the fruitfulness of value analysis in obvious but frequently overlooked areas.

TABLE 2.16   Value Analysis Checklist (22)

General

Can the design be changed to eliminate parts?
Can the present design be purchased at lower cost?
Can a standard part be used?
Would an altered standard part be more economical?
If the part is to improve appearance, is its presence justified?
Is there a less costly part that will perform the same function?
Can the design be changed to simplify the part?
Will the design permit standard inspection equipment to be used?
Can a part designed for other equipment be used?
Can a less expensive material be used?
Can the number of different materials be reduced?
Are new developed materials available for use?
Can the design be modified to permit manufacture on automatic machinery?

Machining

Are all the machined surfaces and finishes necessary?
Will a coarser finish be adequate?
Does design permit the use of standard cutting tools?
Are tolerances closer than they need be?
Can another material be used that would be easier to machine?
Can a fastener be used to eliminate tapping?
Can weld nuts be used instead of tapped holes?

TABLE 2.16 *(Continued)*

Assembly

Can two or more parts be combined?
Can parts be made symmetrical?
Is there a newly developed fastener to speed assembly?
Are minimum numbers of hardware sizes used?
Are stock components called for, if feasible?
Can roll pins be used to eliminate reaming?

Specifications and Standards

Is there a standard part that can replace a manufactured item?
Can an altered standard part be used instead of a special component?
Can any specification be changed to reduce cost?
Is standard hardware used?
Are all threads standard?
Can standard cutting tools be used?
Can standard gauges be used?
Is there available material with tolerances and finish that will eliminate machining?

Quality Assurance

Are inspection standards realistic?
Is the present level of testing necessary?
Can redundant inspections or tests be eliminated?
Would redesign eliminate a quality problem?
Can the design be modified to simplify inspection?

Packaging

Is the present level of packaging needed?
Can the packaging be simplified?
Could different packing materials be used?
Is bulk packing or palletizing possible?
Can packaging be redesigned for automatic machinery?
Is packaging arranged for lowest-cost total material handling?

Source: Defense Logistics Agency, Contract Management Directorate, *Guidebook to DoD Contractors, Value Engineering,* August 1982.

3. INVESTIGATION

The objective of investigation is to gather pertinent information concerning the project including major functions, cost, and functional worth. Examples of data used include drawings, process plans, specifications, purchasing and accounting records, and, if possible, actual samples of hardware.

4. SPECULATION

Having defined the problem and having assessed the relevant facts, one can generate alternative approaches for high-cost design elements through creative thinking and brainstorming and then evaluate these alternatives on a comparative basis.

5. EVALUATION

The objective of evaluation is to analyze the ideas from the creative thinking and brainstorming process, taking into account the effect of the alternatives on functional objectives and on economic constraints. The evaluation process attempts to use quantitative data to the greatest extent possible.

6. DEVELOPMENT

The best alternative is analyzed for implementation and cost. Required changes in design, material, and processes are developed along with a plan to implement the alternative.

7. PRESENTATION

The highlight of presentations is a comparison of before-and-after effect of the proposed improvement. Well-documented cost comparisons lend credibility to the presentation. The format used for industrial engineering estimates (shown in Figure 6.10) is the recommended medium for showing original costs, cost savings, and final costs.

8. IMPLEMENTATION AND AUDIT

Rapid implementation of changes maximizes savings. The team remains involved during implementation to ensure continuity and documentation of the results from implementing the change. Documented savings are shared by the contracting parties and are subject to audit.

2.8.2 Function Analysis System Technique

The function analysis system technique (FAST) concept, illustrated in Figure 2.14, is used for intense study of functions and their interactions. The technique asks three questions and then diagrams the results as shown in the illustration. The questions asked about the functions are: "Why?" "How?" and "When?."

Answers are constrained to two words, a verb and a noun, to ensure that the functions are stated precisely and unambiguously. Answers to the question "Why?" lead ahead to the higher-level function for which this function being performed. Answers to the question "How?" lead back to a prerequisite function that must be performed to accomplish the former function.

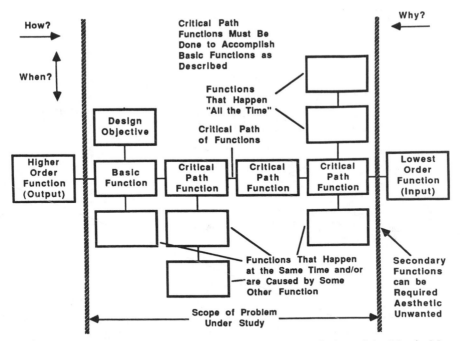

Figure 2.14 The FAST concept (23). (Reprinted by permission of the Martin Marietta Corporation.)

Functions are charted with the highest-level functions, identified by the question "Why?" toward the left, and the functions identified by the question "How?" toward the right. Each function in a given string is annotated on the left by "Why it is done" and on the right by "How it is done."

Next the question "When?" is asked of each function. The answer is diagrammed vertically to indicate those functions that are accomplished at the same time and the sequential relationships of the others.

The power of FAST is its ability to segregate basic functions from secondary functions that contribute little or nothing to the functionality of the product. For example, in Figure 2.15, the secondary function "Rotate beam (electron)" could be traded against rotating a table mechanically.

Additional details on value analysis techniques can be obtained from the classic works by Lawrence D. Miles (24) an Arthur E. Mudge (25).

2.8.3 Contractual Clauses

The U.S. Departments of Defense, Energy, and Transportation and many state agencies encourage or require value engineering in their contracts. Value engineering clauses in such contracts contain either incentive clauses or program requirement clauses to promote the submittal value engineering change proposals. In the case of the latter, the contractor is funded to pursue

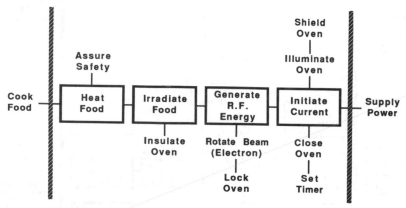

Figure 2.15   FAST diagram of microwave oven (26). (Reprinted by permission of the Martin Marietta Corporation.)

specific cost-reduction initiatives and as a consequence shares less of the saving.

Policy and procedures are spelled out in Parts 48 and 52.248–1 of the Federal Acquisition Regulation (FAR). Provisions for sharing cost savings by the contractor are summarized in Table 2.17. Rewards are greater for voluntary participation under the incentive clause of contracts than under the mandatory program requirement clause.

Instant contracts are those currently in effect with contractors originating the value engineering change proposal (VECP), whereas future contracts are intended for follow-on work with the same contractors. Concurrent con-

TABLE 2.17   Contractor Sharing Provisions (27)

	Value Engineering Contractual Clause		
	Incentive	Program Requirement	
	Instant, Concurrent, or Future Contract	Instant Contract	Concurrent or Future Contract
Type of Contract			
Fixed price other than incentive	50	25	25
Incentive fixed price or cost[a]	50	—	25
Cost reimbursement other than incentive[b]	25	15	25

[a] Same ratio as the contract's cost incentive ratio.

Includes cost plus award fee contracts.

urce: Federal Acquisition Regulation, *Parts 48 and 52.248-1*.

tracts are with contractors other than those originating the VECPs but are for the same items. In addition, contractors share 20 percent of O&S saving in an average year's use. This is called "collateral" saving.

2.9 RISK MANAGEMENT

Risk management ensures that both the producer's and the consumer's goals materialize to the benefit of both. It provides confidence bounds about final costs and identifies actions needed to keep cost and schedule on target.

Risk management is the logical process of assessing uncertainties in achieving cost goals, and quantifying these uncertainties in terms of corrective action cost and taking action to prevent risks from materializing. The rationale for preventive action should be the ROI in terms of reduced corrective-action cost.

2.9.1 Risk Perspective

Each foreseeable item of risk should be evaluated from the perspective of its potential impact on the program of interest. This is necessary to both ensure the optimal balance of cost and effectiveness within the constraints of funding limits and essential functionality and provide the operational capability within the required time frame.

The military has developed a convenient means for evaluating risk that is based on a concept called "isorisk contours." The concept is illustrated in Figure 2.16 by the sequence of isorisk contours denoted by second-order curves.

The curves in Figure 2.16 are plotted using values obtained from solving the following equation for risk factor R_f:

$$R_f = (P_f + C_f) - (P_f C_f) \tag{2.1}$$

where P_f and C_f are factors used to rate the probability of occurrence of a particular risk item and the consequence or cost to the program given the risk does occur.

The next section presents a comprehensive approach to calculating these factors. The objective of this section is to ensure the correct interpretation of the relationship of risk-items and isorisk contours.

The military classifies risk factors as "low," "medium," and "high" with corresponding isorisk contour values of 0 to 0.30, 0.31 to 0.70, and 0.71 to 1.00. It is obvious that were there a risk consequence of the highest possible magnitude, that is, $C_f = 1.00$, and if the probability of occurrence of that particular risk item were certain, that is, $P_f = 1.00$, the risk factor would be

$$R_f = (1 + 1) - (1)(1) = 1 \tag{2.2}$$

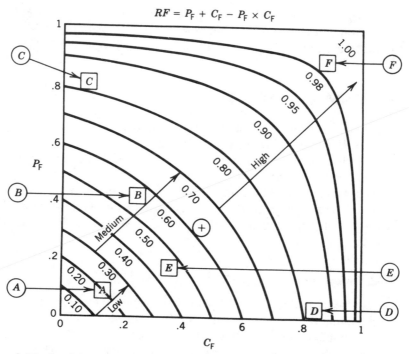

Figure 2.16 Isorisk contours (28). (Source: Defense Systems Management College, *System Engineering Management Guide,* 1982.)

Figure 2.16 depicts a number of such relationships; with the relationship indicated by the letter "F" being essentially the same as the foregoing example. Specifically, the success of the selected approach or solution is extremely critical to the program. There is no known fall-back position should the selected solution not succeed, and there is a high probability that the selected solution will not succeed.

The relationship indicated by the letter "E" is next in the order of adverse situations denoting that the success of the selected solution is extremely critical to the program and that there are a limited number of acceptable fall-back positions. Again, there is a high probability that the selected solution may fail.

Next follows the relationship indicated by the letter "D" denoting that the consequences to the program would still be high were the selected solution to fail and that there are still only a limited number of acceptable fall-back positions. In this case, however, there is a low probability that the selected solution may fail.

The relationship indicated by the letter "C" denotes that the success of the selected solution is not critical to the program and that there are a large number of acceptable fall-back positions. However, there is a high probabil-

TABLE 2.18   Risk Probability (29)

Score	Current Level of Technical Maturity
0.0	Completed system test
0.1	Completed assembly test
0.2	Successful system simulation
0.3	Completed assembly bench test
0.4	Completed subassembly bench test
0.5	Completed brassboard test
0.6	Completed breadboard test
0.7	Completed detailed design
0.8	Completed functional design
0.9	Design approach proved analytically
1.0	No design solution known

Reprinted by permission of the Martin Marietta Corporation.

ity that the selected solution may fail, and one of the other alternative solutions should be considered as the prime candidate.

The relationship indicated by the letter "B" denotes that the success of the selected solution is of moderate importance to the program and that the number of fall-back solutions is limited. In this case, there is a medium probability that the selected solution may fail, and one of the other alternative solutions should be considered in parallel with the one selected.

The relationship indicated by the letter "A" denotes that success of the selected solution is not critical to the program, that there are many acceptable fall-back positions, and that the probability is low that the selected solution may fail. No further action is required.

2.9.2   Risk Assessment

The current level of technical maturity and the schedule criticality of components comprising proposed products or systems are convenient means for assessing risk. Tables 2.18 and 2.19 provide guidelines for scoring these factors in terms of risk probability and risk magnitude.

TABLE 2.19   Risk Magnitude (30)

Score	Schedule Criticality
0.0	Affects only contract closeout
0.1–0.3	Needed for system assembly and test
0.4–0.6	Needed for subsystem assembly and test
0.7–0.9	Needed for assembly fabrication
1.0	Needed for detail fabrication

Reprinted by permission of the Martin Marietta Corporation (22).

Consider, for example, a chassis that houses circuit card assemblies. Detail design of the chassis has been completed, and it is needed at the midpoint of system assembly and test.

From Tables 2.18 and 2.19, risk probability and risk magnitude are 0.7 and 0.2, respectively. These values might suggest that although the risk probability in achieving a fully functional chassis is relatively high, the risk magnitude is sufficiently low for the chassis and thus it should not constitute a major problem.

In the next section, risk probability and risk magnitude are related to corrective action cost that would be incurred if the risk were to materialize. The resultant product is the risk–cost of the undertaking.

2.9.3 Risk–Cost Modeling

The risk–cost concept relates the probabilistic nature of risk to the cost of corrective action. In other words, a risk with a corrective-action cost of $100,000 and a 25 percent probability of occurrence would have a risk–cost of $25,000. Total risk–cost would be the summation of the individual risk-costs of the elements contained in the system.

The risk–cost model shown in Figure 2.17 equates technical maturity to risk probability (Table 2.18). That is, the probability of a risk materializing is a direct function of the current level of technical maturity of the particular component.

The model also equates schedule impact to risk magnitude (Table 2.19). That is, the earlier the need for a component in the design or production flow, the greater is its potential impact on the program.

Estimating corrective action cost is the responsibility of design, manufacturing, and finance personnel. Given such estimates, the model relates risk magnitude to corrective action cost by generating a risk–cost correlation function. The model next derives a risk-probability distribution for the components comprising the product or system.

The correlation function describes the risk–cost sensitivity of the product or system. The risk-probability distribution describes the variability of risk magnitude.

The model then transforms the risk-probabilty distribution by the risk–cost correlation function, generating a cost-probability distribution. This, in turn, is used to predict risk–cost in the form of the S curve shown in Figure 2.18 for a typical high-technology development.

The 50 percent probability value in the illustration is the should-cost estimate for the development and is referred to as the "50/50 cost." The 80 percent probability for what development could cost should risks materialize is referred to as the "80/20 cost." The 20 percent probability for what development might cost as a result of cost-avoidance is referred to as the "20/80 cost." The model treats cost-avoidance as negative risk–cost.

The plateau about the should cost value of $50 million represents an

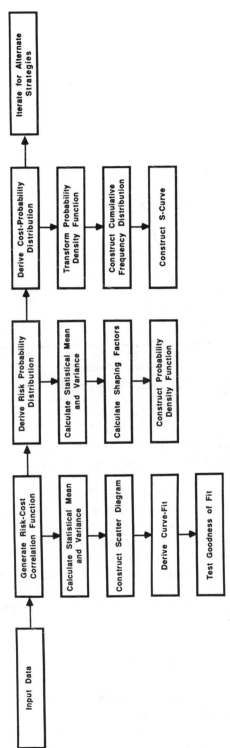

Figure 2.17 Risk–cost model (31). (Reprinted by permission of the Martin Marietta Corporation.)

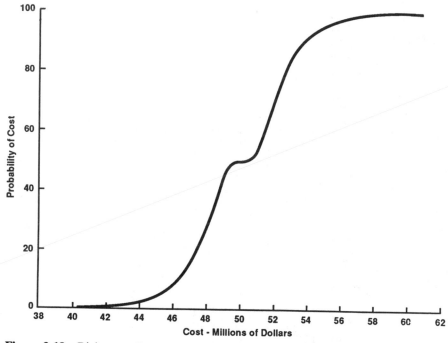

Figure 2.18 Risk–cost S curve (32). (Reprinted by permission of the Martin Marietta Corporation.)

uncertainty region that is a function of the curve order of the corrective action cost correlation function. The lower the curve order, the broader is the plateau.

Values below the 50 percent probability of cost are attributed to cost-avoidance on the premise that cost-avoidance is the inverse of corrective-action cost when operating on the same product or system. Values above the 50 percent probability of cost are attributed to corrective action.

The 80 percent probability of cost value is approximately $52.6 million, or $2.6 million more than the should-cost level. Management may elect to spend some portion of the $2.6 million up-front to achieve the 20 percent probability of cost value of approximately $47.4 million. The minimum ROI would be (52.6–47.4)/2.6, or 2.

2.10 SETTING DESIGN-TO-COST GOALS

The activities described to this point are preparatory for setting design-to-cost goals. In accordance with DoD Directive 4245.3, a design-to-cost goal

A specific cost number, in constant dollars, based on a specific produc-
a quantity and rate, established early during system development as a

management objective and design parameter for subsequent phases of the acquisition cycle.

Goal selection should not be done arbitrarily, but rather should evolve from the best available knowledge of the expected cost of the system tempered by projected budgetary limits. The key to achieving cost goals is to allow designers the freedom of choice to arrive at configurations that satisfy mission objectives. Only end results should be specified, and not the means for accomplishing them.

Design-to-cost goals may be difficult, but they should be achievable. Motivation vanishes if goals are set so low that it is obvious that they cannot be achieved. However, setting goals too high is not only self-denial of the fruits of cost saving but also tends to encourage wasteful practices.

2.10.1   Cost Trade Studies

The conduct of trades studies in general is discussed in Section 3.4. Table 2.20, however, offers some managerial guidelines for specifying their conduct in design-to-cost programs. The objective of such cost trade studies is to strike an optimal balance of cost and effectiveness within the constraints of funding limits and essential functionality.

The objective of this section is to illuminate the nature of the input variables used in trade studies and the accompanying cost-estimating process flow. Cost-estimating techniques are described in Section 6.4.

Figure 2.19 illustrates the nature of the input variables used in trade studies. Note that input variables are required for all alternative solutions (i.e., alternative approaches for meeting requirements) and that, within each alternative solution, input variables are required for each hardware configuration item, for each software configuration item, and for each corresponding operation and support (O&S) item.

Figure 2.20 illustrates the cost-estimating process flow that is inherent in trade studies for design to cost. Each hardware and software configuration item is modeled individually to the extent permitted by the concurrent design effort. Complexity factors are developed for the configuration items, and respective costs are estimated on the basis of these complexity factors.

Typically, cost estimates are within 15 to 25 percent of actual costs during the early stages of the conceptual phase. These estimate are usually within 5

TABLE 2.20   Cost Trade Study Guidelines

Specify the technical performance required, not the technical approach

Specify the time by which operational capability is required, not interim milestones

Schedule for several design iterations, not for 100 percent success on the first attempt

---

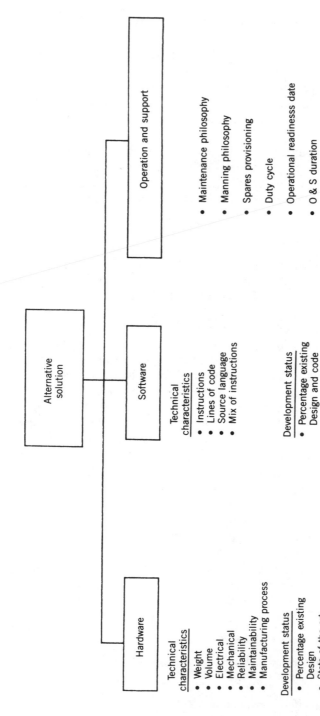

Figure 2.19 Trade study input variables.

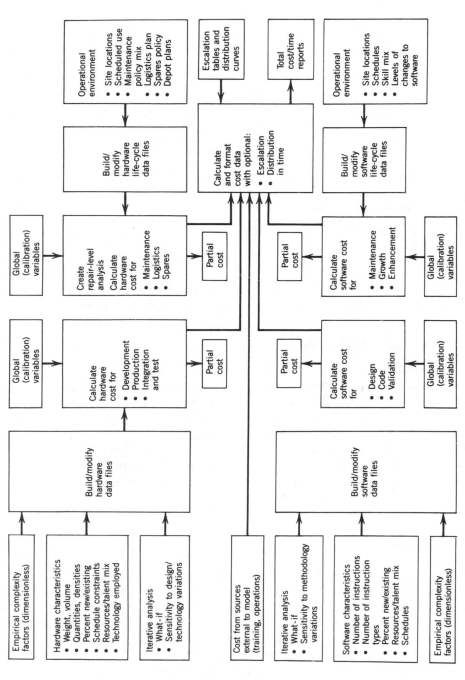

Figure 2.20 Cost-estimating process flow (33). (Source: Defense Systems Management College, *System Engineering Management Guide*, 1982.)

63

TABLE 2.21 Cost Goal Allocations (34)

WBS	Title	CAM[a]	Goal ($)	Quantity
1.0	Transport Equipment	J. Eagen	36,381,300	001
1.1	Handling Equipment	R. Mann	16,048,700	001
1.1.1	Stage IV Equipment	R. Mann	2,783,200	001
1.1.1.1	End Ring Set	D. Deer	761,700	004
	Cost Elements WBS 1.1.1.1			
	Manufacturing Labor		19,840 hr	
	Quality Labor		4,200 hr	
	Test Labor		300 hr	
	Other Technical Services Labor		2,400 hr	
	Material		$180,100	
	Subcontracted Items		$9,100	

Adapted by permission of the Martin Marietta Corporation (25).

[a] Cost account manager.

to 10 percent of actual cost by the end of demonstration and validation and then converge rapidly on the actual costs during fullscale development.

2.10.2 Allocating Cost Goals

The best conceived goals will come to no avail if they are not allocated to those people who ordain final costs, and if performance toward those goals is not pursued relentlessly. The recommended form for allocating design-to-cost goals to specific individuals is given in Table 2.21.

The discussion of allocating goals is continued in Section 3.12 in the context of maintaining an audit trail. In summary, however, goals should be allocated to those specific elements of the work-breakdown structure (WBS) for which costs can be identified and collected and should be assigned to specific individuals, not organizations.

2.11 SUMMARY

Getting started properly in design to cost, the theme of this chapter, requires some fundamental commitments on the part of management and intense up-front analysis that should have the full support of the entire organization.

The first section addressed the compelling need for management to dispel the notion that quality and affordability are mutually exclusive and to adopt the posture that the union of the two aided with the tools and techniques of value analysis can produce cost savings that are electrifying in their magnitude. Key to such success is management's maturity regarding quality, and the means for self-appraisal are provided.

It is also important to understand the posture on affordable quality of the Department of Defense (DoD) that was covered in this section. The DoD epitomizes high technology and is an excellent role model even for the private sector.

The next section continued the elaboration on the continuum of decisions that management must make over the life of the program. The point was made that these decisions are interactive and iterative. The discussion was organized by the contractual phases of the program, and because of the sequential nature of the decisions; the flow is from product to process to programmatic decisions.

During the conceptual phase, the major thrust should be to establish functionality and affordability limits and to select the appropriate product and process concepts. The development phase is the time to solidify activities that will ensure the design-to-cost goals of the program. Production is the time for realizing the fruits of the design-to-cost labors, and the ownership phase is the time to ensure customer loyalty by standing behind systems, products, or services, thus also ensuring continuous and enduring growth in the marketplace.

The next section began the discussion of the numerous activities that characterize successful design to cost starting with the system engineering process. The system engineering process, the fabric from which successful design to cost is woven, provides the basis for each activity discussed subsequently.

Table 2.9 provided a roadmap to the sections in the book giving details on the activities comprising the system engineering process. These activities are also addressed from the perspective of the DoD.

The next section addressed the subject of affordability analysis building from the fundamental concept of affordability as a function of perceived needs. The discussion was extended to the federal government in recognition of the great influence it exerts on the economy.

Federal budget and monetary concepts were explained, and processes were illustrated with the history of congressional action on defense budgets. The actual methodology used in affordability analysis was then covered.

The next activity addressed in the context of the system engineering process was cost-effectiveness analysis. Extensive details were provided on the methodology that has provided favorable results in innumerable high-technology applications.

Included in this section was a step-by-step procedure for estimating preliminary design-to-cost goals with a series of illustrations that start by relating requirements to complexity and conclude with the compilation of development, production, and operation and support cost. The section also provided some insight into Pareto analysis of cost drivers. Pareto analysis separates the vital few concerns from the trivial many and allows for more efficient utilization of resources.

The next section addressed the accommodation of new technology so as to minimize capital investment and to maximize ROI. Some sources of new-technology information were identified and application guidelines and some insight into how to schedule the acquisition of new technology presented.

The section also attempted to illuminate the hesitancy of U.S. industry to pursue the promises of MRP II. A typical MRP II system was presented as the basis of the discussion.

This was followed by the section on value analysis, which has already been proclaimed as an invaluable adjunct to quality control for the ultimate in affordability. This section covers both value analysis, often called "value engineering," techniques and the value engineering clauses encountered in government contracting.

The cost-saving sharing provisions in these clauses are quite generous, amounting to 50 percent for the contractor in many cases. The use of the job plan and an analytical tool [Functional analysis system technique (FAST)] to maximize savings was addressed. Table 2.16 provided a comprehensive checklist for discerning cost-saving candidates.

The next section was concerned with risk management, which is needed to ensure that the fruits of design-to-cost labors are not consumed by unforeseen problems. The approach to maintaining the right perspective on the effects of risk was illustrated with a concept called "isorisk contours."

The section included the methodology for assessing risk in terms of its probability of occurrence and the magnitude of its impact in the event that the risk materializes. Tables 2.18 and 2.19, which are used to score these relationships, were designed to maximize both comprehension and intuitive appeal. The use of these relationships in a probabilistic risk–cost model was described and illustrated in terms of what a particular system could cost with the proper prevention and what it would cost if left to its own resources.

The next section introduced the very important subject of setting design-to-cost goals. The cost trade study process was emphasized as the path to both affordable and realistic goals. Managerial guidelines for implementing such studies were provided.

The point was made that goals may be challenging, but they should be achievable given supportive and timely management decisions and the proper priority. However, management depends on the performance of people, and it is generally fruitless when goals are levied on organizational elements instead of people, and not made part of the appraisal process for people.

2.12 CASE STUDIES AND EXERCISES

The case studies that follow are intended to amplify key points in this chapter. The exercises following the case studies allow the reader to relate the events that are unfolded to personal viewpoints and experiences. The case studies in this chapter highlight the importance of the system engineering process, the cost-saving potential of value engineering, the environmental impact on technology, and the need for continued management emphasis and support in design to cost.

2.12.1 System Engineering at War

This case study illustrates the inherent difficulty in attempting a so-called optimal compromise for a range of missions that at first glance appear to be closely related in terms of operational requirements and environmental constraints. Some years ago, the system engineering process was applied to the problem of protecting transoceanic cargo shipping from enemy antishipping actions during wartime.

The resultant trade studies shown in tree form in Figure 2.21 suggest that antisubmarine warfare systems aboard carrier-based fixed-wing aircraft offered the optimal compromise for the envisioned missions. The decision path is indicated by the triple vertical lines in the illustration.

After several years of concept exploration that included field experimentation, it was concluded that fixed-wing aircraft was a suboptimal solution for the operational concept of magnetic anomaly detection (MAD) curtain and some aspects of the other operational concepts in the protection of shipping mission. It was concluded that a combination of surface ships, submarines, and various forms of aircraft provided a better solution in terms of cost and effectiveness within the constraints of funding limits, minimum essential functionality, and, in particular, the time frame for the required operational capability. Essentially, the same conclusion was reached regarding the mission of offensive action against submarines.

It would appear that the system engineering process had been unwittingly biased in favor of carrier-based fixed-wing aircraft by the way the trade study flow had been structured. The bias could have been avoided had the antisubmarine missions trade studies been elevated from the bottom level as shown in Figure 2.21 to the level that follows enemy antishipping actions trade studies. The relocation would have essentially doubled the number of branches in the trade study tree, but the additional cost would have been recovered manifold by the subsequent economy in the concept exploration effort.

EXERCISE   Relate this application of the system engineering process to attempts by U.S. industry to combat competition from overseas. Speculate on how the choice and ordering of measures of effectiveness could affect the outcome of these attempts.

2.12.2 Value Engineering in Defense

The Undersecretary of Defense for Acquisition announced in August 1987 that value engineering actions, approved in fiscal year 1986, will save almost $1.9 trillion for the Department of Defense (DoD) in its current and future

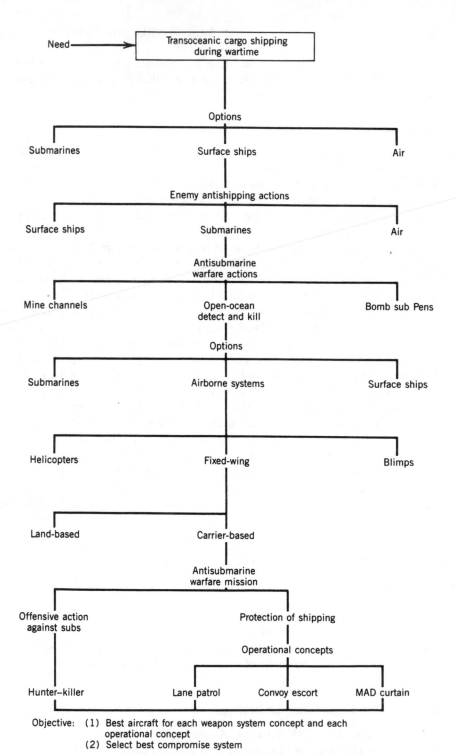

Figure 2.21 Antisubmarine warfare trade study tree (35). (Source: Defense Systems Management College, *System Engineering Management Guide,* 1982.)

obligations. Defense contractors originated about 12 percent of these actions; the balance originated within the various components of the DoD. However, contractor actions accounted for only about 0.02 percent of the saving.

The preponderance of government actions resulting in savings is due to the government's ability to act unilaterally on its own value engineering proposals (VEPs). Contractor actions require contract changes through value engineering change proposals (VECPs) that are approved by the government.

Some of the disparity is due to the fact that operation and support, which account for a large share of the defense budget, and are fertile areas for value engineering action, are under the purview of the military, who establish the operational doctrine and maintenance philosophy. In addition, there has been lack of emphasis in certain components of the DoD.

A recent circular on the subject of value engineering was issued by the Office of Management and Budget to the heads of executive departments and establishments and stated in part: "Over the last several years, reports issued by the General Accounting Office (GAO) and many Inspectors General (IG) have consistently concluded that wider use of value engineering would result in substantial savings to the government. While some agencies have some value engineering programs, other agencies have not utilized value engineering fully. Even for agencies with established programs, the GAO and IG reports conclude that much more can and should be done to realize the benefits of value engineering" (36).

EXERCISE   Legislation has been recently introduced in Congress to make value engineering mandatory in all federal programs and procurement. Proponents claim that cost savings of at least 25 percent are possible through value engineering.

Using the current edition of the *Statistical Abstract of the United States* for a database, project the expenditures at the federal level with and without the value engineering mandate being obeyed over the next 5 years. Assume annual savings of 20 percent from applying value engineering. Calculate the difference and, then, watch history unfold over the next 5 years.

2.12.3   Little Things Save a Lot

This case study is a report on the continuing success of a small business in its prosecution of value engineering change proposals (VECPs). The company, which specializes in ordnance devices for the military, is Martin Electronics, Inc. in Perry, Florida. The secret of its success is to focus on changes in processes, procedures, and materials that are so obvious that they would ordinarily be overlooked. The savings are relatively small on an individual basis but are significant when factored by the quantity of devices delivered (37).

Figure 2.22 illustrates the kind of VECPs that have been submitted by Martin Electronics, Inc (not related to Martin Marietta). The M781 40-millimeter (mm) practice cartridge is a training device that is fired from a M203 or M79 grenade launcher. On impact, the cartridge dispenses orange dye over the target. The cartridge, which weighs about 170 grams (g) and travels almost 247 feet per second (ft/sec) over ranges of 100 to 200 m, was a reasonable design challenge.

The change in piston material from 1018 carbon steel to 121L14 carbon steel provided a per-unit saving of $0.03269. The change in the process for fabricating and inserting spring pads provided a saving of $0.02573, for a total saving of $0.05842.

The company delivers approximately 1.8 million to 2.4 million units per year. This translates into yearly savings of $105,156 to $140,208, 50 percent of which is retained by the company as additional profit that can be treated as a capital gain.

Another example of a practical VECP involved a watertight shipping container for the Air Force, Navy, and Marines. The VECP substituted fiberboard boxes sealed in barriers bags to replace a metal sealed container for a potential saving per-unit of $2.60 in quantities of 100,000 (39).

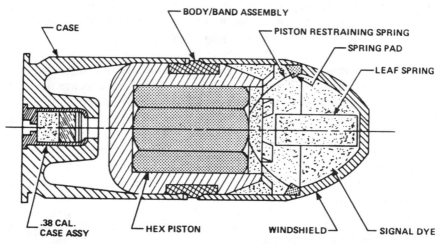

PISTON: CHANGE OF MATERIAL FROM 1018 CARBON STEEL TO 12L14 CARBON STEEL WITH NIB. SAVINGS RESULTED FROM CHANGE IN MATERIAL AND ELIMINATED SECONDARY MACHINING OPERATION.
SAVINGS: $.03269 P/U

SPRING PADS: SEPARATELY MOLDED AND PLACED IN POSITION - ELIMINATED PADS AND MACHINE FORMED SPRING.
SAVINGS: $.02573 P/U

Figure 2.22 Redesign 781 40-mm practice cartridge (38). (Source: Department of Army Contract DAAA09-80-C-0174.)

EXERCISE   Examine both the design features and the packaging of items that are produced and distributed in large volumes. Attempt to emulate the performance of the aforementioned company by searching for changes that would produce relatively insignificant per-unit savings, but would add up to large overall savings.

Factor these savings by the quantities involved, and rank-order the values of total savings. Using Pareto analysis (see Section 2.5.2), establish the point of diminishing return that separates the vital few from the trivial many.

2.12.4   Nuclear Power and the Environment

Environmental protest to nuclear power generation is telling its toll. According to an article in *U.S. News & World Report*, the nation's first large nuclear power plant at Shippingport, Pennsylvania, is being dismantled. Now, the Seabrook, New Hampshire, plant that has already cost $5.5 billion is threatening its owners with bankruptcy. The Department of Energy (DoE) estimates that 16 of the 108 plants in the United States will reach the end of their useful lives by the year 2000 (40).

The nation is at an impasse regarding its energy needs for the third millennium. Construction costs for nuclear plants have spiraled over the past decade, and existing plants are producing at about half capacity. Oil and natural-gas supplies are dwindling and are the victims of international pressures. Coal, while plentiful, poses its own environmental hazards. What can be done to mitigate these problems?

Richard K. Lester (41) asks that very question and provides the following answer in an article in *Scientific American:*

> What changes in reactor design could mitigate these problems? A promising approach that has recently attracted attention both in the U.S. and overseas is to design the reactor so that if normal cooling fails, the heat generated by fission products in the core can safely dissipate through natural heat-transfer processes such as convection or thermal radiation. The passive cooling would suffice to prevent overheating and core damage, eliminating the need for external forced-cooling systems and plant operators to activate them.
>
> Such a strategy would considerably simplify the design and construction of the plant, and in particular its nonnuclear systems, which today are subject to strict regulatory standards because malfunctions there in theory can lead to core damage. A self-protecting reactor would make it possible for the rest of the plant to be designed and built to the standards of conventional fossil-fuel plants, and the savings in equipment and labor costs would be substantial.
> —Reproduced, with permission, from R.K. Lester, "Rethinking Nuclear Power," *Scientific American*, March 1986.

EXERCISE   Can the shift from the current technological approach for nuclear power be considered realistic? Would the combination of commercial standards and nuclear standards in a given installation be satisfactory to both regulatory bodies and the public?

Hypothesize what would have to be done at the levels of the federal government, regulatory bodies, and electric utilities to realize the lower power strategy. In particular, what would have to be done to allay environmental concerns?

2.12.5 Functionality in Transportation

The San Francisco Bay to Stockton, California navigation project included a plan that was approved in December 1981 for widening an existing 5.9-mile (mi) channel from 300 to 450 ft, and for deepening the existing channel from 30 to 45 ft. The objective was to allow two-way traffic and larger vessel passage within the reach of the channel.

Investigation of user requirements in the Stockton Port District revealed need for passage of larger vessels, but no current or future requirement for two-way traffic. The plan was therefore revised to widen the channel to only 350 ft and deepen the channel to 35 ft. As a consequence, construction cost was reduced from $9.3 million to $4.0 million and estimated maintenance cost for 25 years from $8.5 million to $5.5 million (42).

EXERCISE   Can the concept of alternating one-way facilities with a moderate increase in facilities be applied to the problems of metropolitan areas during rush hours? Consider the potential impact on users and speculate on alternative sources of funding.

2.12.6 Design to Cost Downstream

A major weapon system was already in production when a substantial amount of redesign was undertaken to improve range and other performance parameters. Despite the attempt to keep as much as possible of the original design, the unit production cost of the improved system was estimated to be significantly higher than the original.

An aggressive design-to-cost effort was initiated. The team was allowed to challenge as much as necessary of the original design. As shown in Figure 2.23, unit production cost was reduced by 28 percent as opposed to the 12 percent that would have resulted from classical cost reduction attempts.

EXERCISE   Consider the four phases in the life cycle of products or systems: concept, development, production, and ownership. Enumerate the kind of savings that design to cost could effect in investment and in operation and support cost if introduced in successively later phases.

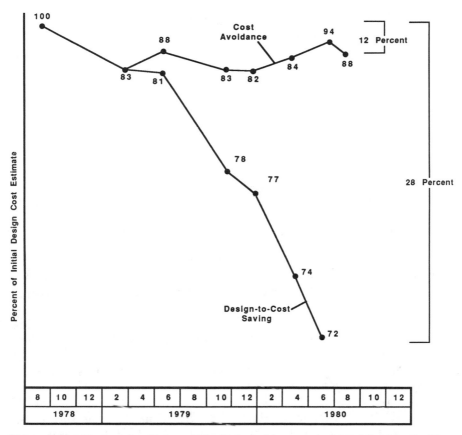

Figure 2.23 Cost-saving history (43). (Adapted by permission of the Martin Marietta Corporation.)

2.12.7 The Sun Shines Bright

The sun may shine bright over the broad land called "America," but the solar collector industry is virtually extinct. Solar collectors are devices for intercepting sunlight, converting the sunlight to heat, and carrying the heat to where it will be either used or stored. Table 2.22 depicts the fluctuation in the number of solar collector manufacturers in the United States.

This case study epitomizes Robert Burns's poem on the best-laid plans of mice and men and underscores the need to expect the unknown when undertaking risk analysis. Included in the 1974 ranks of solar collector manufacturers was a company that by 1979 had become one of the leaders in the field. The company was not among the ranks of the 97 survivors in 1986.

The post-1980 Arab oil embargo and the dramatic increase in crude oil prices motivated the solar collector industry to expand its horizon. The

TABLE 2.22   Domestic Solar Collector Manufacturers (44)

Year	Number	Year	Number
1974	45	1981	203
1975	131	1982	265
1976	186	1983	203
1977	321	1984	224
1978	340	1985	161
1979	349	1986	97
1980	233		

Source: U.S. Bureau of the Census, *Statistical Abstract of the United States: 1988.*

decrease in the number of companies from 349 in the year 1979 to 203 in the year 1981 was due primarily to consolidation in the industry by acquisitions over the 2-year period. Because of continued interest, the number of companies had increased to 265 in the year 1982.

This particular company had acquired three smaller companies following a reasonably precise analysis of the risk in expanding with borrowed capital. What the company had not foreseen was the impact on its customer base of the expiration in 1984 of the federal energy tax credit. Burdened by cashflow problems, the company discontinued operations in 1985.

EXERCISE   Construct trends lines (i.e., least-squares lines) using the techniques given in Section 6.6.2 for the number of solar collector manufacturers and for the number of barrels of crude oil imported daily from the data given in Tables 2.22 and 2.23. Develop the correlation between the number of manufacturers and the number of barrels.

TABLE 2.23   Crude-Oil Imports, 1000 Barrels per Day (45)

Year	Number	Year	Number
1974	3477	1981	4396
1975	4105	1982	3488
1976	5287	1983	3329
1977	5615	1984	3426
1978	6356	1985	3201
1979	6519	1986	4178
1980	5263	1987	4202

Source: U.S. Bureau of the Census, *Statistical Abstract of the United States; 1988.*

Using the premise that reduction in the amount of crude oil imported is conducive to renewed interest in solar energy, predict the state of the solar collector industry in the year 2000.

2.12.8 Concept of Proportionality

A number of cost-driving relationships are so obvious that they should be self-evident to individuals making decisions influencing costs. For example, development and production costs are exponentially proportional to the complexity of the items being produced. In turn, complexity is exponentially proportional to increased performance requirements. Therefore, it can be stated that development and production costs are exponentially proportional to increased performance requirements.

Table 2.24 lists some similar relationships for both direct and indirect cost as functions of schedule and scope of work. Note that there are four classes of proportionality: direct-exponential, direct-linear, inverse-linear, and inverse-exponential. For example, if the scheduled time of a program were doubled, direct cost would be expected to increase not by a factor of 2, but by a factor of 2 raised to some power to account for the increased-time effects of inflation and escalation. Should the scheduled time of a program be halved, however, direct cost would be expected to decrease by a factor of 2 raised to some power to account for the decreased-time effects of inflation and escalation. The foregoing relationships assume that per-unit labor time remains constant.

The schedule impact on indirect costs is linear provided the revised schedule remains within the period of time for which forward pricing rate agreements have been negotiated (see Section 5.3). Otherwise, the relationship is exponential—either direct or inverse, depending on the nature of the schedule change.

The impact of scope changes on direct cost is linear, with direct-charge labor and material increasing or decreasing accordingly. Small-scope

TABLE 2.24 Cost-Driving Relationships

Dependent Variable	Independent Variable	Proportionality
Direct cost	Schedule extension	Direct-exponential
	Schedule compression	Inverse-exponential
	Increased scope	Direct-linear
	Decreased scope	Inverse-linear
Indirect cost	Schedule extension	Direct-linear or direct-exponential
	Schedule compression	Inverse-linear or inverse-exponential
	Increased scope	None or direct-exponential
	Decreased scope	None or inverse-exponential

changes usually have no impact on indirect cost. For example, indirect-charge support and administrative labor can absorb small increases in workload. The impact of increased scope is direct-exponential once the ability to absorb increased workload is exceeded, however, and is inverse-exponential once the workload has decreased to the point where some personnel can be reassigned.

This case study is based on a bilateral agreement between a military customer and contractor to extend a production schedule from 5 to 7 years to compensate for the reduction in funding during the first three fiscal years of the production program. A quantity of 120 systems was to be delivered at the original rate of 24 systems in each of the 5 years. The average unit cost was $1.768 millions.

The revised schedule called for 12 systems to be delivered in each of the first 3 years followed by 21 systems in each of the successive 4 years. The year was 1978, and the extended period of production would start in 1979 and run through 1985.

The customer and contractor wisely took into consideration applicable proportionality relationships such as those given in Table 2.24. New forward pricing rate agreements were negotiated on the basis of the 1978 producer price index (PPI) for machinery and equipment, and the funding incurrence profile was revised.

Table 2.25 lists the producer price indexes (PPI) for machinery and equipment in 1978 and the ensuing years. Note that the PPI rose from 196.1 in 1978 to 298.9 in 1985, the year the last systems were produced and delivered. The producer was protected by an economic price adjustment (EPA) clause in the contract. The increased amounts of the customer's outlays, however, were far more than the reductions in the first 3 years of production.

EXERCISE   Use the PPI values for machinery and equipment given in Table 2.25 for the years 1979 to 1986 and prepare a profile of outlays by the customer for these years from the information given above. Use the time value of money relationships in Section 6.7 to calculate the present values,

TABLE 2.25   Producer Price Indexes for Machinery and Equipment (46)

Year	Number	Year	Number
1978	196.1	1983	286.4
1979	213.9	1984	293.1
1980	239.8	1985	298.9
1981	263.3	1986	303.3
1982	278.8		

Source: U.S. Bureau of the Census, *Statistical Abstract of the United States: 1988.*

from a baseline of 1978 of the series of outlays under the revised schedule of 7 years and of the series of outlays under the original schedule of 5 years.

Which approach would have been least costly to the customer in the long run? Can the expediency of adapting to limited funds in the early part of a production program be justified in light of the increased cost of the overall program?

REFERENCES

1–2. Philip B. Crosby, *Quality is Free—The Art of Making Quality Certain*, Mc-Graw-Hill Book Company, 1979.

3. Martin Marietta Corporation, *Design to Cost/Affordability Manual*, 1986.

4. Department of Defense Instruction No. 5000.2, *Major System Acquisition Procedures*, 1985.

5. Richard J. Schonberger, *Japanese Manufacturing Techniques*, The Free Press, 1982.

6. MIL-STD-499A, *Engineering Management*.

7. Office of Management and Budget, *The Federal Budget Update*, May 1987.

8. U.S. Bureau of the Census, *Statistical Abstract of the United States: 1988*.

9–10. Martin Marietta Corporation, *Design to Cost/Affordability Manual*, 1986.

11. James F. Ogg, *Pareto and Value Analysis*, Proccedings of the 1986 Society of American Value Engineers International Conference.

12. Martin Marietta Corporation, *Design to Cost/Affordability Manual*, 1986.

13. U.S. Department of Commerce, *National Technical Information Service*.

14. Oak Ridge National Laboratory, *Technical Applications Bulletins*, Oak Ridge, Tennessee.

15–17. Martin Marietta Corporation, *Design to Cost/Affordability Manual*, 1986.

18. Robert H. Hayes and Steven C. Wheelright, *Restoring Our Competitive Advantage, Competing Through Manufacturing*, John Wiley & Sons, 1984.

19. Thomas G. Gunn, *Manufacturing for Competitive Advantage, Becoming a World Class Manufacturer*, Balling Publishing Company, 1987.

20. Martin Marietta Corporation, *Manufacturing Resources Planning II, Requirements Definition*, 1985.

21. Martin Marietta Corporation, *Value Engineering Manual*, 1987.

22. Defense Logistics Agency, Contract Management Directorate, *Guidebook for DoD Contractors, Value Engineering*, August 1982.

23. Martin Marietta Corporation, *Value Engineering Manual*, 1987.

24. Lawrence D. Miles, *Techniques of Value Analysis and Engineering*, Mc-Graw-Hill Book Company, 1972.

25. Arthur E. Mudge, *Value Engineering, A Systematic Approach*, Arthur E. Mudge, 1971.

26. Martin Marietta Corporation, *Value Engineering Manual*, 1987.

27. Federal Acquisition Regulation, *Parts 48 and 52.248-1*.

28. Defense Systems Management College, *System Engineering Management Guide*, 1982.

29–32. Jack V. Michaels, *Risk–Cost Model for Bounding System Acquisition Cost*, Proceedings of the 1986 International Society of Parametric Analysts Annual Conference. Copyright 1986 Martin Marietta Corporation.

33. Defense Systems Management College, *System Engineering Management Guide*, 1982.

34. Martin Marietta Corporation, *Design to Cost/Affordability Manual*, 1986.

35. Defense Systems Management College, *System Engineering Management Guide*, 1982.

36. Office of Management and Budget, *Circular A-131, Value Engineering*, February 3, 1988.

37–39. John R. Peterson, *Value Engineering Change Proposals, A Continuing Success Story from a Small Business*, Proceedings of the Value Management Symposium of the Society of American Value Engineers, Winter Park, FL, October 1, 1984.

40. *U.S. News & World Report*, "Death of a Nuclear Plant," November 2, 1987.

41. R.K. Lester, "Rethinking Nuclear Power," *Scientific American*, March 1986.

42. U.S. Army Corps of Engineers Publication EPS 1-3, *Value Engineering Program*, April 1987.

43. Martin Marietta Corporation, *Design to Cost/Affordability Manual*, 1986.

44–46. U.S. Bureau of the Census, *Statistical Abstract of the United States: 1988*.

3
DEFINING ACTIVITIES AND RESPONSIBILITIES

The elements of successful design-to-cost programs are listed in Table 3.1. Success is a direct function of continued management interest, emphasis, and support; of how well activities are defined and organized; and of how well responsibilities are assigned, understood, and pursued over the program lifetime. The concern of this chapter is how to initiate, maintain, and emphasize design to cost throughout the organization as well as over the program lifetime.

The process starts with clear understanding of required design-to-cost activities by contractual phases as enumerated in the following section of this chapter. The major concern should be how to deal with cost growth starting in the preproposal phase of the program and continuing until the final contractual obligation has been fulfilled.

The next concern should be how to organize for design to cost so as to achieve synergistic results from individual organizational commitments to affordability. The guidelines given in this chapter have a proven record of success, and the typical design-to-cost organization described herein is worthy of emulation.

The success, however, depends on how well roles and responsibilities are defined and assigned to individuals. The next section, therefore, presents definitive statements of work for the various functional disciplines involved in the program. Individual performance evaluation should be keyed to these statements of work.

Multiple design solution and trade studies are dictates in design to cost. The conduct of trade studies is the subject of the next section, which describes a proven methodology for effective trades and a technique for evaluating study candidates that are in the embryonic stage.

The following section discusses the reward of supplier participation in design-to-cost programs in terms of eliminating unnecessary cost in procurement. Some insight is provided into the advantages of multiple sourcing,

TABLE 3.1   Elements of Successful Design-to-Cost Programs (1)

Institute effective design-to-cost management
Initiate, maintain, and emphasize design to cost through the program lifetime
Understand affordability limits and functional worth of requirements
Establish realistic but challenging design-to-cost goals
Assign cost goals to individuals, not to organizations.
Establish audit trails for tracking cost growth versus requirements growth and for
 individual accountability
Require multiple design solutions and trade studies.
Design inherently low cost systems
Select optimal tooling and facilities concept
Employ competitive business strategy
Flow down requirements and incentives to suppliers
Use validated and accepted estimating techniques
Motivate personnel
Remember history and benefit from the experience of others

Reprinted by permission of the Martin Marietta Corporation.

which are revisited again in Section 5.4.4 in the context of the business strategy for dealing with suppliers, and the need for constant supplier surveillance to prevent last-minute surprises.

It is impossible to achieve the full fruition of design to cost without rigorous control of technical baselines as well as cost goals. Therefore, a section is devoted to specification practices in the context of MIL-STD-490. Design-to-cost practitioners should gain familiarity with these practices even though they may never work on a military program because of the rigor they ensure in defining products and systems.

Effective design to cost is very dependent on both schedule control and the maintenance of an audit trail that relates technical performance toward achieving specification requirements to cost performance. Both of these activities require absolute control over matters affecting the technical baseline. Therefore, another section is devoted to configuration management in the context of MIL-STD-483A and includes some observations on data management. Both configuration management and data management have the potential for significant cost saving. However, such saving needs to be pursued judiciously.

This is followed by some suggestions on schedule control in the context of preventing cost growth. Schedule control is revisited in Section 5.7 in the context of a cost-saving strategy.

Likewise, reviews are the lifeblood of effective design-to-cost programs, and a section is devoted to technical reviews and audits in the context of MIL-STD-1521A. Again, it would be advantageous for design-to-cost practitioners to gain familiarity with these practices, which have evolved from managing thousands of complex, high-technology programs.

Two other military standards are worthy of consideration by design-to-cost practitioners: MIL-STD-499A, *Engineering Management,* and MIL-STD-1567A, *Work Measurement.* The former is particularly interesting from the viewpoint of technical performance measurement, which is both the counterpart of cost–schedule control systems criteria according to DoD Instruction 7000.2 (see Section 6.8.1) and is a corollary task to risk management as well as cost and schedule control.

Both should be pursued vigorously throughout development. Military Standard 1567A provides the yardstick for measuring the effectiveness of cost-saving effort in the factory.

At this juncture, it is appropriate to discuss audit trails, which should be established at the very onset of programs to allow cost performance to be tracked, responsibility to be maintained, and requirements growth to be separated from cost growth. The degree of formalism may differ in the public and private sectors and as a function of the size of the program, but to achieve both affordability and profitability, the substance should not differ.

Following the summary of its contents, the chapter concludes with a number of case studies and exercises that are intended to amplify key points in the chapter. The exercises allow the readers to relate their experiences and viewpoints to the events that are unfolded in the case studies.

3.1 ACTIVITIES BY CONTRACTUAL PHASE

From the life-cycle viewpoint, the major program phases are concept formulation, development, production, and ownership. This was the framework for the discussion in Chapter 2, starting with the optimum timetable for management decisions and concluding with setting realistic design-to-cost goals.

Where large investments are involved in either the public or private sectors, the aforementioned phases should also be considered from their contractual status—preproposal, proposal or contractual—because these determine how the work is funded and accomplished. This is the framework for this chapter.

The ensuing discussion is in the context of governmental customers and contractors. However, the guidance can serve other customers and producers in the high-technology arena.

3.1.1 Preproposal Phase

Government bodies and their industrial counterparts devote a significant amount of effort to issues of functionality and affordability whenever the acquisition of new products, systems, or services are contemplated. Long before solicitations or propositions are tendered, customers strive to establish the functional worth of their requirements and to determine their should-cost worth. Concurrently, producers explore alternative approaches in the attempt to mitigate cost drivers while satisfying essential requirements of customers.

The preproposal phase is one of the most important and rewarding periods in the program for cost saving, making it imperative that design-to-cost principles be kept foremost in the minds of all concerned. Toward that goal, this is the time to determine the framework of the organization required for design to cost and to select the manager and team members. In addition, it is necessary to estimate and obtain approval of the resources needed to ensure the continuity of the effort.

The flow of activities for the team is shown in Figure 3.1. Initial activities during the preproposal phase are affordability analysis and cost-effectiveness analysis of the new product or system as described in Sections 2.3 and 2.4. Cost-estimating activity that accompanies these analyses and preliminary estimates are usually prepared by the government's Program Management Office (PMO) and sometimes at the headquarters level of the particular service by an independent function, called the Cost Analysis Improvement Group (CAIG).

Contractors with more successful track records become quite involved with their government counterparts during the preproposal phase. Frequently, first cuts at development and production costs come from contractors who possess the necessary skills and facilities to meet the requirements.

Baseline cost estimates that are made during the preproposal phase generally use expert opinion, analogy, or parametric methods that are described in Section 6.4. Although usually gross approximations, these are the most reliable estimates available, and they serve to establish a footing for the proposed program.

A baseline cost estimate implies that a preliminary engineering baseline has been established even though little or no detail design is yet available. It often means that a design-to-cost goal has been imposed by a customer in the contracting domain and by marketing organizations in other ventures.

It is very important to ensure adequate documentation of both the baseline design and the cost estimate. This is where traceability begins, and an audit trail is established to differentiate requirements growth from cost growth as the program matures.

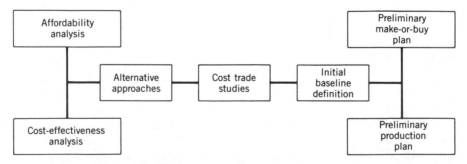

Figure 3.1   Design-to-cost preproposal activity flow.

Cost trade studies should be conducted of all operational and technical requirements, identifying those that are cost drivers. Each element should be reviewed for its contribution to performance versus the cost involved. It is essential that alternatives be found for elements whose costs are greater than their contribution to performance.

A work-breakdown structure (WBS) and generation breakdown (GB) should be established that will serve proposal and contract needs with as little modification as possible. The WBS is a product-oriented family-tree division of hardware, software, services, and other work tasks that organizes, defines, and displays the product to be produced as well as the work to be accomplished toward achieving the specified product. The GB is similar to the WBS except that it is limited to the product to be produced and essentially serves as the architecture for putting the product together.

The WBS and GB in turn provide the framework for the preliminary make-or-buy plan and preliminary production plan that should also be prepared during the preproposal phase. The make-or-buy plan, a formal document that enumerates those components that will be made by the organization producing a particular product and which components will be purchased, is prepared on the basis of organizational capability, component criticality, and other similar factors. The production plan is a formal document governing the manner in which make components will be produced.

The usual procedure is for the manufacturing organization in the company to take the lead in these matters with the cooperation of the functional disciplines. The design-to-cost manager should ensure that the lowest cost approach is followed in deciding the make-or-buy structure within the limit of established company policy, which preordains that certain work will be accomplished in-house.

On the basis of the make-or-buy plan, the procurement organization should begin planning the acquisition of the major subsystems. The design-to-cost manager should ensure that all potential subcontractors are aware of design-to-cost requirements in the program. A large measure of the success of a program is dependent on the cost performance of its subcontractors.

Also at this time, the manufacturing organization should begin initial planning for fabrication and assembly of the product or system. Manufacturing representatives should be members of the design-to-cost team to ensure that the optimum cost-effective manufacturing solution is found. As in other program activities, it is incumbent on the design-to-cost manager to act as coordinator and medium of communication among the various functional entities on the program.

3.1.2 Proposal Phase

If aggressive and comprehensive preproposal activities were pursued, the proposal phase should consist mainly of comparing and verifying accomplished tasks against requirements in the request for proposal (RFP). The typical flow of activities is shown in Figure 3.2. It should be noted that the

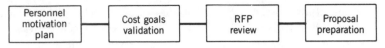

Figure 3.2 Design-to-cost proposal activity flow.

start of the proposal phase, with its typically long working hours, is the most fruitful time to institute and publicize a personnel motivation plan.

Cost goals should be validated during the proposal phase. This usually requires firm quotations from suppliers and industrial engineering estimates of what is to be built.

The method by which the customer states cost goals can vary with program phasing. For conceptual studies, goals may be stated for either unit production cost or total life-cycle cost. Either way, the objective is to assess affordability while exploring alternative system concepts.

If the solicitation is for a later phase, such as advanced or engineering development, cost goals can vary radically, depending on whether the contractor has participated in a previous phase of the program. If the solicitation is for follow-on effort, then examination of the customer's cost goals should allow verification of previous findings.

If there was no participation in an earlier phase, an intense effort should be undertaken to substantiate the customer's cost goals. In addition to substantiating cost goals, it is important to conduct a careful review of the RFP's special provisions relating to design to cost. In particular, be alert for the following:

1. REPORTING LEVEL

Check that the reporting level is appropriate for the type of program. Work-breakdown-structure level 3 or 4 is usually a good choice for a fairly mature design (advanced or engineering development); level 2 is more appropriate for a conceptual design. In any event, the level should not be lower than the one at which costs are accumulated and should be compatible with allocated goals for purposes of tracking and cost responsibility.

2. COST-ELEMENT DEFINITION

Carefully review the cost items included and excluded in the cost target. Preferably, they should be limited to recurring investment contractor costs for manufacturing the product or system.

3. EFFECTS OF INFLATION AND OF TIME VALUE DISCOUNTING

The government is still studying methods for reliably predicting the future effects of inflation, with no indication of consistent success. Also, there are sporadic attempts to introduce into life-cycle cost estimates a discounting schema (see Section 6.8.3) to allow for the time value of money, which appears in cost proposals as capital cost of facilities money (CCoFM). These two factors have a tendency to cancel each other out; however, inflation and CCoFM are so dynamic that they should be treated separately and be expressed in constant dollars.

4. DEFLATION AND DEESCALATION PROCEDURES AND FACTORS

These are very important considerations and, if not properly defined, cost goals rapidly become uncontrollable as inflation escalation pushes costs higher. Deflation and deescalation avoid the danger of predicting the economy and simplify proposal preparation. A diligent effort should be made to identify and obtain approval for producer price indexes (PPIs) and standard industrial codes (SICs) that are compatible with the product under consideration. Experience indicates that although higher and more aggregate indexes and codes more accurately reflect most companies' method of doing business, lower and more disaggregate indexes and codes provide more protection to contractors. This subject is treated in some detail in Section 6.8.3.

5. AWARD FEE PROVISIONS AND TIMING

Customers are generally willing to provide incentives for achieving or bettering specified cost goals. These usually take the form of an award fee, which is an incentive offered by the customer in addition to and separate from any other fee provision in the contract. The dollar amount usually justifies the effort to earn as much of the award fee as possible. One of the keys to this is to have a credible cost history that will withstand the most rigorous audit. In this regard, the special provisions of the request for procurement (RFP) should contain a statement substantially as follows: "Any amount of fee not awarded during any of the designated award periods may be earned in subsequent period(s)."

3.1.3 Contractual Phase

The contractual phase covers a much larger time span than the previous phases and involves a wide range of subphases: concept formulation, demonstration and validation; full-scale engineering development, including production planning and tooling design; and production, including support.

Figure 3.3 shows the typical flow of design-to-cost activities during the contractual process; however, the influence of design to cost on the cost of products is steadily reduced as programs progress toward production. The detail in the illustration shows that design-to-cost activity is at a peak during the contractual phase.

Initial work consists mostly in gathering and checking actual costs against the cost figures generated during the proposal phase. If the actual costs exceed the projected costs, the design-to-cost team should seek solutions

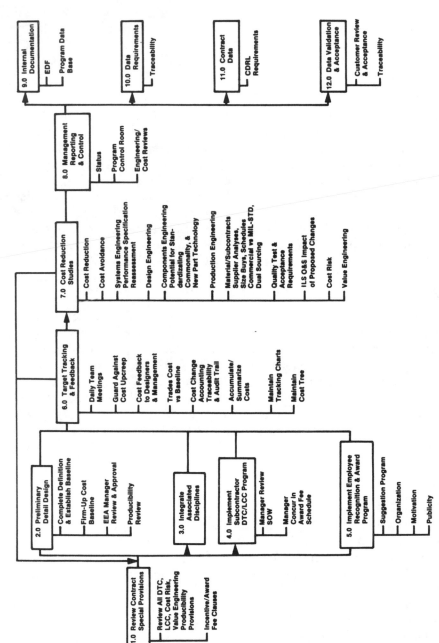

Figure 3.3 Design-to-cost contractual activity flow (2). (Reprinted by permission of the Martin Marietta Corporation.)

that bring the cost under control. Teamwork is key, and the employees recognition and award program should be operational at this point.

The following remarks illuminate activities by contractual subphases:

1. CONCEPT FORMULATION, DEMONSTRATION, AND VALIDATION

In conceptual contracts, there is often no formal design-to-cost goal. However, in many cases the contractor is provided guidance about acceptable cost levels along with design guidance. By the end of this subphase, there should be enough information to establish the design-to-cost goals with reasonable levels of confidence. Estimates from the contractor should be in as much detail and contain as much substantiating data as is consistent with the degree of design definition. Contracts for validation present no great challenge from the standpoint of design to cost if the steps described previously were observed. Typically, customers elect a proposed design and validation program that is considered to be a balance of performance, life-cycle cost, and schedule.

2. FULL-SCALE ENGINEERING DEVELOPMENT

In full-scale engineering development contracts, designs become defined and production configurations established. Opportunities for cost reduction begin to diminish during this phase, and the emphasis shifts toward preventing or minimizing cost growth. Constant and close communication is necessary to avoid cost growth. Cost goals need to be tracked from the start of full-scale engineering development phase with established organizational patterns and cost-tracking techniques. If design to cost has not yet been formally instituted on the program until this phase, effort should begin on the first day of the contract. As stated above, the opportunities for significant cost reductions will be severely limited unless time, money, and the willingness to accommodate sizable changes in direction are given. This, of course, is almost entirely dependent on the thrust and requirements of the contract. If the contract does not provide some flexibility in time and funds to allow cost reduction design iterations, then a viable design-to-cost program is difficult, if not impossible. The cost feedback loop should be fully operational at this point with functional inhibitions overcome to allow a free and frank exchange of cost information. Control of cost against the established baseline should be a continuing process by this time.

Costs and cost changes should be accumulated with respect to the WBS or GB and summarized by cost goal responsibility. Regardless of the operational style of a company or a program, an individual should be identified as responsible for each element of hardware and for attaining the associated cost goal. However, it is the responsibility of the design-to-cost manager to ensure that costs in the aggregate do not exceed overall design-to cost goals for products or systems. A fundamental principle in design to cost is that if costs increase in certain areas, then costs in some other areas must be reduced by commensurate amounts. This should be effected by trades of cost and functionality among the various components of the products or systems.

Continuous visibility into the cost and functionality of maturing designs is essential. Cost performance tracking should be done both daily on a direct interchange basis between the design-to-cost manager and responsible individuals, and at periodic program and design reviews. This daily contact among members of the team ensures a tight feedback loop that allows early detection of potential problems as designs progress.

The problems should be sorted in terms of being product-related, process-related, or both. Once the root causes of the problems have been established as being design-related, material- or parts-related, or both, preferred solutions to the problems should be evaluated in the context of the particular phase of the program and selected so as to introduce the minimum possible delay and increase in cost on the basis of the overall program. For example, an element of product redesign during the development phase would incur some additional nonrecurring cost but could avoid substantially larger increases in recurring cost during the production phase. However, during the production phase it might be preferable to undertake some additional nonrecurring cost of tooling and process changes to avoid the substantially larger nonrecurring costs due to such factors as product redesign and requalification of new suppliers.

The foregoing underscores the importance of the design-to-cost manager having drawing review and approval authority in order to keep abreast of the program at each step of product design and process design. In particular, it is essential that the design-to-cost manager be in the approval channel for trade studies (see Section 3.4). Thus, no change will take place without specific review, assessment, and concurrence of the design-to-cost manager from the standpoint of achieving design-to-cost goals.

3. PRODUCTION

The greatest possible motivation for a company is a market for its products that ensures increased profits and growth, although survival itself may occasionally emerge as the key motivational force. The rewards of properly conducted design-to-cost programs are increased profitability and affordability. The penalties of improperly conducted programs, or no programs at all, are exactly the opposite. The broad range of rewards and penalties associated with design-to-cost make it particularly important that management be kept thoroughly informed of the status of the program. The design-to-cost manager should take the initiative to ensure full consideration of cost performance during program reviews. Contracts for the production phase are structured to reward the contractor for actual cost performance against the unit production cost goal. There should be provisions in the production contract to provide for measurement of actual costs against cost goals established in accordance with an agreed-to set of cost elements and progress milestones. In addition, there should be provisions in the contract to prevent assignment of production-related costs to elements of cost not covered by the cost goals. Examples of such elements of cost are the cost of receiving, inspecting and controlling government-furnished equipment (GFE) used in both development contracts and productions contracts and the cost of initial spares used in initial operation capability (IOC) trials with first articles of production hardware.

The contractor should ensure that deliverable items that are not covered by the unit production cost goal are separately priced line items. This is essential in order to demonstrate the extent to which goals are being achieved. Frequently, development contracts contain a reliability improvement warranty (RIW) clause whereby contractors commit to incorporating in production hardware any design changes developed subsequent to the start of production that will increase the reliability of the produced products. This can become a major cost driver insofar as design changes usually require process changes. There are several approaches toward mitigating the impact of such cost increases, starting with the attempt to negotiate funds for RIW work in the production contracts. Beyond that, it is important to ensure that the contracts contain clauses for value engineering change proposals and cost-reduction-oriented contractual product improvement programs that allow the contractor to share up to 50 percent of the forthcoming net savings (see Section 2.8.3).

Good documentation is especially important during production contracts. This is particularly true for the technical baseline, which is referred to as the "technical data package" (TDP) and the cost baseline that includes firm quotations from suppliers and detailed industrial engineering estimates for each element of the WBS. Complete cost traceability is generally required by customers, and the design-to-cost manager should organize and maintain a complete filing system containing records of every program activity that can have an impact on cost.

The contract data requirements list (CDRL) should be reviewed carefully. The scope and frequency of the technical and administrative reports can have a considerable impact on program costs. This applies to subcontractors as well as to the prime contractor.

3.1.4 Dealing with Cost Growth

Seemingly inevitable situations arise wherein it is suddenly discovered that current cost estimates exceed previous predictions, precipitating intensive cost-reduction exercises. As stated before, it is imperative to have a firmly established baseline that documents in detail previous and current cost estimates and the basis for estimates, so that cost growth can be separated from requirements growth.

If cost growth does occur, all available cost-reduction and cost-avoidance techniques should be exploited by functional disciplines. As described in Section 2.8, a value engineering representative is a valuable adjunct in such investigations.

It may be necessary and perhaps profitable to go back to the beginning to find the means to reduce cost. In particular, the system engineering organization should conduct a rigorous reassessment of requirements, categorizing them by degree of criticality to the mission, and the consequences of varying degrees of performance. From this, it may be possible to develop a rationale for change proposals that have the potential of high dollar savings for limited performance reduction.

The design engineering organization should seek simpler and consequently less costly approaches in designing products or systems. They should examine their designs for undue conservatism and possible material substitutions and, in concert with the manufacturing organization, search for less expensive fabrication techniques.

Designers should be encouraged to take a probabilistic approach to design risk (see Section 2.9). Instead of optimizing risk on each component, a minimum cost approach that has an acceptable overall risk should be found.

The components engineering organization should explore both elemental and composite material costs from the viewpoint of standardization, commonality, and new technology. For example, microelectronic technology takes a quantum leap about every 4 years; therefore, product life expectancy should be reviewed to eliminate cost creep, which accompanies obsolescence.

The manufacturing and industrial engineering organizations should encourage production-line personnel to recommend equipment and process changes for improved productivity and reduced scrap and rework. Solutions to production cost problems should be sought in concert with the other functional disciplines. The institutional approach wherein each functional organization is concerned only with its own responsibilities and prerogatives simply does not produce low-cost products.

The procurement organization should conduct a supplier analysis, exploring avenues for procured parts cost reduction, including larger buys, relaxed schedules, requirements cost-sensitivity reviews (e.g., commericial vs. military quality), and qualification of new sources. In particular, the feasibility of competition for the various procurements should be reexamined. It has been shown repeatedly that competition is the best cost-reduction technique available (see Section 5.4); however, the concern for quality must pervade such pursuits.

Suppliers should be encouraged to conduct cost and schedule trade-offs in search for results that could provide the basis for cost-reducing specification changes such as reduced tolerance and surface finish requirements. Experience shows that suppliers are willing and able to help when they become part of a team, given they understand the team's objectives.

The product assurance organization should examine the cost impact of any unusually severe or overly demanding test and acceptance requirements and recommend alternatives. Since quality-control activities are both critical and significant cost drivers, incorporation of built-in test features in the items being produced and of inspection features in tooling should be considered. An example of the latter would be go–no go devices on mills, drill presses, and other machinery, whereby operations cease if out-of-tolerance items are produced.

As design changes are proposed to reduce production costs, the product support organization should determine the corresponding impact of the proposed change on operation and support (O&S) costs. It is important that O&S models used to determine the cost impact of such changes be derived from the approved O&S concept for the particular product or system.

3.2 ORGANIZING FOR DESIGN TO COST

A comprehensive design-to-cost management plan is a key element of a strong cost-avoidance oriented approach to system acquisition and is usually required by the request for proposal (RFP). The plan should be conceived and implemented early in the deliberations to achieve producibility and pro-

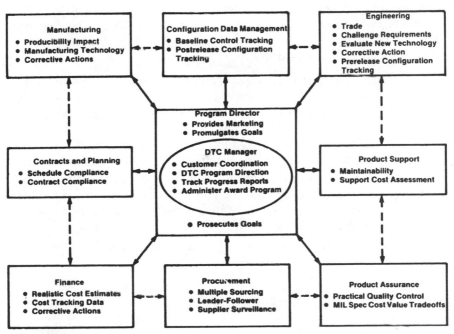

Figure 3.4 Typical design-to-cost organization (3). (Reprinted by permission of the Martin Marietta Corporation.)

TABLE 3.2   Design-to-Cost Team Responsibilities (4)

Entity	Primary Function
Program director	Establishes business strategy and affordability limits; promulgates and prosecute goals
Design-to-cost manager	Executes design-to-cost program; determines corrective actions
Engineering	Formulates baseline design
Industrial Engineering	Estimates production costs
Manufacturing	Provides facilitization, tooling, and production planning
Product Assurance	Ensures quality control
Procurement	Provides control of subcontractors and vendors
Product Support	Fulfills logistical requirements
Planning	Ensures schedule compliance
Configuration and Data Control	Provides change control and data submittal
Finance	Provides cost estimating and cost control
Contracts	Ensures contract compliance

Adapted by permission of the Martin Marietta Corporation.

ductivity in the baseline design and should be applicable through all program phases.

The plan governs the organization and staffing of the design-to-cost team and the functional responsibilities of team members. Figure 3.4 illuminates the functions of a typical design-to-cost organization in high-technology organizations. Team responsibilities are summarized in Table 3.2. Several organizational points are noteworthy.

1. The design-to-cost manager reports directly to the program director to ensure independence. The tendency to appoint the manufacturing manager, or for that matter the engineering manager, can lead to conflicts of interest since the performance evaluation of these individuals is initiated influenced largely by their functional departments, and frequently functional and program objectives are at odds with each other.

2. The functional managers shown in the illustration are those already on-program, fulfilling their respective line responsibilities, ensuring that design to cost is an integral part of their normal functions and avoiding the cost burden of additional staff.

3. The design-to-cost manager is in the approval chain for all matters affecting cost.

3.3   FUNCTIONAL RESPONSIBILITIES

The success of design to cost is a direct function of how well specific cost subgoals are assigned to line-function managers and of the care taken in delineating specific responsibilities. The criteria for cost and schedule control outlined in Section 6.8 can serve as measures for determining how well these tasks have been done.

Above all, it is absolutely essential that these individuals be given authority that is commensurate with the responsibilities for which they are accountable. The following statements of work build from the discussion in Section 3.3 and are offered as role models for high-technology undertakings in both the public and private sectors (5).

3.3.1 Engineering Organization

The actions and decisions of the engineering organization affect every other functional discipline; consequently, it takes the lead during design development and hardware qualification and works closely with manufacturing during the pilot production phase of system acquisition. Table 3.3 is the recommended statement of work (SOW) for the engineering organization.

3.3.2 Manufacturing Organization

Aggressive participation by the manufacturing organization is required during development as well as production. Manufacturing representatives should be members of subsystem task groups and participate in the design and evaluation of the product or system concept. Table 3.4 is the recommended SOW for the manufacturing organization.

TABLE 3.3   Engineering Organization Statement of Work for Design to Cost

Provide leadership in matters relating to MIL-STD-499A, *Engineering Management*

Examine the configuration of the hardware to determine what changes are necessary to ensure optimum producibility of the production design

Develop a priced generation breakdown (GB) of the preliminary production configuration, with assistance from the finance organization and other functional disciplines

Review associated costs of existing designs to be used in the production configuration

Review and challenge specifications

Generate a list of potential trade studies

Conduct approved trade studies and recommend cost-effective changes

Provide inputs to the procurement organization on critical components and assemblies

Provide members for supplier survey team and conduct design critique and value analysis on supplier suggestions

Provide a list of alternative approaches

TABLE 3.4 Manufacturing Organization Statement of Work for Design to Cost

Provide leadership in matters relating to MIL-STD-1528, *Production Management*

Provide preliminary production plan and manufacturing concepts to support the plan

Provide preliminary make-or-buy plan to ascertain procurement needs for production

Provide members for supplier survey teams to provide analysis and recommendations in the areas of supplier equipment, facilities, tooling, testing, manufacturing procedures, labor skills, labor relations, process capability, and producibility programs

Provide final production plan and final make-or-buy plan

Survey industry for commercial processes with potential application to high-technology hardware

Recommend design and process changes to improve producibility and reduce unit production cost

Design tools to make cost goal labor standards realizable

Develop performance and work standards that will enhance achievability of design-to-cost goals

Develop capital equipment acquisition requirements on the basis of return on tooling investment

Track and monitor design changes against baseline for cost goals impact

Provide a list of alternative production approaches

3.3.3 Product Assurance Organization

Quality should be job number one of all disciplines; however, it is the responsibility of product assurance organization to ensure that quality standards are applied properly to delivered products. Equally aggressive participation is required of Product Assurance during development as well as production. The amount of quality touch labor expended in production is a

TABLE 3.5 Product Assurance Organization Statement of Work for Design to Cost

Provide leadership in matters relating to MIL-Q-9858A, *Quality Program Requirements*

Reduce quality touch labor cost to no more than 3 percent of unit cost without compromising product quality

Inject "new quality" considerations such as "tolerance centering" (see Section 4.5.1) at the earliest practical point in the product or system design

Provide members for survey teams to evaluate suppliers' capability for consistent production of quality products

Evaluate subcontractors' and suppliers' quality engineering, inspection, general controls, methods, equipment, skills, and procedures

Evaluate suppliers' previous performance to serve as a basis for predicting their capability of maintaining required quality levels

Work with the procurement organization to establish cost-effective supplier surveillance fertile area for cost saving. Table 3.5 is the recommended SOW for the product assurance organization.

3.3.4 Procurement Organization

Typically, 40 to 60 percent of the cost of high-technology products can be expended on procured items. Efficient use of supplier resources can contribute significantly to achieving design-to-cost goals. Table 3.6 is the recommended SOW for the procurement organization.

TABLE 3.6   Procurement Organization Statement of Work for Design to Cost

Provide cost history of all levels of material requirements and respond to new inquiries and cost-oriented trade studies

Participate in make-or-buy decisions to ensure maximum cost advantage of each decision

Prepare an initial supplier list and lead surveys of potential suppliers to gain comprehensive knowledge of technical and production capabilities, financial stability, and general management strength, stability, and attitude toward the program

Provide source selection data, including recommended dual sourcing where feasible, evaluation of suppliers' capabilities to overcome known areas of weakness, alternate sourcing where significant supplier weakness is discovered, and maximum use of new suppliers where significant contributions (quality, technical, price, delivery) are available

Provide close liaison with suppliers of designed parts to make optimum use of advances in suppliers' technology and maximum efforts to best use suppliers' overall capabilities

Provide supplier producibility inputs and recommendations and communicate any supplier commentary regarding specifications or changes that may affect supplier performance

Conduct intensified supplier surveys and performance analyses before beginning the production program, to discover any supplier weakness previously overlooked, and take action immediately if conditions such as reorganization, new interests, or any other critical change in corporate direction will detract from immediate or long-range interests of the program

Provide a final list of acceptable suppliers with regard to development or production effort

In conjunction with the product assurance organization, implement a supplier early warning system for nonperformance in critical procurement

Recommend sources for dual development when critical high-cost hardware design and fabrication is involved, and continue to survey industry for new suppliers who can contribute to program objectives

Extend design-to-cost requirements, reporting requirements, and award fees and incentives to suppliers

Train suppliers in design-to-cost methodology

Monitor, evaluate, and report supplier progress against assigned cost goals

TABLE 3.7 Product Support Organization Statement of Work for Design to Cost

Assist in validating cost estimates with data from the user's logistical organization

Assist in definition of the production configuration to ensure that logistics cost drivers receive the proper visibility for management review and are tracked accurately

Provide guidance to supplier's logistical personnel to ensure that the objectives of the prime contract can be achieved

Participate in trade studies and initiate logistic-peculiar trades to arrive at the lowest feasible cost to accomplish each function

Provide O&S cost estimates for life-cycle-cost trades

3.3.5 Product Support Organization

Typically, O&S accounts for the largest share of the life-cycle cost. The product support organization should participate in all phases of the program to assist in attaining the best balance of acquisition cost, O&S cost, acceptable performance, and schedule. Table 3.7 is the recommended SOW for the product support organization.

3.3.6 Planning Organization

The role of the planning organization is to ensure timely implementation of the design-to-cost program and to provide design and cost status visibility to management by preparing various levels of schedules and tracking performance to these schedules. Table 3.8 is the recommended SOW for the planning organization.

3.3.7 Configuration and Data Management Organization

The configuration and data management organization has the responsibility for the maintenance of specifications (see Section 3.6) and configuration control of the design-to-cost baseline and production configuration (see Sec-

TABLE 3.8 Planning Organization Statement of Work for Design to Cost

Provide planning leadership in all matters relating to MIL-STD-1521A, *Technical Reviews and Audits of Systems, Equipments, and Computer Programs*

Establish detailed schedules for the implementation of the design-to-cost program

Assess production implementation schedule for impact of long-lead items on critical path and design-to-cost goals, and recommend changes to schedule

Review design and cost performance and report status to management

Provide schedules for internal and external reviews

Provide schedules for contract end item and data item deliveries

In conjunction with the finance organization, and the configuration and data management organization, establish and track the design-to-cost audit trail

TABLE 3.9 Configuration and Data Management Organization Statement of Work for Design to Cost

Provide leadership in matters relating to MIL-STD-490, *Specification Practices;* DOD-STD-480A, *Configuration Control-Engineering Changes, Deviations and Waivers;* and MIL-STD-483A, *Configuration Management Practices for Systems, Equipment, Munitions, and Computer Programs*

Provide recording of the proceedings and documentation and tracking of action items in matters relating to MIL-STD-1521A, *Reviews and Audits for Systems, Equipments, and Computer Programs*

Identify the configuration elements of the WBS impacted by design to cost and provide specifications maintenance for these elements

Maintain control of the production configuration

Establish the change management process to accommodate design-to-cost and value engineering change proposals

Maintain data control in accordance with the contract data requirements list (CDRL)

In conjunction with the finance organization and the planning organization, establish and track the design-to-cost audit trail

tions 3.6 and 3.7). The configuration and data management organization is the only official source for program documentation. Table 3.9 is the recommended SOW for the configuration and data management organization.

3.3.8 Finance Organization

The finance organization is responsible for all cost-estimating and control activities and for maintaining the cost baseline for production configurations. The finance organization is the only official source for cost data and the final authority on the audit trail. Table 3.10 is the recommended SOW for the finance organization.

3.3.9 Contracts Organization

The contracts organization has the responsibility for the contractual aspects of design to cost and is the only entity that can commit the program contractually. Typically, the on-program configuration and data management organization reports to the on-program contracts organization. Table 3.11 is the recommended SOW for the contracts organization.

The next section discusses the management of trade studies. It is essential that all functional disciplines view the respective forgoing statements of work as their charter to participate in and influence the outcome of trades studies so that optimal balances of functionality and affordability are obtained.

TABLE 3.10   Finance Organization Statement of Work for Design to Cost

Provide leadership in matters relating to DoD Instruction 7000.2, *Performance Measurement for Selected Acquisitions,* and performance measurement systems responding thereto (see Section 6.8.2)

Participate in all trade studies and baseline change actions and furnish the cost-impact information for changes under evaluation

Furnish preliminary estimates to provide order of magnitude and relative cost data for selection of candidate approaches

In conjunction with the planning organization and the configuration and data management organization, establish and track the design-to-cost audit trail

Complete baseline updates following significant change decisions and provide cost definition to evaluate impact on goals

Provide members for supplier survey teams

Provide cost and price analysis of suppliers' quotations

Participate in setting supplier goals and evaluating and approving cost goal status reports

Establish funding limits for cost account managers and collect cost

Analyze variance reports and update latest revised estimates (LRE)

TABLE 3.11   Contracts Organization Statement of Work for Design to Cost

Review and negotiate contract and provide direction concerning contractual design-to-cost provisions

Issue operations directives to implement the various activities of the design-to-cost program

Submit and negotiate engineering and value engineering change proposals

Deliver contract end items and data items to customers

3.4   MANAGING TRADE STUDIES

Trade studies are the vehicles for evolving cost-reduction strategies and mitigating program risks. Figure 3.5 illustrates a typical closed-loop process for managing trade studies wherein cost is an argument. A control number is assigned to each study, and a specific statement of work and schedule are prepared and maintained under the configuration control in conjunction with those areas of the baseline that may be impacted by the study findings.

Note the box in the illustration entitled "Analyses and trade studies." The issue is how to assess concepts that are too primitive in terms of design and cost details to consider them as alternative solutions in trade study.

The approach shown in Figure 3.6 is recommended for such cases. No matter how primitive concepts may be, there is always sufficient experience and knowledge on programs to judge intuitively how performance, reliabil-

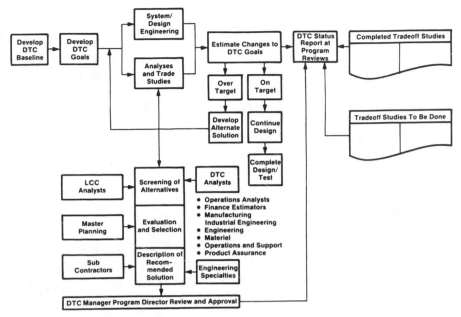

Figure 3.5 Trade study methodology (6). (Reprinted by permission of the Martin Marietta Corporation.)

ity, maintainability, and cost would be affected if the concepts were implemented.

This judgment is indicated in Figure 3.6 by up or down arrows for increases or decreases, or dashes for no expected changes. Concepts that are annotated with up arrows for performance, reliability, and maintainability, and down arrows for cost, are suitable candidates for trade studies.

Date	Control Number	Concept Description	Performance ↑ Up —— Unchanged ↓ Down	Reliability Up ↑ —— Down ↓	Maintainability ↑ Up —— Unchanged ↓ Down	Cost Up ↑ —— Down ↓	Recommend Study √ Yes X No

Figure 3.6 Assessment of trade study concepts (7). (Reprinted by permission of the Martin Marietta Corporation.)

3.5 SUPPLIER PARTICIPATION

Procurement frequently accounts for 40 to 60 percent of production cost in high-technology programs. Therefore, it should be standard practice to require forceful design-to-cost programs at major suppliers. In particular, the statement of work should require cost goal tracking programs and reporting comparable both in scheduling and in content with the requirements on the prime contractor.

Generally, it is both satisfactory and advisable to include language in the subcontract that is essentially indentical to that in the prime contract. The contract should contain incentive provisions similar to those in the prime contract. An equitable and acceptable formula for the appropriate subcontractor award fees is a prorated share of the prime contractor award fee.

There may be exceptions in the case of value engineering incentives to subcontractors. Savings diminish as they flow down from the government to the prime to the subcontractor. When permitted by the Federal Acquisition Regulation (FAR), sharing from implementing value engineering change proposals should be bottom-up to motivate suppliers to submit value engineering change proposals.

3.5.1 Multiple Sourcing

It is axiomatic that the lowest prices are obtained through competition. Therefore, every effort should be made to identify multiple qualified sources and to invite competitive bids whenever possible. In some instances, it may be worthwhile to plan to qualify at least one additional source for each subcontracted item. Even if the plan is not fully implemented, the threat of competition often forces prices down and keeps in line companies who presently have, or believe they have, a lock on the competition. Details on multiple sourcing are provided in Section 5.4 from the viewpoint of business strategy.

As a note of caution, do not allow buy-ins at unrealistic prices that cannot be realized. Carefully analyze bids, and investigate the capability and previous performance record of the bidders.

A useful technique is to prepare a should-cost estimate of the item to be bought. This tends to establish limits of realism for bids. It is also advisable to make an assessment of a bidder's capital equipment requirement to determine if it is realistic and is comparable to that of other offerors.

3.5.2 Supplier Surveillance

Classic business imperatives, performance, schedule, and cost become especially sensitive where critical components must be procured from suppliers. Deficiencies in their process control result in last-minute surprises with costly consequences.

The implementation of a supplier early warning system is highly recommended. It should take advantage of existing test data developed from the supplier's manufacturing processes to effect preventive or corrective action sufficiently early to prevent problems from becoming emergencies.

The emphasis should be on product uniformity in procured items not only to prevent such surprises but also to reduce overall procurement cost. The technique called "tolerance centering" described in Section 4.7.1 is the recommended medium for achieving product uniformity.

3.6 SPECIFICATION PRACTICES

Specifications provide the baseline for the products or systems to be produced. They are maintained under configuration control and may be altered only with the unilateral approval by the customer hopefully following bilateral agreement by the customer and contractor on the need for and the extent of the changes.

Specifications govern the development of hardware or software products that are referred to as "configuration items." The concept of a configuration item (depicted in Figure 3.7) is defined as "an aggregation of hardware and/ or software, or any of its discrete portions, which satisfies an end-use function and is designated by the government for configuration management in terms of its functional and physical characteristics."

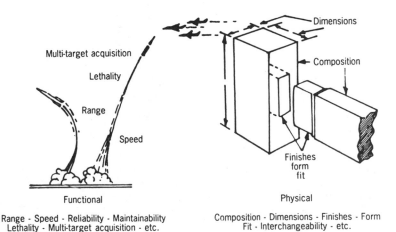

The functional and/or physical characteristics of hardware/software
as set forth in technical documentation and achieved in a product

Dimensions

Multi-target acquisition

Composition

Lethality

Range

Speed

Finishes
form
fit

Functional

Physical

Range - Speed - Reliability - Maintainability
Lethality - Multi-target acquisition - etc.

Composition - Dimensions - Finishes - Form
Fit - Interchangeability - etc.

Figure 3.7 Characterization of a configuration item (8). (Source: U.S. Air Force Systems Division, Directorate of Configuration Management, *Configuration Management, Strategic Systems*, 1985.)

Departures from specifications may be intended for the convenience of either the customer or the contractor, and are termed "deviations" or "waivers." When they are for the convenience of the contractor, the customer usually requests consideration in the form of a reduction in the target cost of the contract. Deviations and waivers are discussed in the next section, on configuration management. The military hierarchy of specifications is outlined in Table 3.12. The structure and contents are recommended for review by design-to-cost practitioners because of the carefully formulated rigor they bring to high-technology products and systems. Review of the terminology given in Table 3.13 is also recommended for better understanding of the discussion that follows.

3.6.1 System Specification

The system specification, which is designated Type A, states the technical and mission requirements for a system as an entity, allocates requirements to functional areas and defines the interfaces among the functional areas. Normally, the initial version of this specification is based on parameters developed during concept formulation or during exploratory preliminary design by feasibility studies and analyses.

The initial version is used to establish the general nature of the system that is to be further defined during a contract definition, development, or design period. The system specification is maintained current during these periods, culminating in a revision that forms the future performance base for

TABLE 3.12 Military Specification Hierarchy (9)

Type	Specification
A	System specification
B	Development specifications
B1	Prime item
B2	Critical item
B3	Noncomplex item
B4	Facility or ship
B5	Computer program
C	Product specifications
C1a	Prime item function
C1b	Prime item fabrication
C2b	Critical item function
C3	Noncritical item fabrication
C4	Inventory item
C5	Computer program
D	Process specification
E	Material specification

Source: MIL-STD-490, *Specification Practices.*

TABLE 3.13 Specification Practices Terminology (10)

Allocated configuration identification (ACI). Current, approved performance-oriented specifications governing the development of configuration items that are part of a higher level configuration item, in which each specification (1) defines the functional characteristics that are allocated from those of the higher level configuration item; (2) establishes the tests required to demonstrate achievement of its allocated functional characteristics; (3) delineates necessary interface requirements with other associated configuration items; and (4) establishes design constraints, if any, such as component standardization, use of inventory items, and integrated logistic support requirements

Configuration. The functional and physical characteristics of hardware or software as set forth in technical documentation and achieved in a product

Configuration item (CI). An aggregation of hardware and/or software, or any of its discrete portions, that satisfies an end-use function and is designated by the government for configuration management in terms of its functional and physical characteristics; CIs are only those specification items that are referenced directly in a contract

Configuration management. A discipline applying technical and administrative direction and surveillance to (1) identify and document the functional and physical characteristics of a configuration item, (2) control changes to those characteristics, and (3) record and report change processing and implementation status

Critical item. An item within a configuration item that, because of special engineering or logistical considerations, requires an approved specification to establish technical or inventory control at the component level

Form, fit, and function. That configuration representing the physical and functional characteristics of the item as an entity but not including any of the elements making up the item

Functional configuration identification (FCI). The current approved technical documentation for a configuration item (CI) that prescribes (1) all necessary functional characteristics; (2) the tests necessary to demonstrate achievement of specified functional characteristics; (3) the necessary interfaces characteristics with associated CIs; (4) its key lower-level CIs; and (5) design constraints such as envelope dimensions, component standardization, use of inventory items, and integrated logistics support policy

Product configuration identification (PCI). The current approved or conditionally approved technical documentation that defines the configuration of a CI during the production, operation, maintenance and logistic support phase of its life cycle, and that prescribes (1) all necessary form, fit, and function characteristics of a CI; (2) the selected functional characteristics designated for production acceptance testing; and (3) the production acceptance tests

Source: MIL-STD-480A, *Configuration Control-Engineering Changes, Deviations and Waivers.*

the development and production of configuration items with their performance being allocated from the system requirements.

The system specification serves for what is called the "functional configuration identification" (FCI). As stated in Table 3.13, the FCI defines (1) all essential system functional characteristics, (2) necessary interface characteristics, (3) specific designation of the functional characteristics of key configuration items, and (4) all the tests required to demonstrate achievement of each specified characteristic.

The Type A specification, as do all the other specifications, contains the following six numbered sections plus appendixes as required:

1. Scope
2. Applicable documents
3. Requirements
4. Quality assurance provisions
5. Preparation for delivery
6. Notes
10. Appendix

3.6.2 Development Specification

Development specifications, which are designated Type B, state the performance and environmental requirements to be achieved in the design or engineering development of a product. Each development specification must be in sufficient detail to describe effectively the performance characteristics that each configuration item is to achieve when a developed item is to evolve into a detail design for production.

Development specifications serve for what is called "allocated configuration identification" (ACI). As stated in Table 3.13, the ACI defines the functional requirements for each major configuration item, including (1) all essential configuration item functional characteristics, including delineation of interfaces; (2) physical characteristics necessary to assure compatibility with associated systems, configuration items, and inventory items; (3) all the tests required to demonstrate achievement of each specified functional characteristic; and (4) design constraints.

Development specifications should be maintained current during production, when it is desired to retain a complete statement of performance requirements. Since the breakdown of a system into its elements involves items of various degrees of complexity that are subject to different engineering disciplines or specification content, it is desirable to classify development specifications by subtypes. Details regarding each subtype follow.

1. PRIME ITEM DEVELOPMENT SPECIFICATION

The prime item development specification, which is designated Type B1, is applicable to a complex item such as an aircraft, missile, launcher equipment, fire-control equipment, radar set, or training equipment. A prime item development specification may be used as the ACI for a single-item development or as part of the ACI where the item covered is part of a larger system development program. Normally, items requiring Type B1 specifications meet the following criteria:

Items will be accepted on a DD Form 250 (the form used by components of the DoD for accepting delivery of products).

Provisioning action will be required.

Manuals covering operation and maintenance will be required.

Quality conformance inspection of each item, as opposed to sampling, will be required.

2. CRITICAL ITEM DEVELOPMENT SPECIFICATION

The critical item development specification, which is designated Type B2, applies to an item that is below the level of complexity of a prime item but that is engineering-critical or logistics-critical. An item is engineering-critical where one or more of the following applies:

The technical complexity warrants an individual specification.

Reliability of the item significantly affects the ability of the system or prime item to perform its overall function, or where safety is a consideration.

The prime item cannot be adequately evaluated without separate evaluation and application suitability testing of the critical item.

Repair parts will be provisioned for the item.

The procurement activity has designated the item for multiple-source reprocurement.

3. NONCOMPLEX ITEM DEVELOPMENT SPECIFICATION

The noncomplex item development specification, which is designated the Type B3, applies to items of relatively simple designs. Examples are special tools, work stands, fixtures, brackets, and dollies. Type B3 specifications are optional for the procuring activity for items meeting the following criteria:

Acceptance testing to verify that performance is not required.

Acceptance can be based on verification that the item as fabricated conforms to the drawings.

4. FACILITY OR SHIP DEVELOPMENT SPECIFICATION

The facility or ship development specification, which is designated Type B4, applies to each item that is both a fixed or floating installation and an integral part of a system. Examples are as follows: basic structural, architectural, or operational features designed specifically to accommodate requirements that are unique to the system and that must be developed in close coordination with the system; the facility or ship services that form complex interfaces with the system; facility or ship hardening to decrease the total vulnerability of the system; and ship speed and maneuverability.

5. COMPUTER PROGRAM DEVELOPMENT SPECIFICATION

The computer program development specification, designated Type B5, applies to the development of computer programs. The specification must describe in operational, functional, and mathematical language all the requirements necessary to design and verify the required computer program in terms of performance criteria. The specification must provide the logical, detailed descriptions of performance requirements and the tests required to assure development of a computer program satisfactory for the intended use.

3.6.3 Product Specification

A product specification, designated Type C, applies to any item below the system level and may be oriented toward procurement of a product through specification of primarily function (i.e., performance) requirements or primarily fabrication (i.e., detail design) requirements.

A product function specification covers form, fit, and function and defines the complete performance requirements of the product for the intended use and the necessary interface and interchangeability characteristics. A product fabrication specification provides a detailed description of the parts and assemblies of the product, usually by prescribing compliance with a set of drawings, and the performance requirements and corresponding test and inspections necessary to assure that proper fabrication, adjustment, and assembly techniques are employed. Tests normally are limited to acceptance tests in the shop environment.

Description of subtypes of product specifications to cover equipments of various complexities or requiring different outlines of form follow.

1. PRIME ITEM PRODUCT SPECIFICATION

The prime item product specification, designated Type C1, applies to an item meeting the criteria for prime item development specifications. It may be prepared as product function or fabrication specifications as warranted by the procurement conditions.

2. PRIME ITEM PRODUCT FUNCTION SPECIFICATION

The prime item product function specification, designated Type C1b, applies to the procurement of prime items when a "form, fit, and function" description is acceptable. Normally, the Type C1b specification would be prepared only when a single procurement is anticipated and training and logistics considerations are not paramount.

3. CRITICAL ITEM PRODUCT SPECIFICATION

The critical item product specification, designated as Type C2, applies to engineering or logistic critical items meeting the criteria for the critical item development specification. It may be prepared as a product function or fabrication specification.

4. CRITICAL ITEM PRODUCT FUNCTION SPECIFICATION

The critical item product function specification, designated Type C2a, applies to critical items where the performance characteristics of the items are of greater concern than part interchangeability or control over the details of design. Generally, a "form, fit, and function" description is adequate.

5. CRITICAL ITEM PRODUCT FABRICATION SPECIFICATION

The critical item product fabrication specification, designated Type C2b, applies to a critical item when detailed design disclosures need to be made available, or where it is considered that adequate performance can be achieved by adherence to a set of detail drawings and required processes.

6. NONCOMPLEX ITEM PRODUCT FABRICATION SPECIFICATION

The noncomplex item fabrication specification, designated Type C3, applies to an item meeting the criteria of the noncritical item development specification. When acquisition of a noncomplex item to a detailed design is desired, a set of detail drawings may be substituted for the specification.

7. INVENTORY ITEM SPECIFICATION

The inventory item specification, designated Type C4, applies to an item that exists in the DoD inventory and will be incorporated in a prime item or system being developed. The purpose of the inventory item specification is to stabilize the configuration of items in the DoD inventory and to achieve standardization among systems and prime items.

8. COMPUTER PROGRAM PRODUCT SPECIFICATION

The computer program product specification, designated Type C5, applies to the production of a computer program and defines their implementing media such as punched tape, magnetic tape, disk, or drum. It does not cover detailed requirements for material or manufacture of the implementin media. Where two-part specifications are used (see below), the Type B5 specification forms Part I and the Type C5 specification forms Part II. Such two-part specifications provide a transition of the performance requirements into programming terminology and the quality assurance provisions necessary to assure production of a satisfactory program.

3.6.4 Process Specification

The process specification, designated Type D, applies to a service that is performed on products or materials. Examples are heat treatment, welding, plating, microfilming, packing, and marking.

Process specifications cover manufacturing techniques that require a specific procedure designed to achieve a satisfactory result. Normally, the process specification applies to production but may also be used to control the development of a process.

3.6.5 Material Specification

The material specification, designated Type E, applies to raw material such as metals and chemicals, mixtures such as paints and cleaning agents, and semifabricated material such as chemical tubing and electrical wire. Normally, a material specification applies to production but may also be used to control the development of materials.

Specification Types C, D, and E constitute what is called "product configuration identification" (PCI), when supplemented with engineering drawings and related data. The PCI, which is alternatively called the "technical data package" (TDP), provides a set of documents adequate for the procurement, production, test, evaluation, and acceptance of an item without requiring further development work (see Table 3.14).

3.6.6 Two-Part Specification

The two-part specification, which combines both development (i.e., performance) specifications and product fabrication (i.e., detail design) specifications under a single specification number as Part I and Part II, respectively, may be selected as a procuring activity option. This practice requires both parts for a complete definition of both performance requirements and detailed design requirements governing fabrication.

Under this practice, the development specification remains applicable during the life of the item as the complete statement of performance requirements. Proposed design changes must be evaluated against both the development part and the product fabrication part of the specification. Two-part specifications are not applicable where the product specification is a product function specification.

TABLE 3.14 Configuration Management Terminology (11)

Advance change study notice. A notification by the contractor to the procuring activity of the intention to submit an engineering change proposal

Allocated baseline. The approved allocated configuration identification

Allocated configuration identification (ACI). Current, approved performance-oriented specifications governing the development of configuration items that are part of a higher-level configuration item, in which each specification (1) defines the functional characteristics that are allocated from those of the higher level configuration item; (2) establishes the tests required to demonstrate achievement of its allocated functional characteristics; (3) delineates necessary interface requirements with other associated configuration items; and (4) establishes design constraints, if any, such as component standardization, use of inventory items, and integrated logistic support requirements

Change control board (CCB). The functional body within the system program office, composed of representatives of the various commands concerned with the procurement and with the responsibility of configuration control; Class I engineering change proposals are the prerogative of only the CCB, which is chaired by the system program manager

Computer program component (CPC). A functional or logically distinct part of a computer program configuration item (CPCI)

Computer software component (CSC). A functional or logically distinct part of a computer software configuration item (CSCI)

Configuration. The functional and physical characteristics of hardware or software as set forth in technical documentation and achieved in a product

Configuration item (CI). An aggregation of hardware and/or software, or any of its discrete portions, that satisfies an end-use function and is designated by the government for CM in terms of its functional and physical characteristics; CIs are only those specification items that are referenced directly in a contract

Configuration management (CM). A discipline applying technical and administrative direction and surveillance to (1) identify and document the functional and physical characteristics of a CI, (2) control changes to those characteristics, and (3) record and report change processing and implementation status

Configuration status accounting. The recording and reporting of the information that is needed to manage configurations effectively, including a listing of the approved configuration identifications and the implementation status of approved changes

Critical Design Review (CDR). A review to determine that the detail design of the CI satisfies the performance and specialty engineering requirements of its development specification

Critical item. An item within a configuration item that, because of special engineering or logistical considerations, requires an approved specification to establish technical or inventory control at the component level

TABLE 3.14 (*Continued*)

Deviation. A specific written authorization, granted prior to the manufacture of an item, to depart from a particular performance or design requirement of a specification, drawing, or other document for a specific number of units or for a specific period of time; a deviation, unlike an approved engineering change, does not require corresponding revision of the specification, or drawing of the item in question

Engineering change. An alteration in the configuration of a configuration item after formal establishment of its CI

Engineering change proposal (ECP). A term that includes both a proposed engineering change and the documentation by which the change is described and suggested

Engineering release record. The official data file that records and interrelates engineering data and changes thereto, which technically describe and are used to build, operate, and maintain configuration items

Formal qualification review (FQR). A review to verify that the product has met specific contractual performance requirements

Form, fit, and function. That configuration constituting the physical and functional characteristics of the item as an entity but not including any of the elements making up the item

Functional configuration audit (FCA). An audit to validate that the development of the configuration item has been completed satisfactorily and that the configuration item has achieved the performance and functional characteristics in the functional or allocated identification

Functional baseline. The approved functional configuration identification.

Functional configuration identification (FCI). The current approved technical documentation for a configuration item (CI) that prescribes (1) all necessary functional characteristics; (2) the tests necessary to demonstrate achievement of specified functional characteristics; (3) the necessary interfaces characteristics with associated CIs; (4) its key lower-level CIs; and (5) design constraints such as envelope dimensions, component standardization, use of inventory items, and integrated logistics support policy

Material review board. The functional body similar to the change control board, except that it includes a representative of the contractor and its prerogative is limited to Class II engineering change proposals and is advisory regarding Class I engineering change proposals

Notice of revision (NoR). A form used to propose revisions to a drawing or list and, after approval, to notify users that the drawing or list is revised accordingly

Product baseline. The approved product configuration identification

Physical configuration audit (PCA). An audit to verify that the "as-built" configuration item conforms to its defining technical documentation

Preliminary design review (PDR). A review to evaluate the progress, technical adequacy, and compatibility and risk resolution of the selected design approach

Product configuration identification (PCI). The current approved or conditionally approved technical documentation that defines the configuration of a CI during the production, operation, maintenance, and logistic support phase of its life cycle, and that prescribes (1) all necessary forms, fit, and function characteristics of a CI; (2) the selected function characteristics designated for production acceptance testing; and (3) the production acceptance tests

Production readiness review (PRR). A review to verify satisfactory completion of specific actions prior to executing a production go-ahead decision

System allocation document. A document that identifies the aggregation of configuration items by serial number and the system configuration at each location

Specification change notice (SCN). A document used to propose, transmit, and record changes to a specification; in proposed form, prior to approval, the SCN (P) supplies proposed changes in the text of each page affected

System design review (SDR). A review to evaluate the optimization, correlation, completeness, and risks associated with the allocated technical requirements

System requirements review (SRR). A review to ascertain the adequacy of the contractor's efforts in defining system requirements

Waiver. A written authorization to accept a configuration item or other designated items that during production or after having been submitted for inspection are found to depart from specified requirements but nonetheless are considered suitable for use "as is" or after rework by an approved method

Source: MIL-STD-480A, *Configuration Control-Engineering Changes, Deviations and Waivers*.

3.7 CONFIGURATION AND DATA MANAGEMENT

Configuration management and data management are generally provided by a single organization both for the procuring activities of the government and for contractors. A typical SOW for such an organization is given in Table 3.9.

Configuration management is a management approach to give order, visibility, and control to life-cycle management of hardware and software. It can be paraphrased simply as "knowing what you have and keeping track of it."

Configuration management is a discipline that must be learned, applied, and—above all—supported by management to be successful in any high-technology program. This is particularly so in programs with design-to-cost requirements, and the case study in Section 3.14.5 dramatizes the dire consequences of management deemphasis of configuration management.

Data management is the function that governs and controls the selection, generation, preparation, acquisition, and use of data by functional managers to support their various technical and administrative activities. In terms of design to cost, these data should be the minimum essential for carrying out the respective responsibilities.

3.7.1 Configuration Management

Military Standard 483A, *Configuration Management Practices for Systems, Equipment, Munitions, and Computer Programs,* is part of a hierarchy of standards defining both configuration management and change control. The other documents are DOD-STD-480A, *Configuration Control-Engineering Changes, Deviations and Waivers;* MIL-STD-481, *Configuration Control-Engineering Changes, Deviations and Waivers (Short Form);* and MIL-STD-482, *Configuration Status Accounting Data Elements and Related Features.*

The objective of MIL-STD-483A is to establish uniform configuration management (CM) practices in all systems and configuration items procured by the military agencies. Configuration management requirements apply during the applicable life-cycle phases of configuration items (CI), whether part of a system or independent CIs. Contractors are required to ensure that all hardware, firmware, and software documentation procured from subcontractors is generated in accordance with the requirements of this standard.

It should be evident that CM can consume a large portion of overall program funding, and typically ranges from 5 to 15 percent in defense contracts. It is therefore recommended that design-to-cost practitioners become sufficiently familiar with CM practices in order to ensure the greatest possible cost-effectiveness in their implementation. Review of the CM terminology given in Table 3.14 is also recommended for better understanding of the discussion that follows.

Military Standard 483A establishes CM requirements in the following areas, which are discussed below:

Configuration management plan
Configuration identification
Configuration control
Configuration audits
Interface control
Engineering release control
Configuration status accounting

1. CONFIGURATION MANAGEMENT PLAN

Contractors are required to establish, within their organizations, responsibility for implementing requirements of CM evoked by the procuring activities. The statement of responsibilities and procedures are subject to the approval of the procuring activities. Baseline management is one of the more important aspects of CM and is formally required at the beginning of acquisition programs. The baselines are documented by approved configuration identifications that are the bases for control of changes in systems and configuration items.

2. CONFIGURATION IDENTIFICATION

Configuration identification is required for every configuration item in the form of technical documentation. Initially, functional configuration identifications are used to establish performance-oriented requirements for the design and development of higher-level configuration items. These requirements are translated into allocated configuration identifications for selected configuration items that are part of the higher-level configuration items. Ultimately, for developed configuration items, product configuration identifications are used to prescribe "build-to" or form, fit, and function requirements, and acceptance tests appropriate to these requirements.

3. CONFIGURATION CONTROL

Configuration control provides the systematic evaluation; coordination approval or disapproval; and implementation of (1) the initial configuration, (2) all changes to that configuration after the formal establishment of baselines, and (3) all changes to that configuration during the operational period (particularly modifications and changes for maintenance). The objectives for change processing, which should be shared by the contractor as well as the customer, is to provide early visibility to forthcoming changes and meet realistic need dates for change authorization. All engineering change proposals, as well as advance change study notices and requests for deviations and waivers, are processed by the change control board (CCB).

It is important to understand the salient differences between Class I and Class II engineering change proposals (ECPs) and between deviations and waivers. The requirements constituting Class I ECPs are verified needs to correct deficiencies, affect significant operational or logistic support changes, effect substantial life-cycle-cost saving, or prevent slippage in production schedules. Only the CCB can approve Class I ECPs. Class II ECPs pertain to such items as the correction of documentation errors; minor design changes that do not effect form, fit, and function; and material substitutions. Class II ECPs are usually approved by the material review board (MRB) and rarely submitted to the CCB for concurrence. It should be noted that the MRB has the responsibility for dispositioning nonconforming material and failures during development and production. The salient difference between a deviation and a waiver is the time relationship to production. Deviations are used prior to the manufacture of a given item to temporarily depart from a requirement to preclude a slip in the delivery schedule. Waivers are used after manufacture of a given item to temporarily depart from, or permanently change, a requirement as the result of an error during manufacture of the item. In either case, the procuring activity usually requests consideration in the form of a reduction in the target cost of the contract.

4. CONFIGURATION AUDITS

Configuration audits consist of the functional configuration audit (FCA) and physical configuration audit (PCA). The FCA and PCA are chaired by a representative of the CCB and are discussed in Section 3.9, on the review process in accordance with MIL-STD-1521A, *Technical Reviews and Audits for Systems, Equipments, and Computer Programs.*

5. INTERFACE CONTROL

Interface control is the coordinated activity required to ensure that the functional and physical characteristics and systems are compatible. Typically, an interface control contractor is assigned the responsibility to ascertain that configuration item identifications conform to the functional interfaces established by the system engineering process, and that the configuration items, including computer software as finally designed, are physically and logically compatible, will assemble together, and can be operated and supported as intended. The interface-control contractor is usually supported in these endeavors by an interface-control working group (ICWG), which consists of representatives of the various contractors producing those configuration items that must interoperate and of the various procuring activities. These representatives are usually provided with resources to undertake related studies, and design-to-cost practitioners should be alert to the opportunity to participate in these deliberations.

6. ENGINEERING RELEASE CONTROL

It is mandatory that contractors maintain current engineering release records of all specifications and drawings for configuration items accepted or to be accepted by the procuring activity. The engineering release records must interrelate with the contractor's internal system of controls to assure that all approved Class I engineering changes have been incorporated in production items as specified. Unreleased engineering is one of the most costly aberrations in production, and should also be accounted for in the release system in the form of part numbers to be completed. The uncertainty represented should also be documented in the form of an engineering change curve showing the cumulative percentage of engineering changes that may occur during the process of completing and releasing the outstanding part numbers. This is another area requiring close scrutiny by design-to-cost practitioners.

7. CONFIGURATION STATUS ACCOUNTING

Configuration status accounting provides the reporting and recording of (1) the status of systems and equipment after the establishment of documented baselines in order to provide the visibility essential to program management and (2) the status of the implementation of approved changes to established configurations to ensure that the initial configurations and all subsequent changes match the technical descriptions. Configuration status accounting is essentially an automated bookkeeping function that can be extremely costly if not constantly monitored for duplicative data and duplicative reports that may be required by the contract data requirements list (CDRL). This concern, however, should be extended to the greater subject of data management.

3.7.2 Data Management

As stated in Section 3.7, data management is the function that governs and controls the selection, generation, preparation, acquisition, and use of data by functional managers to support their various technical and administrative activities. From the standpoint of design to cost, these data should be the minimum essential for carrying out the respective responsibilities.

The basic cost-saving guideline is to immediately recommend deleting from the CDRL any data that do not contribute to (1) maintaining visibility in progress and problems; (2) controlling the program from the viewpoints of performance, schedule, and cost; (3) making decisions on corrective actions and alternative approaches; and (4) defining product designs and manufacturing processes.

This guideline should be viewed as only the starting point. Those data items surviving the screening should next be challenged with regard to the frequency of reporting and the number of recipients for the same data items.

The thrust should be to limit the recipients to those with authority to act on the information contained in the data items in matters concerning the specific contract or closely related contracts.

There are essentially two different classes of cost involved in the preparation of data items: (1) a class covering the cost of the technical work that has to be done irrespective of the work being reported in the data items and (2) a class covering the cost of preparing and submitting the data items. Again, the emphasis should be on minimizing the latter.

3.8 SCHEDULE CONTROL

Schedule control is not only mandatory to avoid cost growth but also, as indicated in Section 5.7, is an effective strategy for reducing cost. The administrative responsibility for schedule control may be vested in the planning organization of companies, but all functional and program elements bear the responsibility for their respective portions of the schedules.

This is why the hierarchy of schedules for a given program should be consistent with not only the work breakdown structure of the program and the generation breakdown of the products but also the operational flow in development, manufacturing, and procurement. One of the most vital program interfaces is between the planning organization and the production control organization.

The hierarchy of schedules consists of the top-level program schedule, intermediate-level schedules for each major task constituting the program and detailed schedules for each work element making up the tasks. Figure

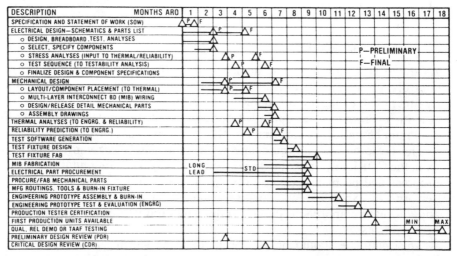

Figure 3.8 Intermediate-level schedule for switching-mode power supply (12). (Source: NAVMAT P4855-1, *Navy Power Supply Reliability*, 1982.)

3.8 illustrates an intermediary-level schedule for developing a switching-mode power supply and is rendered in months after receipt of order (ARO).

Each line item in Figure 3.8 is a work element and the subject of a detailed schedule that is rendered in weekly increments and tracked on a weekly basis. Typically, tracking uses a system called "page and line." In the system, a page is devoted to each work element and the lines on the page to the respective subelements. There are columns on each page for the "scheduled date," "actual date," and "promised date."

Deviations from the scheduled dates require schedule variance reports. These, in turn, are the subject matter of the "page and line summary report" prepared weekly for program management.

These comments are offered to emphasize the serious need for schedule control in general and, in particular, for design to cost. The scheduling strategies discussed in Section 5.7 would be counterproductive and not merely ineffective without absolute control of scheduled events.

3.9 THE REVIEW PROCESS

Reviews take on a whole new dimension and a whole new meaning in programs with design-to-cost requirements. The new dimension results from elevating cost goals, and not just the projected costs of the current designs, to the same level as performance and schedule in decisions regarding corrective actions or alternative approaches.

The new meaning on an overall basis is that progress toward meeting cost goals must also be satisfactory in order to deem that technical performance and schedule performance are satisfactory. Insufficient progress in meeting cost goals is sufficient to warrant trade studies and redirection of designs.

The specific meaning to the ranks of management is that they have granted authorization to those people conducting the reviews to expend additional funding on the pursuit of alternative approaches if warranted. Typically, this has added up to 25 percent to the original estimate for the development cost.

The key word is "rigor"—rigor in maintaining cost goals as a top criterion and rigor in conducting reviews. It is for this reason that MIL-STD-1521A, *Technical Reviews and Audits for Systems, Equipments, and Computer Programs,* is recommended to design-to-cost practitioners as a guidance document. This standard and its predecessor, MIL-STD-1521, have guided thousands of reviews and audits of complex high-technology weapon systems and other equipments. These standards are at the heart of military procurement, and it has become customary to refer to the acquisition of a complex system as a "MIL-STD-1521 program."

A strict admonition is in order. Military Standard 1521A defines and mandates technical reviews and audits in military acquisition. It does not, however, address the urgency for prompt and accurate resolution of action items resulting from discrepancies revealed in the reviews and audits. Prolonging the action item closure process can do nothing but add to the cost of programs, and design-to-cost practitioners should act to hasten the process to the extent possible.

Table 3.15 lists the reviews and audits covered by the MIL-STD-1521A along with summary definitions of the events. The order follows the life-cycle path in system acquisition. The flow is illustrated in Figure 3.9 (see Appendix 2 for definition of abbreviations) which shows the sequence of tests, technical reviews and audits, and specifications leading to the definitization of product baselines.

Somewhat more detail is provided in this section on the system requirements review since it is the most formative review in shaping the evolving system in terms of cost-effectiveness. Reference is made to MIL-STD-1521A for similar details on the other reviews and audits, with the exception of the PRR, which is defined in MIL-STD-1528, *Production Management,* and in Section 4.9 of this book.

It will be noted in MIL-STD-1521A, however, that the amount of required detailed information increases almost exponentially for each successive review and audit, and that they can become extremely costly vehicles for reporting progress. Therefore, guidelines for tailoring the reviews and audits to the needs of the particular program are also given in this section.

TABLE 3.15 MIL-STD-1521A Technical Reviews and Audits (13)

System requirements review (SRR). A review to ascertain the adequacy of the contractor's efforts in defining system requirements

System design review (SDR). A review to evaluate the optimization, correlation, completeness, and risks associated with the allocated technical requirements

Preliminary design review (PDR). A review to evaluate the progress, technical adequacy and compatibility, and risk resolution of the selected design approach

Critical design review (CDR). A review to determine that the detail design of the configuration item satisfies the performance and specialty engineering requirements of its development specification

Functional configuration audit (FCA). An audit to validate that the development of the configuration item has been completed satisfactorily and that the configuration item has achieved the performance and functional characteristics in the functional or allocated identification.

Physical configuration audit (PCA). An audit to verify that the "as-built" configuration item conforms to its defining technical documentation

Formal qualification review (FQR). A review to verify that the product has met specific contractual performance requirements

Production Readiness Review (PRR). A review to verify satisfactory completion of specific actions prior to executing a production go-ahead decision

---

Source: MIL-STD-1521A, *Technical Reviews and Audits for Systems, Equipments and Computer Programs.*

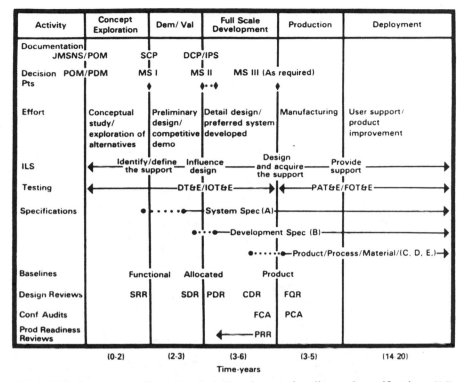

Figure 3.9 Sequences of tests, technical reviews and audits, and specifications (14). (Source: MIL-STD-1521A, *Technical Reviews and Audits for Systems, Equipments and Computer Programs.*)

3.9.1 System Requirements Review

The objective of the system requirements review (SRR) is to ascertain the adequacy of efforts in defining system requirements. The SRRs are normally conducted during the conceptual or validation phase of the system.

Such reviews may be conducted at any time in this period but normally are conducted after the accomplishment of functional analysis and preliminary requirements allocations to determine initial direction and progress of the contractor's system engineering management effort and convergence on an optimum and complete configuration. The requirements allocations are in the areas of operational, maintenance, and hardware configuration items (CIs); computer program CIs (CPCI); facility CIs; manufacturing; personnel; and human factors.

Table 3.16 lists representative items reviewed at the SRRs. The intent is to assess the total system engineering management activity for responsiveness to the statement of work and system or system segment requirements.

TABLE 3.16 System Requirements Review Items (15)

Mission and requirements analysis
Functional flow analysis
Preliminary requirements allocation
System–cost-effectiveness analysis
Trade studies
Synthesis
Logistics support analysis
Specialty discipline studies
Generation of specifications
Program risk analysis
Integrated test planning
Producibility analysis plans
Technical performance measurement planning
Engineering integration
Configuration management plans
System safety
Human-factors analysis
Value engineering studies
Life-cycle-cost analysis
Preliminary manufacturing plans
Manpower requirements and personnel analysis

Source: MIL-STD-1521A, *Technical Reviews and Audits for Systems, Equipments and Computer Programs.*

Direction to the contractor from the procuring activity is provided as necessary for continuing the technical program and system optimization.

The trade studies indicated in Table 3.16 address system functions in terms of hardware, software, and firmware. The specialty discipline studies address hardware and software reliability, maintainability analysis, armament integration, electromagnetic compatibility, survivability, and vulnerability, including nuclear inspection methods and techniques analysis.

3.9.2 System Design Review

The objective of the system design review (SDR) is to ensure that (1) the updated, completed system specification is adequate and cost-effective in satisfying validated mission requirements; (2) the allocated requirements represent a complete and optimal synthesis of the system requirements; and (3) the technical program risks are identified, ranked, and avoided and reduced through trades, hardware proofing, tests, and analysis.

The SDR is normally conducted as the final review prior to the submittal of validation phase products. The outcome of the SDR should be technical understanding and agreement between the customer and the contractor on the validity and degree of completeness of the following items:

System specification
System segment specifications
Engineering cost estimate for the system
Prime item development specifications
Critical item–development specifications

3.9.3 Preliminary Design Review

The objective of the preliminary design review (PDR) is to (1) evaluate the progress, technical adequacy, and risk resolution on the basis of performance, schedule, and cost of the selected design approach; (2) determine its compatibility with performance and engineering specialty requirement of the configuration item (CI) or computer program configuration item (CPCI) development specifications; (3) evaluate the degree of definition and assess the technical risk associated with the selected manufacturing methods and processes; and (4) establish the existence and compatibility of the physical and functional interfaces among the CI and/or CPCI and other items of equipment, facilities, computer programs, and personnel.

The PDR is a formal technical review of the basic design approach for a CI or CPCT, or for a functionally related group of CIs and/or CPCIs. It is held after the development specifications are available, but prior to the start of detailed design.

3.9.4 Critical Design Review

The objective of the critical design review (CDR) is to (1) determine that the detail design of the CI or CPCI satisfies the performance and engineering specialty requirements of the CI or CPCI development specifications; (2) establish the detail design compatibility among the CI and/or CPCI and other items of equipment, facilities, computer programs, and personnel; (3) assess CI and/or CPCI risk areas on the basis of performance, schedule, and cost; assess the results of the producibility analysis conducted on system hardware; and (5) review the preliminary product specifications.

The CDR is conducted on each CI or CPCI prior to fabrication or coding and test release to ensure that the detail design solutions as reflected in the product specifications and engineering drawings satisfy performance requirements established by the development specifications. As the result of a successful CDR for a hardware CI, the contractor is permitted to use the detail design as presented in the CDR and reflected in the product specification for production planning and, if specifically authorized, for initial production of the CI.

The CDR for a CPCI is conducted for the purpose of establishing the integrity of computer program designs at the level of flowcharts and program design languages. The outcome of a successful CDR for a CPCI is the formal identification of specific computer programming documentation that will be released for coding and testing.

3.9.5 Functional Configuration Audit

The objective of the functional configuration audit (FCA) is to verify that the actual performance of the CI complies with development specifications. Test data are reviewed to verify that the item has performed as required by its functional and/or allocated configuration identification.

The FCA of a complex CI may be conducted on a progressive basis and culminates at the completion of the qualification testing of that item with a review of all discrepancies at the final FCA. Included in the final FCA are the minutes of the PDR and CDR to ensure that all findings have been incorporated and completed.

3.9.6 Physical Configuration Audit

The objective of the physical configuration audit (PCA) is to verify that the as-built CI conforms to the technical documentation that defines the CI. The PCA is conducted on the first article of CIs in order to establish the CIs product baseline.

The PCA also determines that the acceptance testing requirements prescribed by the documentation is adequate for subsequent acceptances of CIs by quality assurance activities. The PCA includes an audit of released engineering documentation to ensure that the as-built configuration is reflected by this documentation. After a successful PCA, all subsequent changes are processed by engineering change action.

3.9.7 Formal Qualification Review

The objective of the formal qualification review (FQR) is to verify that the actual performance of the CI as determined through test complies with its development specification, and to identify the test data that document results of qualification tests of the CI. When feasible, the FQR is combined with the FCA at the completion of development tests.

If sufficient test results are not available at the FCA to ensure that the CI will perform in its system environment, the FQR is conducted after the PCA using the first article test results. Duplication is avoided, however, for non-combined FCAs and FQRs.

The outcome of a successful FQR is certification by the procuring activity that the CI has been officially qualified for entry into the government's inventory.

3.9.8   Tailoring Guidelines

As stated in Section 3.9, reviews and audits in accordance with MIL-STD-1521A can be extremely costly to conduct from the standpoint of both the customer and the contractor. Accordingly, MIL-STD-1521A offers guidelines for tailoring the requirements to maximize the cost-effectiveness of the reviews and audits. The guidelines are centered on the (1) relationship to the statement of work, (2) elimination of redundancy and ambiguity, (3) contractor participation in tailoring, (4) complexity, and (5) scheduling of reviews and audits.

1.   RELATIONSHIP TO THE STATEMENT OF WORK

The key to tailoring MIL-STD-1521A is to match its requirements against the details of the contractual statement of work. It should become immediately obvious that some of the technical review factors are not applicable to the contract under consideration. As an extreme example, if a contract does not include computer software, then all references to computer program material in MIL-STD-1521A would not apply. By carefully going through this process, requirements will become program-specific rather than constitute an all-purpose document to be continuously negotiated during contract performance.

2.   ELIMINATION OF REDUNDANCY AND AMBIGUITY

Whereas MIL-STD-1521A is the broad program document for technical reviews and audits, other applicable standards, such as for reliability and maintainability, also require reviews and audits. If such standards are stipulated contractually together with MIL-STD-1521, then the statement of work should contain a provision indicating how the reviews can be combined. Combining reviews does not nullify any of the standards. The contract should require the minimal integrated review effort that will provide the desired visibility and assurance of contract compliance.

3.   CONTRACTOR PARTICIPATION IN TAILORING

Contractors should be encouraged to participate in tailoring of the requirements of MIL-STD-1521A. The diversity of viewpoints provide a synergism for more cost-effective implementation of the review and audit processes.

4. COMPLEXITY

Configuration item complexity and the nature of the program should be central in determining the need for and the number of reviews and audits. For example, a newly developed, complex item would require the majority of the review topics, whereas an off-the-shelf item would require few or none. In the case of modified designs, judgment should be based on the modified areas and the degree of modification.

5. SCHEDULING OF REVIEWS AND AUDITS

The schedule for technical reviews and audits is extremely important. If they are conducted too early, the item for review will not be defined adequately. Conversely, if the reviews are conducted too late, the program commitments could have been made erroneously, and correction will be both difficult and costly. A good method for scheduling reviews is to relate them to the documentation requirements. For example, schedule the preliminary design review (PDR) after the development specification is available since the essence of the PDR is to assess the approach to meeting the requirements of this specification. Scheduling of audits is dependent on the availability of not only documentation but also hardware and software.

3.10 TECHNICAL PERFORMANCE MEASUREMENT

Program management must be cognizant of three basic program areas: technical performance, schedule performance, and cost performance. In military acquisitions, the last two areas are controlled through such schema as the cost–schedule control system criteria discussed in Section 6.8.1. The first area is controlled with technical performance measurement (TPM) system in accordance with MIL-STD-499A, *Engineering Management*.

The complexity of modern major weapon systems requires conscientious application of such precepts to ensure producible operable, supportable, and—above all—affordable systems that satisfy mission requirements. Despite the military origin, the principles of TPM are generic and can be applied to practically any system, civilian as well as military (16).

This section addresses the principles and applications of TPM whose purpose is to (1) provide management visibility of actual versus planned performance, (2) provide early detection or prediction of performance that requires management attention, and (3) support the assessment of the impact on the program of proposed changes.

The framework for TPM is derived from the contract work-breakdown structure (CWBS), which defines all the tasks to be accomplished on the program and follows the system hierarchy and program specification tree. Technical performance measurement selects elements of the CBWS for their

TABLE 3.17 Technical Performance Measurement Values (17)

Planned value. The anticipated value of a parameter at a given point in the development cycle; a plot of planned value versus time is called the "planned value profile"; it is often desirable to indicate a range of acceptable values versus time, and this range is called a "tolerance band"

Demonstrated value. The value estimated or measured in a particular analysis or test

Specification requirement. The value or range of values contained in a contractual performance specification or allocated from such a specification, with a verification requirement for the end product.

Current estimate. The value of a parameter predicted for the end product of the contract

Demonstrated technical variance. The difference between the planned value and the demonstrated value of a parameter

Predicted technical variance. The difference between the specification parameter and the current estimate of the parameter

Work-breakdown element. Element of the contract work breakdown structure selected for TPM

Source: Defense Systems Management College, *Systems Engineering Management Guide,* 1982.

criticality to the product and monitors their technical status throughout the development of the product. Table 3.17 lists the values of measurement used in implementing TPM.

The analytical flow in TPM is shown in Figure 3.10. Work-breakdown elements, the basic kernels of analysis, are usually at the subsystem level. These elements are used to prepare a master parameter list, and profiles are derived for each parameter on the list. The performance against profile forecasts are tracked, interactions among profiles are summed in system models, and the results are presented in TPM status reports.

3.10.1 Master Parameter List

In implementing TPM, only a few key parameters should be selected at the top level because the lower-level parameters supporting the key parameters may be one or two orders of magnitude greater in number. Table 3.18 lists some typical key parameters that have been critical on numerous programs and are good indicators of system effectiveness.

It is necessary to consider the lower-level parameters, and interactions among them, in forecasting key parameter profiles. Lower-level parameters are identified through the process of requirements flowdown and represent the allocation of system-level requirements to lower levels within the system hierarchy. For example, consider the key parameter called "pointing error" in Table 3.18.

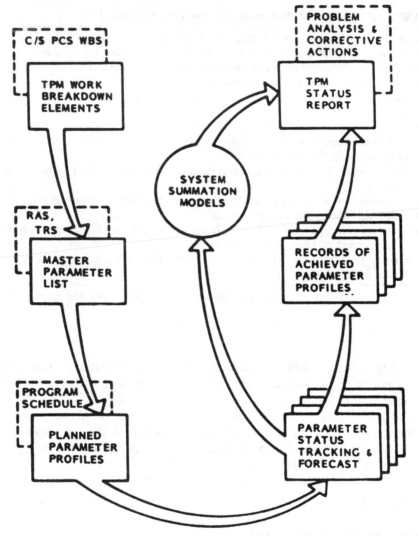

Figure 3.10   Technical performance measurement flow (18). (Source: Defense Systems Management College, *System Engineering Management Guide,* 1982.)

Allowable pointing accuracy is a critical issue in the cost-effectiveness of all spacecraft and missile programs. Typical allowable pointing errors range from several tenths of a degree to a few seconds of arc for astronomical observatory spacecraft. In establishing an error budget for pointing accuracy it is first necessary to define those hardware and software characteristics that contribute to the error, otherwise known as "error sources."

The flowdown process for pointing error results in the allocations given in Table 3.19. It can be seen that the one key parameter decomposes into

TABLE 3.18 Typical Technical Performance Measurement Key Parameters (19)

Weight
Payload
Range
Ranging accuracy
Pointing error
Target location error
Reaction time
Reliability, availability, maintainability
Survivability
Computer throughput
Computer memory
Processing time
Telemetry allocations
Command allocations
Power

Source: Defense Systems Management College, *System Engineering Management Guide,* 1982.

TABLE 3.19 Pointing Error Parameter Decomposition (20)

Subsystem	Lower-Level Parameter	Error Source
Payload	Alignments	Feed-to-antenna
		Antenna-to-mount
	Thermal distortion	Same
	Structural flexure	Same
Structure	Alignments	Payload-to-gyro[a]
	Star sensor-to-gyro[a]	Same
	Thermal distortion	Same
	Dynamic flexure	Same
Attitude control	Star sensor	Random errors
		Aberrations
	Gyros	Scale factor estimation
		Scale factor stability
		Scale factor nonlinearity
	Control dynamics	Same
Command and control	Data processing	Star database storage
		Round-off
		Timing
Ground system	Tracking ephemeris	Target location uncertainty
	Command	Same
	Margin	Error source values inaccuracy

Source: Defense Systems Management College, *System Engineering Management Guide,* 1982.
[a] Gyroscope.

fourteen lower-level parameters, each of which possesses one or more error sources.

3.10.2 Parameter Profiles

In Figure 3.11, which illustrates planned and achieved TPM parameter profiles for allowable pointing error, the ordinate represents the percentage of allowable error and the abscissa indicates time. Note that the percentage difference between the planned value profile and current estimate at a given point in time is the demonstrated variance in technical performance. Also note how error margin is treated.

As indicated in Table 3.19, many error sources contribute to pointing error. When error sources are independent, their combined effect on pointing error is calculated by taking the square root of the sum of the squares (RSS) of the individual sources. When there is interaction among the individ-

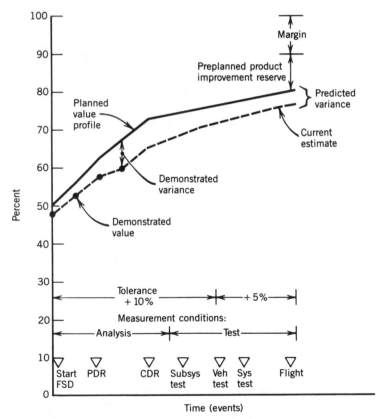

Figure 3.11 Pointing-error parameter profiles (21). (Source: Defense Systems Management College, *System Engineering Management Guide*, 1982.)

TABLE 3.20   Test Performance Measurement Status Report (22)

Element Parameter	Current Report			End Product		
	Demonstrated Value	Planned Value	Demonstrated Variance	Current Estimate	Specification Requirement	Predicted Value
			Engine			
Thrust, lb	26,000	28,000	−2,000	29,000	30,000	−1,000
Weight, lb	5,400	5,500	−100	4,900	5,000	−100
Specific fuel consumption, lb/hr · lb	0.045	0.05	+0.005	0.04	0.04	0

Source: Defense Systems Management College, *Systems Engineering Management Guide*, 1982.

ual error sources, it is necessary to use techniques that account for the correlation among these sources such as the one described in Section 4.7.4 for multiparameter devices.

Technical performance measurement status is always included in the agenda for those technical reviews discussed in Section 3.9 and is usually presented in the format given in Table 3.20. This example is part of the report for a missile; the work-breakdown element is the engine. The entries in the columns under "Current Report" relate to the current performance. The entries under "End Product" relate to forecast performance at completion of development.

3.11 WORK MEASUREMENT

It is important that accurate means for measuring the work accomplished in factories be consistently employed in all production programs. The purpose of MIL-STD-1567A, *Work Measurement*, is to increase discipline in work measurements with the objective of improved productivity and efficiency in production operations. This section conveys the essence of the military standard to familiarize design-to-cost practitioners in an aspect of the business that is often neglected. Experience has shown that excess labor and lost time can be identified, and reduced, and that continued method improvements made where work measurement programs have been implemented and conscientiously pursued.

Work measurement in the context of MIL-STD-1567A is keyed to the specification of "Type I Engineered Labor Standards." These standards are defined as "being established by a predetermined time system and reflecting an accuracy of ±10 percent with a 90 percent or greater confidence at the operation level." Standards with lesser accuracy or with lesser confidence are called "Type II."

Type II standards are acceptable only for initial coverage, and plans for upgrading to Type I standards are required in what is called the "Work Measurement Touch Labor Coverage Plan." Table 3.21 defines the terminology and parameters used in the plan and work measurement programs.

TABLE 3.21   Work Measurement Terminology (23)

Actual hours. An amount determined on the basis of time incurred as distinguished from forecast time; includes standard time adjusted for applicable variance

Earned hours. The time in standard hours credited to a worker or group of workers as the result of successfully completing a given task or group of tasks; usually calculated by summing the products of applicable time standards multiplied by the number of completed work units

Element. A subdivision of the operation composed of a sequence of several basic motions and process activities, which is distinct, describable, and measurable

Labor efficiency. The ratio of earned hours to actual hours spent on the same increments of work during a reporting period

Methods engineering. The analysis and design of work methods and systems, including technological selection of operations or processes, specification of equipment types, and locations

Operation. A job or task consisting of one or more work elements, normally done in one location; also, the lowest level grouping of elemental times at which allowances are applied

Operation analysis. A study that encompasses all procedures concerned with the design or improvement of production, including the purpose of the operations, inspection requirements, materials used and material handling, setup, tooling, and working conditions

Predetermined time system. An organized body of information, procedures, and techniques employed in the study and evaluation of manual work elements; the system is expressed in terms of the motion used, their general and specific nature, the conditions under which they occur, and their previously determined performance times

Realization factor. The ratio of actual labor hours to the earned hours; also a factor by which labor standards are multiplied when developing projected requirements

Standard time data. A compilation of all elements used for performing a given class of work with normal elemental time values for each element; the data are used as the basis for determining time standards on work similar to that from which the data were determined

Touch labor. Production labor that can be reasonably and consistently related directly to a unit of work being manufactured, processed, or tested; involves work affecting the composition, condition, or production of a product

Touch labor normal time. The time required by a qualified worker to perform a task at a normal pace or to complete an element, cycle, or operation using a prescribed method

Touch labor standard. A standard time set on a touch labor operation.

Touch labor standard time. Touch labor normal time plus an allowance for fatigue and unavoidable delay

Type I engineered labor standards. Standards established by using a predetermined time system, and with stated requirements for accuracy and confidence level

Type II labor standards. Standards not meeting the requirements of Type I labor standards, and to be used on an interim basis

Source: MIL-STD-1567A, *Work Measurement*.

Minimum requirements to be met in the coverage plan are as follows: (1) explicit definitions of standard times that apply throughout the jurisdiction of the work measurement program; (2) procedures to be used for maintaining engineered labor standards to known accuracy; (3) procedures for the use of labor standards as inputs to budgeting, estimating, production planning, and performance evaluation; (4) designation of the organization and personnel responsible for the execution of the work measurement program; and (5) schedule and plan for the aforementioned upgrading of Type II to Type I engineered labor standards.

Operations analysis is an integral part of the development of Type I engineered labor standards. The documentation of the operations analysis provides a record of standard time computations including allowances and a record of observed times or predetermined time system time values used in determine the final labor standards.

Design-to-cost practitioners are advised to become familiar with MIL-STD-1567A in conjunction with MIL-STD-1528, *Production Management* (see Section 3.11), because of interrelated requirements for the selection of labor standards, the audit of labor standards, and reporting of earned hours versus actual hours.

3.12 MAINTAINING AN AUDIT TRAIL

Maintenance of an audit trail is an essential ingredient in design to cost. The audit trail provides traceability of all factors influencing cost from the initial baseline to final delivery.

Avoiding goal slippage is a near impossible task without an audit trail, as is the matter of imposing cost accountability on people. The audit trail clearly differentiates cost variance due to requirement growth versus that due to design maturation.

Audit trails cannot be established without clear understanding of who is responsible for what elements of cost. The first decision, once a baseline estimate is available, is to what levels of detail in the work-breakdown structure (WBS) or generation breakdown (GB) goals should be assigned. In making this decision, a balance should be achieved among the following factors:

1. Cost goals should be allocated to those specific elements of the production configuration for which costs can be identified and accumulated.
2. The element should be assigned to specific individuals for total responsibility, not to organizations. Individuals must have control over the costs relating to the goals assigned them.
3. The element should represent a sufficiently high percentage of overall system cost to make tracking worthwhile.

The recommended form of documentation for allocating goals to specific individuals, (see Table 2.21) is repeated in Table 3.22. The table constitutes a matrix of allocations. The allocation of cost goals should be keyed to the WBS. Cost account managers (CAM) are responsible for mitigating the cost impact of changes and for tracking and reporting status in the respective WBS elements.

3.12.1 Change Control and Accountability

A realistic approach to design to cost recognizes the dynamic nature of changes necessitated by a process of development and refinement and pro-

TABLE 3.22   Cost Goal Allocations (24)

WBS	Title	CAM[a]	Goal ($)	Quantity
1.0	Transport Equipment	J. Eagen	36,381,300	001
1.1	Handling Equipment	R. Mann	16,048,700	001
1.1.1	Stage IV Equipment	R. Mann	2,783,200	001
1.1.1.1	End Ring Set	D. Deer	761,700	004

Cost elements WBS 1.1.1.1	
Manufacturing labor	19,840 hr
Quality labor	4,200 hr
Test labor	300 hr
Other technical services labor	2,400 hr
Material	$180,100
Subcontracted items	$9,100

Adapted by permission of the Martin Marietta Corporation.

[a] Cost account manager.

vides for mechanisms to maintain control of configuration changes and systems for tracking and reporting change data. This is essential to sort requirements growth from cost growth.

Members of design-to-cost teams are urged to become thoroughly familiar with their organization's change flow and procedures as well as the essence of specification practices and configuration and data management described in Sections 3.6 and 3.7. The point to remember is that cost account managers bear the responsibility for mitigating the cost impact of changes at every step in the flow.

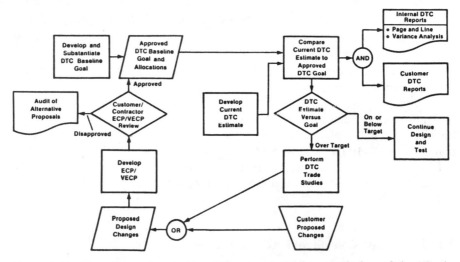

Figure 3.12 Tracking and reporting (25). (Reprinted by permission of the Martin Marietta Corporation.)

CONTRACTOR _____

ADDRESS _____

CONTRACT # _____

FY DOLLARS

DESIGN TO COST

COST ELEMENT/CWBS DATA

PERIOD _____

DATE _____

Contract Work Breakdown Structure / Cost Elements								TOTAL
Production Nonrecurring (includes all those non-recurring production costs, i.e., tooling, necessary to acquire a production capability)								
Production Recurring 2/								
• Production (includes all engineering, tooling, manufacturing, quality control, G&A, and profit associated with the cost of production capability)								
• Engineering Changes								
Current DTC Estimates								
DTC Goal								
Variance								1/

NOTE: 1/ Should be reconcilable to total specified contract Design to Cost goal. Other CWBS columns represent contractor allocated cost goals.

2/ Appropriate cost elements will include cost by: direct labor, material, overhead, other direct charges.

Figure 3.13 Reporting format A (26). (Source: Departments of the Army, the Navy, and the Air Force, *Joint Design-to-Cost Guide*, 1977.)

CONTRACTOR _____

ADDRESS _____

CONTRACT # _____

FY DOLLARS _____

DESIGN TO COST

VARIANCE ANALYSIS

PERIOD _____

DATE _____

Contract DTC Work Breakdown Structure (Note a)	Allocated DTC Goal	DTC Estimate Previous Report	DTC Estimate Current Report	Variance (Note b)		Analysis of Variance/Reallocation (Note c)
				from alloc. DTC Goal	fm prev. DTC Est.	

Notes: (a) List each WBS element indicated on Format A having a DTC goal variance beyond threshold.

(b) Variance is difference between current DTC estimate and allocated DTC goal and between current DTC estimate and that included in the prior DTC report.

(c) In a narrative analysis, provide rationale for variance from established DTC goal, changes in DTC goal allocation, and difference between current estimate and previous estimate. State impact on other elements (i.e., Technical, Cost, Performance, Schedule, etc.) and provide a schedule for corrective action or specify corrective action accomplished.

Figure 3.14 Reporting format B (27). (Source: Departments of the Army, the Navy, and the Air Force, *Joint Design-to-Cost Guide*, 1977.)

134

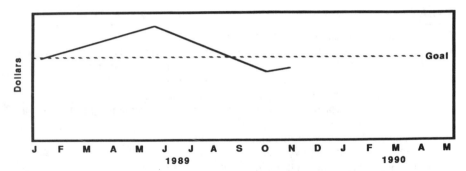

Figure 3.15 Cost goal tracking chart (28). (Adapted by permission of the Martin Marietta Corporation.)

3.12.2 Tracking and Reporting

Tracking and reporting provide the last leg of the audit trail for assessing and directing design-to-cost performance. The tracking and reporting process provides the status of the approved cost goal in terms of current cost estimates and variances and various internal and customer reports. Recommended tracking and reporting processes are shown in Figure 3.12.

The minimum requirement for internal reporting should be weekly for cost performance status and monthly for cost variance analysis. Reports should be sent to line managers and program personnel with cost goal responsibility as well as to the program director. These reports provide visibility of the current design-to-cost estimates, variances between current estimates and approved goals, and most important of all, the basis for the cost estimates.

Formal reporting to the customer may also be required on certain programs. Departments and agencies of the federal government generally specify the formats shown in Figures 3.13 and 3.14. Format A is used for periodic cost status reporting; format B, for explaining the cause of cost goal variances.

It is also advantageous to publicize progress toward achieving design-to-cost goals within both the program and the company. The tracking chart shown in Figure 3.15 is one such motivational tool.

3.13 SUMMARY

The elements of successful design-to-cost programs that were given in Table 3.1 are repeated in Table 3.23 to emphasize their importance. The concern of this chapter was how to initiate, maintain, and emphasize design to cost throughout the organization as well as over the program lifetime, and to

TABLE 3.23   Elements of Successful Design-to-Cost Programs (29)

Institute effective design-to-cost management
Initiate, maintain, and emphasize design to cost throughout the life of the program
Understand affordability limits and functional worth of requirements
Establish realistic but challenging design-to-cost goals
Assign cost goals to individuals, not to organizations
Establish audit trails for tacking cost growth versus requirements growth and for
    individual accountability
Require multiple design solutions and trade studies
Design inherently low cost systems
Select optimal tooling and facilities concept
Employ competitive business strategy
Flow down requirements and incentives to suppliers
Use validated and accepted estimating techniques
Motivate personnel
Remember history and benefit from the experience of others

Reprinted by permission of the Martin Marietta Corporation.

ensure that certain essential activities, functions, and practices are both understood and undertaken at the proper time and with the proper thrust.

Section 3.1 defined activities by contractual phases: preproposal, proposal, and contractual. The work in each phase can be for concept formulation, development or production, which together with ownership constitute the life cycle of systems or products. The flow of activities within and between phases is highlighted and areas that should be of particular concern are identified.

The vital issue of separating cost growth from requirements growth was also addressed in Section 3.1. This concern continued throughout the chapter and coalesced in Section 3.12 on audit trails as the means for maintaining the integrity of the cost baseline and for maintaining the accountability of individuals.

It is with this objective that Section 3.2 enumerated responsibilities for the various functional disciplines involved in the program. The key message is that both responsibility with commensurate authority should be stated clearly and tied to performance evaluation.

Section 3.2 provided guidance on how to organize for design to cost so as to achieve synergistic results from individual expectations and contributions to affordability. The importance of the design-to-cost manager reporting directly to the program director was underscored as one of the most important attributes of successful design-to-cost programs. Definitive statements of work were also provided for the broad range of functional disciplines that may be involved in the program. Again, the message was that success depends on how well roles and responsibilities are defined and assigned to individuals and individual performance is measured.

Section 3.4 is concerned with the management of trade studies since multiple design solutions and trade studies are dictates in design to cost. Both the methodology for effective trades and a technique for evaluating the cost saving potential of concepts that are in the embryonic stage were described in the section.

Management commitment to the pursuit of multiple design solutions and trade studies is essential since the process can add up to 25 percent to the typical cost of a single-approach development effort. On the other hand, the return on investment (ROI) in terms of balanced affordability and functionality will invariably warrant the up-front investment. In addition, trade studies are the vehicles for evolving cost-reduction strategies when problems arise and for mitigating risks that can add an untold amount of cost.

Section 3.5 addressed the reward of committed supplier participation in the design-to-cost program in terms of eliminating unnecessary cost in procurement. However, a balanced approach was recommended in seeking the participation of suppliers since competition is still one of the more effective means for reducing cost.

Some insight was provided into the advantages of multiple sourcing, which are revisited in Chapter 5.4 in the context of the business strategy for dealing with suppliers. In any regard, however, Section 3.5 stressed the need for constant supplier surveillance to prevent last-minute surprises.

It is impossible to achieve the full fruition of design to cost without rigorous control of technical baselines as well as cost goals. Therefore, Section 3.6 was devoted to specification practices in the context of MIL-STD-490. The hierarchy of military specifications was presented and the purpose of each type of specification illuminated.

The key point made in the section is that the rigor imposed on the definition of products and systems by the hierarchy of military specifications is worthy of emulation in the private sector. In addition, such specifications are the basis for configuration management (CM), which is essential in both military and civilian enterprises involving high technology.

Section 3.7 extended the concern for specification practices to CM, which is the next essential element in the maintenance of an audit trail. Configuration management consists of both configuration control and data management. The former was discussed in the context of MIL-STD-483A.

Both of these activities require absolute control to maintain the integrity of the technical baseline but can become cost drivers in their own right if not balanced against the essential requirements of the particular program. Both configuration management and data management have the potential for significant cost saving. However, the need to pursue such savings judiciously was stressed.

Section 3.8 then provided some suggestions on schedule control in the context of preventing cost growth that could be attributable to delays in specification practices and CM actions as well as slippages in development tasks. Schedule control is revisited in Section 5.7, but this time in the context of a cost-saving strategy.

Section 3.9 defined reviews as the lifeblood of effective design-to-cost programs and discusses the subject of technical reviews and audits in the context of MIL-STD-1521A. The organization and conduct of these reviews have evolved from managing thousands of complex high-technology programs and are also worthy of emulation in nonmilitary high-technology undertakings.

Sections 3.10 and 3.11 are based on two other military standards worthy of consideration by design-to-cost practitioners: MIL-STD-499A, *Engineering Management* and MIL-STD-1567A, *Work Measurement*. The former is particularly interesting from the viewpoint of technical performance measurement (TPM), which is a corollary task to both risk management and to cost and schedule control, and which should be pursued vigorously throughout development. Military Standard 1567A provides the yardstick for measuring the effectiveness of cost-saving effort in the factory.

With the background provided to this point, Section 3.12 discussed the maintenance of audit trails. Audit trails should be established at the outset of programs to allow cost performance to be tracked, responsibility to be maintained, and requirements growth to be separated from cost growth.

The roles of change control and tracking and reporting were described on an integrated basis. The message was that only the degree of formalism should differ in the public and private sectors and as a function of the size of the program. However, the substance should not differ for both affordability and profitability to be achieved.

3.14   CASE STUDIES AND EXERCISES

The case studies that follow are intended to amplify key points in this chapter. The exercises following the case studies allow the reader to relate these points to personal viewpoints and experiences. The case studies in this chapter stress the need to eliminate to the greatest extent possible tiers of management and labor that do not add to the value of products or services and to ensure that individual responsibilities and authorities are made known with the utmost clarity.

3.14.1   Manufacturing to Compete

Contemporary works give excellent guidance on using manufacturing as a competitive tool (30, 31). The question is how many enterprises in the United States heed such guidance.

The inability of the United States to compete in the world market as well as domestically is attributed in large measure to the loss of productivity. An article in *Business Week* reported that U.S. productivity in terms of the index of output per hour worked only increased from about 100 to 105 over the years 1980 to 1986. In contrast, the index of international competitive-

**TABLE 3.24 "Leanest and Meanest"
Companies (32)**

Company	Annual Percentage Increase
Marion Laboratories	37.0
Corning Glass Works	26.6
Walt Disney	26.3
Squibb	22.7
Circuit City Stores	20.5

Reprinted from the October 5, 1987 issue of *Business Week* by special permission © 1987 by McGraw-Hill, Inc.

ness of U.S. manufacturers over the same time period decreased from about 100 to 92.

The survey identified 70 major organizations that have made significant inroads in using labor more profitably, principally from a combination of eliminating tiers of management, reducing support labor, and increasing touch labor efficiency. The companies listed in Table 3.24 were cited "the leanest and meanest" on the basis of their annual percentage increase in inflation-adjusted operating income per employee through the years 1981 to 1986.

EXERCISE Average the annual percentage increase in operating income per employee for the five companies listed in Table 3.24. Obtain the percentage changes in annual producer price indices for the years 1981 to 1986 from the *Statistical Abstract of the United States*.

Average the wholesale price indices and compare to the average percentage increase in operating income per employee. Will the difference increase or decrease over the next decade?

3.14.2 Organizing for Profit

It is axiomatic that integrated control is more cost-effective than fragmented control. This is particularly true in the control of material that accounts for a large share of cost of goods sold.

Labor devoted to material handling is called "support labor," as opposed to "touch labor," which is expended in production. Support labor contributes relatively little value to products, yet generally equals and often exceeds touch labor.

EXERCISE Elwood S. Buffa, in *Modern Production Management*, describes the reorganization in a major corporation to achieve integrated and less costly material control. Figures 3.16 and 3.17 show the organizational structure before and after reorganization.

Assume cost of goods sold was $450-millions of which material procurement and handling accounted for 60 percent. Use the decrease in the number of boxes from Figure 3.16 and Figure 3.17 as the measure of handling labor reduction, and estimate the cost saving to the company.

3.14.3   Prospering in Adversity

At the time when large, integrated steel mills were closing, smaller plants called "minimills" were flourishing. Jack Robert Miller (35) reports the following in an article in *Scientific American:*

> Since 1977 the 10 American companies that make up what is often called Big Steel, have closed, idled, transferred, or sold some 20 plants or parts of plants, shrinking their production capacity by about 10 million metric tons, or 8.3 percent, from 12.3 million metric tons per year. Another consequence was a reduction in the number of workers in the steel industry from 453,000 in 1979 to 247,000 at the end of 1982, a decline of 45 percent in three years. In 1982 the steel industry as a whole lost $3.2 billion, far more than it had in any previous year. The focus in Big Steel is on "restructuring," which has been described by David M. Broderick, the chairman of the U.S. Steel Corporation, as a "state of accelerating self-liquidation." More specifically, restructuring includes facilities closed, projects deferred or cancelled, production consolidated, and products added or dropped.

> In contrast, the segment of the industry represented by what are called minimills has expanded and prospered since about 1960. In that year there were 10 or 12 minimills sharing about 2 percent of the U.S. steel market; at the beginning of this year, 50 minimills accounted for between 15 and 18 percent of the market. Their total capacity (reckoned in terms of plants that can produce up to 800,000 metric tons per year) approximates 14 million metric tons per

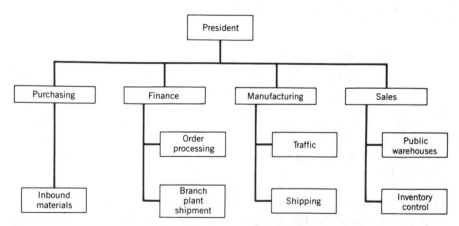

Figure 3.16   Original organizational structure (32). (Adapted by permission of John Wiley & Sons, Inc.)

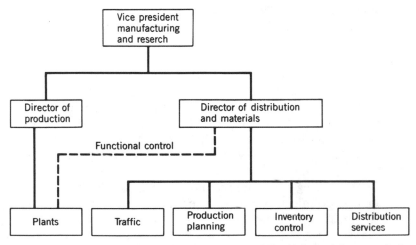

Figure 3.17   Integrated organizational structure (28). (Adapted by permission of John Wiley & Sons, Inc.)

year. The focus among the operators of minimills is on the expansion of plants and markets and on enlarging the range of products.

> —Reproduced, with permission, from Jack Robert Miller, "Steel Minimills," Scientific American, May 1984.

Minimills are characterized by little investment in raw material; scrap steel is bought only when needed. Transportation and energy costs are minimal; minimills are located close to customers and sources of scrap and low-cost energy. Product mixes are relatively restricted but can be varied easily.

Support labor and tiers of management are minimal in minimills. Foundry personnel generally handle the paper work and maintenance, and paths are short from the foundry floor to the executive suites.

EXERCISE   A number of minimills have gone out of business since 1985 despite the focus on expansion of plants, markets, and product lines. Can the failures be attributed to a shift toward the integrated mill concept? Consider the difference between the concept of integrated operations brought out in the previous case study and this case study.

3.14.4   Equal Partners

There is a saying that "All partners are equal except some partners are more equal than others." The element of truth in this saying can be evidenced by the rivalry for influence and resources between functional managers who are supposedly of equal importance to a given program and ostensibly equally dedicated to the objectives of the program. These instances are only microcosms of what often happens when companies form partnerships to pursue ventures with great economic potential, but both situations are organizational challenges.

This case study concerns a joint venture formed by companies from four different NATO (National Alliance Treaty Organization) nations to pursue a high-technology program with enormous production potential. The four companies formed a corporation to serve as the integrating contractor, with each company an equal partner in the corporation. The arrangement was approved by the respective nations with the stipulation that the work division among the four companies would constitute a single production line when production was undertaken.

The concept of a single production line envisions the integration of production in four different places into a single flow of processes and tests. This necessitates almost complete disclosure of technology among the participants. As can be expected, work division became a matter of contention as each company became increasingly familiar with the technology of the others and as the time for production neared. The issue was exacerbated by a cutback in the anticipated production funding. In essence, each partner company became a competitor for the single production line.

Thus, what often happens within a particular program happened here in the macrocosm. However, much of the same organizational pressures prevailed.

EXERCISE   Examine several programs known to involve a broad range of functional disciplines. Ascertain the program organizations and determine the relative distributions of resources and responsibilities by functional disciplines. Compare the distributions by programs and rationalize any differences.

3.14.5 Configurational Faux Pas

Instances of wrong spare parts and transmissions from lower-priced automotive vehicles showing up in higher-priced models are evidence of configuration management (CM) failures. The problems reported in the case studies of Sections 5.12.1 and 6.10.1 were also exacerbated by such failures.

The NIMBUS project, discussed in Section 5.12.3, involved eight companies under associate contractor contracts with the National Aeronautics and Space Administration (NASA), an integration contractor, and NASA serving as the program manager. Interface control among the eight cocontractors and the integration contractor posed the more serious problems and prevailed even after individual subsystems were qualified. The most serious of all was the lack of electromagnetic compatibility among the systems that ultimately required the redesign of all input and output circuits as well as the spacecraft harnesses. A significant part of the 2-year schedule slip, and a major part of the multimillions of dollars overrun, was due to this configurational faux pas.

The tactical communication system, discussed in the case study of Section 6.10.1, was more the victim of overt deemphasis of configuration management. It is unfortunate that disciplines such as CM, data management, and planning are referred to as "other technical services" in the military and aerospace contract domains. The expression connotes a certain lack of importance in contrast to the design disciplines, and, as a result, the resources devoted to the aforementioned disciplines are usually reduced in times of austerity to an amount less than the critical mass needed to do the job.

As early as 1976, it was foreseen that production of the tactical communication system would be delayed for more than 2 years, and, in an attempt to keep the program alive during the stretchout, both the procuring activity and the contractor cut back significantly in the "other technical services" disciplines. The effect on configuration management was the occurrence of substantial delays in preparing and approving engineering change proposals (ECPs) that were essential to finalizing the production design.

EXERCISE   As stated in Section 6.10.1, the production cost estimate of $294 million in then-year dollars was prepared in 1976. By the start of production, this estimate had grown to $594 million in 1983 dollars. Assume that 25 percent of the cost growth was due to untimely configuration management, and that the reduction of resources in CM was uniformly distributed over the period of time from 1976 to 1983, amounting to a total of $5 million.

Using the time value of money relationships given in Section 6.7, calculate the present value (i.e., in 1976) of a series of seven uniform annual expenditures amounting to a total of $5 million at a discount rate of 10 percent compounded annually.

Obtain producer price indexes (PPI) for the years 1976 to 1983 from the *Statistical Abstract of the United States*. Using the percent changes in the PPI, convert the 1983 production budget estimate of $594 million in 1983 dollars to 1976 dollars. Take 25 percent of the difference between the two budget estimates and calculate the leverage that was lost by reducing the configuration management support by the amount of the present value. Note that the term "leverage" denotes the control of financial transactions involving substantial sums of money by significantly smaller sums of money.

REFERENCES

1–7. Martin Marietta Corporation, *Design to Cost/Affordability Manual*, 1986.

8. U.S. Air Force Air Systems Division, Directorate of Configuration Management, *Configuration Management, Strategic Systems*, 1985.

9. MIL-STD-490, *Specification Practices*.

10. MIL-STD-480A, *Configuration Control-Engineering Changes, Deviations and Waivers.*

11. DOD-STD-480A, *Configuration Control-Engineering Changes, Deviations and Waivers.*

12. NAVMAT P4855-1, *Navy Power Supply Reliability,* 1982.

13–15. MIL-STD-1521A, *Technical Reviews and Audits for Systems, Equipments, and Computer Programs.*

16–22. Defense Systems Management College, *System Engineering Management Guide,* 1982.

23. MIL-STD-1567A, *Work Measurement.*

24–25. Martin Marietta Corporation, *Design to Cost/Affordability Manual,* 1986.

26–27. Departments of the Army, the Navy, and the Air Force, *Joint Design-to-Cost Guide,* 1977.

28–29. Martin Marietta Corporation, *Design to Cost/Affordability Manual,* 1986.

30. Robert H. Hayes and Steven C. Wheelright, *Restoring Our Competitive Edge,* John Wiley & Sons, 1984.

31. Thomas G. Gunn, *Manufacturing for Competitive Advantage,* Ballinger Publishing Company, 1987.

32. *Business Week.* "America's Leanest and Meanest," October 5, 1987.

33–34. Elwood S. Buffa, *Modern Production Management,* 4th ed., John Wiley & Sons, 1973.

35. Jack Robert Miller, "Steel Minimills," *Scientific American,* May 1984.

4
DESIGNING FOR INHERENTLY LOW COST

It is characteristic of high-technology industries that performance requirements lead and determine the ability to produce. Designs typically reflect the leading edge of the state of the art in manufacturing technology and materials. Consequentially, there is much potential for cost growth because of design features that rely on technological breakthroughs in devices and materials, and frequently in processes.

This can result in numerous design iterations that prolong engineering development to the point where the window of opportunity for life-cycle-cost saving (see Figure 2.1) is virtually closed. Ideally, the design effort would converge rapidly on the producibility objectives given in Table 4.1, thus economizing on development cost while optimizing nonrecurring and recurring costs for the lowest production cost. Such a design is called an "inherently low cost design."

The essence of low-cost production is ease of fabrication, assembly, and test. The relative ease of these activities is a measure of the design efficiency of the product being produced. Products with greater design efficiency are produced more economically and in general their ownership requires lower life-cycle cost. This is particularly true of high-technology products.

Design efficiency is characterized by the degree to which product simplification and work simplification can be effected. This chapter advocates that design efficiency be elevated to the same level of concern as product performance and, following the perspective on advanced technology's role in low-cost production, presents guidelines for achieving product simplification.

The first section in this chapter is devoted to technology from the perspective both of increasing design efficiency and reducing work in process. Work in process (WIP), the antithesis to affordable quality, has become an anathema to the Japanese. Technology is addressed again in Section 5.2 from the viewpoint of the business strategy of participating in the industrial modernizations incentives program (IMIP) of the U.S. Department of Defense.

TABLE 4.1   Producibility Objectives (1)

Maximize
>   Simplicity of design
>   Economical parts and materials
>   Standardization of parts and materials
>   Economical manufacturing technology
>   Simplicity of processes
>   Process repeatability
>   Process inspectability and testability
>   Manufacturing yield

Minimize
>   Design changes for production
>   Number and variety of parts and materials
>   Critical materials
>   Critical processes
>   Scrap and rework
>   Procurement lead time
>   Support and other nontouch labor
>   Work in process
>   Energy consumption

Adapted by permission of the Martin Marietta Corporation.

The next section addresses product simplification with emphasis on the cost-driving relationships inherent in product specifications. These are organized in the context of material selection, detail fabrication, and assembly.

The cost advantage of castings, introduced in the context of product simplification, sets the stage for a section devoted to casting processes and cost comparison of the various processes with forgings that are usually employed when high mechanical properties are desired. It is important for design-to-cost practitioners to understand both the technical and financial aspects of the casting technology to do justice to its cost-saving potential.

The next two sections address approaches for quantifying the efficiency of designs in terms of assembly ease and testability. These are highly compatible design characteristics; products that are easy to assemble are easy to test. A parametric approach to testability is presented as a tool for both assessing the inherent testability of existing designs and determining the degree of testability needed in new designs to achieve cost goals. This is followed by a brief introduction to MIL-STD-2165, whose thrust is integrated diagnostics in military equipment that is offered as guidance for other high-technology products and systems.

Next, guidelines for work simplification are presented, bringing in the relationships between production equipment and the human element. The very important subject of automation and robotics is included.

Perhaps the greatest cost driver in the aerospace industry has been the approach to product quality, which is paramount because of the intended applications. Product quality has not been an inherent characteristic in aerospace, but rather has been achieved by the very expensive process of weeding out defects, starting with the costly business of 100 percent rescreening of procured parts.

Section 2.1 proclaims that affordability and quality are compatible and, given the proper organizational mind-set and cohesiveness of purpose, that quality could be free. This section supplements these thoughts by describing a concept that has emerged in recent years and that provides a new approach to quality by replacing the notion of conformance-to-specification limits by the idea of reduced variability regarding targets for greater product uniformity. The chapter advocates the adoption of this concept as the cornerstone for the just-in-time strategy discussed under technology perspective in Section 4.1, and provides insight into a technique called "tolerance centering."

Another section in this chapter is devoted to power supplies. In the subsystem hierarchy of high-technology products and virtually all industrial and consumer products, no subsystem is more ubiquitous than the power supply. Yet, few subsystems are appreciated less as design, schedule, and cost challenges.

Up to this point, the thrust has been on designing for inherently low cost. The next section shifts to the question of the design's readiness for production. The subject is discussed according to the rationale that the affordability of even the lowest cost designs will not be fully realized if designs and processes are not proved at the time of production. An overview is provided of the production readiness criteria contained in Department of Defense Directive 5000.34.

Despite the hardware orientation of the book, it recognizes that software cost is no less important than hardware cost, including the software activity leading to firmware implementation. There is a tendency to think that software cost is a nonrecurring one-time expenditure, when recurring expenditures on the maintenance of both production and mission software have been large cost drivers in many instances. Therefore, an insight into some aspects of software maintenance cost is provided.

Following the summary of its contents, the chapter provides a number of case studies and exercises with the intent of amplifying key points in the chapter. The exercises allow the reader to relate personal views and experiences to the events unfolded in the case studies.

4.1 TECHNOLOGY PERSPECTIVE

It has been the desire of every manufacturer since the Industrial Revolution to replace costly stockpiling of raw material, WIP, and other inventory with a productive flow of finished goods that exactly matches demand. In large measure, this has been accomplished by the Japanese, who serve as a measure of effectiveness for the rest of the world (2).

4.1.1 Potential

It would now appear that all factories worldwide could achieve this goal as beneficiaries of the dramatic advances in design and manufacturing technology and of innovations in production management that have been evolving over the past decade. The promise is centered about flexible manufacturing and just-in-time (JIT) manufacturing and procurement.

Flexible manufacturing systems are characterized by the ability to change products produced by given assembly lines on a lot-by-lot basis. For example, steel minimills shift from specialty to specialty in this fashion.

Just-in-time manufacturing is typically understood to mean that at every point in the production flow the right items are being either procured or produced with the right quality and at the right time, thus avoiding stockpiling and reducing WIP to almost insignificant levels. The true meaning of JIT is more subtle, however, in that WIP or other inventory no longer "pushes" or establishes factory output, but rather that the required factory output "pulls" the production and procurement flow with zero inventory as the goal.

Group technology and in-process controlled quality are needed to realize the full potential of JIT and flexible manufacturing. In group technology, a series of processes providing different functions are grouped so that they operate similar to an assembly line. In-process controlled quality, inspection, and test are integral parts of the production process at each point in the flow.

The importance of in-process quality control is the motivation for including a section in this chapter on product uniformity based on the concept of tolerance centering. Tolerance centering is a derivative of statistical quality control with the added dimension of criteria for real-time management intervention.

The concept of in-process controlled quality extends beyond the factory floor to the overall operations of the organization from order-taking through postdelivery support of products and includes administrative and support phases of the business. This concept is referred to as "total quality control" (TQC). It connotes doing everything right and doing it right the first time and is thus a key element in a commitment to excellence.

Computer-aided design (CAD) provides design efficiency and is a prerequisite for computer-aided manufacturing (CAM) in order to ensure maximum producibility within the constraint of existing production capability. Computer-aided design can serve as the driver for numerically controlled operations, robotics, and conveyers, as well as providing the product-design function. In this case, the process is called "computer-aided design–computer-aided manufacturing" CAD–CAM.

In essence, CAD–CAM ensures producibility of given designs, flexible manufacturing provides quick reaction to the demands of the marketplace and JIT efforts strive to eliminate WIP and other inventories.

The key point to remember, however, is that there is an inherent limit to the production economy that can be realized in any given design. This limit is established by the aforementioned design efficiency of the product being produced.

4.1.2 Timing

Successive program phases present diminishing opportunities for realizing the cost-containing potential of advanced technology. As noted in Section 2.2, however, advanced technology for the purpose of reducing cost should be considered in the context of the long-range strategy for the overall organization rather than for an individual program or product.

It is during the conceptual phase of a new program that an assessment of how it fits into existing capability and capacity should be made and the need for advanced technology quantified in terms of cost and lead time. The consideration should include the capability and capacity of suppliers, which leads to the conclusion that make-or-buy and advanced technology decisions should be made on an integrated basis and should be prerequisite for undertaking the expense of the proposal phase of the program.

As stated in Section 2.2.1, the conceptual phase is the optimal period for cogent management action in the interest of affordability with profitability. Interesting parallels can be drawn from the current state of the art in integrated-circuits technology

Figure 4.1 illustrates the substantial saving that can be realized from very-large-scale integration in quantity production of gate arrays, standard cells, and even custom devices. Standardization is key to achieving full economy of scale.

A new frontier of technology is evolving in MIMIC, an acronym for microwave–millimeter wave monolithic integrated circuits. The use of gallium arsenide in MIMIC portends shrinking both size and cost of analog components operating at frequencies approaching 100 gigahertz (GHz).

It is usually advantageous to use devices with more capability than needed in certain product applications in the interest of standardization. Timely management action is needed to ensure that proper trades are made toward obtaining the greatest possible cost benefits.

On the other hand, there are high-usage areas where inadequate technology precludes the benefits from economy of scale and where timely management intervention by directing applied research could result in significant saving. For example, large numbers of complex castings are used in high-technology products, but the state-of-the art in multicavity casting necessitates extensive welding and machining to finish end products (see Section 4.3).

There is need for management to intervene in such areas early in program life cycles. For example, consider castings that generally are cost drivers because of the need for subsequent welding and machining. A research goal

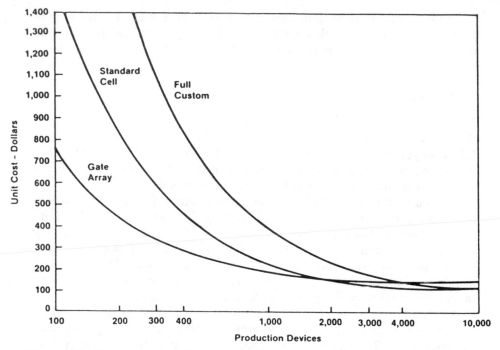

Figure 4.1 Economy of scale in very large scale integration (3). (Reprinted by permission of the Martin Marietta Corporation.)

could be to effect the equivalent of welding in the wax phase of the process thus yielding complex castings without the need to weld sections and with substantially less secondary machining.

In most instances, it is possible to delay actual monetary outlay for production facilities and equipment until sometime during the development phase. The funding commitment, however, should be understood and made by management during the proposal phase. This is key to the viability of design-to-cost programs. Facilities and equipment that will be in place at the start of production are as much part of the baseline as the design requirements for the product to be produced.

4.1.3 Break-Even

Significant financial investment is involved in realizing the promise of flexible manufacturing and JIT manufacturing if they are centered on automation and robotics. Generally, an automated line must be designed from the ground up to perform its specific function. Granted, its operation will reduce unit cost; however, the development of the concept, with its inherent trials and errors, can increase investment out of proportion to expectations for quantities that can be handled by more conventional methods, especially when there are design variations in the product line.

One major advantage of CAD–CAM is adaptability to design variations. For example, consider the assembly of a printed wiring board into a circuit-card assembly. Component stuffing, soldering, and testing are involved and each different assembly requires different numerically controlled tapes for sorting, sequencing, and insertion. Such tapes, however, are by-products of CAD. But even the cost-effectiveness of CAD is a function of quantity.

Figure 4.2 illustrates the break-even relationship for the various approaches as a function of the quantity to be produced. It is evident that the quantity needed to be produced to achieve a target unit cost is a function of the slope of the respective lines in the figure. When only target cost is specified, quantity is traded against the nonrecurring cost of the respective approaches. The opposite applies when only quantity is specified. When both target cost and quantity are specified, they are traded against their respective nonrecurring costs.

Robots are a form of flexible automation, somewhat adaptable to product variations, and by themselves are relatively inexpensive. However, interfacing equipment and controls add from one to two times the cost to the overall robot.

In typical manufacturing shops, work is processed in batches or lots. Changeover or setup time therefore becomes significant, depending on lot size and the nature of the process. For example, in a small-batch operation, changeover on automatic equipment could take a long time in relation to run time because of the need for precise orientation to do the job repeatedly.

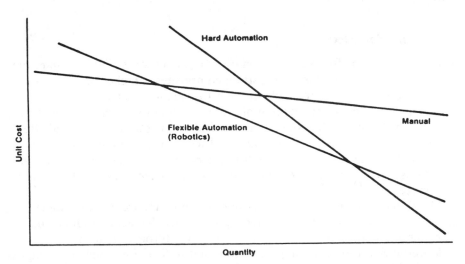

Figure 4.2 Break-even relationships (4). (Reprinted by permission of the Martin Marietta Corporation.)

A single-purpose unit is more accurate and faster than a robot or a human. If flexibility is required or product changes are likely, however, robots or people should be considered. As a general rule, people should be used for very short runs, hard automation for very long runs, and robotics for intermediate runs.

4.2 PRODUCT SIMPLIFICATION

Production consists of processes that convert material into details and, with the addition of other parts, assemble these details into complete products. A detail is a single electrical or mechanical part that cannot be disassembled further without being destroyed.

Some processes are material-intensive; some, labor-intensive; some energy-intensive; and others, all three. Product simplification should therefore address material selection, detail fabrication, and assembly, along with the necessary inspection and test to ensure product integrity and quality.

Product simplification should also be considered from the aspect of energy consumption, which influences production cost in two ways. First is the energy cost associated with converting raw materials into usable form for production purposes. Secondly, as energy cost rises, certain raw materials may become cost drivers.

Other energy-related cost drivers are the cost of metal removal, hot process steps, heat-treating, and welding operations. Projection of energy cost is thus an important element in evaluating alternative designs and manufacturing processes.

4.2.1 Material Selection

Material selection affects production costs in many ways. For example, the current cost of such materials as carbon composites is higher than for metallic materials, especially for high-strength-to-weight designs.

Among metal materials, there is also a wide variation of material cost and availability. Trade studies should be undertaken to determine the final effect of selecting a higher performance material with correspondingly higher unit cost versus selecting a material with lower performance characteristics and lower cost but for which the total cost may be higher because of tolerance allowances.

Metal matrix composites such as boron aluminum are good examples of costly materials with cost-effective applications. Typical products made from these composites are blades and vanes for turbine engines.

Material cost trends are important to monitor. The time frame of production should influence the selection of materials for a design. For instance, composite material costs continue to decrease as volume increases and re-

TABLE 4.2 Material Waste Factors (5)

Material	Percentage
Sheet metal	50–55
Machine plate	15–25
Machine bar and rod	20–25
Forgings	15–25

Adapted by permission of the Martin Marietta Corporation.

lated manufacturing technology matures. Concern should also be exhibited for material waste. This is particularly important in the high-technology industries that are heavy users of costly materials such as stainless steel and titanium.

As much as 55 percent of sheet metal stock may go to waste in the manufacturing process. Table 4.2 gives other typical material waste factors in high-technology industries. Designs that favor greater material usage have the potential for lower production costs.

In recent years, minimization of material waste has become an important by-product of computer-aided engineering (CAE). The process can be envisioned as the solution of a linear programming problem (see Section 5.8.1) wherein material utilization is the objective function and the numbers of the different details to be cut are the constraint equations. In essence, cutting patterns are optimized on the basis of all mechanical details to be fabricated starting with the largest sizes and progressing down to the smallest sizes. This practice has effectively reduced the waste factors given in Table 4.2 to about one-half their values.

It is relatively inexpensive to sort scrap material so that it can be sold to a salvage company at a higher price than ordinary waste. Depending on the commodities market, it may be advisable to stockpile the sorted scrap until commodity prices are on the rise. Salvage companies typically provide transportation of scrap as part of the purchase agreement which is usually prepared on an annual basis.

4.2.2 Detail Fabrication

A "detail" has been defined as a single electrical or mechanical part that cannot be disassembled further short of being destroyed. For example, a printed wiring board prior to insertion of components is a detail. On the insertion of components, it becomes a circuit-card assembly.

The major factors influencing the cost of detail fabrication are tolerance and surface finish requirements, detail complexity, and fabrication techniques employed. These factors are evidenced in tooling and quality-control costs, particularly where large quantities are involved.

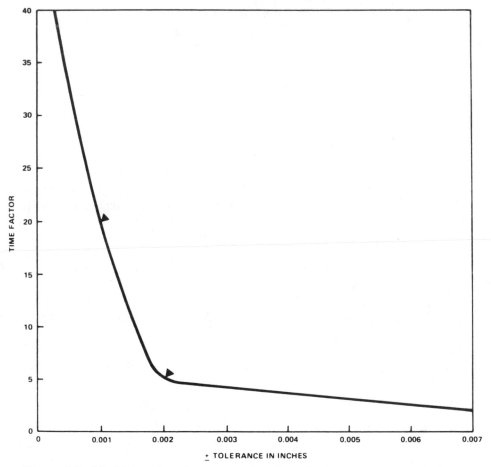

Figure 4.3   Machining time factor as a function of tolerance (6). (Reprinted by permission of the Martin Marietta Corporation.)

1. TOLERANCE

Figure 4.3 shows machining time as a function of tolerance. It should be noted that the machining time factor increases from about 5 to 20, or is approximately quadrupled, when plus or minus 0.001-inch (in.) tolerances are used instead of plus or minus 0.002-in. tolerances. In some instances, it may be better to tighten detail tolerances to increase yield at the assembly level (see Section 4.7).

2. SURFACE FINISH

Figure 4.4 shows time factor for finishing the surface of details as a function of the allowable roughness of the finished detail. Time is also influenced by the physical size and the number of dimensions of the details to be

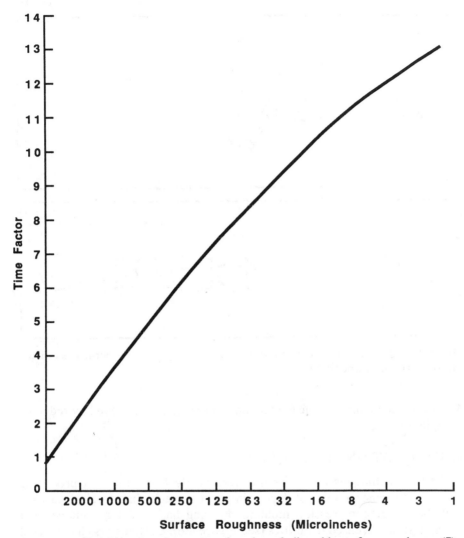

Figure 4.4 Finishing time factor as a function of allowable surface roughness (7). (Adapted by permission of the Martin Marietta Corporation.)

finished. It should be noted, however, that surface finish is not as great a cost driver as tolerance. A decrease in allowable surface roughness from 1000 to 125 μin., or 8 to 1, increases the time factor from only about 3.7 to 7.3, or a little more than 1 to 2.

3. COMPLEXITY

Complexity is the product both of the number and of the variety of details used in an assembly and of the complexity of the individual details. Figure

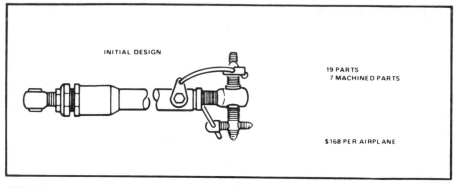

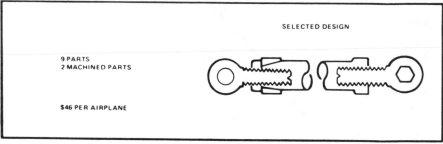

Figure 4.5   Cost as a function of complexity (8). (Reprinted by permission of the Martin Marietta Corporation.)

4.5 shows an example of the cost reduction that can be achieved by reducing complexity.

4. FABRICATION TECHNIQUES

Certain techniques are inherently less costly than others in producing details. The general order of decreasing cost is machining, forging, casting, and thermoset compression molding. Forging has a cost advantage over machining at increased quantities (see Figure 4.6). Castings also have a cost advantage over machining (see Figure 4.7), except when more than one casting is needed to fabricate a detail and secondary welding and machining are required (see Figure 4.8). Castings have a cost advantage over forgings at increased quantities, and in numerous cases, die castings have a cost advantage over investment castings (see Figure 4.9).

The die casting industry has achieved process controls for heat, pressure, and cycle time that can ensure acceptable products for many applications previously reserved for investment castings and forgings. Nonetheless, care should be exercised in structural applications of die castings. The use of compression molding of thermoset plastic in fabricating enclosure details instead of the more conventional sheet metal buildup and honeycomb sand-

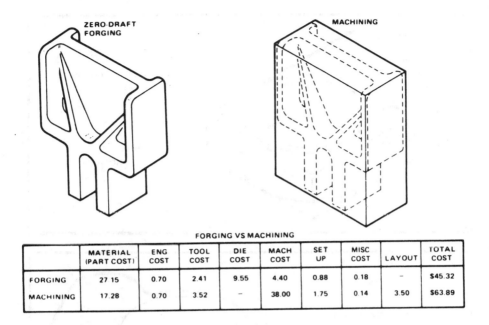

FORGING VS MACHINING

	MATERIAL (PART COST)	ENG COST	TOOL COST	DIE COST	MACH COST	SET UP	MISC COST	LAYOUT	TOTAL COST
FORGING	27.15	0.70	2.41	9.55	4.40	0.88	0.18	–	$45.32
MACHINING	17.28	0.70	3.52	–	38.00	1.75	0.14	3.50	$63.89

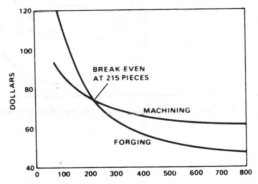

Figure 4.6 Cost of forging versus machining (9). (Reprinted by permission of the Martin Marietta Corporation.)

wiching should be examined from a cost viewpoint when large quantities are involved. Figure 4.10 compares the cost of fabricating an enclosure cover by each of the three techniques. The figure shows that each technique provides the same radio-frequency attenuation at the frequency region of interest. Honeycomb construction has a weight advantage over the other two, and thermoset compression molding has a slight weight advantage over sheet-metal construction. However, the cost advantage of thermoset compression molding over the other two is significant at the larger quantity.

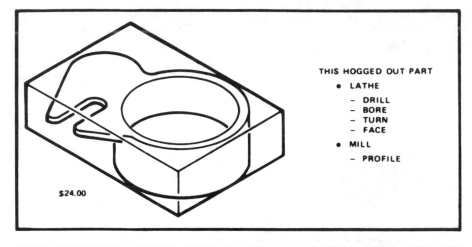

THIS HOGGED OUT PART
- LATHE
  - DRILL
  - BORE
  - TURN
  - FACE
- MILL
  - PROFILE

$24.00

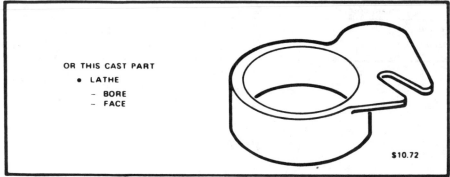

OR THIS CAST PART
- LATHE
  - BORE
  - FACE

$10.72

Figure 4.7 Cost of casting versus machining (10). (Reprinted by permission of the Martin Marietta Corporation.)

5. OTHER FACTORS

Other factors influencing the cost of detail fabrication are its geometry and the material used to build it. These factors are particularly significant where castings are involved (see Section 4.3). Figure 4.11 illustrates the general relationship between geometry and cost. The geometry, size, and shape, of the part have a direct bearing on the tooling, equipment, and processes required. Large parts may limit the use of castings and forgings. Compound contours create the need for special techniques. Stiffening beads, lightening holes, and special trims add to the costs of both tooling and processes. Materials used for the details are critical to their cost of fabrication. Conventional forming and metal removal are not appropriate for some commonly used metals. For example, titanium and some stainless steels require hot forming and slow speed metal removal techniques. In addition, these metals cannot be butt-welded for loadbearing applications. In contrast,

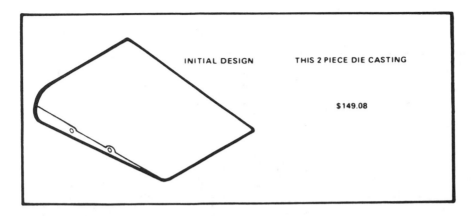

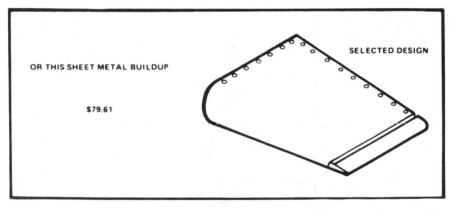

Figure 4.8 Cost of multiple-piece casting (11). (Reprinted by permission of the Martin Marietta Corporation.)

most nonmetallic details require labor intensive processes or expensive special tooling.

6. RESIDUAL EFFECTS

Residual effects of the aforementioned can be experienced in several areas. Support and other nontouch labor costs increase as touch labor increases. Maintenance, repair and tool replacement factors increase with increased complexity of details.

4.2.3 Assembly

There is a direct correlation between assembly ease and low-cost production. Ease of assembly is established by a number of factors, including accessibility, materials to be joined, joining processes, special processes such as sealing, parts count and diversification, tolerance, and geometry.

	INVESTMENT CASTING	DIE CASTING
FTU = ULTIMATE TENSILE STRENGTH FTY = YIELD TENSILE STRENGTH FSU = ULTIMATE SHEAR STRENGTH E = MODULUS OF ELASTICITY	FTU = 38,000 PSI FTY = 28,000 FSU = 27,000 E = 10.4 ELONG = 5%	FTU = 46,000 PSI FTY = 23,000 FSU = 28,000 E = 10.0 ELONG = 2.5%
COMPONENT CONFIGURATION	356-T6 ALUM	380 ALUM CASTING
PITCH WING 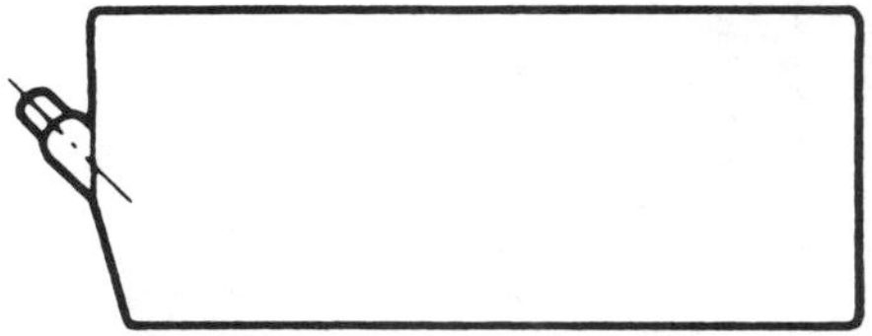 WT = 0.20 LB QUANTITY = 600,000	EVALUATION PHASE: 200 PIECES = $35 EA WITH MACH – USE PRODUCTION TOOLING PRODUCTION: 600,000 PIECES: = $26 EACH WITH MACH TOOLING = $20,000	EVALUATION PHASE: 200 PIECES = $4.65 EA WITH MACH TOOLING = $9,000 PRODUCTION: 600,000 PIECES: = $2 EACH WITH MACH TOOLING = $50,000
YAW WING  WT = 0.15 LB QUANTITY = 600,000	EVALUATION PHASE: 200 PIECES = $35 EA WITH MACH – USE PRODUCTION TOOLING PRODUCTION: 600,000 PIECES: = $26 EACH WITH MACH TOOLING = $20,000	EVALUATION PHASE: 200 PIECES = $4.65 EA WITH MACH TOOLING = $9,000 PRODUCTION: 600,000 PIECES: = $2 EACH WITH MACH TOOLING = $50,000

Figure 4.9 Cost of investment versus die-casting (12). (Adapted by permission of the Martin Marietta Corporation.)

CONTROL FIN

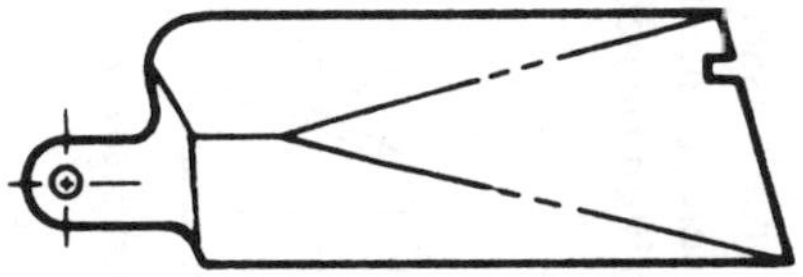

WT = 0.15 LB
QUANTITY = 1,200,000

2 PIECE CONST	
200 PIECES = $40 EA WITH MACH – USE PRODUCTION TOOLING	200 PIECES = $5.00 EA TOOLING = $12,000
PRODUCTION = $30 EACH	PRODUCTION = $2.25 EA
TOOLING = $30,000	TOOLING = $75,000

CENTER SUPPORT

WT = 20.4 LB
QUANTITY = 50,000

2 PIECE CONST	1 PIECE CONST	
200 PIECES = $300 EA = $600/SET TOOLING = $25,000 EA = 50,000 TOTAL	200 PIECES: $100/SET 50 EA TOOLING = $130,000	
PRODUCTION = $270 EA = $540 SET	PRODUCTION: $45 EA 90 SET	
TOOLING: $100,000	TOOLING = $210,000	
200 PIECES = $500 EA $25,000 TOOLING	200 PIECES = $85 EA TOOLING = $170,000	
PRODUCTION: $450 EACH	PRODUCTION: $75 EACH	
TOOLING = $100,000	TOOLING = $210,000	

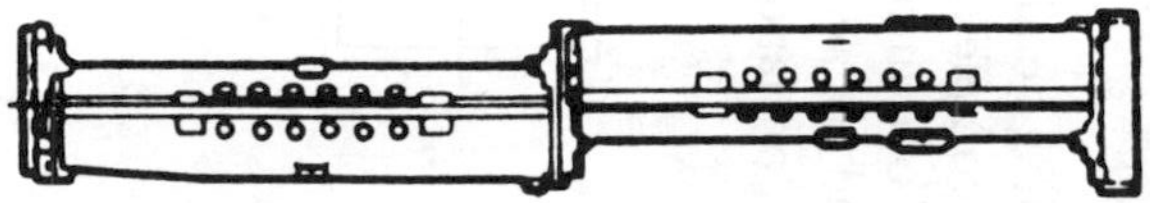

Figure 4.9 (*Continued*)

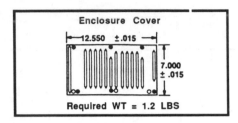

Quantity	Honeycomb "Sandwich" Aluminum Construction	Sheet Metal Solid Aluminum Construction	Thermoset Compression Modeling
120	Unit Cost $2,608 WT = 1.2 LBS	Unit Cost $663 WT = 1.6 LBS	Unit Cost $390 WT = 1.5 LBS
25	$3,390 WT = 1.2 LBS	$861 WT = 1.6 LBS	$1,395 WT = 1.5 LBS

Figure 4.10 Cost of enclosure fabrication techniques (13). (Adapted by permission of the Martin Marietta Corporation.)

1. ACCESSIBILITY

Accessibility for installing details establishes tooling, sequence, and process requirements. Tool complexity and cost increase as accessibility decreases. The sequence of operations and the need to break assemblies into subassemblies are affected by accessibility. Process selection, such as robotics, automatic riveting, or hand assembly, is also driven by accessibility.

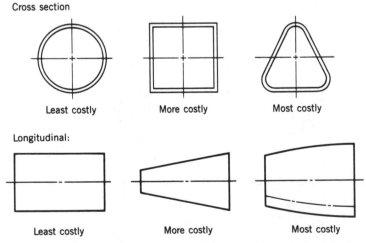

Figure 4.11 Relationship between geometry and cost.

2. MATERIALS JOINED

The selection of materials to be joined and the process of joining directly affect costs. Environmental controls, capital equipment, and special tools must be matched to materials and required joining processes. Exotic metals and high-temperature composite materials require the development of new joining processes and techniques. For example, adhesives for high-performance composites are based on epoxy, epoxy novolac, nylon epoxy, epoxy phenolic, and vinyl phenolic resins; selection depends on the properties of the particular composite. Adhesives are usually applied in the form of films. Uniform pressure is applied over the entire bonding area, typically under autoclave bagging pressures, and parts are cured at elevated temperatures. An example of this process is the fabrication of sandwich panels. There are related effects on inspection and test when such materials are employed. Inspection equipment and techniques need to be enhanced as the manufacturing processes become more complex.

3. SPECIAL PROCESSES

Special processes such as sealing and wet fastener installation also add to the cost of manufacturing and inspection and test of assemblies. Tooling and equipment costs are also adversely affected.

4. PARTS COUNT AND VARIETY

The number and the variety of both manufactured and procured parts affect tooling costs. Tooling complexity and quantities are driven by the number and variety of parts to be located and installed. The variety of parts affects labor cost. For example, in a paced production line used to maintain a constant daily output, the number of different parts in an assembly usually establishes the number of operators needed on-line.

5. TOLERANCE

Tight tolerances increase the need for hard tooling and tool complexity and increase overall tooling costs. Master tools and coordinating tools are commonly used to maintain tolerance requirements throughout the assembly process. It is imperative that detail part and assembly tolerances be compatible.

6. GEOMETRY

Shape and size of the assembly will establish fixture complexity and size. The size and weight of details and assemblies will also increase the cost of manufacturing labor and the need for special-handling equipment.

7. RESIDUAL EFFECTS

Residual effects of the aforementioned can be experienced in several other areas. Both direct and indirect support labor costs increase as touch labor increases. Repair and replacement factors increase with complexity of the assembly. Nonlabor support cost, such as maintenance and perishable tool replacement, can also be expected to increase.

4.3 ROLE OF CASTINGS

The discussion in Section 4.2 leads to the conclusion that the proper use of castings can fulfill many of the requirements for mechanical detail fabrication and assembly at substantially reduced cost. Program personnel usually accept this statement intuitively but generally lack the background to gauge the true cost savings after allowances have been made for design and other nonrecurring costs associated with castings.

Design-to-cost practitioners should, therefore, become sufficiently familiar with casting technology to render valid judgment on potential applications and concurrent savings. This section provides an overview of casting processes in the various forms encountered, specifically, sand casting, permanent mold casting, plaster mold casting, investment casting, die casting, shell mold casting, and composite mold casting.

The advantages and disadvantages of the various processes are discussed along with the precautions each process requires. The advantages from the viewpoint of design, metallurgy, and production are summarized in Table 4.3. The section then presents the cost comparison of these processes with respect to forgings that are viewed as the standard for mechanical properties.

Castings are produced in foundries and a unique terminology for the casting processes has emerged. Definitions of terms commonly encountered in foundries are given in Table 4.4 and should be remembered because of the specific meanings.

4.3.1 Casting Processes

Metals suitable to the various casting processes are listed in Table 4.5. These are identified again in the subsequent discussion of specific processes and from the standpoint of precautions to be taken. For example, castings from titanium, which is a reactive metal, require chemical etching to remove exterior deposits on the castings.

1. SAND MOLD CASTING

The sand mold casting process is illustrated in Figure 4.12. Sand combined with a binder suitable for the casting metal is packed densely about a

TABLE 4.3   Casting Advantages (14)

Design

Minimum number of constraints on size and complexity of designs
Mass can be located only where needed, resulting in overall weight saving
Prototype parts can be provided for proof of design and test and evaluation
Design requirements can be satisfied with a wide range of metal properties
Appearance of parts can be enhanced without restricting the design of castings

Metallurgy

The equiaxis grain structure of castings results in isotropic properties for improved performance
Controlled cooling rates offer grain size control in high-stress areas to provide performance which is specifically tailored to the stress areas

Production

Amenable to high volume and high production rates and large economy of scale
Secondary machining can be reduced or eliminated

Adapted by permission of the Martin Marietta Corporation.

rigid pattern so that when the pattern is removed a cavity corresponding to the shape of the pattern remains. Molten metal is poured through the sprue into the cavity and, when solidified, forms a cast replica of the pattern. The sand forming the mold cavity can be broken away readily for removal of the casting. The molds used for sand mold casting are green sand molds, dry sand molds, and dry sand core molds. Green sand molds are the most commonly used of the sand molds; the word "green" connotes that the sand mixture is allowed to remain moist. Dry sand molds are oven dried. The dried layer is usually 0.5 in. or more thick depending on the section thickness and may extend through the entire section of the mold. Dry sand core molds are made from assemblies of sand cores. Dry sand core molds are used when flasks would be too large to fit into ovens or when the cost of drying large masses of sand would be prohibitive. Dry sand mold casting is suitable with all the metal alloys listed in Table 4.5 and may also be used with iron and nickel alloys. Advantages and disadvantages of sand mold casting are given in Table 4.6. Precautions to be taken in sand mold casting are (1) design the cavity for uniform section thicknesses; (2) avoid abrupt changes in cross sections; (3) avoid sharp corners and use generous fillets; and (4) avoid cores, undercuts, and deep pockets and, when these are necessary, make their shape as simple as possible. When designing sand molds, it is important to visualize the casting in the mold and attempt to effect the design so that (1) the parting line is straight; (2) natural draft is provided; (3) heavier portions, the portions to be machined, or the entire part may be cast in the drag; and (4) both thick and thin portions of the casting can be fed easily and progressive solidification achieved.

TABLE 4.4   Foundry Terminology (15)

Chaplet. A metal device for holding a core or section of a mold in place; normally used to brace a core in the drag or in the cope

Chill. A metallic object, usually of steel or cast iron, placed in the wall of the mold or on the surface of the core to solidify the casting more rapidly at that point

Cope. The upper section of a mold or flask; for sand castings, usually made of sand plus a binder; for permanent mold castings, usually made of metal or sand plus a binder; for die castings, always made of metal; for investment castings, usually made of plaster, soluble wax, metal, and ceramic

Core. A separable part of the mold used to create openings or cavities in the casting that are not otherwise possible

Core box. The pattern equipment used to make cores

Core Shift. The displacement of the core in the mold caused by closing the mold, or by the pressure of molten metal that tends to dislodge the core

Drag. The lower or bottom section of a mold or flask

Dry sand mold. A mold thoroughly dried, baked, or chemically bonded

Fin. Thin ragged appendages on rough castings formed by metal running into the mold joints or cracks in the mold or cores

Flask. A metal or wood container without top or fixed bottom used to retain the material in which the mold is formed

Gate. The connected columns and channels that carry the metal from the top of the mold to the casting cavity; frequently denotes parts of the gate assembly between the runner and casting cavity called the *in-gate, down-gate,* or *sprue*

Green sand core. Core used in the as-mixed, moist condition

Green Sand Mold. Mold used in the as-mixed, moist condition

Mismatch. Lateral offset at the parting line caused by misalignment of the cope and the drag

Mold. Cavity in the matrix where the casting is shaped; also the matrix that contains the cavity.

Parting line. The joint where one section of the mold meets the other

Pattern. The model that forms the casting cavity when placed in the mold; it is oversize to compensate for shrinkage due to solidification and contraction of the cast material.

Riser. A reservoir of molten metal to supply the mold cavity and to compensate for the contraction of cast metal as it solidifies.

Runner. That portion of the gate assembly that connects the sprue, or down-gate, with the in-gate

Sprue. An opening in the mold into which the molten metal is poured; also called *down-sprue* or *down-gate*

Tie bar. A column of metal connecting two webs or extended lugs to reduce warping, or to assist in the proper feeding of metal

Adapted by permission of the Martin Marietta Corporation.

TABLE 4.5 Casting Metal Alloys

Process	Aluminum	Magnesium	Copper	Steel	Titanium
Sand mold casting	X	X	X	X	X
Permanent mold casting	X	X	X		
Investment casting	X	X	X	X	X
Die casting	X	X			
Plaster mold casting	X	X	X		
Shell mold casting	X	X	X	X	
Composite mold casting	X	X	X		

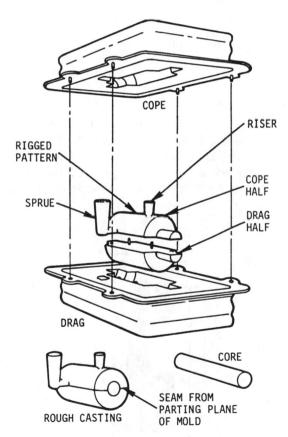

Figure 4.12 Sand mold casting process (16). (Reprinted by permission of the Martin Marietta Corporation.)

TABLE 4.6   Sand Mold Casting (17)

Advantages

Suitable for all casting alloys
Greatest availability of foundries
Shortest delivery time
Lowest cost for limited quantities
Most adaptable to varieties of shapes and sizes
Good physical properties obtainable
Intricate and multiple coring possible

Disadvantages

Largest tolerances required
Lowest dimensional accuracy
Poorest process consistency
Thickest sections required
Not adaptable to cast-in inserts
Secondary machining usually required

Adapted by permission of the Martin Marietta Corporation.

2. PERMANENT MOLD CASTING

Compared to sand mold casting, permanent mold casting produces more uniform castings with closer dimensional tolerances, superior surface texture, and improved mechanical properties. Permanent mold casting is well suited for high-volume production of small simple castings that have fairly uniform wall thickness, no intricate internal coring, and no undercuts. The

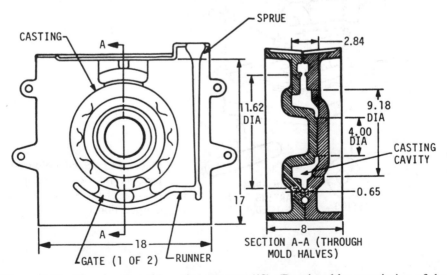

Figure 4.13   Permanent mold casting process (18). (Reprinted by permission of the Martin Marietta Corporation.)

TABLE 4.7 Permanent Mold Casting Process (19)

Advantages

Suitable for broad variety of shapes
Denser grain structure possible than in sand mold casting
Better mechanical properties than in sand mold casting
Closer dimensional tolerances and consistency than in sand mold casting
Better surface texture than in sand mold casting
Less machining required than in sand mold casting
Thinner sections possible than in sand mold casting
Adaptable to cast-in inserts

Disadvantages

Limited to nonferrous alloy
Tooling cost greater than in sand mold casting
Reduced availability of foundries over sand mold casting
Increased delivery time over sand mold casting

Adapted by permission of the Martin Marietta Corporation.

process can also produce moderately complex castings; however, quantities should be sufficiently large to justify substantially greater mold costs.

The permanent mold casting process is illustrated in Figure 4.13. A metal mold consisting of two or more parts is used repeatedly for the production of many castings of the same form. The molten metal enters the mold by gravity. Only relatively simple cores are made of metal for permanent mold casting. More complex cores are made of sand or plaster, and when these are used, the process is called "semipermanent mold casting."

As indicated in Table 4.5, alloys used in permanent mold casting are limited to those of the nonferrous metals. The advantages and disadvantages of permanent mold casting are given in Table 4.7.

The major precaution to be taken from the viewpoint of production is the provision of adequate draft in the permanent mold. Section uniformity is also important since the process is restrictive in the use of gates and risers to feed critical sections. Small deep pockets and small fillet radii should be avoided in the design of permanent molds.

3. PLASTER MOLD CASTING

The plaster mold process produces castings that have greater dimensional accuracy, smoother surfaces, and more finely reproduced details that can be obtained with either sand mold or permanent mold casting. As stated before, the latter is called "semipermanent mold casting" when plaster cores are used. The advantages and disadvantages of the plaster mold casting process are given in Table 4.8. The process is suitable only with aluminum and cooper alloys. The major precaution is to use the process only for short runs where close tolerances are required because of the fragility of the plaster.

TABLE 4.8 Plaster Mold Casting Process (20)

Advantages

Suitable for intricate shapes with variable thickness sections
Closer dimensional tolerances and consistency than with sand mold castings or
  permanent mold castings
Better surface texture than with sand mold castings or permanent mold castings
Less secondary machining required than with sand mold castings or permanent
  mold castings
Thinner sections possible than with sand mold castings or permanent mold cast-
  ings
Adaptable to cast-in inserts

Disadvantages

Process limited to aluminum and copper alloys
Tooling cost greater than with permanent mold castings
Reduced availability of foundries from permanent mold castings
Increased delivery time over permanent mold castings
Mechanical properties slightly inferior to permanent mold castings

Adapted by permission of the Martin Marietta Corporation.

4. INVESTMENT CASTING

Figure 4-14 illustrates the investment casting process. Investment casting
uses a mold that has been produced by surrounding an expendable pattern
with a refractory slurry. The pattern, which is usually made of wax or
plastic, is melted or burned out, leaving a monolithic mold cavity. Internal-
cored recesses and cavities are integral parts of the mold and are not subject

TABLE 4.9 Investment Casting Process (22)

Advantages

Suitable for all metal alloys
Suitable for very intricate shapes with variable thickness sections
Greater dimensional accuracy and consistency than with sand mold castings or
  with permanent mold castings
Better surface texture than with sand mold castings or with permanent mold cast-
  ings
Less secondary machining required than with sand mold castings or permanent
  mold castings

Disadvantages

Tooling cost greater than with permanent mold castings
Increased delivery time over sand mold castings

Adapted by permission of the Martin Marietta Corporation.

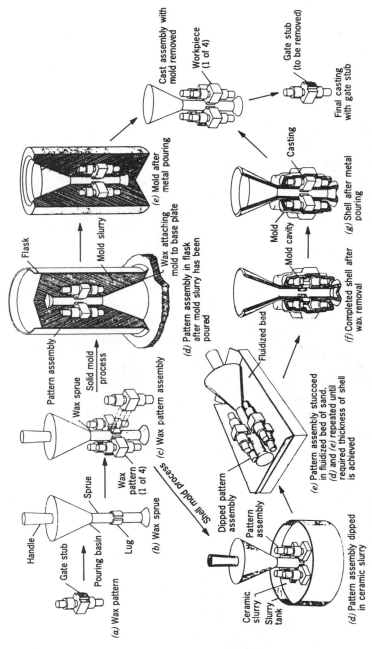

Figure 4.14 Investment casting process (21). (Reprinted by permission of the Martin Marietta Corporation.)

(a) Wax pattern

Handle
Gate stub
Pouring basin
Sprue
Lug

(b) Wax sprue

Wax sprue
Wax pattern (1 of 4)

(c) Wax pattern assembly

Pattern assembly
Wax sprue

Solid mold process

Flask
Mold slurry

(d) Pattern assembly in flask after mold slurry has been poured

Wax attaching mold to base plate

(e) Mold after metal pouring

Shell mold process

Ceramic slurry
Slurry tank

(d) Pattern assembly dipped in ceramic slurry

Dipped pattern assembly
Pattern assembly
Fluidized bed

(e) Pattern assembly stuccoed in fluidized bed of sand. (d) and (e) repeated until required thickness of shell is achieved

(f) Completed shell after wax removal

Mold
Mold cavity

(g) Shell after metal pouring

Casting

Cast assembly with mold removed
Workpiece (1 of 4)

Gate stub (to be removed)
Final casting with gate stub

to the instabilities experienced in the other processes. Investment casting is also called "lost-wax process." In sand mold casting, wood or metal patterns are used to make the impressions in the molding material. The patterns are reusable, but the mold is expendable. In investment casting, a metal pattern die is used to form expendable patterns that in turn are used to produce ceramic molds that are also expendable. The ceramic molds are formed as a shell that is created by dipping the pattern in mold material until the shell is of adequate thickness, and then the shell is cured. Molds are also produced by a flask method called "solid molding." The investment casting process is suitable for all the metal alloys listed in Table 4.5 plus iron and cobalt and nickel alloys. The advantages and disadvantages of the investment casting process are given in Table 4.9. The precaution to be taken with the process is one of economics. Investment casting should be considered only when castings are of such shapes and to be made of such alloys that they cannot be produced economically by other processes.

5. DIE CASTING

Die castings are produced by forcing molten metal under pressure into metal molds called "dies." Die casting is similar to permanent mold casting in that the two processes employ reusable metal molds. The two processes differ in mold-filling methods. Whereas mold filling in permanent mold casting depends on the force of gravity, die casting involves metal flow at high velocities induced by the application of pressure. Because of this high-velocity filling, die casting can produce shapes that are more complex than those produced by permanent mold castings. The die-casting process is suitable to production rates of up to 500 parts per hour. For lower rates, a variation of die casting called "squeeze casting" can be used. Squeeze casting (Figure 4.15) begins by pouring a quantity of molten metal into the bottom half of a die set mounted in a press. The dies are then closed, filling

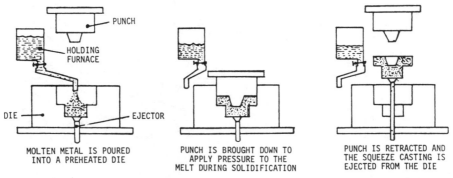

Figure 4.15 Squeeze-casting process (23). (Reprinted by permission of the Martin Marietta Corporation.)

TABLE 4.10   Die-Casting Process (24)

Advantages

Suitable for very intricate with thinner sections than any other casting process
Better dimensional accuracy and consistency than with any other casting process
Usually no secondary machining required
Better surface texture than with any other casting process
Adaptable to cast-in insert
Lowest per-unit recurring cost at very high production rates

Disadvantages

Greatest tooling cost of all casting processes
Limited to nonferrous alloys
Subject to extensive porosity in heavier sections
Should not be surface machined to a depth greater than 0.03 in.
Restricted to lower-strength, nonstructural applications

Adapted by permission of the Martin Marietta Corporation.

the die cavity with molten metal. Pressure is applied on the solidifying casting, accelerating the solidification and producing a pore-free, fine-grained part whose mechanical properties exceed those of conventional die casting. As indicated in Table 4.5, the die-casting process is suitable only for nonferrous alloys because of the difficulty in accommodating the high pouring temperatures required for the ferrous alloys. The advantages and disadvantages of the die casting process are given in Table 4.10. The major precaution to be taken with die castings is their use in structural applications requiring high strength. If such applications are attempted, make sure that proper process control is enforced in making the castings, particularly with temperature and pressure.

6. SHELL MOLD CASTING PROCESS

The shell mold casting process (Figure 4.16) is a variant of the sand mold casting process that allows high-rate casting with closer dimensional control. In the process, the mold is formed from a mixture of sand and a thermosetting resin binder that is placed against a heated metal pattern. When the mixture is heated in this fashion, the resin becomes tacky, causing the grains of sand to adhere to each other. As the heat penetrates to a predetermined depth, a shell is formed. The shell, when cured by the heat, becomes sturdy and constitutes half of the mold. The shell is stripped from the pattern and any required cores are set. The cope and drag halves of the mold are secured together and placed in a flask. Backup material is added, and the model is ready for castings. The shell mold casting process has been used to produce castings weighing from a few ounces to almost 500 pounds (lb). Limited

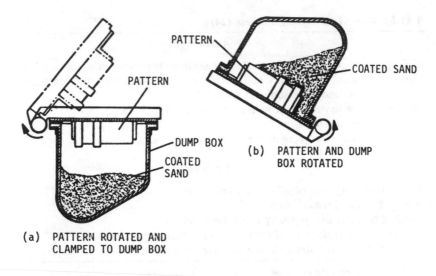

(a) PATTERN ROTATED AND
    CLAMPED TO DUMP BOX

(b) PATTERN AND DUMP
    BOX ROTATED

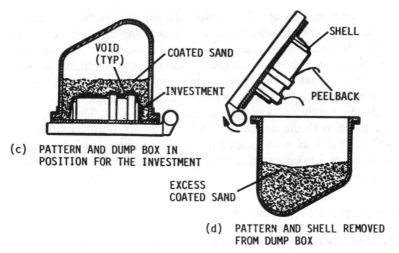

(c) PATTERN AND DUMP BOX IN
    POSITION FOR THE INVESTMENT

(d) PATTERN AND SHELL REMOVED
    FROM DUMP BOX

Figure 4.16   Shell mold casting process (25). (Reprinted by permission of the Martin Marietta Corporation.)

quantities of castings weighing in excess of 1000 lb have been produced with the shell mold casting process. The process is suitable for both nonferrous and ferrous alloys, and shell cores, made with this technique, may be used with sand molds or semipermanent molds. Advantages and disadvantages of the shell mold casting process are given in Table 4.11. The precaution to be taken in using the shell mold casting process should be based on economic considerations which usually limit use of the process to ferrous alloys.

TABLE 4.11 Shell Mold Casting Process (26)

Advantages

Suitable for complex shapes
Closer dimensional control and consistency in large quantities than with sand
  mold castings
Better surface texture than with sand mold castings

Disadvantages

Reduced availability of foundries over sand mold casting
Increased delivery time over sand mold casting
Part sizes smaller than with sand mold casting

Adapted by permission of the Martin Marietta Corporation.

7. COMPOSITE MOLD CASTING PROCESS

The objective in using the composite mold casting process is to benefit from the advantages of other processes without the penalties of their disadvantages. The use of three or more different mold or core materials in one composite mold is not unusual (Figure 4.17). Aluminum alloy castings made with the composite mold casting process are referred to as "premium-quality castings" and "engineered castings." These castings are costly in limited quantities. The restriction on suitable casting alloys depends on the materials used in the composite mold. For example, the use of plaster limits

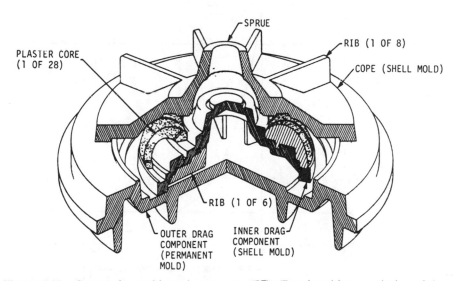

Figure 4.17 Composite mold casting process (27). (Reprinted by permission of the Martin Marietta Corporation.)

TABLE 4.12   Composite Mold Casting Process (28)

Advantages

Suitable for more intricate shapes than with sand mold castings or permanent
   mold castings
Closer dimensional tolerances and consistency than with sand mold castings or
   permanent mold castings
Less secondary machining required than with sand mold castings or permanent
   mold castings
Better surface texture than with sand mold castings or permanent mold castings
Thinner sections possible than with sand mold castings or permanent mold cast-
   ings
Better mechanical properties than with investment castings
Adaptable to cast-in inserts

Disadvantages

Greater cost than with sand mold castings or permanent mold castings
Reduced availability of foundries over permanent mold casting
Increased delivery time over sand mold casting

Adapted by permission of the Martin Marietta Corporation.

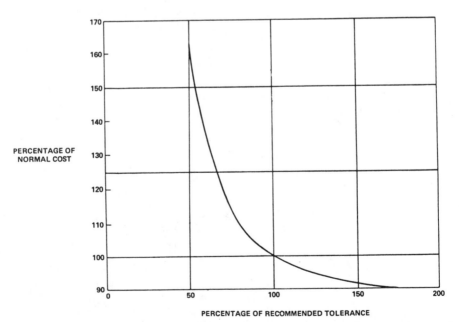

Figure 4.18   Casting cost as a function of tolerance (29). (Adapted by permission of
the Martin Marietta Corporation.)

application to nonferrous metal alloys. The advantages and disadvantages of the composite mold casting process are given in Table 4.12. The precaution to be taken in using the composite mold casting process should be based on economic considerations that usually limit the use of the process to very large production quantities.

4.3.2   Casting Cost Considerations

The most significant cost drivers in castings are dimensional tolerances that are more stringent than the casting process is capable of providing routinely. The relationship between tolerance and cost of castings is shown in Figure 4.18.

For example, doubling the allowable tolerance from the nominal value of 100 to 200 percent reduces casting cost to 50 percent of the nominal value,

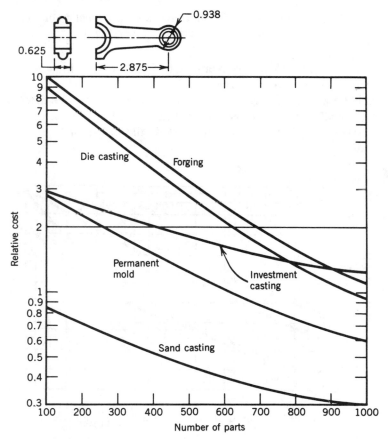

Figure 4.19   Relative cost of casting processes (30). (Reprinted by permission of the Martin Marietta Corporation.)

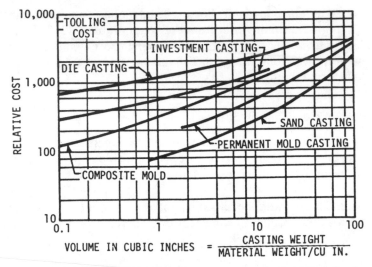

Figure 4.20   Relative tooling cost of casting processes as a function of volume (31). (Reprinted by permission of the Martin Marietta Corporation.)

whereas reducing the allowable tolerance to 50 percent of the nominal value increases casting cost by 65 percent.

It should be noted that Figure 4.18 addresses only one of the three dimensions of a typical casting and assumes that the other two dimensions are held constant. Were all three dimensions varied, the effect on cost would be compounded.

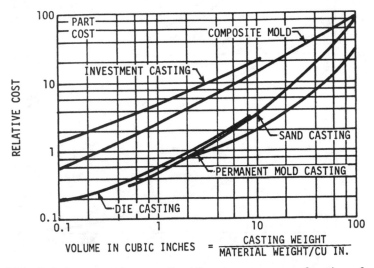

Figure 4.21   Relative per-unit cost of casting processes as a function of volume (32).(Reprinted by permission of the Martin Marietta Corporation.)

Specific requirements may limit the choice of processes to produce some casting. However, most design can be produced by several processes, and the choice should be based on the comparative costs of these processes. Figure 4.19 shows the relative cost as a function of the number of parts produced for the particular part shown in the illustration. Dimensions are given in inches.

It can be seen that forgings do not become competitive until quantities approach one thousand. In addition, the significant advantage of sand mold casting over the other processes is clear.

Figures 4.20 and 4.21 show the relative cost as a function of casting volume for nonrecurring tooling cost and recurring per-unit cost of parts produced. It is interesting to note that the relative costs of the various processes converge as the casting volume approaches 100 cubic inches (in.^{3}). In essence, large castings are costly.

4.4 WORK SIMPLIFICATION

Manufacturing processes must be examined critically to ensure the most economical and profitable products. Mandating manufacturing processes without considering alternatives including manual labor usually results in high production costs.

4.4.1 Work Design Principles

This section addresses the issue of integrating the worker into the production process. A checklist to simplify work and improve productivity is given in Table 4.13. The work to be done should, in large measure, dictate the workplace design. Highly automated production lines should be designed before buildings are designed to house the lines.

Industrial engineering time-and-motion study is important in establishing the capacity of the production process and determining the standard output

TABLE 4.13 Work Simplification Checklist (33)

Is the task necessary?
Can the task be shortened?
Can tasks be combined?
Can handling be minimized?
Can automation, flexible or hard, be used?
Are working conditions best for the task?
Is idle time employed usefully?
Is fatigue minimized?
Are worker skill levels appropriate for the task?

Reprinted by permission of the Martin Marietta Corporation.

rate of the operation. Actually, these are two separate areas of study: motion study is oriented toward improving productivity, and time study toward measuring productivity.

The purpose of motion study is to increase the worker's efficiency of movement, and to decrease fatigue and errors. Table 4.14 presents general guidelines for economy of motion in the form of a checklist.

When human labor is part of production operations, it is necessary to know the productivity of that labor for capacity planning, process design, and scheduling. Thus there is a strong need for work measurement to establish standards for output rates. Time study and predetermined standards are two widely used methods of standard time development.

Time study analysis involves observations of the repeated performance of a work task that is broken down into elemental motions. A subjective performance rating in comparison to an average worker is factored into the observed average elemental times to derive a normal time for each job element. Allowances are then added for fatigue and unavoidable time loss. Time standards for similar work tasks are useful sources of labor estimates.

Predetermined time data concern the movement involved in a task. A knowledge of the movements allows synthesis of known normal times to arrive at a total normal time for the task. Methods-time measurement (MTM) provides the most popular set of standard time elements. This system uses predetermined times called "time measurement units" (TMU) to measure various elementary micromotions such as reach, grasp, and turn. These times (each TMU) are stated in 0.000001 hr.

Finally, human-factors analysis should be undertaken with the goal of optimizing the work environment for efficient operation and worker convenience. Table 4.15 is a checklist of human factors that should be addressed in workplace design.

Throughout all these determinations, however, it is essential that workers receive both visual and oral feedback on how well they are doing against the

TABLE 4.14   Economy of Motion Checklist (34)

Minimize movements, including eye movements, by shortening movements, combining movements, and eliminating unnecessary movements

Make movements smooth, continuous, curved, and rhythmic rather than zigzag, angular, stop and go, and erratic in other fashions

Work with the smallest muscle group possible; use gravity as much as possible

Provide variety with foot controls, intermittent muscle use for tension relief, and perceptual variety with shapes and colors

Use holding fixtures, guides, and stops to minimize muscular effort

Locate tools and equipment conveniently to the task

Use easy-to-operate tools and equipment

Coordinate work benches and chairs for operator ease and comfort

Adapted by permission of the Martin Marietta Corporation.

TABLE 4.15   Checklist of Human Factors in Workplace Design (35)

Illumination	Neurological responses
Noise	Average body dimensions
Temperature	Safety
Humidity	Health
Muscular abilities	

Adapted by permission of the Martin Marietta Corporation.

established benchmarks. To ensure proper motivation and, in turn, optimum productivity, the feedback should be objective, candid, and timely.

4.4.2   Tooling Principles

Production facilities include facilities, equipment, and tooling required to accomplish the program objectives. Facilities are defined as physical plant requirements that include buildings, space, layout, utilities, and environmental and ancillary requirements.

"Equipment" is defined as machinery and special materials necessary for the manufacture of specific products of a given variety. "Tooling" is defined as those devices such as fixtures and gauges needed for the manufacture and test of a specific product.

Tooling falls into three general categories: employee-supplied tools, general-purpose tools, and special tools. The latter are the subject of this section.

Special tools and special test equipment are designed and built for application on a specific product or contract. They range in complexity from a perishable special cutter to a floor assembly jig and automated test station.

Costs for such tools are normally amortized against the product. If a contract to develop a product is involved, the costs may be charged to the customer and the tools become the customer's property. Customers, particularly those in the public sector, are also required to pay normal maintenance and replacement costs for the tools.

1. CONTROLLING TECHNICAL FACTORS

Engineering requirements such as tolerances, materials, and geometry leave few alternatives for the choice of tooling concepts. As an example, compound contours on sheet-metal parts may limit forming the parts to stretching or drop-hammer applications. In contrast, a cylindrical contour could use either of these processes or simply be roll-formed. A similar example in assembly can be seen in the decision to use a close tolerance shear-bolt instead of the standard driven rivet. This affects the quality of the special tooling required and the amount of manufacturing labor involved in the installation.

2. CONTROLLING PROGRAM FACTORS

Quantities to be produced and the scheduled period of performance bear a direct relationship to the tooling philosophy adopted on a program. Low production rates lead to planning a job with open setups and hand layouts. Medium rates lend themselves to "soft" or short-life tools. Both of the above normally require more manufacturing labor. Large rates of production create the need for "hard" or long-life tools that will ensure repeatability and minimize manufacturing labor.

4.4.3 Automation and Robotics

There is a fundamental difference between automation and robotics, and they should not be considered interchangeable. Automation provides dedicated functions such as insertion of specific components in assemblies, whereas robotics can accommodate a multitude of tasks, albeit of a similar nature.

Generically, robotics is a form of flexible automation. Dedicated automation is referred to as "hard automation."

Reprogrammability is the salient characteristic of robots; it allows the incorporation of artificial intelligence for effecting process changes. Many robots are equipped with a host of sensors for their adaptive role.

The choice of automation or robotics and the extent to which the choice is implemented should be dictated by need and economics. The customary factors that favor the use of automation and robotics are the need for reduced touch labor or for sustained high-rate production.

There are situations, however, where automation or robotics is required to maintain both yield and product quality because of the delicate processes and materials involved. There are also processes involving hazardous materials that are performed in unstaffed, remote locations with automation or robotics. In addition, the need for manufacturing flexibility is a basic reason for choosing robotics.

Table 4.16 builds from the perceived need for flexibility and gives a broad range of robotics criteria including justification. In essence, a searching analysis in terms of need, capability, cost, and risk should be made.

For example, an automated transfer-type machine may perform many operations on the same assembly; therefore, a breakdown can lead to complete line shutdown. An approach to minimize the effect of a shutdown is to develop a bank of assemblies as a buffer. This requires more space and increases inventory. Such costs should be considered in the overall evaluation.

TABLE 4.16   Robotics Criteria (36)

Application

Parts should be delivered in a precise, oriented manner

Operations should be performed with a maximum of six axes of motion

Production volume should be sufficient; explore parts variability and families of parts

Consider the life expectancy of products

Keep robot applications simple

Operations should require no human judgment

Compare present cycle times and production rates to those of robots

Know everything about operations; itemize what could go wrong

Develop backup systems

List all safety requirements

Review the complexity of installations

Define working parameters including: physical layout, upstream operations, downstream operations, and operating patterns

List special-purpose equipment required for operations

Survey viable alternatives to robotics, including conventional machines and manual labor; modification to existing equipment, tooling, and fixtures; other forms of flexible automation such as numerical control; and hard automation

Selection

Become familiar with available robots and compare capabilities; list special equipment required, including controls, actuators, end-of-arm tooling, and interfacing equipment

Determine effects of hostile environment on robots

Provide safety guards for operators and passersby

Select robots with extra capacity for weight carrying, memory, strokes per axis, and number of axes

Determine spare parts availability

Justification

Estimate investment, including engineering, robots, auxiliary equipment, training, switchover, spares, maintenance, and utilities

Estimate economic benefits, including reduced hiring, training, and labor cost; reduced setup time; increased machine utilization; reduced rework and scrap; increased throughput, capacity, and productivity; increased flexibility; reduced work in process and inventory; investment tax credit; and depreciation

Estimate noneconomic benefits, including increased quality and safety and improved working conditions

Implementation

Develop application plan, including workstation layout; utility services; and safety systems

Develop preventive maintenance program

Train personnel

Effect upstream and downstream operations changes

Reprinted by permission of the Martin Marietta Corporation.

4.5 DESIGN EFFICIENCY

This section addresses techniques for determining the design efficiency of alternative designs in terms of their assembly ease. Section 4.6 addresses testability from the same viewpoint.

4.5.1 Scoring

A systematic approach has been devised that allows objective rating of designs for ease of assembly. It is called "design for assembly" (DFA), although it addresses superfluous parts as well as assemblies (37).

For example, unless a part must move relative to other parts in the assembly, be made of different material, or be removed for service, the numerical score reveals that the design should be changed to eliminate the particular part by incorporating its function in another part.

The technique relates the number of times a particular operation is carried out to part handling and insertion times and labor cost and develops a rating that ranges from 0 to 1.0 as the measure of design efficiency. The lower the rating, the greater is the design efficiency.

4.5.2 Application

The technique can be applied with either a computer program or a manual routine. The example in this section was the result of a manual application; the beneficiary was the piston assembly shown in Figure 4.22.

Table 4.17 is the worksheet used to score the design efficiency of the original piston at 0.23. Subsequent modification to the piston is shown in Figure 4.23, and the resultant design efficiency of 0.74 is scored in Table 4.18.

The seemingly simple changes provide a reduction in touch labor of 100[(0.74 − 0.23)/0.743], or 69 percent. In addition, the number of parts in the assembly is reduced from five to three.

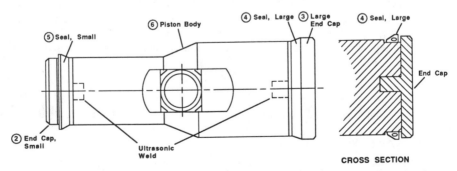

Figure 4.22 Original piston assembly (38). (Reprinted by permission of the Martin Marietta Corporation.)

TABLE 4.17 Original Piston Assembly Worksheet (39)

			Design for Manual Assembly Worksheet						
1	2	3	4	5	6	7	8	9	
Part No.	Number of Times the Operation is Carried Out Consecutively	Two-Digit Manual Handling Code	Manual Handling Time per Part	Two-Digit Manual Insertion Code	Manual Insertion Time per Part	Operation Time, Seconds $(2) \times [(4) \cdot (6)]$	Operation Cost, Cents $0.4 \times (7)$	Figures for Estimation of Theoretical Minimum Parts	Name of Assembly (Part No. 1, Piston)
6	1	00	1.13	00	1.5	2.63	1.05	1	Piston body
5	1	12	2.25	01	2.5	4.75	1.90	1	Seal, small
4	1	12	2.25	01	2.5	4.75	1.90	1	Seal, large
3	1	11	1.80	93	12.	13.8	5.52	0	End cap, large
2	1	11	1.80	93	12.	13.8	5.52	0	End cap, small
						39.73 TM	15.89	3 NM	

$$\text{Design efficiency} = \frac{3 \times \text{NM}}{\text{TM}} = .23$$

Adapted by permission of the Martin Marietta Corporation.

TABLE 4.18 Modified Piston Assembly Worksheet (41)

Design for Manual Assembly Worksheet

1	2	3	4	5	6	7	8	9	Name of Assembly (Part No. 1, Piston)
Part No.	Number of Times the Operation is Carried Out Consecutively	Two-Digit Manual Handling Code	Manual Handling Time per Part	Two-Digit Manual Insertion Code	Manual Insertion Time per Part	Operation Time, Seconds $(2) \times [(4) \cdot (6)]$	Operation Cost, Cents $0.4 \times (7)$	Figures for Estimation of Theoretical Minimum Parts	
6	1	00	1.13	00	1.5	2.63	1.05	1	Piston body
5	1	12	2.25	01	2.5	4.75	1.90	1	Seal, small
4	1	12	2.25	01	2.5	4.75	1.90	1	Seal, large
						12.13	4.85	3	
						TM		NM	

$$\text{Design efficiency} = \frac{3 \times \text{NM}}{\text{TM}} = .74$$

Adapted by permission of the Martin Marietta Corporation.

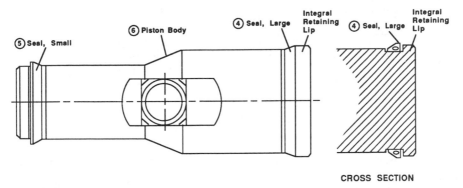

CROSS SECTION

Figure 4.23 Modified piston assembly (40). (Reprinted by permission of the Martin Marietta Corporation.)

4.6 TESTABILITY

There is a direct correlation between low production cost and the ease of product testing, particularly in the final assembly form. This characteristic, called "testability," is an essential element in producing products that are both affordable and profitable.

The issue in incorporating testability into product design concerns cost recovery expressed by (1) what the product cost should be to ensure the sale of the quantity produced; (2) what the nonrecurring cost of incorporating the degree of testability that realizes the product cost is, and (3) whether the profit on the anticipated sales will at least offset the investment in testability.

This section presents a parametric approach to (1) expressing testability of alternative designs in terms of figure of merit (FoM) and (2) optimizing FoM in terms of return on investment.

The nonrecurring investment and recurring cost savings as a function of (FoM) vary among diverse products. They do, however, follow the general form of the relationships described in this section, and the examples can serve as role models for other applications.

Testability is a design characteristic of systems or products in concert with the test processes. Where there is built-in test equipment (BITE) in the unit under test (UUT), testability is primarily a design characteristic of the UUT.

Testability can also be defined as "the ability to probe a system or a product, and assess the functionality of the probed portion." Figure of merit is the measure of effectiveness of the process and is derived from the probabilistic performance of the test process over a given period of time.

From the viewpoint of testability, "probabilistic performance" connotes the relative frequency in the UUT of the four states of functionality that are listed in Table 4.19. It should be noted that functional versus nonfunctional

TABLE 4.19 Testability States of Functionality (42)

State	Definition
S_0	Functional and functional status indicated
S_1	Functional and nonfunctional status indicated
S_2	Nonfunctional and nonfunctional status indicated
S_3	Nonfunctional and functional status indicated

Reprinted by permission of the Martin Marietta Corporation.

status is governed by the inherent failure rate of the UUT and not of the test process.

Figure of merit can thus be defined as "being proportional to the relative frequency of states S_0 and S_2 and inversely proportional to the relative frequency of states S_1 and S_3." The element of time enters the formulation of transition probabilities for the four states that are used to derive the equation for FoM.

4.6.1 Probabilistic Performance

The approach for determining probabilistic performance builds on established techniques for analyzing the accuracy of built-in test equipment. These techniques start by delineating the state transitions shown in Figure 4.24 as the basis for deriving transitional probabilities and the summed probabilities of correct and incorrect status indications (43).

The notations p_0, p_1, p_2, and p_3 denote the transitional probabilities of the process remaining in state S_0, or transitioning from state S_0 to states S_1, S_2, or S_3, given that the process is in state S_0 at time $t = 0$. The assumptions given in Table 4.20 are used to simplify the derivation of the transitional probabilities; however, they are reasonable from the aspect of representing test processes.

Next, the state probability equations for the four Markov processes are derived. By taking the limit of these equations as incremental t approaches

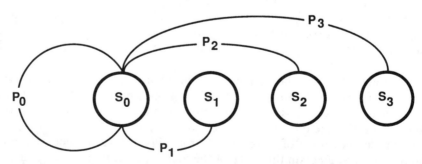

Figure 4.24 State transitions diagram (44). (Reprinted by permission of the Martin Marietta Corporation.)

TABLE 4.20   Analytical Assumptions (45)

The UUT is functional at the start of test
Transitions are from state S_0 to one of the other states and not among the other states
State transitions are Markov processes wherein future states are completely determined by present states and not at all by the way in which present states arose

Reprinted by permission of the Martin Marietta Corporation.

0, one obtains four differential equations. Their solution yields the following equations for state probability as functions of time:

$$P_0(t) = e^{-(\lambda_u + \lambda_f)t} \tag{4.1}$$

$$P_1(t) = \frac{\lambda_f}{(\lambda_u + \lambda_f)} (1 - e^{-(\lambda_u + \lambda_f)t}) \tag{4.2}$$

$$P_2(t) = \frac{\lambda_d}{(\lambda_u + \lambda_f)} (1 - e^{-(\lambda_u + \lambda_f)t}) \tag{4.3}$$

$$P_3(t) = \frac{\lambda_n}{(\lambda_n + \lambda_f)} (1 - e^{-(\lambda_u + \lambda_f)t}) \tag{4.4}$$

where λ_u is UUT inherent failure rate; λ_f, false alarm rate; λ_d, fault detection rate; and λ_n, fault nondetection rate.

Since the four states are mutually exclusive, the probability of correct status indication, denoted by $P(t)$, is the sum of p_0 and p_2. The probability of incorrect status indication, denoted by $Q(t)$, is the sum of p_1 and p_3. The equations for $P(t)$ and $Q(t)$ are as follows:

$$P(t) = e^{-(\lambda_u + \lambda_f)t} + \frac{\lambda_u}{(\lambda_u + \lambda_f)} (1 - e^{-(\lambda_u + \lambda_f)t}) \tag{4.5}$$

$$Q(t) = \frac{(\lambda_n + \lambda_f)}{(\lambda_u + \lambda_f)} + (1 - e^{-(\lambda_u + \lambda_f)t}) \tag{4.6}$$

From a testability viewpoint, it is desirable to express these relationships in terms of fault detection requirement (FDR), fault nondetection requirement (FNR), and false-alarm requirement (FAR). These requirements are defined in Table (4.21). Substitution of these definitions in Equations (4.5)

TABLE 4.21   Definition of Requirements (46)

Fault detection requirement, FDR $= \lambda_d / \lambda_u$
Fault nondetection requirement, FNR $= \lambda_n / \lambda_u$
False-alarm requirement, FAR $= \lambda_f / \lambda_u$

Reprinted by permission of the Martin Marietta Corporation.

and (4.6) yields the following equations for $P(t)$ and $Q(t)$ as functions of FDR, FNR, and FAR:

$$P(t) = e^{-\lambda_u t(1 + FAR)} + \frac{FDR}{(1 + FAR)} (1 - e^{-\lambda_u(1 + FAR)t}) \qquad (4.7)$$

$$Q(t) = \frac{(FNR + FAR)}{(1 + FAR)} (1 - e^{-\lambda_u(1 + FAR)t}) \qquad (4.8)$$

Equations (4.7) and (4.8) enable a wide range of trades among the requirements leveled on products, BITE, and test processes. Requirements FDR and FNR are essentially functions of the sensitivity of test circuitry, and FAR, of error-control logic. Costs can be associated with these parameters and balanced against test and rework costs.

Table 4.22 illustrates the use of Equations (4.7) and (4.8) with a set of assumed product requirements that are used to calculate paired values of $P(t)$ and $Q(t)$. These, in turn, provide the baseline for deriving the equation for FoM. The value of $t = 8$ hr typifies production shift duration.

For the examples, the probability of the correct status being indicated, $P(t)$, over an 8-hr time period is .9998. The probability of the incorrect status being indicated, $Q(t)$, over the same period of time is .00015. These values serve as the baseline for deriving the expression for FoM.

4.6.2 Figure of Merit

The range of values for FoM is 1 to 10, with FoM = 1 being unacceptable and FoM = 10 being ideal. The equation for FoM can be expressed in the following general form:

$$FoM = \alpha P(t) + \beta Q(t) \qquad (4.9)$$

where α and β are constants that are equated to the values of $P(t)$ and $Q(t)$ for both the unacceptable case and the ideal case.

The values of $P(t) = 0.5$ and $Q(t) = 0.5$ are deemed unacceptable and are applied to cases where FoM = 1. The values $P(t) = .9998$ and $Q(t) = .00015$ are deemed ideal and are applied to cases where FoM = 10.

Next, the following two equations are solved simultaneously, yielding the approximate values of $\alpha = 10$ and $\beta = -8$ for use in the expression for FoM:

$$10 = \alpha(.9998) + \beta(.00015) \qquad (4.10)$$

$$1 = \alpha(.50) + \beta(.50) \qquad (4.11)$$

Substituting $\alpha = 10$ and $\beta = -8$ in Equation 4.9 yields

$$FoM = 10P(t) - 8Q(t) \qquad (4.12)$$

TABLE 4.22   Examples of $P(t)$ and $Q(t)$ Calculations (47)

$\lambda_u = .01 \text{ hr}^{-1}$

$\text{FDR} = .999$

$\text{FNR} = .001$

$\text{FAR} = .001$

$t = 8 \text{ hr}$

$$P(t) = e^{-(.01)(1+.001)(8)} + \frac{.999}{(1 + 0.001)} (1 - e^{-(.01)(1+.001)(8)})$$

$$= .9998$$

$$Q(t) = \frac{(.001 + .001)}{(1 + .001)} (1 - e^{-(.01)(1+.001)(8)})$$

$$= .0015$$

Reprinted by permission of the Martin Marietta Corporation.

As an example, for a product design that satisfies the requirements of $P(t) = 0.8$ and $Q(t) = 0.2$, the rating would be:

$$\text{FoM} = 10(0.8) - 8(0.2) = 6.4 \tag{4.13}$$

The value of FoM = 6.42 is somewhat better than average in terms of testability. However, the significance in terms of life-cycle cost of the product needs to be assessed. Figure 4.25 illustrates the general form of the relationship of testability investment and inspection and test cost with respect to life-cycle cost.

From the customer's point of view, the issue is to achieve the degree of testability that provides the lowest life-cycle cost as shown in the illustra-

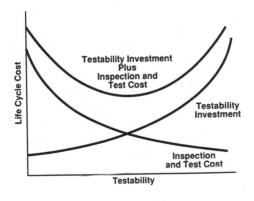

Figure 4.25 Life-cycle cost as a function of testability (48). (Reprinted by permission of the Martin Marietta Corporation.)

tion. For the producer, however, this point may not ensure cost recovery of the nonrecurring investment in testability.

4.6.3 Application

Consider, for example, the cost breakdown shown in Figure 4.26 of a typical high-technology product used in an aerospace application. Given that the unit cost of the product is $50,000 when produced in a buy of 10,000, then approximately 33 percent, or $16,509, could be attributed to inspection and test. A good goal for cost saving would be to reduce this cost by about an order of magnitude.

The motivation to reduce cost is competition. The cost recovery issue can be expressed by (1) how much the product cost should be reduced to ensure the sale of the quantity produced, (2) what the nonrecurring cost of incorporating the degree of BITE to realize the cost reduction is, and (3) whether the profit on the anticipated sales would at least offset the nonrecurring investment.

As stated previously, nonrecurring technology investment and recurring inspection and test cost as functions of FoM vary widely among systems or products of interest. They do, however, follow the general form of the relationships shown in Figure 4.27 and provide the bases for trades between these elements of cost, with life-cycle cost as the argument.

The left ordinate in the illustration is the inspection and test cost factor that varies as a function of figure of merit shown on the abscissa. The values of the left ordinate range from .1 to 1.0 and are used as multipliers of the baseline recurring cost. The right ordinate is the testability investment factor that establishes FoM. These values also range from .1 to 1.0 and are used as multipliers of the baseline nonrecurring cost. There is no particular significance to the crossover point of the two curves in the figure.

The example of the high-technology product for an aerospace application

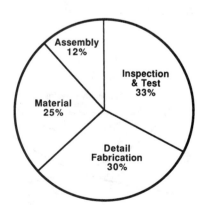

Figure 4.26 High-technology product cost breakdown (49). (Reprinted by permission of the Martin Marietta Corporation.)

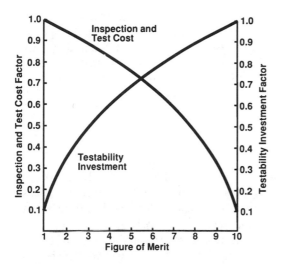

Figure **4.27** Interaction between inspection and test cost factor and testability investment factor (50). (Reprinted by permission of the Martin Marietta Corporation.)

continues. Assume that the baseline nonrecurring testability investment is $500,000 and profit is 10 percent. The goal is to reduce the cost of the product from $50,000 to $40,000 to ensure an award of the next purchase. The issues are how great an investment is needed and when cost can be recovered with the per-unit profit reduced to $4000 from $5000.

The reduction of $10,000 could be obtained by reducing inspection and test cost from $16,500 to $6500, for a cost reduction of .39 ($6500/$16,500). It is assumed that the baseline design has an FoM of about 5.0, which is equivalent to an inspection and test cost factor of about .75 as indicated in Figure 4.27. The product of .39 and .75, or .2925, is the inspection and test cost factor that would yield the per-unit recurring cost of $6500.

As shown in Figure 4.27, .2925 is equivalent to an FoM of about 9.3. In contrast, an FoM of 9.3 is equivalent to a testability investment factor of about .97 versus .67 for the original FoM of 5.0.

The baseline investment, which is $500,000, would become $500,000(.97/.67), or $723,881, for an additional investment of $223,881 ($723,881 − $500,000). Cost recovery could be expected after the delivery of the fifty-sixth ($223,881/$4000) product.

4.6.4 Integrated Diagnostics

Military Standard 2165, *Testability Program for Electronic Systems and Equipment,* is recommended to design-to-cost practitioners because of its salience to a broad range of high-technology applications other than military. The standard provides uniform procedures and methods for assessing testability in designs and for integrating testability in the acquisition process.

In particular, Appendix A of the military standard is a virtual treasure trove of testability program application guidance. Extensive details are given on (1) testability program planning, (2) testability reviews, (3) testability data collection and analysis planning, (4) testability requirements, (5) testability preliminary design and analysis, (6) testability detail design and analysis, and (7) testability demonstration.

4.7 PRODUCT UNIFORMITY

The eminent Dr. William Edwards Deming, honored by the Emperor of Japan for his contribution to that nation's economy, proclaimed many years ago that quality control based on conformance to tolerance limits was the antithesis of true quality and served only to increase costs to consumers. He postulated that the tolerance-oriented approach guaranteed excessive tolerance buildup with attendant waste of material and labor. He was describing the contemporary approach in high-technology enterprises of building in quality by iterations of inspection, test, rework, and scrap.

The Japanese were quick to respond to Dr. Deming's message and have capitalized on production strategies such as just-in-time (JIT) that are possible only with consistently high product uniformity. It is only under the competitive pressure of recent years that the western world has started to realize that the classical approach to quality costs money, whereas the new approach of reducing variability is lucrative.

The Japanese use the concept of loss function to expose unnecessary cost (51). For example, parts and labor costs would about double if each part in a product needed to be replaced before integration in the next higher assembly. The loss function expresses the cost of replacing or reworking parts with excessive variability within the limits of tolerances used as design parameters. Variability is a function of the process-control state of the processes producing the parts.

The concept called "tolerance centering" builds from the same relationship to provide a relatively simple means for designating process-control states on a lot-by-lot or sample-by-sample basis. Tolerance centering is not intended to replace specification limits that are essential elements of product definition and contracting. It is recommended, however, as a primary performance measure for ensuring production savings (52).

4.7.1 Tolerance Centering

The basic difference between tolerance centering and classical quality control is the former's reliance on success data as well as failure data. Typical inspection schema in military procurement are based on MIL-STD-105, *Sampling Procedures and Tables for Inspection by Attributes,* and are go–

no go in nature. Tolerance centering is patterned after MIL-STD-414, *Sampling Procedures and Tables for Inspection by Variable for Percent Defective,* and uses actual data values.

The thesis is that variations in success data portend changes in process control that may lead to defective products. The ability to anticipate such eventualities is the essence of the cost advantage of tolerance centering over the classical approach (inspection by attributes), which is after the fact. Need for corrective action is revealed only after an excessive number of defects are encountered.

The concept of tolerance centering envisions production output as a normally distributed population. Each successive lot constitutes a distribution. The manner in which the lot distribution fits within tolerance limits describes the process control state under which the lot was produced.

Table 4.23 lists criteria for designating process control states by relating statistical measures of lot distributions to tolerance limits that are divided into six equal increments. For example, the increments would each be 0.0167 in. for a bolt specified by 3 ± 0.1 in. Under Process Control State I, the lot distribution mean would fall within 3 ± 0.0167 in., and the lot distribution ± 3-sigma (standard deviation) values would fall within 3 ± 0.0334 in.

TABLE 4.23   Process Control States Criteria (53)

Process Control State I

Lot distribution mean falls within the ± 1 tolerance increments of the specification
Lot distribution ± 3-σ values fall within the ± 2 tolerance increments of the specification
Out-of-specification items are not found by inspection

Process Control State II

Lot distribution mean falls within the ± 2 tolerance increments of the specification
Lot distribution ± 3-σ values fall within the ± 3 tolerance increments of the specification
Out-of-specification items are not found by inspection

Process Control State III

Lot distribution mean falls within the ± 3 tolerance increments of the specification
One or both lot distribution 3-σ values fall beyond 3 tolerance increments of the specification
Out-of-specification items are not found by inspection

Process Control State IV

Process Control State III
Out-of-specification items are found by inspection

Adapted by permission of the Martin Marietta Corporation.

Process Control State I signifies proper process control. Departures from this ideal condition are called Process Control States II, III and IV, where State II is marginally acceptable and all inspected items are within tolerance limits, State III is unsatisfactory but all inspected items are within the limits and the lot may be acceptable, and State IV is unsatisfactory and some inspected items are outside the limits and therefore unacceptable.

4.7.2   Procedure

The application of tolerance centering is first illustrated with a simple item, a switch, that has only one parameter of interest in order not to obscure the relatively simple procedure. The item is an electrical switch and the parameter of interest is the dc resistance of the switch. The approach for multiparameter items is illustrated in Section 4.7.3.

The direct-current (dc) resistance specification for the switch is 50 ± 1 ohms (Ω). The manufacturer draws a sample lot of 50 from the production run before encapsulating the switches. The dc resistance test results are given in Table 4.24.

The first step in the procedure is to construct a frequency table from the data in Table 4.24. The frequency table, given in Table 4.25, is used to construct a histogram for a quick look at the state of process control. This involves grouping the data in classes. For this example, a class interval of $0.20 \ \Omega$ is adequate.

TABLE 4.24   DC Resistance Test Results (54)

Class No.	Ohms	Class No.	Ohms	Class No.	Ohms
1	49.91	18	49.48	35	49.27
2	50.83	19	50.60	36	50.21
3	50.33	20	49.89	37	49.26
4	49.55	21	49.75	38	49.62
5	49.61	22	50.18	39	49.55
6	49.95	23	49.35	40	50.29
7	48.38	24	49.40	41	49.42
8	49.68	25	49.38	42	49.70
9	49.75	26	49.14	43	49.65
10	49.66	27	50.50	44	49.93
11	49.44	28	49.53	45	50.93
12	50.14	29	49.50	46	49.01
13	49.60	30	49.29	47	49.85
14	49.53	31	50.24	48	49.70
15	49.82	32	49.43	49	50.00
16	49.25	33	49.30	50	49.62
17	49.47	34	49.50		

Reprinted by permission of the Martin Marietta Corporation.

TABLE 4.25   Frequency Table (55)

Class No.	Class Boundaries	Midvalues	Frequency
1	49.01–49.20	49.095	2
2	49.21–49.40	49.295	8
3	49.41–49.60	49.495	12
4	49.61–49.80	49.695	11
5	49.81–50.00	49.895	6
6	50.01–50.20	50.095	3
7	50.21–50.40	50.295	5
8	50.41–50.60	50.495	1
9	50.61–50.80	50.695	1
10	50.81–51.00	50.895	1

Reprinted by permission of the Martin Marietta Corporation.

The next step in the procedure is to divide the specification limits into six equal increments. These six increments are plotted in Figure 4.28 along with the histogram constructed from the data in Table 4.25, both to the same scale. A quick look indicates that the data are within the tolerance limits, suggesting an adequate state of process control in manufacturing the switches.

The subsequent steps, however, are more revealing. The mean $\bar{X}$ and standard deviation s of the sample are calculated with the data in either Table 4.24 or 4.25, with the former providing slightly more precision. Using the data in the Table 4.24, $\bar{X}$ and s are 49.71 and 0.41 Ω, respectively. These values uniquely define the normal curve, which is also plotted to the same scale in Figure 4.28.

As previously stated, histograms can provide a quick look at the current state of process control on a lot-by-lot basis, but true insight into process variation requires the tolerance centering distribution that is depicted by the normal probability distribution for the data plotted in relationship to the tolerance limits. Note that the -3-σ value of the distribution falls beyond the -3 tolerance increment. Since all the inspected items are within the specified limit (see Tables 4.24 and 4.25), Process Control State III is declared.

4.7.3   Cost Advantage

The concept of tolerance centering that envisions product output as a normally distributed population gives rise to a powerful technique for estimating the relative cost advantage of the various states of process control. It thus provides design-to-cost practitioners a valuable tool for trading process costs against product costs.

Figure 4.29 shows the normal probability density function and the areas under the curve for the respective minus and plus values of standard deviation. It follows from the process control state designations in Table 4.23 that

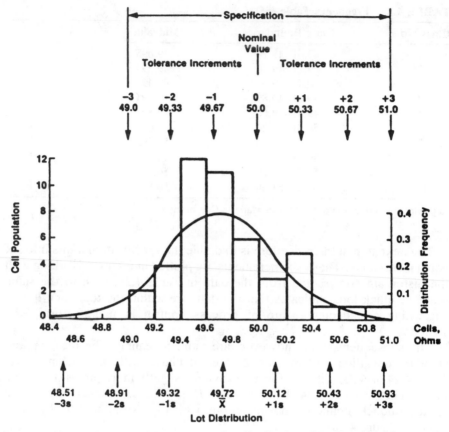

Figure 4.28   Resistance tolerance centering distribution (56). (Reprinted by permission of the Martin Marietta Corporation.)

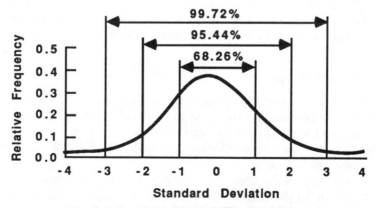

Figure 4.29   Normal probability distribution.

99.72 percent of the production output resides within −2 to +2, or four tolerance increments for Process Control State I, and within −3 to +3, or six tolerance increments for State II. For State III, 99.72 percent of the production output resides in seven or eight tolerance increments. Process Control State IV is not considered in this deliberation because it is completely unacceptable.

The boundaries of the lot distribution means given in Table 4.23 are used to arrive at the relative cost advantage of the various states of process control. The boundary displacements are characterized by (1) dividing .9972 by the number of tolerance increments encompassed by the ±3-σ values of the lot distribution and (2) multiplying the quotients by the number of tolerance increments encompassed by the boundaries of the mean of the lot distribution.

Starting with Process Control State I, the standard of excellence, first .9972 is divided by 4, obtaining .2493 unit of area under the curve per tolerance increment. The mean production output value in State I lies within minus and plus 1 tolerance increments, which equates to 2 × .2493, or .4986 unit of area under the curve. This calculation is repeated for States II and III, yielding .6648 and .7479 units of area under the curve.

These values are used as variability indices of the three process-control states. Next, the indices are normalized with respect to State I to serve as variability measures. Table 4.26 presents the results of these calculations.

The product cost function can now be expressed in the following form:

$$c = kV \qquad (4.14)$$

where k denotes the basic cost of the process and V, the normalized variability measure. Note that in State I, where $V = 1$, product cost c equals the basic process cost k, whereas in States II and III product cost can be 1.33 and 1.5 times the basic process cost.

For example, a system with a per-unit cost of $100,000 when produced under Process Control State I might, if produced under State III, cost as much as $100,000 × 1.5, or $150,000. Conversely, a system with a per-unit cost of $100,000 when produced under Process Control State III might, if produced under State I, cost as little as $100,000 ÷ 1.5, or $66,667.

TABLE 4.26 Variability Computations (57)

Process Control State	Variability Index	Normalized Variability Measure
I	0.4986	1.00
II	0.6648	1.33
III	0.7479	1.50

Reprinted by permission of the Martin Marietta Corporation.

Tolerance centering can be applied profitably to all processes in production. As a case in point, consider the cost breakdown of typical aerospace products shown previously in Figure 4.26. The 33 percent for inspection and test is based on submitting every item produced to full scrutiny. Military Standard 414 allows reduction in sampling given a certain number of acceptable lots, but even this option is after the fact, being keyed to the percentage defectives by lot.

Tolerance centering can be at the heart of more positive strategies such as those given in Table 4.27. For example, if a number of successive lots are designated Process Control State (PCS) I, then reduced inspection and test to 50 percent from 100 percent might be implemented. Consequently, the inspection and test cost of that particular product could be reduced from 33 percent of the total cost to 16.5 percent.

4.7.4 Multiparameter Items

This section presents the methodology for tolerance centering for items such as transistors whose acceptance is based on more than one parameter. Consider an NPN transistor such as the 2N2222 for use as an amplifier. The transistor is accepted only if all its parameters are within tolerance limits.

The approach is to first determine the key parameter for the item and then treat the remaining parameters as contributors to the key parameter. For example, the key parameter for the 2N2222 transistor is gain.

Variability analysis techniques can provide the statistical distribution for gain that takes into account the variations and interactions of the contributing parameters. Thus, one test can replace many, provided devices are tested in their intended applications.

Dynamic transistor gain is essentially a function of the h parameters of the transistor. Gain is the quotient of input and output. For unity input, the gain

TABLE 4.27 Inspection and Test Strategies (57)

Event	Strategy
Initial PCS I	Continue normal inspection and test
Repeated PCS I	Implement reduced inspection and test
Initial PCS II	Implement preventive action
Repeated PCS II	Implement tightened inspection and test
Initial PCS III	Implement preventive action and tightened inspection and test
Repeated PCS III	Evolve corrective action and maintain tightened inspection and test
Initial PCS IV	Evolve corrective action and implement tightened inspection and test
Repeated PCS IV	Implement corrective action

Adapted by permission of the Martin Marietta Corporation.

TABLE 4.28 Typical Transistor h Parameters (59)

	Minimum	Maximum	Unit
Input impedance h_{ie}	0.25	1.25	Kilohms
Small signal current gain h_{fe}	75	375	—
Output admittance h_{oe}	25	200	Microhms

Reprinted by permission of the Martin Marietta Corporation.
[a] Specified at collector-emitter voltage, V_{CE} + 10 V dc; collector current, I_C = 10 mA dc; frequency, f = 1.0 kHz; and ambient temperature, T_A = 25°C.

is simply the output voltage. Therefore, the gain g of the transistor is some function of input impedance h_{ie}, current h_{fe}, and output admittance h_{oe} as follows:

$$g = a_1 h_{ie} + a_2 h_{fe} + a_3 h_{oe} \qquad (4.15)$$

where a_1, a_2, and a_3 relate the sensitivity of v to the h parameters.

Typical manufacturer's data given in Table 4.28 serve as the specifications for the h parameters. The performance curves shown in Figure 4.30 serve for variability data.

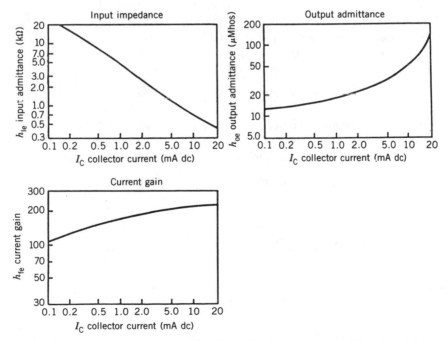

Figure 4.30 The h paremeter as a function of collector current (60). (Reprinted by permission of the Martin Marietta Corporation.)

TABLE 4.29 Typical _h_ Parameter Data (61)

I_C, mA dc	h_{ie}, $\kappa\Omega$	h_{fe}	h_{oe}, $\mu\mho$ [a]
0.2	16	130	13
0.5	8	160	15
1.0	4.8	180	18
2.0	2.5	190	22
5.0	1.4	210	32
10.0	0.7	220	52
15.0	0.5	230	85
20.0	0.4	270	140
Σx_i	34.3	1590	377
$\bar{X}_i$	4.3	199	47.1
s_i^2	29.3	1898	199.8
s_i	5.4	43.6	44.7

Reprinted by permission of the Martin Marietta Corporation.
[a] Micromhos.

Table 4.29 lists these data as functions of collector current. Also listed are computed values of the mean X, variance s^2, and standard deviation s.

The procedure also uses partial derivatives and the correlation among variables. The partial derivatives can be obtained from the slopes of the performance curves at the midpoint of minimum and maximum specification values. These values, given in Table 4.30, serve as the values for the constants a_1, a_2, and a_3 in Equation (4.15).

Equation (4.15) can now be written as

$$g = -0.7h_{ie} + 2.4h_{fe} + 6.4h_{oe} \tag{4.16}$$

In addition, the mean values of h_{ie}, h_{fe}, and h_{oe} can be calculated from the minimum and maximum values in Table 4.33 and substituted in Equation (4.16), yielding the following nominal gain for the 2N2222 transistor:

$$g = (-0.7)(4.3) + (2.4)(199) + (6.4)(47.1) \tag{4.17}$$
$$= 776$$

TABLE 4.30 Typical Performance Curve Slopes (62)

h Parameter	Equation Symbol	Specification Midpoint Value	Slope m
h_{ie}	a_1	0.75 $\kappa\Omega$	-0.7
h_{fe}	a_2	225	2.4
h_{oe}	a_3	112.5 $\mho$	6.4

Reprinted by permission of the Martin Marietta Corporation.

The next step is to compute the covariances of the h parameters that are used to compute the variance of the output voltage v. The covariance cov_{ij} is the mean of the cross products CP_{ij} of the variables i and j. The expression for cross products is:

$$CP_{ij} = (x_i - X_i)(x_j - X_j) \qquad (4.18)$$

where x_i and x_j are the values of the variables i and j and $\bar{X}_i$ and X_j are their means.

The expression for covariance is

$$cov_{ij} = \frac{(\Sigma CP_{ij})}{(n - 2)} \qquad (4.19)$$

Table 4.31 lists the computed cross products and covariances for the h parameters. The variance of the output voltage s_v^2 can now be computed with the following expression:

$$s_v^2 = \qquad (4.20)$$

Applying the data in Tables 4.29, 4.30, and 4.31, Equation (4.20) yields

$$s_v^2 = 82,225 \qquad (4.21)$$

and the standard deviation of the output voltage s_v is

$$s_v = 287 \qquad (4.22)$$

Equation (4.17) yielded a nominal gain of 776 for the 2N2222 transistor. The gain for the device can now be specified as 776 ± 287.

Consider the data in Table 4.32 from gain tests of a sample lot of 10 transistors. The mean X and standard deviation s of the sample are 664 and 272, respectively. These values uniquely define the normal probability density function shown in Figure 4.31.

The standard deviation of 287 determined with Equation (4.22) is divided by 6 for incremental values of the tolerance limits. These increments of 47.83 are also plotted in Figure 4.32 and together with the density function, constitute the tolerance centering distribution for the sample date.

It can be seen that the -1σ value of the density function falls outside the -3 tolerance increment of the specification and the value of the function falls outside the $+3$ tolerance increment of the specification. Since, out-of-specification transistors were found by inspection (Nos. 4, 7, 8, and 9 in Table 4.32), Process Control State IV is designated and corrective action is initiated.

TABLE 4.31 h Parameter Cross Products and Covariances (63)

h Parameter Pairs	Cross Products $(x_i - X_i) \times (x_j - \bar{X}_j) = CP_{ij}$		Covariance cov_{ij}
h_{ie}, h_{fe}	(16–4.3)(130–199)	−807	
	(8–4.3)(160–199)	−144	
	(4.8–4.3)(180–199)	−10	
	(1.5–4.3)(190–199)	16	
	(1.4–4.3)(210–199)	32	
	(0.7–4.3)(220–199)	76	
	(0.5–4.3)(230–199)	118	
	(0.4–4.3)(270–199)	277	
	ΣCP_{ij}	−442	74
h_{ie}, h_{oe}	(16–4.3)(13–47.1)	−399	
	(8–4.3)(13–47.1)	−199	
	(4.3–4.3)(18–47.1)	−15	
	(2.5–4.3)(22–47.1)	45	
	(1.4–4.3)(32–47.1)	44	
	(0.7–4.3)(52–47.1)	−18	
	(0.5–4.3)(85–47.1)	−144	
	(0.4–4.3)(140–47.1)	−362	
	ΣCP_{ij}	−968	−16
h_{fe}, h_{oe}	(130–199)(13–47.1)	2,353	
	(160–199)(15–47.1)	1,252	
	(180–199)(15–47.1)	553	
	(190–199)(22–47.1)	226	
	(210–199)(32–47.1)	−166	
	(220–199)(52–47.1)	103	
	(230–199)(85–47.1)	1,175	
	(270–199)(140–47.1)	6,596	
	ΣCP_{ij}	12,092	2,015

Reprinted by permission of the Martin Marietta Corporation.

TABLE 4.32   Transistor Gain Test Data (64)

Class No.	Gain	Class No.	Gain
1	525	6	820
2	850	7	400
3	890	8	350
4	430	9	375
5	1,050	10	950

Reprinted by permission of the Martin Marietta Corporation.

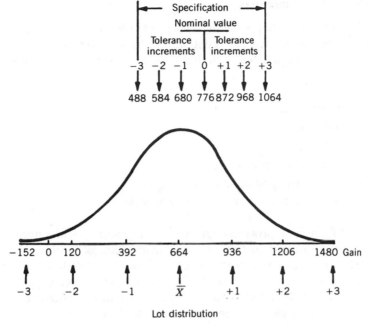

Figure 4.31   Transistor gain tolerance centering distribution (65). (Reprinted by permission of the Martin Marietta Corporation.)

4.8   THE UBIQUITOUS POWER SUPPLY

As stated in the introduction to this chapter, few subsystems are as commonplace as power supplies. They are encountered in just about every product using energy, and have become high-technology products in themselves; the modern-day switching-mode power supply is a prime example.

Yet, few subsystems are as unappreciated as design, schedule, and cost challenges until such time as programs encounter complications because of power-supply problems. Usually, specification and design of power supplies are not considered seriously until the host system reaches substantial maturity, and then a very cost-ineffective catch-up game is played.

Reliable power supplies require an average development time of 18 months (shown in Figure 3.8). Be suspicious of anything less. Twenty-four months is not an unreasonable amount of time for completing designs involving circuit innovations.

The notion that power supplies are simple items to design and produce leads to schedule delays and cost. Design-to-cost practitioners should be on guard against this tendency.

4.8.1 Design Considerations

The thesis is that reliable power supplies are the least costly power supplies from the viewpoint of life-cycle cost should be promulgated in every program and in every organization. Reliable power supplies are characterized by

Proved circuit design

High reliability parts

Parts derating

Low hot-spot temperatures

Printed wire boards and connectors

Avoidance of point-to-point and wire harnesses

Causes of failures in power supplies are not generally understood. Table 4.33 identifies a number of failure mechanisms. Sneak circuits should be considered in the design of power supplies since most failures are due to peak instantaneous transients. Most high-technology power supplies use a switching-mode schema. The guidance given in Table 4.34 should be considered when designing switching-mode power supplies.

TABLE 4.33 Switching-Mode Power-Supply Failure Mechanism (66)

Instantaneous power dissipation
Secondary breakdown limits
Voltage peaks
Current peaks
Thermal peaks
Ripple current
Skin effects
Leakage inductance
Stray capacitance
Common-mode noise
Magnetic interaction
Electronic field interaction
Parasitic inputs and oscillatory effects
Inadequate phase gain margin
Worst-case tolerance effects
Source impedance effects
Interaction between systems on same power source
Poor grounding practices
Differential noise effects
Electrostatic interaction
Uncontrolled power-up and power-down

Source: NAVMAT P 4855-1, Navy Power Supply Reliability, 1982.

TABLE 4.34   Switching-Mode Power Supply Design Guidance (67)

Put voltage transient protection on the input power lines

Put an in-rush limiting circuit in series with the input capacitor to avoid input rectifier damage during turn-on

Build an internal housekeeping power supply to isolate sensitive circuits from the hostile power line and to improve safety

Incorporate a soft-start circuit to relieve component stressing during turn-on

Tailor the turn-on and turn-off load lines for minimum peak power in semiconductors during turn-on and turn-off intervals

Incorporate a crossover interlock circuit in the power stage that is connected across the power line so that two devices can never be on simultaneously across that power line

Incorporate input electromagnetic interference filtering that is incompatible with negative resistance loads and variable input source impedances

Incorporate a fast-attack current limit circuit to protect power devices from control logic anomalies

Design inductors, transformers and magnetics to avoid saturation during peak loads and transient states

Design the turn-on–turn-off logic for orderly and controllable sequencing

Analyze and measure worst-case parameters and compare rated limits of components

Perform worst-case thermal and hot-spot analysis

Design printed wire boards and packaging for optimal heat transfer and to minimize common-mode and differential-mode noise

Package magnetics and other heavy current carrying conductors with adequate thermal interfaces.

Avoid ground loops and develop grounding to minimize crosstalk and interaction.

Analyze and measure loop stability to ensure adequate phase gain margin under all line, load, temperature, and component tolerance limits.

Avoid the use of power semiconductors in hot-case packages that are susceptible to assembly errors and could cause secondary failures from their high-energy handling capacity.

Use beryllia isolation where possible for its low thermal resistance.

Use parts standardization to the extent possible.

Use only hard-solder die bonding

Avoid parallel operation of active bipolar devices

Avoid parts that are sensitive to electrostatic discharge

Use parts screening on active components

Use environmental stress screening that can improve reliability of the product by a factor of 4–8

Source: NAVMAT P4855-1, *Navy Power Supply Reliability*, 1982.

4.8.2   Manufacturing Considerations

The maintenance objective of minimizing handling, tear-down, and reassembly should be extended to the factory environment through the medium of simplified packaging design. The guidance in Table 4.35 should be considered in the packaging design.

TABLE 4.35   Power Supply Packaging Guidance (68)

Use printed wire boards and multilayer interconnection boards instead of point-to-point wiring and wiring harnesses

Avoid the use of sheet-bond material because it absorbs moisture

Design boards for automatic parts insertion

Use keyed connectors for input–output interfaces

Limit wire connections to the component side of boards to simplify assembly and minimize handling

Ensure that solder joints are all visible for inspection by eliminating blind-hole solder joints

Avoid cavities that collect moisture and loose particles

Ensure that each subassembly is testable as an entity without the complete assembly

Ensure that torque specifications are adequate for heat transfer without causing damage

Source: NAVMAT P4855-1, *Navy Power Supply Reliability*, 1982.

4.9   PRODUCTION READINESS

At this juncture, the concern in design-to-cost programs relates to the production readiness of both product and process designs. The approach of the Department of Defense (DoD) is offered as a role model in this regard.

It is the intent of the DoD that no acquisition shall proceed into production until it is determined that the principal contractors have the physical, financial, and managerial capacity to meet the cost and schedule commitments of the proposed procurement. Assessment is required of the contractors' capabilities to meet surge (i.e., peacetime) and mobilization (i.e., declared national emergency) requirements and their commitments to participate in the DoD industrial preparedness planning program for these requirements.

This direction, which is spelled out in DoD Directive 5000.34, *Defense Production Management*, is addressed in this section. However, it is advisable to first review the production management terminology given in Table 4.36, and then to review the production-related program milestones given in Table 4.37, in order to better comprehend the directive and to more fully utilize it in nonmilitary high-technology undertakings.

4.9.1   Management Guidelines

Department of Defense Directive 5000.34 requires that explicit and timely assessments of production risks be made throughout the acquisition process beginning with the exploration of alternative design concepts. Consideration shall be given to production feasibility, availability of materials, and utiliza-

TABLE 4.36 Production Management Terminology (69)

Producibility. The relative ease of producing an item or system governed by the characteristics and features of a design that enable economical fabrication, assembly, inspection, and testing using available production technology

Production engineering. The application of design and analysis techniques to produce a specified product; includes functions of planning, specifying, and coordinating the application of required resources; performing analyses of producibility and production operations, processes, and systems; applying new manufacturing methods, tooling, and equipment; controlling the introduction of engineering changes; and employing cost-control techniques

Production feasibility. The likelihood that a system design concept can be produced using existing production technology while simultaneously meeting quality, production rate, and cost requirements

Production management. The effective use of resources to produce on schedule the required number of end items that meet specified quality, performance, and cost

Production readiness. The state or condition of preparedness of an item or system to proceed into production; an item or system is ready for production when the completeness and producibility of the production design and the managerial and physical preparations necessary for initiating and sustaining a viable production effort have progressed to the point where a production commitment can be made without incurring unacceptable risks that thresholds of schedule, performance, or other established criteria will be breached

Production readiness review. A formal examination of a program to determine whether the design is ready for production, production engineering problems have been resolved, and the producer has accomplished adequate planning for the production phase

Source: Department of Defense Directive 5000.34, *Defense Production Management.*

TABLE 4.37 Production-Related Program Milestones (70)

Milestone 0, program initiation. Production management shall be specifically addressed at each program milestone decision point subsequent to Milestone 0

Milestone I, demonstration and validation. Production feasibility of candidate system concepts shall be addressed and areas of production risk shall be evaluated; manufacturing technology needed to reduce production risk to acceptable levels shall be identified.

Milestone II, full-scale engineering development. The potential producibility of the design approach shall be reviewed and production risk determined acceptable; requirements for long-lead procurements and limited production shall be identified and evaluated; the full-scale engineering development phase shall include provisions to attain producibility of the design utilizing cost-effective manufacturing methods and processes

Milestone III, production and deployment. Production decisions shall be supported by an assessment of the program readiness for production based on a formal production readiness review; plans and provisions for accomplishing cost reduction during production shall be described

Source: Department of Defense Directive 5000.34, *Defense Production Management.*

tion of energy for the projected system life cycle. Voids and deficiencies in required manufacturing technology shall be identified.

Manufacturing technology deficiencies shall be addressed concurrently with concept demonstration and validation through the use of manufacturing technology projects or other means. The producibility of each system design concept shall be considered at the full-scale engineering decision point.

Contractor previous performance (to the extent that it has a bearing on the concept involved) potential to execute the production program and demonstrated production management capability shall be among those factors included in the contractual solicitations and evaluated thereafter in the source selection.

Production engineering and production planning shall be accomplished throughout full-scale engineering development. Industrial preparedness planning shall be effectively integrated with production management and production planning. Production risks, which should be identified as early as possible in the acquisition cycle, shall be reduced to acceptable levels prior to a production decision.

Production decisions shall be supported by an independent assessment of production readiness, including evaluation of the findings of a formal production readiness review. Production readiness reviews shall confirm the stability and producibility of the design; progress toward meeting reliability and maintainability characteristics; the adequacy of supporting manufacturing technology; the refinement of manufacturing methods, techniques, and processes; and the suitability of provisions for control of manufacturing, cost, and quality assurance.

Competition, value engineering, tailoring of specifications and standards, trade studies, constant workforce approach, and other techniques shall be used to minimize production, operation, and support costs. Standardization, commonality and interchangeability shall be promoted throughout the acquisition cycle to reduce lead time and life-cycle cost. Continued emphasis shall be placed on life-cycle-cost reduction during the production phase through the use of contractual incentives and other means.

Production management planning and implementation shall include provisions for measuring progress in meeting design-to-cost and life-cycle-cost commitments. Cost and schedule control systems to be used in the production phase shall satisfy the requirements of DoD Instruction 7000.2, *Cost/Schedule Control Systems Criteria* (see Section 6.8.1).

4.9.2 Readiness Criteria

Production readiness reviews encompass all considerations that relate to the completeness and producibility of the production design and to the managerial and physical preparations for initiating and sustaining a viable production effort. This section provides representative listings of areas of concern

TABLE 4.38 Product Design Production Readiness Criteria (71)

The design is low-risk from the standpoint of producibility

Design change activity has stabilized at a low level

Validation demonstration of the design has been accomplished, including qualification of subsystems and components as appropriate and the demonstration of performance and reliability and maintenance (R&M) characteristics

Incomplete portions of the design are identified and do not introduce significant risks to production

A system configuration audit has been accomplished and discrepancies resolved

The design is in consonance with operational, maintenance, and support concepts

The technical data package supports competitive acquisition where appropriate

Standardization has been accomplished in the design to maximize production economies derived from the use of standard parts, materials, and processes

Critical and scarce materials are used only where dictated by required performance, and such use is compatible with established priorities and allocations

Alternates for critical materials or processes are identified in the design

Production cost projections have been made and are well supported

in production readiness reviews, together with functional statements and conditions appropriate to these areas.

These areas are representative insofar as the extent of conformance required is dependent on the point in time at which the assessment is made and whether the assessment is in support of a limited or full production release decision. The criteria are presented by area in Tables 4.38 through 4.44 for product design, industrial resources, production engineering and planning, materials and purchased parts; quality assurance; logistics; and contract administration.

TABLE 4.39 Industrial Resources Production Readiness Criteria (72)

Plant capacity is adequate for the required production rate taking into consideration other production efforts

Consideration has been given to meeting surge and mobilization production requirements; a commitment to participate in the DoD industrial preparedness planning program has been made.

Contractor and government owned facilities, production equipment, special tooling, and special test equipment have been identified in terms of specifications, quantity, and finances; acquisition and installation plans meet program requirements

Needed plant modernization and productivity enhancements have been accomplished, including advantageous employment of CAD–CAM and other advanced techniques; associated computer software has been developed

Skilled production personnel is available

Necessary personnel training and certification are programmed

No major labor relations problems are anticipated

Source: Department of Defense Directive 5000.34, *Defense Production Management.*

TABLE 4.40   Production Engineering and Planning Production Readiness Criteria (73)

A comprehensive production plan has been developed

The nature and sequence of manufacturing methods and processes, together with associated facilities, equipment, tooling and plant layout, represent economical applications of proven technology consistent with

    Product specification and quality requirements

    Quantity and rate requirements

    OSHA,[a] environmental, and energy-conservation requirements

Alternative production approaches are available to meet contingency needs

Production schedules are compatible with end-item delivery requirements

Drawings, standards, and shop instructions are sufficiently explicit for correct interpretation by manufacturing personnel

Provisions have been made for determining producibility and cost impacts of engineering changes introduced during production

Configuration management is adequate to assure configuration identification, control, and status accounting during production

A program manager has been assigned the authority and responsibility for manufacture and delivery of the system and the functional elements, and the staff of this manager's organization has been identified

Policies and procedures implementing production requirements have been fully identified and documented

A management information system exists that provides current status of production effort and sufficient visibility of existence, cause, and extent of production problems to enable responsive management action

Source: Department of Defense Directive 5000.34, *Defense Production Management.*

[a] Occupational Safety and Health Administration.

TABLE 4.41   Materials and Purchased Parts Production Readiness Criteria (74)

A complete and accurate bill of materials has been prepared

Make-or-buy determinations have been made for all significant or critical elements of the system and are supported by sound justification

Long-lead-time materials have been identified and action initiated for advance procurement where appropriate

Sole-source items are identified and continuity of supply is assured

Government-furnished material (GFM) and government-furnished equipment (GFE) are identified with program and production plans, including associated lead time and schedule requirements

The contractor's material control and material inventory system are adequate

The contractor's material procurement plan provides

    Criteria for selection of subcontractors and vendors who emphasize timely delivery of acceptable material at a reasonable cost

    Effective procedures to determine material needs, lead times, and delivery schedules

    Multisourcing of critical items to the extent possible

    Economic lot-size orders

    Visibility and control of subcontractors and vendors

TABLE 4.42 Quality Assurance Production Readiness Criteria (75)

The quality assurance function is organizationally placed and structured to permit independent objective judgments

The contractor's quality program is in accordance with the contract requirements and the quality plan is appropriate for the production program

Necessary quality-control procedures and quality acceptance criteria have been established

The quality assurance organization is a participant in the production planning and facilitization effort

Source: Department of Defense Directive 5000.34, Defense Production Management.

TABLE 4.43 Logistics Production Readiness Criteria (76)

Production capacity exists to manufacture initial spares, including contingencies for high-usage items during initial deployment

Operational support, test, and diagnostic equipments have been developed and their state of production readiness will meet the system deployment schedule

Training aids, simulators, and other devices for operator and maintenance personnel have been developed and can be produced to support the system deployment schedule

Source: Department of Defense Directive 5000.34, *Defense Production Management.*

TABLE 4.44 Contract Administration Production Readiness Criteria (77)

Adequate government representation (i.e., numbers, capabilities, and functional responsibilities) will be provided at the major production sites

Appropriate liaison exists between the DoD component program manager's office, the on-site government representative, and the contractor's production organization

Effective government procedures have been established for timely processing of change proposals and issuance of change orders

Source: Department of Defense Directive 5000.34, *Defense Production Management.*

4.10 SOFTWARE MAINTENANCE COST

Software maintenance is more accurately described as postdelivery software support. History shows a disproportionately high cost for software maintenance, when the magnitude of its tasks of error correction and upgrading is compared to that of development. This phase can account for a large percentage of total life-cycle cost and, therefore, should be a major affordability concern (78).

The nature of software maintenance changes over the life cycles of the supported systems and products. During the early stages of ownership, emphasis is on debugging or corrective action. As products approach obsolescence the emphasis shifts more toward upgrading the software.

1. CORRECTIVE MAINTENANCE

Corrective maintenance includes the discovery, isolation, and correction of defects that prevent the system from operating according to its specification. A major concern of corrective maintenance is that although the incidence of defects diminishes with time, the relative complexity of the defects increases.

2. ADAPTIVE MAINTENANCE

Adaptive maintenance includes changes to the software necessary to enable the system to continue performing its specific function. Examples are changes to accommodate new hardware, new software and existing software changes, and changes in the environment that, in turn, change the form of the data processed.

3. PERFECTIVE MAINTENANCE

Perfective maintenance includes changes that alter the manner in which functions are performed while retaining the same functional results. Such changes are usually performed in order to restore or enhance efficiency.

4. SOFTWARE ENHANCEMENT

Software enhancement includes changes that are needed to carry out altered system functions. This is a major cost driver and is due to the lack of stable requirements. Ensure at all times that the product is clearly defined and that cost estimates fully reflect the product.

4.11 SUMMARY

The essence of low-cost production is ease of fabrication, assembly, and test. Product and process designs that maximize these features are referred to as "inherently low cost designs."

This chapter addressed the characteristics of and the techniques for achieving inherently low cost designs. In the aggregate, these characteristics define producibility in terms of which aspects of production operations should be maximized and which aspects should be minimized.

It is in this context that the potential of advanced design and manufacturing technology was explored with some emphasis on flexible and just-in-time (JIT) manufacturing. The roles of group technology, in-process quality control, computer-aided design (CAD), and manufacturing were illuminated.

Guidelines were given for timing the introduction of technology to render it supportive of organizational long-range plans as well as the particular program or product of interest at the moment. In addition, break-even points for technology investments were discussed.

The next section addressed product simplification in the context of the cost-driving relationships inherent in product specifications that translate into material selection, detail fabrication, and assembly tasks. Material costs were discussed from the viewpoints of energy consumption, material waste, and material properties.

The major factors influencing the cost of manufacturing details—tolerance and surface finish requirements, detail complexity, and the fabrication techniques employed—were discussed. Assembly costs were discussed from the viewpoints of accessibility, materials to be joined, joining processes and other special processes, parts count and variety, tolerance, and geometry.

An entire section was devoted to the role of castings in product simplification. First, casting advantages were enumerated with respect to design, metallurgy and production; then various casting processes were described.

The advantages and disadvantages of the various casting processes were enumerated and casting costs considered. It was pointed out that the most significant cost drivers in castings are dimensional tolerances that are more stringent than the casting process is capable of providing routinely.

The next section addressed work simplification, emphasizing the relationships between production equipment and the human element. The subjects covered were work design principles and tooling principles, and checklists were provided for work simplification, economy of motion, and human factors in the workplace.

Included in this section was the very important subject of automation and robotics. Robotics is a form of flexible automation; an extensive list of robotics criteria was provided.

The next two sections covered approaches for quantifying the efficiency of designs in terms of assembly ease and testability. These are highly compatible design characteristics; products that are easy to assemble are easy to test.

A technique called "design for assembly" (DFA) was presented as a relatively easy method for scoring the assembly ease of alternative designs. The techniques was illustrated with an application to a piston assembly.

The subject of testability was treated from the theoretical viewpoint and from the practical viewpoint of estimating costs of various degrees of testability based on the concept of figure of merit. In addition, MIL-STD-2165, whose thrust is integrated diagnostics in military equipment, was introduced as guidance for high-technology products and systems in the nondefense domain.

The next section described a concept that has emerged in recent years and that provides a new approach to quality by replacing the notion of conformance-to-specification limits by the concept of reduced variability about targets for greater product uniformity. A technique called "tolerance centering" is at the heart of the concept.

Tolerance centering is a derivative of statistical quality control that allows near real-time determination of the state of process control. The relationship between process control states and production costs was illustrated.

The next section in the chapter was devoted to power supplies since few subsystems are appreciated less as design, schedule, or cost challenges. Both design and manufacturing considerations were included in the discussion.

At this juncture, the subject of production readiness was introduced according to the rationale that the affordability of even the lowest inherent cost design will not be fully realized if design is not validated and processes are not on-line and proved at the time of production. Production readiness criteria and management guidelines for ensuring readiness were provided.

The criteria were presented in the form of tables that were adapted from DoD Directive 5000.34, *Defense Production Management*. Included were criteria for judging the readiness of the product design, industrial resources, production engineering and planning, materials and purchased parts, quality assurance, logistics, and contract administration.

The next section provided an insight into some aspects of software maintenance cost. Despite the hardware orientation of the book, it recognizes that software cost is no less important than hardware even beyond the development phase of programs. The elements of software cost that were considered are essentially recurring and are usually overlooked when design-to-cost goals are first established.

4.12   CASE STUDIES AND EXERCISES

The case studies that follow are intended to amplify key points in this chapter. The exercises following the case studies allow the reader to relate these points to personal viewpoints and experiences. The case studies in this chapter address the issue of increasing productivity and offer practice in some of the techniques presented in the chapter.

4.12.1   In Search of Productivity

A team from Harvard Business School recently completed a multiyear study of 12 factories in three companies for the purpose of clarifying the variables that influence productivity at the micro level. The salient conclusion was that internally generated confusion and the ensuing disruption in operations are the greatest obstacle to productivity. The report cited that no amount of capital investment can improve competitiveness without first building clarity into operations, eliminating unnecessary disruptions, and nurturing technical competence.

Engineering change orders were found to have the most negative effect on productivity, and in one plant an increase in change orders from 5 to 10 in one particular month was accompanied by a reduction in productivity of about 5 percent. Contrary to the popular belief that block changes are more economical, the study concluded and recommended that change orders should be released in a steady fashion to minimize confusion and disruption (79).

EXERCISE Investigate the policies and procedures for implementing engineering change orders in a known company in terms of clarity and conciseness. Obtain yield statistics from a production program in the company and correlate them to the engineering change curve for the program.

Conclude whether the policies and procedures serve to enhance or degrade productivity. Recommend appropriate changes.

4.12.2 The Promise of Technology

Thomas G. Gunn, in *Manufacturing for Competitive Advantage,* uses the expression "world class manufacturer" to denote organizations that view manufacturing as a competitive asset, employ technology to enhance overall operations as well as manufacturing, and thus compete effectively in the international marketplace (see Table 4.45).

A cited example of a world class manufacturer is General Electric's Louisville dishwasher plant, which was redesigned at a cost of $60 million. The new plant has a daily capacity of 1000 dishwashers and can produce 13 different models (80).

At the same time, the company increased its share of the market to 31 percent and reduced service calls by 50 percent. Some of the operational advantages of the new facility over the old are given in Table 4.45.

EXERCISE Key among the many characteristics that discriminate world class from conventional manufacturers are the number of raw material and work-in-process (WIP) inventory turns per year and the cost of quality as a percentage of sales. Cited guidelines for inventory turns are 2 per year for conventional and up to 50 per year for world class manufacturers. For cost

TABLE 4.45 Operational Advantages of a World Class Manufacturer (81)

Factor	Percentage
Material cost reduction	12
Parts reduction on assembly line	61
Raw material and work in process inventory reduction	66
Productivity improvement	20
Product cycle time	83
Conveyor length reduction	75
Quality improvement	45

Adapted by permission from Gunn's *Manufacturing for Competitive Advantage: Becoming a World Class Manufacturer,* Copyright 1987, Ballinger Publishing Company.

of quality, the guidelines are 12 percent of sales for conventional and as little as 1.5 percent of sales for world class manufacturers (82).

Examine the records of a known company in the areas of inventory turns and quality costs. On a scale of 1 to 10, how does the company rate as a world class manufacturer? Relate the finding to the company's share of the worldwide market for its products.

4.12.3   One Step Forward

Computer-aided design–computer-aided manufacturing (CAD–CAM) was cited in Section 4.1.1 as prerequisite for maximum producibility within the constraint of existing production capability. In its own right, CAD–CAM can provide substantial saving during development and early phases of production by increased productivity in design drafting and subsequent checking and administration.

Table 4.46 lists work-hour per square foot of drawings for conventional drafting. Table 4.47 gives productivity improvements that can be expected from using CAD–CAM in the drafting process.

EXERCISE   Estimate the area and types of drawings in a program known to be using conventional drafting. Estimate the cost of drawing preparation from the relationships in Table 4.46, compare to actual drawing cost, and develop a factor for the difference between the two costs.

Apply the productivity improvement relationships in Table 4.47 to the estimated cost of drawing preparation. With the improvement ratio, estimate the saving that might have been realized in the actual cost.

4.12.4   Less is Better

Figure 4.32 illustrates how high-technology products can be the beneficiary of product simplification and ensuing work simplification. The figure shows the before-and-after configurations of a missile that was the subject of an intensive value analysis effort.

TABLE 4.46   Work-Hours per Square Foot for Conventional Drafting (83)

Task	Hours per Square Foot
Preparation	1.0
Drawing	2.2
Checking	2.7
Administration	1.4
	7.3

Adapted by permission of John Wiley & Sons, Inc.

TABLE 4.47   CAD–CAM Productivity Improvement in Drafting (84)

Drawing Type	Improvement Ratio
Simple logic drawings	4.5–5.0
Single-line drawings	3.5–4.0
Piping and instrumentation diagrams	3.0–3.5
Revision of diagrams	10.0
Stock drawings	4.3
Assembly–detail	3.7
Sheet-metal drawings	3.7
Extrusion drawings	3.2
Numerical control tapes	2.7
Detail aircraft drawings	2.4
Layout drawings	1.7–2.2
Structural steel	1.5–2.0
Piping layout	1.25–1.75

Adapted by permission of John Wiley & Sons, Inc.

Table 4.48 lists specific elements of product simplification that resulted. Performance of the missile was not degraded; however, the unit cost was reduced by about 25 percent. This was due to the combination of reduced parts and of simplified processes that allowed steeper learning curves to be realized.

EXERCISE   Apply value analysis techniques to a known product. Ascertain the functional worth of the product, and discriminate the secondary functions from the basic function the product is intended to perform.

Hypothesize alternative means for implementing the basic function and estimate the respective costs. Select the preferred approach, and estimate the investment needed to modify the product and the payback period.

TABLE 4.48   Missile Simplification (86)

Was	Is Now
Four fins	Three fins
Two folding fin and mechanism	One folding fin and mechanism
Non-round-nosed cone	Spun circular ogive
Flexible duct splice	Fixed duct splice
Ordnance activated dome	Passive dome
Cast fuel tank	Formed and welded tank
Canted air duct	Horizontal air duct
Submerged INCO 718 Combustor	One piece titanium booster
Structural fairing	Nonstructural fairing

Reprinted by permission of the Martin Marietta Corporation.

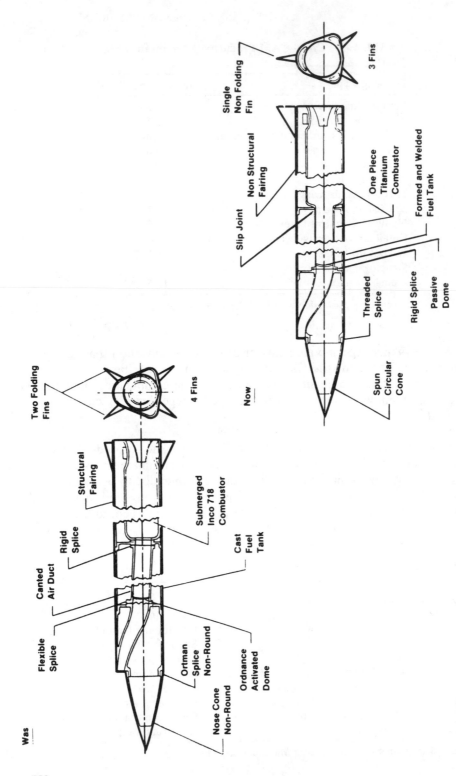

Figure 4.32 Missile simplification (85). (Reprinted by permission of the Martin Marietta Corporation.)

4.12.5 All for One and One for All

A state-of-the art navigation pod for an attack aircraft had been developed successfully when the military service in charge of the development realized that the probable production cost for the quantities required would exceed the obligated funding for the program. Investigation of the potential cost overrun was undertaken, which revealed that the major cost drivers were forgings used for the structure of the pod.

There were 32 forgings used in each pod with an average unit recurring cost of $2000 based on a production quantity of 500 pods. Subsequent redesign replaced the 32 forgings with 8 complex castings.

EXERCISE Considering the application, which of the casting processes discussed in Section 4.3.1 would be the preferred approach?

Assume that each of the eight castings replaced a group of four forgings each with the individual cost of $2000. Using the cost data in Section 4.3.2, estimate the unit recurring cost saving using castings by the preferred process for the production quantity of 500 pods.

4.12.6 The Machine That Walked Like a Human

This case study depicts an attempt to utilize a robot for an application that should have been reserved for humans. One of the military services sponsored the development of an airborne antitank weapon with all-weather performance. This requirement led to the selection of millimeter wave radar in the missile for target acquisition and tracking.

A contract, which was awarded for both development and production, contained a requirement for design to cost and specified the unit cost goal to be attained. A substantial award fee was tied to the cost goal to ensure its prosecution.

The millimeter wave requirement resulted in a production design of the radar subsystem that was extremely labor intensive. The average component was less than 50 cubic centimeters (cm^3) in volume and required placement, orientation, and adjustment to within a tenth of a milliradian. The operation was not only time-consuming but also conducive to error.

The millimeter wave components were the major cost drivers in production. The investment of almost $1 million in a robot appeared justifiable in relationship to the award fee that would obtain from realizing the unit cost goal.

The robot was acquired and did an excellent job of installing and integrating the components comprising the radar subsystem of the missile. Unfortunately, the job of aligning the component electronically had not been appreciated fully.

Necessary, but seemingly incompatible requirements for minimum voltage standing-wave ratio (VSWR), maximum gain, and minimum noise required many iterative adjustments in order to decrease thresholds to sufficiently low levels. The robot's computer program for this operation invariably went into a loop, causing the robot to oscillate.

Ultimately, the robot experienced the equivalent of a nervous breakdown, and the adjustment part of the process was restored to human hands. It evolved that less than 25 percent of the labor could be saved in the final assembly and test of the radar subsystem.

EXERCISE   Examine several production processes that are labor-intensive for the potential of using automation or robotics. Search for repeated operations with changing criteria that would impact the use of automation or robotics and define the extent to which they could be used without problems.

4.12.7   Hope Springs Eternally

A long-established manufacturer of bedroom furniture began to experience an increasing number of returns of mattresses from retailers. Most of the complaints were that the inner coil springs were protruding, suggesting that either the springs were too stiff or the covering was too weak.

Both possibilities were disturbing since the springs were procured from the open stock of a particular vendor, and the design of the mattress line was based on the vendor's specification for the spring; namely, 50 ± 10 on the Rockwell Hardness C Scale. In addition, the pricing structure of the mat-

TABLE 4.49   Hardness Test Results (87)

Class No.	Hardness	Class No.	Hardness	Class No.	Hardness
1	53	18	42	35	59
2	50	19	50	36	53
3	58	20	51	37	53
4	57	21	41	38	54
5	44	22	47	39	50
6	45	23	55	40	56
7	60	24	51	41	60
8	55	25	54	42	59
9	51	26	60	43	49
10	52	27	54	44	54
11	53	28	47	45	53
12	56	29	59	46	51
13	48	30	52	47	49
14	51	31	55	48	58
15	46	32	60	49	60
16	52	33	58	50	47
17	49	34	50		

Reprinted by permission of the Martin Marietta Corporation.

tresses was based on the cost of open-stock coil springs as opposed to special designs.

The alternatives were that either the design was at fault or that the springs were not conforming to the specification. The manufacturer hoped that the latter was the case and that only a procurement problem needed to be rectified.

Receiving inspection records, however, indicated that all the springs used in manufacturing the returned mattresses were within the specification limits. Nonetheless, 50 unbroken springs were randomly removed from the returned mattresses and subjected to hardness testing.

Test results are given in Table 4.49. The larger numbers denote harder spring material and, consequently, stiffer springs.

EXERCISE   Apply the procedures given in Section 4.7.1 to determine the process control state for the sample data in Table 4.49. Define which process control state should be acceptable to the manufacturer on the basis of the criteria presented in Table 4.23.

If the process control state proves acceptable, make a recommendation regarding the mattress design. If the process control state proves unacceptable, make a recommendation regarding the procurement of the coil springs.

REFERENCES

1. Martin Marietta Corporation, *Design to Cost/Affordability Manual,* 1986.
2. Richard J. Schonberger, *Japanese Manufacturing Techniques,* The Free Press, New York, 1982.
3–13. Martin Marietta Corporation, *Design to Cost/Affordability Manual,* 1986.
14–32. Martin Marietta Corporation, *Engineering Practices Manual, Mechanical.* Volume 2, 1985.
33–36. Martin Marietta Corporation, *Design to Cost/Affordability Manual,* 1986.
37. G. Boothroyd and P. Dewhurst, *Design for Assembly,* Boothroyd & Dewhurst, 56 Sheerman Lane, Amherst, MA 01002.
38–41. Martin Marietta Corporation, *Design to Cost/Affordability Manual,* 1986.
42. Jack V. Michaels, *Parametric Approach to Testability,* Proceedings of the 1988 International Conference. International Society of Parametric Analysts. Copyright 1988, Martin Marietta Corporation.
43. Captain Dennis Gleason, USAF, *Analysis of Built-in Test Accuracy,* 1982 Proceedings of the Annual Reliability and Maintainability Symposium.
44–50. Jack V. Michaels, *Parametric Approach to Testability,* Proceedings of the 1988 International Conference. International Society of Parametric Analysts. Copyright 1988, Martin Marietta Corporation.
51. L. P. Sullivan, *Reducing Variability: A New Approach to Quality,* Quality Progress, July 1984.
52. Jack V. Michaels, *Parametric Approach to Testability,* Proceedings of the 1988 International Conference. International Society of Parametric Analysts. Copyright 1988, Martin Marietta Corporation.

53–65. Jack V. Michaels, *Tolerance Centering: The Quality Control Alternative*, Proceedings of the 1988 International Conference, Society of American Value Engineers. Copyright 1988 Martin Marietta Corporation.

66–68. NAVMAT P4855-1 *Navy Power Supply Reliability*, 1982.

69–77. Department of Defense Directive 5000.34, *Defense Production Management*.

   78. Martin Marietta Corporation, *Design to Cost/Affordability Manual*, 1986.

   79. Robert H. Hayes and Kim B. Clark, "Why Some Factories More Productive than Others," *Harvard Business Review*, September–October 1986.

80–82. Thomas G. Gunn, *Manufacturing for Competitive Advantage: Becoming a World Class Manufacturer*, Ballinger Publishing Company, 1987.

83–84. Theodore Taylor, *Handbook of Electronics Industry Cost Estimating Data*, John Wiley & Sons, 1985.

85–86. Martin Marietta Corporation, *Design to Cost/Affordability Manual*, 1986.

   87. Jack V. Michaels, *Tolerance Centering: The Quality Control Alternative*, Proceedings of the 1988 International Conference, Society of American Value Engineers. Copyright 1988 Martin Marietta Corporation.

5
CHOOSING BUSINESS STRATEGIES

The competitive posture of contractors and the bargaining posture of customers can be enhanced significantly by selecting the proper business strategy. For example, in situations requiring teaming among contractors, competitiveness can be increased by proposing alternatives to the classical prime-subcontractor relationship. Customers may stipulate an associate contractor relationship with integration provided by the customer. Contractors may propose a joint venture with integration provided by an entity created by the contractors solely for that purpose. Either approach avoids factoring the prime's burden and profit on the subcontractor's cost that results in an attendant increase in overall program cost.

This chapter addresses elements of business strategy for low-cost production starting with the discussion of three very important subjects relating to doing business with the federal government and that, in themselves, are fundamental elements of business strategy: (1) best and final offers in the procurement process, (2) involvement in the industrial modernization incentives program of the Department of Defense (DoD), and (3) indirect cost management. The consequences of actions regarding the first two issues need to be fully understood before any such actions are taken. Indirect cost management becomes an issue when contracts are negotiated, and it is essential that design-to-cost practitioners understand government cost regulations in this regard.

These subjects are followed by the discussion of procurement alternatives and the comparison of these alternatives using the classical prime-subcontractor relationship as a baseline. The discussion is in the context both of dealings between customers and contractors and of dealings between prime contractors and subcontractors.

The next section, therefore, addresses the issue of the flowdown of requirements and incentives to suppliers. The insight should be valuable to all high-technology organizations, however, because frequently contractors and subcontractors reverse roles in the pursuit of business opportunities.

The discussion of make-or-buy decisions that follows is also universally applicable. The implications of company policy and criteria for make-or-buy decisions are discussed, and some suggestions for a rational policy are outlined.

There are several scheduling strategies that can be conducive to lower cost and better utilization of resources provided the attendant risks are understood and anticipated. These are presented following a brief introduction to techniques of schedule management used in these strategies.

Similarly, capacity planning can be conducive to lower cost and improved utilization of resources. Therefore, the next section provides an introduction to linear programming that is a powerful tool with a host of applications in design-to-cost programs as well as in capacity planning.

Inventory practices can exert a profound influence on cost. As expected, inventory strategies range from optimizing the balance of inventory and demand with the concept of economic order quantity (EOQ) to the total elimination of inventory in the penchant of the Japanese. Some guidelines in this regard are given.

The subject of motivating personnel is covered in the next section. The saying "People are our principal asset" is particularly true in high-technology enterprises, and it is never too early to institute a system of recognition and reward for the benefit of the undertaking.

Following the summary of its contents, the chapter concludes with a number of case studies and exercises that are intended to amplify key points in the chapter. The exercises allow the readers to relate their experiences and viewpoints to the events that are unfolded in the case studies.

5.1 BEST AND FINAL OFFERS

It has become a common practice for customers, particularly governmental entities, to require best and final offers (BAFOs) from competing contractors when nearing the conclusion of the proposal phase of the acquisition process. This requirement has become as prevalent in solicitations for development as in solicitations for production, and has even pervaded the fixed-price arena.

The intent of these customers is clear: to promote sharing by contractors of the near-term cost of both development and tooling in anticipation of future production work. The process is intended to be carried out overtly. Offerers are required to provide a roadmap of how they arrived at their BAFOs from their original proposal, the purpose being to expose attempts at buy-in.

The BAFO process has been known to be repeated two or more times on a given acquisition. Again, offerers have been required to provide a roadmap showing how they arrived at their current BAFO from their previous BAFO.

It would appear that these customers wished to ensure that essential requirements were not sacrificed in the attempt to reach their funding ceilings.

It should be understood that the BAFO process conveys only the anticipation and not the promise of follow-on work unless total package procurement is involved. The winning contractor does enjoy a competitive advantage for follow-on work, but this advantage was bought with the investment of the contractor's money and does not included a guarantee.

There are several other equally serious consequences of the BAFO process both from the contractor's perspective and from the customer's perspective. To begin with, the original technical and cost proposals, submitted in today's competitive market place, were undoubtedly well thought out and realistically priced from the viewpoint of work content. Some elements of work must be deleted from the proposals and become the subjects for company funding in response to the BAFO.

Typically, such deletions are made in the area of process design rather than product design. The presumption is that by the time production arrives, the best way to build the product will be known. Unfortunately, process design and product design are as integral in full-scale engineering development as they are in production, and inadequate process control can be equally devastating in both domains. The case study in Section 5.12.1 illustrates this point.

There is also a psychological aspect to the BAFO process that needs to be remembered. People begin to believe a number, such as a BAFO, after it has been around for a while, and tend to forget both the original value of the number and the manner in which the revised number was derived, until such time as problems start to occur. These problems are exacerbated by a series of BAFOs for a given acquisition and are equally prevalent in both the customer's shop and the contractor's shop.

Carried to an extreme, BAFOs will invariably result in "lose–lose" situations both for the customer and for the contractor. Customers should ensure that contractors presently have the capability and resources to support their BAFOs. The caution exercised by contractors in providing BAFOs should be directly proportional to the technical challenges involved and the financial commitments required. There comes a time to stand firm when treading in uncharted waters for economic reasons in the present and credibility in the future.

5.2   INDUSTRIAL MODERNIZATION INCENTIVES PROGRAM

The subject of industrial productivity has been a major concern during the past decade as the United States has lost significant ground to international competitors. This has also been a major concern of the Department of Defense (DoD) with respect to its industrial contracting base.

The defense industry can be characterized to a large measure as being outmoded, inefficient, very labor intensive, and very reluctant to modernize. The latter has been attributed primarily to the high degree of program uncertainties in the DoD and to the cost-based profit policy of the DoD.

The cost-based profit policy means that productivity improvements initiated by contractors permit recovery of a portion of early cost savings but reduce the profit potential of future contracts. This policy has lead to emphasis in the defense industry on short-term return on investment and conservative capital asset management.

The DoD instituted the industrial modernization incentives program (IMIP) to help focus contractor resources on industrial modernization and to support the development of more cost-efficient production systems for military materiel. Under IMIP, incentives are provided to motivate contractors to invest their own funds in improvements that result in reducing acquisition costs.

The major incentives under IMIP are the contractor's share in the savings and protection of the contractor's investment, which involves the government's commitment to buy from the contractor the undepreciated portion of the capital asset of interest in the event that the particular program is terminated. In a few instances, protection is provided by a guarantee of a long-term business base against which investment cost can be recovered. It should be noted, however, that the approval chain for contingent liabilities greater than $10 million includes the Congress of the United States.

Contractors may wish to consider IMIP as part of their business strategy for a particular program area. The government's thrust is to consider IMIP early in the acquisition cycle as part of the acquisition strategy for the program area, although the ultimate decision depends on the funding profile over the program's life cycle.

Typically, IMIP is accomplished in three phases as shown in Figure 5.1. Phase I is a structured analysis of the contractor's total manufacturing capability to identify the interaction of the functional systems. Once the existing systems are understood, a conceptual design of the most cost-efficient factory for the program is developed along with the projected cost savings.

The objective of Phase II is to identify and validate all the technology needed to realize this cost-efficient factory. The output of Phase II includes the design of the factory and plans for purchase and installation of the capital equipment and supporting software.

The objective of Phase III is the physical realization of this cost-efficient factory and bringing it on-line. Phase III includes the purchase and installation of the aforementioned capital equipment and supporting software, and the integration of individual manufacturing subsystems into an optimized system for the particular program.

The shared savings shown in Figure 5.1 are the primary IMIP contract incentives. Sharing relationships are similar to those used for implemented value engineering change proposals (see Section 2.8.3) ranging from about 25

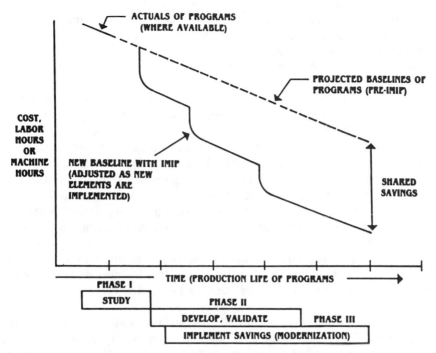

Figure 5.1 Industrial modernization incentives program (1). (Source: Defense Systems Management College, *Industrial Modernization Incentives Program*, 1985.)

percent for the contractor where upfront government funding or guarantees are provided to about 50 percent in their absence.

Industry decisions to participate in IMIP should consider not only the needs of the factory but also the long-range plan of the particular company. Significant investment is involved, and cost–benefit analysis should be conducted using the time value of money relationships in Section 6.7.

It should also be noted that substantial amounts of financial analysis and verification are required in IMIP and that the government is both an investigative and approving participant in these matters. Both the cost of these efforts and their implications in a marketplace that is almost all fixed-price and where such revelations are normally not made should also be considered before participating in IMIP.

5.3 INDIRECT COST MANAGEMENT

Understanding the concept of indirect cost management is important because, while the services provided by indirect costs are needed by either the program in question or by the business as a whole, the services themselves make very little direct contribution to the value of what is being produced.

From the perspective of the customer, the cost of these services appears somewhat unnecessary and the issue essentially concerns how much of the indirect cost should be borne by the customer.

In the government contracting arena, indirect costs are usually subdivided into the cost categories of overhead and general and administrative (G&A). Overhead costs support specific parts or functions of a company but not the whole company. For example, factory maintenance is included in what is called the "manufacturing overhead pool" along with costs such as quality control support. In contrast, planning support and configuration and data management, which are referred to as "other technical services," would be included in what is called the "engineering overhead pool."

The G&A costs are required to support the business as a whole and cannot logically be assigned to any particular grouping of cost objectives. Typical examples of G&A costs are executive salaries and legal and accounting fees.

The term "cost objective" is used to denote a specific cost account such as for a product or a contract. Direct costs can be identified with a single cost objective, whereas indirect costs need to be related to two or more cost objectives.

The factors commonly used to allocate indirect costs to cost objectives are (1) direct labor cost to allocate manufacturing or engineering overhead, (2) direct material cost to allocate material handling costs, and (3) total cost to allocate G&A costs. The resultant overhead and G&A rates are used for (1) pricing and negotiating proposals, (2) progress payments during the period of contract performances, and (3) contractor's fiscal year end determination of final allowable costs on cost reimbursable contracts.

Indirect costs typically represent between one-third to one-half of the cost of contracts with components of the DoD. From the perspective of the customer, indirect costs appear somewhat unnecessary relative to the value of the desired products or systems and thus are subjected to much scrutiny for their allowability. Design-to-cost practitioners should remember and apply the measures of reasonableness and allocability used to determine allowability by government.

A reasonable cost in its nature and amount does not exceed that which would be incurred by a prudent person in the conduct of competitive business. A cost is allocable to a contract if

It is assignable to one or more cost objectives on the basis of relative benefits received.

It is incurred specifically for the contract.

It benefits both the contract and other work but can be distributed to them in reasonable proportion to the benefits received.

It is necessary to the overall operation of the business even though a direct relationship to any particular cost objective cannot be shown.

TABLE 5.1 Principles of Overhead Control (2)

Prospective pricing. Priority emphasis must be placed on prospective pricing of overhead costs; government officials must strive for cost avoidance, using fair and reasonable criteria, before contractor overhead costs are incurred; the most effective cost control will be realized through sound forward pricing rate agreements and advance agreements negotiated between the government and the contractor

Continuous evaluation. Effective overhead cost control begins with forward pricing and ends with final settlement; the validity of forward pricing projections must be constantly assessed, and actions to correct such projections shall be promptly undertaken by government officials

Business base. Future business forecasts are important in developing accurate, cost-effective overhead rates; it is imperative for government officials to understand the contractor's budgetary systems used to estimate overhead allocation bases; the business volume underlying forward pricing agreements shall be regarded as cost and pricing data certified by the contractor

Discrete-cost analysis. Overhead costs must be evaluated on an element-by-element basis that concentrates on where management decisions are made; pricing methods which place undue emphasis on historical costs must be avoided; evaluation tools such as should cost, cost-monitoring reviews, and operation audits should be used to their fullest extent

Personnel cost. The factors associated with contractor personnel cost, which include employee population, wage and salary structure, and fringe-benefit plans, represent nearly two-thirds of all overhead costs; while there must be no interference with industry's collective bargaining process, the government has a responsibility to insure that costs absorbed on defense contracts are fair and reasonable; the contractor employee compensation system review is an important tool for evaluating these costs

Accounting system. Government officials must possess a thorough understanding of the cost accounting system used by the contractor; the cost accounting system must provide overhead allocation on a credible benefits-received basis in the aggregate and on individual items; government officials must also fully understand contractor management accounting systems, particularly as they relate to overhead planning and control

Team approach. Top-management commitment to the team approach is absolutely essential; contracting officers, cost and price analysts, functional experts, program managers, buying activities, and contract auditors must actively participate in all aspects of overhead cost control, and effective communications is vital

Government requirements. Government officials must be sensitive to the impact of their requirements on contractor overhead costs; care should be taken through solicitation review processes to ensure that contract requirements and their attendant administration genuinely contribute to program objectives

Contractor incentives. Government officials are challenged to be creative in employing incentives and techniques that will give the contractor a credible inducement to reduce overhead costs; such incentives could include contract incentive fee structure, industrial modernization incentives program, special productivity profit factor, and source selection consideration

People. Meaningful overhead cost control can be accomplished only by the diligent efforts of individual people; top management shall ensure that adequate personnel resources are applied to this area, not only in numbers but in talent as well; recruitment, training, and retention of qualified people is a priority responsibility

Source: Deputy Secretary of Defense, *Initiative to Reduce Overhead,* 1984.

It should be recognized that the issue of allowability serves as the basis for negotiating forward pricing (i.e., future fiscal year) rates and that forward pricing rate agreements are the biggest cost drivers in the fixed-price contracting arena. Two of the most difficult areas to evaluate in determining forward pricing rates are the reasonableness of the proposed level of indirect cost and the associated allocation base. This applies equally to contracting with the government and with subcontractors.

The negotiation of forward pricing rates provides the best leverage to influence contractor and subcontractor cost containment. Under some circumstances, contract delays, work stoppages, or even program cancellations should be considered if favorable forward pricing rate agreements cannot be attained.

It is interesting to note that the DoD has begun to examine the relationship between overhead and the cost-based profit policy that is promulgated by the DoD (see Section 3.2). This is part of an ongoing initiative to reduce the overhead structure of DoD contractors.

The approach of the DoD in containing such costs is summarized by the principles of overhead cost control given in Table 5.1. Note that priority emphasis is placed on prospective pricing (i.e., negotiated future pricing) of overhead costs. It is incumbent on the defense industry to ensure that these principles are emulated to the extent required in the respective organizations as part of their overall business strategy.

5.4   PROCUREMENT ALTERNATIVES

Various alternatives can be used to increase competition and lower the cost of procurement. Those used most often by customers to reduce cost are leader–follower, associate contractor, multiple source, breakout, and total package procurement. Those used most often by contractors to improve competitiveness are teaming and joint venture.

Table 5.2 summarizes the advantages and disadvantages of the various procurement alternatives. Additional details are given in the sections referenced in the parentheses. Note that the just-in-time (JIT) concept is included in the table since it can be used advantageously by both the customer and the contractor.

The alternatives should be assessed from a baseline of the classic business arrangement of continuous relationships between customers and contractors and between primes and subcontractors that continue from program conception through production.

5.4.1   Baseline

As stated above, the baseline for comparative purposes is the classic business arrangement wherein a prime contractor is selected and leads the pro-

TABLE 5.2 Procurement Alternatives

Alternative	Advantage	Disadvantage
Baseline (Section 5.4.1)	Best history Lowest risk Traditional rules Administrative ease	Reduced competition Higher cost
Leader–follower (Section 5.4.2)	Increased competition Lower recurring cost	Management difficulty Configuration control difficulty Higher nonrecurring cost
Associate contractor (Section 5.4.3)	Eliminates prime burden Lower cost	Integration difficulty Work share allocation Schedule difficulty Software difficulty
Multiple source (Section 5.4.4)	Increased competition Greater supply Lower recurring cost	Management difficulty Higher nonrecurring cost
Breakout (Section 5.4.5)	Increased competition Lower recurring cost	Management difficulty Schedule difficulty Higher nonrecurring cost
Total package procurement (Section 5.4.6)	Cost established up-front	Greater risk
Teaming (Section 5.4.7)	Better technical solution	Subcontractor commitment Production difficulty
Joint venture (Section 5.4.8)	Better technical solution; lower cost	Management difficulty Integration difficulty
Just-in-time (Section 5.4.9)	Lower cost	Supplier commitment

gram through the conceptual, development, and production phases. In essence, the prime contractor is in a sole source mode after a challenging competition to win the conceptual and development phases because of the customer's inability to sustain the nonrecurring cost of parallel sources at the prime and subcontractor levels.

Prime contractors utilize key technologies of various subcontractors and perform all the integration functions. This posture requires large investments on the part of prime contractors in whatever technologies and facilities are needed to become viable competitors. The motivation to make such investment is the anticipation of production and its attendant profit.

Large investments are also required on the part of customers. Research-and-development contracts are typically cost plus incentive fee or cost plus fixed fee due to the uncertainty in high-technology development. However, these contracts are relatively easy to administer and usually present the least technical risk because of the extensive history and experience in the approach.

The procurement alternatives described in the following sections are referred to as "creative procurement" in the government contracting arena. Some notable applications of these alternatives either by or with the concurrence of the government are

Leader–follower:	Hellfire Missile
Associate contractor:	NIMBUS Meteorological Spacecraft
Multiple source:	Main Battle Tank
Breakout:	Pershing Missile
Total package procurement:	C-5A Aircraft
Teaming:	Federal Telecommunication System FTS-2000
Joint venture:	Terminally Guided Weapon for the Multiple Launched Rocket System

5.4.2   Leader–Follower

"Leader-follower" is a procurement technique under which the developer and sole source producer of a system or complex high-technology product (the leader company) is required to transfer the necessary production technology and technical data base to a second source (the follower) selected by the customer, thus allowing the follower to become a competing source, and perhaps eventually a sole source for production. This approach is limited to situations satisfying the following conditions:

The leader company possesses the necessary know-how and is able to furnish requisite assistance to the follower.

No source of supply other than the leader company would be able to meet the customer's requirements without the leader's assistance.

The assistance required of the leader is limited to that which is essential to enable the follower company to produce the product.

Customers reserve the right to approve ensuing leader–follower contracts.

The leader–follower approach is worthy of consideration by companies as a competition fostering approach in procurement. The programmatic and economic issues listed in Table 5.3 should be considered in establishing such arrangements.

The advantage of the leader–follower approach is that it transfers part or all of the production of complex systems or products to a second source. Competition determines the most economical split of the acquisition for the

TABLE 5.3 Leader–Follower Issues (3)

Programmatic Issues

Realistic annual buy quantities and rates
Manufacturing complexity
Degree of manufacturing automation
Learning curves for material and labor
Design stability
Importance of proprietary data and processes
Prime contract content
Facility requirements
Multiple sourcing for critical components
Multiple sourcing for market demand
Multiple sourcing for war mobilization

Economic Issues

Cost of technology transfer
Cost of production qualification
Cost of reduced quantity base
Cost of lost learning
Reduced profit expectation
Reduced allocated burden
Multiple sourcing for competition
Financial stability of companies

Adapted by permission of the Martin Marietta Corporation.

customer. The follower is encouraged to improve the leader's baseline for increased cost-effectiveness and competitive posture.

The major disadvantage of the leader–follower concept from the customer's perspective is the high nonrecurring cost of duplicate tooling and other production items. From industry's perspective, the major disadvantage is the lack of royalty provisions for proprietary data and of the protection present in licensing agreements. Finally, problems can arise between the leader and follower when the leader is required by the customer to warrant the product.

5.4.3 Associate Contractor

This strategy is similar to that of joint ventures by contractors except that the customer is now responsible for schedule and interface control among the associate contractors, and for the integration of the system components. In many cases, the customer may execute a hardware-exclusion contract with another company to provide these functions.

The key advantage is that the burden and profit of a prime contractor are avoided. Problems frequently arise in the design, documentation, and control of the interfaces among associate contractors, particularly in software and hardware–software integration and test. Even more problematic, however, is enforcing schedule adherence.

There have been more instances of schedule slips and overruns in associate contractor relationships than in the other forms of contracting. The case study in Section 5.12.3 illustrates this point.

5.4.4 Multiple Sourcing

Multiple sourcing is discussed in this section from the perspective of customers; however, the observations are pertinent to contractors in their dealings with suppliers.

The promise of profit motivates entrepreneurs to enter their products into competition in the marketplace. Companies make and sell products inexpensively to obtain as large a share of the market as possible. To accomplish this objective, companies invest capital and operate with narrow profit margins. Customers would like to have this market force working for them to reduce procurement costs.

Competition usually reduces cost, but occasionally the result is increased overall cost caused by the effort needed to bring on board additional suppliers. Careful planning and analysis of the sensitivity to the risks of competition are necessary to ensure that competition does, indeed, reduce cost. Each case needs to be analyzed to determine whether the investment in competition will really pay (4).

Table 5.4 lists the factors to be considered in multiple sourcing decisions. The case study in Section 5.5.3 illustrates the military's experience in such endeavors.

TABLE 5.4   Multiple Sourcing Considerations (5)

Quantity to be procured
Duration of production
Slope of learning curves
Complexity of the system
State of the art
Other potential applications of products
Degree of privately funded R&D required
Cost of transferring unique tooling and equipment
Supplier capacity
Maintenance concept to be employed
Production lead time
Number type of suppliers available
Contractual complexity

Adapted by permission of the Martin Marietta Corporation.

Several points in Table 5.4 warrant amplification. The less steep the learning curve, the more adaptable to multiple sourcing the product becomes; the steeper the learning curve, the less likely a second source can effectively compete with the original producer. The more complex the system, the more essential is cooperation and liaison between multiple production sources, and the less adaptable the system is to multiple sourcing.

If the technology employed in the system leads the state of the art, it is unlikely that another source will be able to produce the system without significant difficulty, unless there is extraordinary cooperation between original and other suppliers.

Multiple sourcing can have significant impact on the maintenance concept for the system. Whenever two systems of the same type are not identical, the ability to support those systems with repair parts and maintenance personnel becomes more difficult and costly.

The more complex the original production contract the less adaptable it becomes to multiple sourcing. With warranties, for example, it may be necessary to keep all sources capable of performing warranty work throughout the lifetime of the program.

5.4.5 Breakout

Breakout is a cost reduction technique used by customers, particularly the federal government, following successful development of systems. The customer contracts directly with subcontractors for items that were subcontracted by the prime.

The problem frequently encountered by customers is the inadequacy of the technical data package (TDP) to enable contracting with suppliers other than the original subcontractors. The governing specification for contracting with the military is DOD-D-1000B, *Drawings, Engineering and Associated Lists*. The specification defines the following three levels of documentation, but it is the procuring activity that specifies which level shall apply in a particular contract:

Level 1:   Conceptual and developmental design
Level 2:   Production prototype and limited production
Level 3:   Production

In the interest of economy, it has been customary to contract for Level 2 documentation through the period of full production. This situation tends to perpetuate the limited competition environment that may have existed between the prime and the subcontractors and limit the cost-saving potential of breakout.

From the prime contractor's perspective, care should be taken that the prime is relieved of responsibility and that the customer now assumes the risk. In addition, the prime contractor should take advantage of the opportunity to obtain a service contract to support the breakout item with the additional technical detail lacking in the TDP.

5.4.6   Total Package Procurement

The total package procurement schema was fostered in the Department of Defense (DoD) by Robert S. McNamara as an extraordinary cost-saving strategy for the acquisition, operation and support of major systems. The approach is to contract for the entire program from development through production and support, including spares, at a single price based on the lowest bid for the total package, prior to the start of the program. The experience with the C-5A aircraft was extremely costly.

The firm fixed price with options strategy is a variation of total package procurement. Whereas total package procurement is both for development and for production, the former consists of only a firm fixed price contract for the first production buy and initial spares and includes priced options for some, but not all, subsequent buys. Generally, support equipment and operational spares are not included, but are procured by another command under a separate contract.

The major problems both with total package procurement and with firm fixed price with options are accommodating design changes whose need are uncovered during qualification testing, compensating for delays brought about by external circumstances, and dealing with inflation and escalation. The approach to the latter is discussed in Section 6.8.3.

5.4.7   Teaming

Teaming is primarily a contractor strategy, although there have been several teaming agreements among nations within the North Atlantic Treaty Organization (NATO) and within the European Common Market. Teaming agreements are legal commitments that define the various work shares and who will be prime and who will be subcontractor in the event the contract is awarded to the team. Teaming agreements are usually exclusive, meaning that team members will not enter into agreements with other competitors.

These agreements are becoming more common as more companies acquire in-depth technical specialties and teams are generally superior technically. Such corporate marriages serve the mutual interest of the team members during the early phases of programs.

These relationships, however, seldom remain healthy as competition for production approaches. The case study in Section 3.14.4 illustrates this point on an international level.

5.4.8   Joint Venture

Joint venture is also a contractor strategy, although there is a parallel to the customer's attempt to use the associate-contractor strategy for cost saving.

A joint venture, sometimes referred to as a consortium, is a business structure formed when two or more contractors combine their efforts to complete a business transaction without the cost penalty of the prime-subcontractor relationship.

In a joint venture, prime-level contractors join legally to provide various parts of complex systems with agreed-on investments and work shares. Because of the broad capability base, joint ventures exhibit a high degree of technical superiority.

A variation of this strategy features the formation of a holding company that becomes responsible for integration and interface with the customer. This tends to minimize some of the legal exposure of the members of the joint venture.

In recent times, U.S. and offshore companies have formed such joint ventures, usually in response to a teaming agreement among their respective nations. Typically, the nations require technology exchange among the members of the joint venture, which often poses a problem. As frequently in teaming agreements, relationships in joint ventures become testy as production approaches.

5.4.9   Just-in-Time Procurement

Just-in-time (JIT) procurement is a concept wherein the flow of parts and material goes directly from suppliers to workstations on production lines at precisely the time that these items are needed at the workstations. Furthermore, the quality of the parts and material is such that no further inspection is required after they are shipped by the supplier.

In this regard, JIT procurement has been referred to as a "pull system" rather than the "push system" represented by the classical procurement approach of receiving, inspecting, stocking, and issuing parts and material. Just-in-time procurement is somewhat synonymous to the system called "zero inventory" that is discussed below and in Section 5.5.3.

Just-in-time procurement is a powerful concept for reducing cost and improving quality by reducing the cost associated with work in process and other elements of inventory. Pioneered by the Japanese, it has been adopted by some manufacturers in the U.S. automotive industry with excellent results.

The prerequisite for JIT is a group of very dependable suppliers who are willing to assume considerable responsibility for both quality and timeliness of their deliveries. The implementation of JIT procurement as well as JIT manufacturing requires a commitment on the part of the prime contractor to the new quality and to the concept of product uniformity discussed in Section 4.5.

The discussion of JIT procurement continues in Section 5.9.2 in the context of zero inventory. The concept of zero inventory goes beyond JIT procurement to include zero work in process in any inventory. Items are fabricated precisely at the time that they are needed for the next higher assembly in a given product. The concept of zero inventory is particularly appealing to high-technology enterprises because of the high proportion of expenditures on parts and material, the large amount of work in process (WIP) because of yield problems, and, of course, the substantial amount of capital that needs to be committed to inventory acquisition and control.

5.5 FLOWDOWN TO SUPPLIERS

The flowdown of both requirements and incentives to subcontractors and major suppliers is essential in achieving cost goals. Government policy requires such flowdown for value engineering in subcontracts of $100,000 or more, and does not prevent the flowdown in contracts of a lesser amount if warranted. The government often requires the flowdown of requirements and directs that award fees and incentives for design to cost as well as value engineering be in accordance with the work-share division among the prime contractor and subcontractor.

Notwithstanding externally imposed requirements, it is essential for programs to flow down requirements and incentives to subcontractors and suppliers to ensure the maximum possible cost reduction in procurement. To do so, it is important to understand the difference between subcontractors and vendors.

A subcontractor supplies goods or services to the buyer's specifications under contract. Buyers are responsible for the design and compatibility of such goods and services with their system; subcontractors are responsible for quality and schedules but not for design faults.

A vendor supplies goods or services to the buyer under a simple purchase order. The buyer is responsible only for the suitability of such items to the intended purposes; the supplier is responsible for design and performance, resulting from invention and expertise, as well as for quality and schedule.

5.5.1 Requirements Flowdown

Requests for proposals (RFPs) are typically too general and lacking in the specificity needed for flowdown. Design-to-cost requirements should be explicitly stated in contracts with subcontractors and other major suppliers. The schema for measuring and tracking performance and the method for computing award and incentive fees should be included in the statement of requirements.

Table 5.5 is a checklist of design-to-cost requirements that should be incorporated in such contracts. There should be absolutely no ambiguity in the stated requirements nor in the expected results. Above all, there should be no question on the part of the subcontractor or supplier of how performance will be rated. It is appropriate to rate performance with a numerical score to facilitate the computation of award and incentive fees. Table 5.6 provides suggested rating and scoring guidelines.

TABLE 5.5 Design-to-Cost Requirements Checklist (5)

Define Contractual Requirements

Specify work-breakdown structure (WBS)
Specify nonrecurring and recurring cost elements
Specify schedule
Specify production quantity and rate
Specify learning curve and cumulative average unit cost

Define Measurement Schema

Specify adjustments for schedule and production quantity and rate changes
Specify treatment of inflation and escalation
Specify performance rating and scoring criteria
Specify key measurement milestones

Define Tracking Schema

Specify frequency of reporting
Specify level of detail and formats

Define Award and Incentive Fees Schema

Specify evaluation periods
Specify formulation
Specify cost and fee sharing limits

Adapted by permission of the Martin Marietta Corporation.

TABLE 5.6 Performance Rating and Scoring (6)

Rating	Points
Outstanding. Performance exceeds the general level of competence expected of a qualified contractor in this field by a wide margin, approaching the highest achievable standard; demonstrates a pattern of meritorious and noteworthy accomplishment	96–100
Above average. Performance significantly exceeds the general level of competence expected of a qualified contractor in this field; areas of deficient performance, if any, are few in number and low in importance	86–95
Average. Performance achieves the approximate general level of competence expected of a qualified contractor in this field. Areas of deficient performance, if any, are approximately of the same number and importance as areas of performance that exceed the average competence level	76–85
Below average. Performance is adequate on an overall basis but does not achieve the general level of competence expected of a qualified contractor in this field.	66–75
Minimum. Performance is deficient in a number of important areas	

Adapted by permission of the Martin Marietta Corporation.

5.5.2   Incentives Flowdown

Suppliers can be motivated by award fees or incentives, which are two different contractual strategies. Both may be employed on the same contract between the customer and the prime contractor and consequentially can be used on the same subcontract.

Award fees are based on an appraisal of the overall performance of the contractor in balancing performance, schedule, and cost within contractual requirements. An award fee is not a fee to which the contractor is automatically entitled by achievement of a single objective. Award fee appraisals are both subjective and objective.

The subjective appraisal represents the customer's opinion of the contractor's performance and is expressed in terms of adjective ratings ranging from minimum competence (or poor), to outstanding competence as defined in Table 5.6. The objective portion of the appraisal is keyed to cost performance in terms of variance from cost goals. At the conclusion of any evaluation period, either estimated or actual costs are compared to goals, and the objective scoring is computed on the basis of the variance.

Incentives are above any award fee structure in the contract. Typical incentives are structured in terms of a sharing ratio as shown in Figure 5.2. For example, 70/30 signifies that the customer's share of cost underrun or overrun is 70 percent whereas the contractor's share is 30 percent.

An upper limit to cost overruns is specified beyond which contractors are not reimbursed for cost. This limit, referred to as the "point of total assumption," is indicated in Figure 5.2 as 1.2 times the negotiated target cost.

Incentives flowdown to suppliers has provided mixed results, with award fee arrangements faring somewhat better. The relatively poor performance of incentives has been due to the top-down nature of the arrangements, generally expressed in terms of a percentage of the prime contractor's share of savings. By the time the savings share filters down to the supplier, the dollar amount is insufficient to motivate the effort needed for serious cost

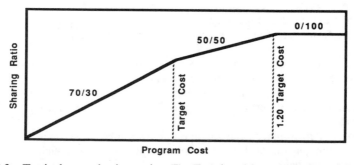

Figure 5.2   Typical cost-sharing ratios (7). (Reprinted by permission of the Martin Marietta Corporation.)

reduction. In addition, the prime contractor's burden on the supplier's selling price inflates the cost baseline for computing incentive fees.

The relatively better performance of award fee arrangements is due to specifying work-share division as the basis for allocating fee. However, these arrangements are also top-down in nature, and the award fees available to suppliers are eroded by the manner in which costs are compounded.

The alternative business strategy employing bottom-up arrangements will go a long way toward motivating suppliers to extend the effort to reduce cost. With regard to value engineering, it should be noted that the Federal Acquisition Regulation (FAR) does not preclude the bottom-up approach application in instant contracts, only in concurrent and future contracts. Notwithstanding the restrictions, positive response can be expected from suppliers, because they are not necessarily involved in concurrent contracts and future contracts.

5.6 MAKE-OR-BUY DECISIONS

Make-or-buy decisions in the U.S. high-technology industry are typically in a state of flux because of the nature of the business. A large portion of the business base of major high-technology concerns is assembly, integration, and test of components that are obtained mostly from abroad. However, the industry has substantial tooling investment, which it needs to continue to maintain its technology edge.

The burden of investments increases overhead and, in turn, competitiveness. Make-or-buy decisions become trade-offs of putting work on the factory floor and lower cost components in the stockroom. A certain amount of value-added work-in-process (WIP) is essential to maintain both expertise and fiscal soundness, but should not be carried to an extent that causes costs to be noncompetitive. However, putting all the work outside increases inordinately the overhead on indirect labor.

The question of how to achieve the optimal balance of make-and-buy with respect to functionality, quality, and affordability is the thrust of this section. The process should start with the enunciation of company policy that is conducive to correct decisions. Then, unequivocal make-or-buy decision criteria should be delineated as guidance to both program and functional organizations within a company and sister companies.

5.6.1 Company Policy

Company policy in the make-or-buy area is sometimes viewed as being detrimental to achieving design-to-cost goals despite the mutual objective of growth and profitability. The following suggestions can be the bases of a rational policy that considers design to cost as an income-producing asset similar to capital investment:

Fabrication, assembly, and test operations that are within the company's capability, are appropriate to its facilities, and are cost-competitive should be "make" items.

Manufacturing operations that cannot be performed with facilities existing during the time frame of the particular program; standard, off-the-shelf, and brand name items; raw materials; and items proprietary to other firms should be "buy" items.

There should be a standing make-or-buy committee to ensure uniform observance of the policy and make-or-buy decision criteria. In addition, the committee should maintain liaison with other divisions of the company to ensure that their products and services are also considered when attempting to achieve the most competitive vantage point.

5.6.2 Decision Criteria

Full consideration of the make-or-buy decision criteria given in Table 5.7 should be mandatory for all functional disciplines in the company, not those on only the particular program of interest. In addition, both the design-to-cost manager and the program director should be signatory to the make-or-buy decision.

Once a decision has been reached to buy, it is important to undertake an aggressive and sustained effort to select the most competitive among the qualified suppliers, and to implement the system of supplier surveillance discussed in Section 3.5.2 to prevent last minute surprises. The selected suppliers should understand and express the willingness to perform under the concept of the "new quality."

TABLE 5.7   Make-or-Buy Decision Criteria (8)

Previous manufacturing experience on like items
Compatibility and fit with planned lines of business and existing or planned facilitization
Plant labor load and the resulting effect on burden rate
Learning retention value in shop performance and internal shop training
Compatibility with customer objectives
Future requirements and market projections
Competitive considerations and proprietary aspects
Comparative cost and schedule considerations
Susceptibility to change during production phase
Quality control and product reliability aspects
Fragility of items, packaging and transportation problems, and cost
Existence and availability of competent suppliers

Adapted by permission of the Martin Marietta Corporation.

5.7   SCHEDULING STRATEGIES

It is axiomatic that time is money, and it would appear that schedule compression should result in reduced overall cost of products or systems. The true answer, however, can be gleaned only by scheduling programs with utmost realism, ensuring that no element of work is overlooked, and assessing the cost consequences on an overall program basis of manipulating the time duration of the various elements of work.

This section introduces schedule planning and control techniques that are the means for such manipulation and assessment. Potential economies in resource leveling, payment progressing (with subcontractors), and least-cost scheduling are then explored.

5.7.1   Schedule Management Techniques

Schedule management entails planning and control. Although there are many diverse techniques in use, they are based mostly on the early work of two different organizations.

The program evaluation and review technique (PERT) was developed in the 1950s by the U.S. Navy for planning and control of the Polaris Missile Program. At about the same time, the duPont Company (E. I. DuPont de Nemours & Co.) developed the critical-path method, (CPM) for planning and control of chemical plant maintenance. Success of PERT and CPM may be gauged by the 2-year reduction in the Polaris development cycle and the more than 37 percent reduction in maintenance downtime at the duPont Louisville works (9).

Figure 5.3 provides a comparison of PERT and CPM to the classical bar-chart form of scheduling. The letters denote activities and the numbers are the time duration of the respective activities. The bar chart shown in part *a* of the illustration does not reveal the precedence of activities and culminating events (encircled numbers) as do PERT and CPM, which are shown in parts *b* and *c*.

Although PERT and CPM are based on substantially the same concept, there are some differences in details. Whereas PERT uses probabilistic estimates of activity duration times along the various paths constituting a network of activities, referred to as "pessimistic," "expected," and "optimistic," CPM is characterized as being deterministic in that it uses constant estimates of activity duration times. While CPM is usually encountered in the form shown in part *c* of Figure 5.3, emphasizing the critical path in the network, PERT usually appears in the form in part *b*. In either case, the heavy lines represent the critical path and the forms can be used interchangeably.

The salient difference in classical PERT would be the appearance of three estimates of time for each activity rather than only one. For example, in part *b* of Figure 5.3, the notation under E could be respectively 0.8, 1.0, and 1.2

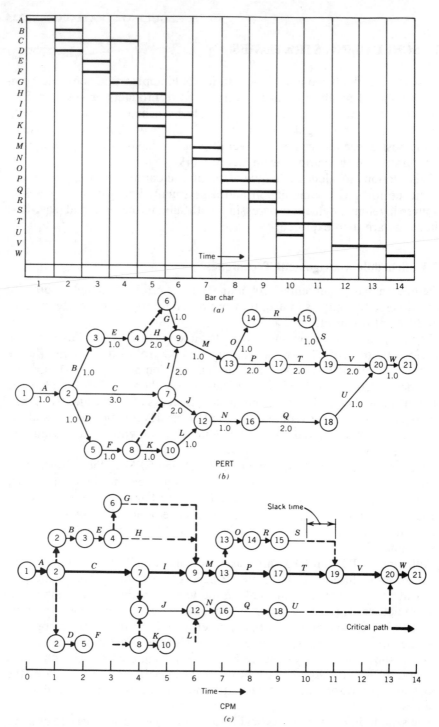

Figure 5.3 Comparison of bar chart, PERT, and CPM (10). (Adapted by permission of John Wiley & Sons, Inc.)

for the optimistic, expected, and pessimistic estimates of duration time for that activity.

The procedure for developing PERT and CPM networks consists of activity analysis, arrow diagramming, and path enumeration. The latter step reveals the critical path of the network.

1. ACTIVITY ANALYSIS

The objective of activity analysis is to illuminate the interrelationships of the activities making up the program. This is done by discerning answers to the following questions:

What activities need to be performed?
What is the duration of each activity?
Which activities immediately precede other given activities?
Which activities immediately succeed other given activities?

Answers to these questions appear in the form given in Table 5.8. The answers to the third and fourth questions may appear redundant; however,

TABLE 5.8   Activities Precedence and Duration

Activity	Duration	Predecessor	Successor
a	0	None	b
b	4	a	c
c	2	b	d,f,r
d	4	c	e,i,j
e	6	d	p
f	1	c	g,h
g	2	f	j
h	3	f	k
i	2	d	k
j	4	d,g	k
k	10	i,j,h	l
l	3	k	m,n,o
m	1	l	r
n	2	l	r
o	3	l	s
p	2	e	q
q	1	p	v
r	1	c	v
s	2	o,t	x
t	3	m,n	s,u
u	1	t	x
v	2	q,r	w
w	5	v	x
x	0	s,u,w	None

they are used to facilitate "arrow diagramming" as well as providing checks on the activity and precedence listings. Units of time in the "Duration" column of Table 5.8 should be compatible with the way costs are estimated and collected in the particular program.

2. ARROW DIAGRAMMING

This step portrays the precedence relationships among the activities comprising the network. The usual practice is to work backward through the list of activities, delineating each successive immediate predecessor activity until reaching the beginning of the network that has no predecessors. Alternatively, the network can be developed by delineating each successive immediate successor activity until reaching the end of the network that has no successors.

Activities in the network terminate at nodal points that are referred to as "events." As shown in Figure 5.4, it is sometimes necessary to introduce dummy activities and events to eliminate ambiguity regarding precedence. Transforming the arrangement in part *a* of the illustration to that of part *b* reveals the correct predecessors for activities *u* and *s*. Similarly, transforming part *c* to part *d* clarifies the end events of activities *m* and *n*. The end product of this step is shown in Figure 5.5. This is the PERT diagram for the activities and precedences listed in Table 5.8.

3. PATH ENUMERATION

Figure 5.5 reveals many alternate paths that progress from beginning event 1 to ending event 20. Path enumeration is simply the task of summing

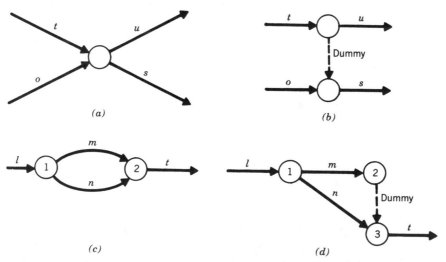

Figure 5.4 Dummy activities and events in PERT (11). (Adapted by permission of John Wiley & Sons, Inc.)

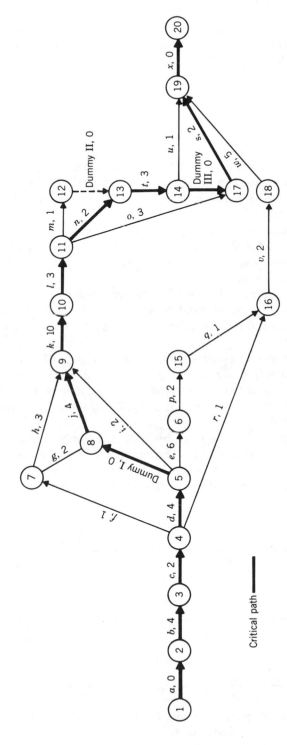

Figure 5.5 Performance evaluation and review technique diagram (12). (Reprinted by permission of John Wiley & Sons, Inc.)

Critical path ——

the total time required along each path. The path requiring the greatest amount of time is the critical path. The critical path is indicated by the heavy line in the illustration and requires 34 units of time. Relative to the critical path, there is slack in the other paths and nodes of the network. Slack analysis provides the basis for resource leveling, payment progressing, and least-cost scheduling, which are discussed next.

5.7.2 Resource Leveling

The critical path in the network identifies activities that must be completed on time for the on-time completion of the program. The corollary to this statement is that the critical path in the network requires the longest amount of time to complete.

Activities that are not on the critical path have some slack, or float time, and could be delayed without adverse effect on the program. Some of the resources in the non-critical-path activities could be devoted to accelerating those on the critical path.

Figure 5.6 and Table 5.9 demonstrate the application of resource leveling. The illustration is a small segment of a hypothetical network rendered in CPM form. The critical path is indicated by the heavy line and consists of activities B and E.

The slack at a node, or event, is simply the latest time that the event could occur, without affecting the critical path, less the earliest time of occurrence. The slack in an activity equals the latest time that the activity could be completed (also without affecting the critical path) less the earliest time it could be completed.

Events in Figure 5.6 are denoted by encircled numbers and activities by uppercase letters of the alphabet. The number directly below the activity letters and path lines is the duration of the respective activity.

The numbers in the parentheses above the path lines are the start and

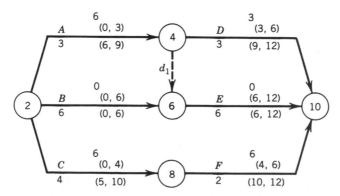

Figure 5.6 Critical-path method network for resource leveling (13). (Reprinted by permission of John Wiley & Sons, Inc.)

TABLE 5.9 Resource Leveling Worksheet (14)

Activity	Normal Duration	Worker-Days	Crew Normal	Size Minimum	1	2	3	4	5	6	7	8	9	10	11	12		Total
A	3	15	5	3	5	5	5											15
B	6	24	4	4	4	4	4	4	4	4								24
C	4	16	4	1	4	4	4	4										16
D	3	9	3	1				3	3	3								9
E	6	24	4	4							4	4	4	4	4	4		24
F	2	12	6	4					6	6								12
Total	Worker-days	100			13	13	13	11	13	13	4	4	4	4	4	4	=	100
A	3	15	5	3		3	3	3	3	3								15
B	6	24	4	4	4	4	4	4	4	4								24
C	4	16	4	1	2	2	2	2	2	2	2	2						16
D	3	9	3	1							3	3	1	1	1			9
E	6	24	4	4							4	4	4	4	4	4		24
F	2	12	6	4									4	4	4			12
Total	Worker-days	100			6	9	9	9	9	9	9	9	9	9	9	4	=	100

Adapted by permission of John Wiley & Sons, Inc.

completion times of the respective activity, and the number above and to the left of the parenthetical numbers is the slack, or float time, in the respective activity. Note that the latter are zero along the critical path. Finally, the numbers in parentheses below the path lines are the start and completion times that resulted from resource leveling.

The top part of Table 5.8 depicts the original labor loading that went from a peak of 13 worker-days to a low of 4 worker-days. The bottom part of the table reveals the results of resource leveling. With the exception of the first and last days, labor loading is constant at 9 worker-days, avoiding the penalty of overtime or increasing crew size. Note also that the labor loading of critical path activities is not reduced.

5.7.3 Payment Progressing

The rationale and approach for resource leveling is equally applicable to work scheduling for suppliers and their progress payments for work completed or items delivered. Considering the large percentage of high-technology product costs expended on procurement, significant reduction in cash flow and overall program cost may be achievable.

In payment progressing, it is necessary to reach an advance agreement with participating suppliers on percent completion milestones for each item on the purchase order or subcontract, and on a delivery schedule that has been derived along the lines of resource leveling.

Figure 5.7 illustrates the concept of payment progressing. The heavy line

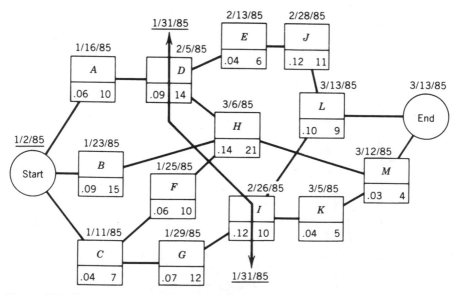

Figure 5.7 Payment progressing example (15). (Reprinted by permission of John Wiley & Sons, Inc.)

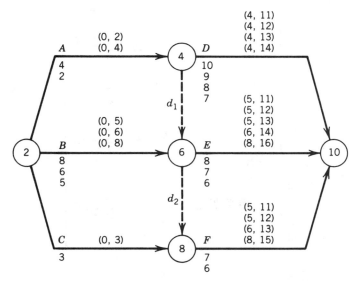

Figure 5.8 Least-cost scheduling example (16). (Reprinted by permission of John Wiley & Sons, Inc.)

represents the current progress line and the occasion for the current payment to the supplier. The value in place for each activity, expressed as a percentage of the purchase order or subcontract, is shown in each activity box, and the dates above the upper right corner of the boxes are schedule activity completion dates.

The progress line shows that the value received from the supplier is the percentages depicted for activities A, B, C, D, F, and G and a prorated share of the percentages for activities D and I. With this arrangement, cash flow can be minimized and procurement saving maximized.

5.7.4 Least-Cost Scheduling

The rationale for least-cost scheduling is that a relatively small increase in direct cost for accelerating critical path activities may result in a far greater cost saving from indirect cost (overhead) reduction in the overall program. The approach is essentially one of schedule compression.

The assumption made regarding the linearity of the relationship between schedule compression and direct cost increase is a major risk causative. The assumption of linearity—meaning that one unit of schedule compression induces one unit of direct cost increase and, therefore, x units of compression, induces x units of increased cost—can be off dramatically. It is advisable, therefore, to attempt least-cost scheduling only with proven cost-estimating relationships.

Figure 5.8 and Table 5.10 demonstrate the application of least-cost scheduling. The process is carried out with the following steps:

TABLE 5.10 Least-Cost Scheduling Worksheet (17)

Activity	Cost ($)		Duration, Days		Difference, ($)	Difference in Duration	Dollars/Day	Days	Cut		
	Crash	Normal	Crash	Normal							
A	500	400	4	2	100	2	50				
B	980	800	8	5	180	3	60	2			
C	700	600	3	2	100	1	100		1		
D	600	500	10	6	100	4	25				
E	950	800	8	6	150	2	75			1	1
F	1000	700	7	4	300	3	100			1	1
Project duration							16	14	13	12	11
Days reduced								2	1	1	1
Dollars/day								60	85	100	200
Dollars increase								120	85	100	200
Direct cost							3800	3920	4005	4105	4305
Indirect cost							1600	1400	1300	1200	1100
Total cost							5400	5320	5305	5305	5405

Adapted by permission of John Wiley & Sons, Inc.

1. Figure 5.8 shows that there is one critical path consisting of activities B and E with a duration of 16 days. According to Table 5.10, it costs $60 per day to shorten activity B and $75 per day to shorten activity E.

2. Activity B is shortened by 2 days, thus shortening the program duration from 16 to 14 days. Increasing direct cost from $3800 to $3920, decreasing indirect cost from $166 to $1400, and decreasing program cost from $5400 to $5320.

3. As a result of step 2, there are now two critical paths consisting of activities A and D and activities B and E. The approach is to shorten activities D and B by 1 day each, which reduces the program duration to 13 days and the program cost to $5305 as shown in Table 5.10.

4. There are still two critical paths consisting of activities A and D and activities B and E. Activity B, however, is at its crash duration, so activities D and E are shortened by 1 day each. The program duration is reduced to 12 days, but the program cost remains at $5305.

5. As shown in Table 5.10, the next attempt at shortening results in the increase of program cost to $5405. The exercise should be terminated at either step 3 or 4.

5.8 CAPACITY PLANNING

Capacity planning is an important element in maximizing affordability and profitability for two points of view: in the short term, it can ensure the most cost-efficient utilization of material, labor, and other resources in manufacturing the particular product of interest; in the long term, it can ensure both the optimal capital investment strategy and the maximum return on investment in concert with the long-range plan of the organization.

This section presents an overview of linear programming as a recommended tool for capacity planning. Linear programming provides an analytical methodology for allocating limited resources among competing alternative applications so that some predetermined objective, such as minimizing cost or maximizing profit, is realized. Table 5.11 lists some of the wide-ranging applications for linear programming.

The principal limitation of linear programming is the requirement for relationships to be linear. Usually, however, a straight-line relationship is an adequate approximation of most situations and linearity can be assumed with small loss of precision.

5.8.1 Linear Programming

A linear programming model consists of three components: (1) the decision variables, (2) the objective function, and (3) the constraints. The decision variables depend on the kind of problem for which a linear programming

TABLE 5.11   Linear Programming Applications (18)

Allocation of production facilities when alternate machine routes are available to
  maximize output or profit, or to minimize incremental cost
Allocation of limited funds to various items of inventory to minimize losses from
  less than optimal inventory levels
Solution of blending problems to minimize cost
Effecting make-or-buy decisions to maximize profit within company policy and
  capacity restrictions
Scheduling production to meet sales forecasts using inventory fluctuations and
  overtime work to absorb random and seasonal variations in load
Maximizing material utilization by determining the combination of cuts that will
  provide the amounts of different sizes required with minimum trim loss

Reprinted by permission of John Wiley & Sons, Inc.

solution is being sought. They generally relate to resources to be allocated in
cost-minimization problems or to the number of units to be produced in
profit-maximization problems.

The objective function is a mathematical expression of the single goal to
be optimized by the linear programming solution. It can be stated in the form
typified by $P = \$60.0x + \$45.50y + \$72.00z$ for profit maximization, or $C =
\$10.50x + \$9.00y + \$12.50z$ for cost minimization. The symbols or letters x,
y, and z denote either the resources consumed for each type produced, or
the number of units of each type that are produced, and are the decision
variables. The same decision variables appear both in the objective function
and in the constraints.

The constraints are mathematical expressions of the groundrules under
which objective functions are to be optimized. They are usually expressed as
inequalities [i.e., equal to or less than (symbolized $\leq$) or equal to or greater
than (symbolized $\geq$)], although equalities are also used when applicable.
Constraints can be stated in the form typified by $2x + 5y + 3z \geq 100$ or $2x +
5y + 3z \leq 100$, denoting that for every two units of x, five units of y and three
units of z must be produced, and that the total number of all types produced
must be equal to or less than 100 in the first case or must be equal to or more
than 100 in the second case.

There are a number of approaches to solving linear programming problems, including systematic trial and error, graphical solutions, and the simplex method. The first approach should be limited to very small scale problems. The second approach is limited to three decision variables by the
nature of the process, but is suitable for a wide range of applications. The
simplex is more general and powerful than the other approaches by providing an iterative algorithm to converge on optimal solutions.

The following discussion of graphical solutions illuminates the basic operation of the simplex method. Amplifying details of the simplex method are
available in the classic work on linear programming by N. Paul Loomba (19).

TABLE 5.12   Graphical Solution Constraints (20)

Department	Washing Machines		Driers
Stamping	10,000	or	10,000
Motor and transmission	16,000	or	7,000
Washing-machine assembly	9,000		
Drier assembly			5,000
Per-unit profit contribution	$90		$100

Adapted by permission of John Wiley & Sons, Inc.

5.8.2   Graphical Solutions

The graphical solutions approach is illustrated with an application to a plant that manufactures washing machines and driers and wishes to optimize the mix of the products for maximum profit. That is to say, how many of each product should be produced monthly within the constraints given in Table 5.12, assuming what is produced can be sold.

There are two decision variables: the number of washing machines and the number of driers to be produced, which are denoted by the symbols x and y. This constitutes a two-dimensional linear programming problem.

It is appropriate to first set up the restrictions to the problem in the form of the constraint equations. For the washing-machine assembly department and the drier assembly department, these are:

$$x \leq 9,000 \tag{5.1}$$

$$y \leq 5,000 \tag{5.2}$$

These constraints are plotted as horizontal and vertical lines in Figure 5.9. The cross-hatched area in the figure is called the "feasible region," and the solution to the problem must lie in this region in order to satisfy the constraints of assembly capacity.

Next, the constraints for the stamping department and the motor and transmission department are derived in the form of inequalities. For the stamping department, this is

$$x + y \leq 10,000 \tag{5.3}$$

Equation (5.3) states that if 10,000 washing machines are produced, then no driers could be produced, or if 5000 washing machines are produced, then 5000 or less driers could be produced.

Similarly, the inequality for the capacity constraint of the motor and transmission department is

$$1.4375x + 3.2857y \leq 23,000 \tag{5.4}$$

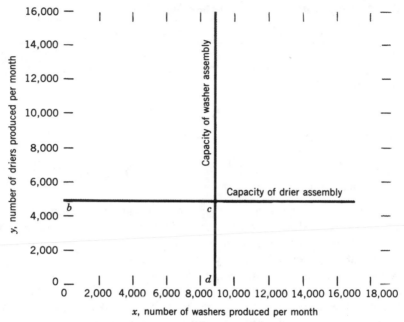

Figure 5.9 Assembly capacity constraints (21). (Reprinted by permission of John Wiley & Sons, Inc.)

where the constraints 1.4375 and 3.2857 are derived from $(16,000 + 7,000) \div 16,000$ and $(16,000 + 7,000) \div 7,000$.

Equation (5.4) states that if 10,000 washing machines are produced, then

$$(1.4375)(10,000) + 3.2957y \le 23,000 \tag{5.5}$$

$$y \le \frac{23,000 - 14,375}{3.2857} \tag{5.6}$$

$$\le 2,625$$

Equations (5.3) and (5.4) are then plotted as overlays to Figure 5.9. The intercepts on the ordinate and abscissa are determined by alternately setting the values of x and y in the equations equal to zero and solving for the other values. In Equation (5.3), when $x = 0$, then $y = 10,000$, and when $y = 0$, then $x = 10,000$. In Equation (5.4), when $x = 0$, then $y = 7,000$, and when $y = 0$, then $x = 16,000$.

The resultant plots are shown in Figure 5.10. The feasible region is now described by the four inequalities representing the four constraints of capacity. The inequality signs (i.e., $\le$) are convenient mnemonic aids for remembering that the feasibility region is to the left and below the plots of the inequalities.

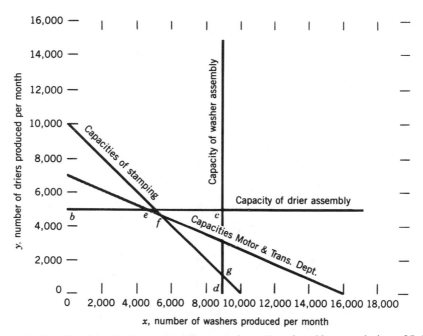

Figure 5.10 Overlay of other capacity constraints. (Reprinted by permission of John Wiley & Sons, Inc.)

The next consideration is that of the objective function, which is to maximize the value of $90x + $100y. The intent is to overlay the objective function on Figure 5.10 so that the objective function intersects the point f, the outermost point on the feasibility region in the figure. When this is done, the intersections of the objective function with the ordinate and abcissa are at the values of y and x that maximize the profit.

This can be done graphically by first determining the slope of the objective function and then constructing a series of plots with this slope until one of the plots intersects point f. The procedure is to arbitrarily assume some value of profit P and solve for x and y by alternately setting x and y equal to zero in the following:

$$P = \$90x + \$100y \qquad (5.7)$$

Assuming $P = \$450,000$, when $x = 0$, then $y = \$4,500$, and when $y = 0$, then $x = 5,000$. Assuming $P = \$63,000$, when $x = 0$, then $y = \$6,300$, and when $y = 0$, then $x = \$7,000$. Assuming $P = \$900,000$, when $x = 0$, then $y = \$9,000$, and when $y = 0$, then $x = \$10,000$.

These values of x and y are used to plot the three objective functions shown in Figure 5.11. These plots are called "isoprofit lines" because they are parallel to each other. Were the objective functions intended to minimize cost, the plots would be called "isocost lines."

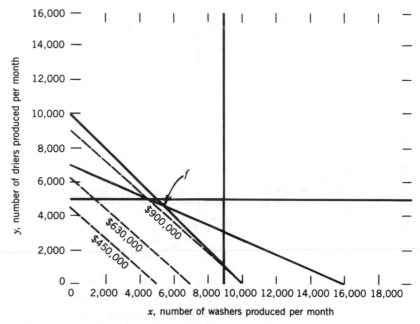

Figure 5.11 Plots of isoprofit lines (23). (Reprinted by permission of John Wiley & Sons, Inc.)

This procedure can be continued until the assumed value of P = $946,670 is attempted, yielding y = 4667, when x = 0, and x = 5333, when y = 0, and a plot that just intersects point f on the feasible region. The preferred approach, however, is to simultaneously solve the two inequalities [Equations (5.3) and (5.4)] that intersect at point f because at this point, and only at this point, their respective values of x and y are equal.

Solving Equations (5.3) and (5.4) simultaneously yields x = 5333 and y = 4667, or the values that were obtained graphically. The profit realized when these quantities of washing machines and driers are sold is therefore $90(5333) + $100(4667), or $946,670.

It is quite feasible to extend graphical solutions to three-dimensional linear programming problems, that is, with three decision variables. There is no restriction on the number of constraints that may be used, except for the physical rendition of the plots. There is always only one objective function, be it to maximize profit or minimize cost.

5.9 INVENTORY STRATEGIES

Just as time is money, so is inventory. A progressive design-to-cost approach also looks to economies in inventory as the additional means for achieving affordability with profitability.

The high cost of capital due to the surging interest rates of the past several decades has prompted a changed attitude regarding inventory and its associated cost. Inventory includes raw material waiting to be converted into assemblies and finished products, work in process (WIP) on the assemblies and products, and finally completed work consisting of items awaiting delivery and spare parts used for service and repair.

The ability to reduce inventory to the absolute minimum needed to sustain production operations on a real-time basis is constrained by both intrinsic and extrinsic factors. An example of the former is the fabrication of microwave integrated circuits such as IMPATT diodes that experience extremely low yields throughout the production processes, necessitating large stockpiles of raw material and WIP. An example of the latter are products of seasonal demand such as air conditioners that require large inventories of finished items.

In both extremes, however, there is a need to optimize the balance of inventory costs, operational needs, and the demands of the marketplace. This is akin to seeking optimal answers to the following questions:

When should particular items be ordered?

How many of the items should be ordered?

What will be the procurement cost?

What will be the holding cost?

What will be the minimum, average, and maximum inventory levels?

The initial objective of this section is to ensure a basic understanding of the concept of economic order quantity (EOQ) as the tool for accommodating the opposing inventory-related pressures. From this base, the underlying rationale and the approach to just-in-time (JIT) procurement are presented. Just-in-time procurement, practiced so successfully by the Japanese, epitomizes zero inventory.

5.9.1 Economic Order Quantity

The concept of EOQ attempts to balance optimally the opposing forces driving inventory costs. The first concern of EOQ is inventory level, since this is the common denominator of the various opposing forces.

Figure 5.12 illustrates the effect on a given inventory item of operational demands and ordering policy. Part *a* of the illustration relates an annual requirement R of 2400 units, or an average of 200 per month, to an ordering lot size Q of 200. The average inventory level is one-half the quantity ordered, or $Q/2 = 100$ units.

Part *b* of Figure 5.12 shows the effect of an ordering lot size of $Q = 150$ units. It can be seen that the average inventory level falls in proportion to the number of units ordered at one time.

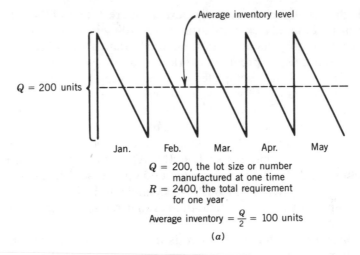

Q = 200 units

Q = 200, the lot size or number
manufactured at one time
R = 2400, the total requirement
for one year

Average inventory $= \dfrac{Q}{2} = 100$ units

(a)

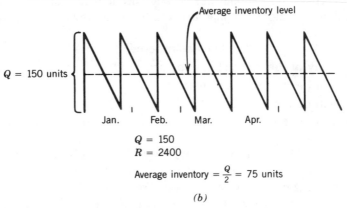

Q = 150 units

Q = 150
R = 2400

Average inventory $= \dfrac{Q}{2} = 75$ units

(b)

Figure 5.12 Effect of ordering lot size on inventory level (24). (Reprinted by permission of John Wiley & Sons, Inc.)

Since inventory level affect the incremental cost of holding inventory, the cost of carrying inventory is proportional to the ordering lot size Q. In addition, the incremental cost of preparing purchase orders increases as the number of units ordered at one time decreases for a constant number of units ordered annually.

It can be noted in Figure 5.12 that if Q were halved, then the average inventory level would also be halved. If the unit inventory holding cost C_H were $0.60 per year, then the annual incremental holding cost would be

$$\left(\frac{Q}{2}\right) C_H = \left(\frac{Q}{2}\right) (\$0.60) = \$0.30Q \qquad (5.8)$$

The results obtained by substituting various values of Q in this equation provide one of the curves needed to construct the EOQ model that is discussed below.

The incremental cost of preparing purchase orders C_P can be prepared in a similar fashion. The number of orders prepared annually is determined by R/Q, where R is the total annual requirement. For the data in Figure 5.8, the relationship is therefore $R/Q = 2400$. If $C_P = \$20.00$ were assumed, the following equation would be obtained:

$$\left(\frac{R}{Q}\right) C_P = \frac{2400(\$20.00)}{Q} = \frac{\$48,000}{Q} \tag{5.9}$$

Plotting the results obtained by substituting various values of Q in this equation is the next step in constructing the EOQ model. Figure 5.13 shows the plots of this and the previous equation and the summations of the results from both equations for various values of Q.

It can be seen that the lowest total cost for this example prevails when the ordering lot size $Q = 400$. A more general relationship for total incremental cost C_T can now be considered as follows:

$$C_T = \left(\frac{Q}{2}\right) C_H + \left(\frac{R}{Q}\right) C_P \tag{5.10}$$

From this equation, the following equation for optimum quantity can be developed.

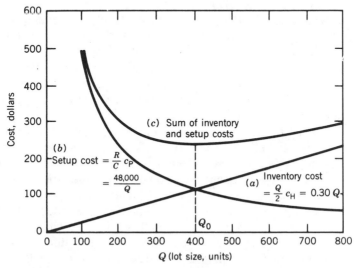

Figure 5.13 Economic order quantity model (25). (Adapted by permission of John Wiley & Sons, Inc.)

$$Q_O = \frac{\sqrt{2RC_P}}{C_H} \tag{5.11}$$

Applying this equation to the previous example yields:

$$Q_O = \frac{\sqrt{2(2400)(\$20.00)}}{(\$0.60)} = 400 \text{ units} \tag{5.12}$$

This is the optimum quantity appearing in Figure 5.9.

The preceding example is only a partial solution to the problem of opposing forces influencing inventory-related cost, but it can serve as a role model for the other factors. In particular, extrinsic factors such as quantity discounts and inflation and intrinsic factors such as production line setup times and learning curves should be considered.

5.9.2   Zero Inventory

Zero inventory is the ultimate fulfillment of JIT as a procurement strategy. As stated in Section 5.4.9, the concept of zero inventory is particularly appealing to high-technology enterprises because of the high proportion of expenditures on parts and material, the large amount of work in process because of yield problems, and, of course, the substantial amount of capital that needs to be committed to inventory acquisition and control.

The concept of zero inventory through a combination of JIT procurement and JIT manufacturing is just now being appreciated and implemented in the United States. However, it has been popular for some time in Japan; the classic example is Toyota's *Kanban*.

The motivation for *Kanban* was the basic belief that inventories are not only unnecessary but are counterproductive with respect to achieving low cost. The drive in *Kanban* is to eliminate the attractiveness of large batches by reducing setup costs. Changeover time at Toyota is measured in minutes as opposed to hours at U.S. plants. In addition, buffer inventories that serve to mask production problems are eliminated, thus giving such problems the immediate attention they deserve (26).

Table 5.13 lists the guidelines under which the Japanese pursue inventory reduction. These guidelines should be considered from the positive rather than the negative point of view. In other words, rather than state that marketing and engineering personnel will never standardize parts and components, search for ways to encourage these people to do so.

The goal should be to turn every production line into a continuously flowing system of procured or manufactured items; with items passing through the system one by one and never being held in storage. Just-in-time procurement and manufacturing can be described as a "pull" system, as opposed to the conventional "push" system in classical production.

TABLE 5.13   Guidelines for Zero Inventory (28)

Encourage marketing and engineering personnel to standardize parts and components

Increase the frequency of vendor deliveries 1–4 times per day instead of 1–4 times per month

Develop a mixed-model assembly line for low-volume models

Reduce setup and changeover times through equipment and procedure modifications

Reduce lot sizes and increase the frequency of model changes

Promote discipline and commitment to the policy throughout all operations and over time

---

Reprinted by permission of John Wiley & Sons, Inc.

The immediate cost benefit of zero, or little inventory is obvious. There are, however, a number of exciting side benefits.

In an operation where each production line operator immediately passes completed items to the next operator, rather than to a storage bin, defects are caught immediately and the causes eliminated. Also, as scrap becomes immediately apparent, the cause is eliminated. Furthermore, production scheduling and control is simpler and less costly without inventories to transport, store and issue (27).

5.10 PERSONNEL MOTIVATION

Total commitment to design to cost is necessary, especially in personnel who can make or break goals. There are both reactive and proactive methods of motivating personnel. The key example of the former is keying personal performance appraisal to cost performance. A mix of both methods is necessary, but the emphasis should be on the latter.

Recognition and award plans that motivate personnel are an essential part of the business strategy for affordability. An example of the former is buyer-of-the-month recognition for the person accomplishing significant procurement economy. The individual is afforded amenities such as reserved parking for the month and dinner with a vice president or director.

In addition, cash or gift award programs keyed to cost savings can be effective when tailored to individual contributions. For example, the policy of a certain aerospace company with regard to savings from value engineering change proposals (VECPs) is noteworthy. When a VECP is approved for submittal to the customer by the program's change board, the originator receives a token gift such as a pocket knife. When the VECP is implemented by the customer, the company's share of net savings raised to the two-thirds power is awarded to the originator. With a company share of $1 million, the award would be $10,000.

TABLE 5.14   Reportable Cost Savings (29)

Change in design
Change in operational or technical requirements or specifications that enable cost-
  reducing design alterations
Change in manufacturing processes
Material substitutions
Relaxation of tolerances
Standardization
Reduction in operation and support effort
Dual-source development
Reduced packaging requirements
Elimination or reduction of test or inspection requirements
Elimination or reduction in services ⁻

Adapted by permission of the Martin Marietta Corporation.

Plans should be adapted to the particular circumstances; however, in all cases, clear definitions of cost saving and reward should be provided, and above all plans should be publicized. To qualify as a reportable cost saving, the idea must reduce some element of life-cycle cost while still allowing the specified mission to be fulfilled. Examples of reportable savings are given in Table 5.14. In addition, recognition should be given for error-cause removal that eliminates or reduces conditions contributing to wasteful practices.

5.11   SUMMARY

This chapter addressed elements of business strategy for low-cost production starting with the discussion of three very important subjects relating to doing business with the federal government and, that, in themselves, are fundamental elements of business strategy: (1) best and final offers in the procurement process, (2) involvement in the industrial modernization incentives program of the Department of Defense (DoD), and (3) indirect cost management.

Section 5.1 discussed the current tendency of customers, particularly governmental entities, to require best and final offers (BAFO) from competing contractors when nearing the conclusion of the proposal phase of the acquisition process. This requirement has become as prevalent in solicitations for development as in solicitations for production, and has even pervaded the fixed-price arena.

The point is that, carried to an extreme, BAFOs will invariably result in "lose–lose" situations for both the customer and the contractor. Customers should ensure that contractors have the capability and resources to support their BAFOs in the current time frame rather than accept such promises for the future. The caution exercised by contractors in providing BAFOs should be directly proportional to the technical challenges involved and the financial commitments required.

The industrial modernization incentives program of the DoD was the subject of Section 5.2. The defense industry can be characterized to a large measure as being outmoded, inefficient, very labor intensive, and very reluctant to modernize. The latter has been attributed primarily to the high degree of program uncertainties in the DoD and to the cost-based profit policy of the DoD.

The DoD instituted the industrial modernization incentives program (IMIP) to help focus contractor resources on industrial modernization and to support the development of more cost-efficient production systems for military materiel. Under IMIP, incentives are provided to motivate contractors to invest their own funds in improvements that result in reducing acquisition costs. Contractors may wish to consider IMIP as part of their business strategy for a particular program area.

Indirect costs typically represent 33 to 50 percent of the cost of contracts with components of the DoD, and Section 5.3 illuminated the important concept of indirect cost management. In the government contracting arena, indirect costs are usually subdivided into the cost categories of overhead and general and administrative (G&A). Overhead costs support specific parts or functions of a company but not the whole company, whereas G&A costs support the business as a whole and cannot logically be allocated to any particular grouping of cost objectives. Some principles of overhead cost control were given.

Forward pricing rate agreements were cited as the biggest cost drivers in the fixed-price contracting arena. The negotiation of forward pricing rates provides the best leverage to influence contractor and subcontractor cost containment. Under some circumstances, contract delays, work stoppages, or even program cancellations should be considered if favorable forward pricing rate agreements cannot be attained.

Section 5.4 addressed the various alternatives that can be used to increase competition and lower the cost of procurement. Those used most often by customers to reduce cost are leader–follower, associate contractor, multiple-source, breakout and total package procurement. Those used most often by contractors to improve competitiveness are teaming and joint venture.

These procurement alternatives were compared to the classical business arrangement of prime contractor and subcontractors from the viewpoint of advantages and disadvantages. The concept of JIT procurement was also discussed since it can be used advantageously both by the customer and the contractor.

Section 5.5 was on the subject of the flowdown of requirements and incentives to suppliers. The insight should be valuable to all high-technology organizations, however, because frequently contractors and subcontractors reverse roles in the pursuit of business opportunities.

Suggested contractual wording was provided, along with the use of award fees and incentives in motivating suppliers. Guidelines were given for rating and scoring the cost performance of suppliers.

The discussion of make or buy followed in Section 5.6. The cost sensitivity of the U.S. high-technology industry to make-or-buy decisions was explored.

The implications of company policy and criteria for make-or-buy decisions were discussed. Some suggestions for a rational policy were outlined, and some guidelines were given for decision criteria.

Section 5.7 addressed scheduling strategies that can be conducive to lower cost and better utilization of resources provided the attendant risks are understood and anticipated. These were presented following a brief introduction to techniques of schedule management using program evaluation and review technique (PERT) and critical-path method (CPM).

Specifically, the section covered resource leveling, payment progressing, and least-cost scheduling. The latter strategy is essentially one of schedule compression, and an example of its effectiveness was provided.

Capacity planning that can also be conducive to lower cost and better utilization of resources was the subject of Section 5.8. The next section provided an introduction to linear programming, which is a powerful tool with a host of applications in design-to-cost programs as well as in capacity planning.

The three components of linear programming problems—the objective function, decision variables, and constraints—were discussed. The procedure was illustrated with an application using the graphical solution approach.

The thesis of Section 5.8 was that inventory is money that is not working, and the section addressed inventory practices that can exert a profound effect on the cost of products and systems. As expected, inventory strategies range from optimizing the balance of inventory and demand with the concept of economic order quantity (EOQ) to the total elimination of inventory in the penchant of the Japanese.

Specific guidelines were given in regard to EOQ and zero inventory. From this base, the underlying rationale and the approach to JIT procurement were presented.

The very important subject of motivating personnel was addressed in Section 5.9. The saying "People are our principal asset" is particularly valid for high-technology enterprises.

It was noted that people make or break cost goals and it is never too early to institute a system of recognition and reward for the benefit of the undertaking. Both reactive and proactive approaches were discussed.

5.12   CASE STUDIES AND EXERCISES

The case studies that follow are intended to amplify key points in this chapter. The exercises following the case studies allow the reader to relate these points to personal viewpoints and experiences. The case studies in this chapter explore the subtleties of various business strategies with emphasis on procurement alternatives.

5.12.1 Best but Not Final

A component of the Department of Defense (DoD) contracted for both the development and limited production of a supersonic low-altitude missile with heretofore unparalleled capability. The procurement strategy, however, was based on fixed-price contracts both for development and limited production. The process of best and final offers (BAFO) was involved in the competition that narrowed down to two offerers.

The BAFO of the winning offerer evolved from process, not design, economies and allowed only an extremely moderate profit from development. The expectation was that production would amply compensate for both these factors.

Three years were devoted to the development of the missile. The gate for transitioning from development to production was the successful flight test of three prototype missiles. There were three flight test failures before the first successful test occurred. Each of the failures was attributed to process control during fabrication of the prototype missiles and was in no way inherent in the design.

EXERCISE   The flight test failures resulted in an overall program delay of 12 months, the three failures and one successful flight being scheduled 3 months apart. Approximately five range days were consumed at the launch site for each of the four attempts.

It is estimated that each range day had cost the customer approximately $100,000 and the increase in administrative costs to the customer and contractor for each month of delay in the program were $50,000 and $250,000.

Using the time value of money relationships given in Section 6.7, calculate the present value (at the start of development) of the additional costs to the customer and contractor. Use a discount rate of 10 percent compounded annually.

5.12.2 Leader–Follower at Work

The U.S. Army is enjoying financial success with an interesting leader–follower variation. In the mid-1970s, the Army awarded the development of a certain air-to-surface and air-to-air missile to an aerospace company that proceeded to become the leader in a relationship with another company that had developed the seeker portion of the missile as a subcontractor to the first company as the prime contractor. The first company was also awarded the first production buy of 5000 missiles with a directed subcontract to the second company.

Concurrently, the Army negotiated contracts with the two companies whereby they would exchange technical data and production technology and compete for subsequent buys of 5000 all-up rounds (ready-to-fire missiles). The arrangement was that the low bidder would be awarded more than 50 percent of the buy and the remainder would be awarded to the other company.

The larger award has cycled between the leader and the follower. The Army is now at buy 6; 75 percent is awarded to the follower at an average unit cost of $26,000, and 25 percent is awarded to the leader at an average unit cost of $27,000.

EXERCISE   Assume that a 90 percent learning curve applies to both companies, and estimate the average unit cost of the first buy that was produced under the baseline procurement strategy of a prime-subcontractor relationship. Absent the competitive pressure of leader–follower, predict what the 6 buys of 30,000 rounds might have cost the Army.

5.12.3   Associate Contractors at Large

The NIMBUS project was the follow-on to TIROS in the National Aeronautics and Space Administration (NASA) meteorological satellite program. After NIMBUS I was successfully launched in 1964, it became the forerunner of today's operational weather satellites.

Beyond question, the design of NIMBUS was the greatest aerospace challenge ever undertaken to that time, and NASA sought the expertise of the foremost companies in aerospace. Eight companies were placed under contract to develop subsystems for the satellite while NASA concentrated on its system design (30).

The preliminary design was completed in 1960, and NASA was ready to undertake the development of a test prototype and fabrication of a flight model. An integration contractor was selected in anticipation of a mid-1962 flight.

In the interest of economy, NASA retained its original contractual relationships with the subsystem developers, so that they and the integration contractor became associate contractors (then called "cocontractors"). Thus, NASA retained schedule control.

It evolved that there were more than the few problems envisioned in the subsystems and only the integration contractor was able to adhere to the program schedule. Unfortunately, the interfaces designed by the integration contractor did not reflect subsequent design changes in the subsystems.

The launch-date slip of two years was accompanied by an attendant overrun in program cost. An additional increase in cost resulted from the large staff of specialty engineers that NASA was obliged to assign to the integration contractor.

EXERCISE Considering the state of the art in the 1960s, what would have been preferred contractual strategies for cost saving and for early launch? Were the two goals compatible at that time, and are they compatible at the present time?

5.12.4 Reverse Engineering

Reverse engineering is the process whereby the design of a particular product or component is reduced to drawings that allow the product or component to be duplicated without the benefit of the original technical data package. Reverse engineering has also been used to circumvent the proprietary aspects of the item by introducing some changes in the design. This practice is referred to as "wrinkling."

The intent in both cases is to avoid the payment of royalties to the original manufacturer and owner of the technical data package (TDP). In recent years, the Department of Defense (DoD) has turned to reverse engineering as a cost-saving alternative to buying the TDP from the contractor who developed and produced the first production buy. In particular, the DoD views reverse engineering as the means for fostering competition in its replenishment parts breakout program (31).

By law, reverse engineering in the DoD is restricted to items that are in the public domains. Thus, in purchasing the item, the DoD has paid for the right to use these items in an unrestricted fashion.

EXERCISE List both the legal issues and the ethical issues that may arise from the use of reverse engineering. Do patent disclosures provide adequate protection to the original contractor for proprietary investment? How would contract wording differ from the perspective of the customer and the perspective of the contractor where there is concern about reverse engineering in either quarter?

5.12.5 Competitive Balance

A competitive balance is as important to the customer as competitive edge is to the contractor. Table 5.15 summarizes the findings of a study by the DoD Product Engineering Services Office of cost savings from competition experienced by the military during the past decade. The systems are listed in the order of decreasing loss and increasing saving from the undertakings that resulted from multiple source procurement.

EXERCISE Note that losses were experienced in 5 of the 16 systems, and note the relative inconsistency between percentages of saving and the magnitude of dollars saved.

TABLE 5.15   Cost Saving from Competition (32)

System	Saving Percentage (Loss)	Saving, $ Million (Loss)
Mark 46 Torpedo	(13.2)	(52.9)
Standard Missile	(3.9)	(11.8)
AIM-9B Sidewinder Missile	(4.0)	(6.7)
AIM-9D Sidewinder Missile	(2.7)	(1.9
ARC-131 Radio	(2.1)	(0.6)
UPM-98 Test Set	3.0	0.08
FAAR TADS	18.2	2.0
FAAR Radar	16.6	4.8
Dragon Round	2.7	8.0
Dragon Tracker	12.0	12.2
Shillelagh Missile	5.9	18.3
AGM-12B Bullpup Missile	16.0	38.3
PRC-77 Radio	34.8	52.6
TOW Missile	8.5	61.3
TOW Launcher	30.2	83.5
Shrike Missile	51.0	103.2

Source: U.S. Army Procurement Research Office, *APRO Report 709-3*, 1978.

Calculate the means and standard deviations of the percentage and dollar values. How should the list of systems be modified to decrease the relative inconsistency between the two sets of values?

5.12.6   Marriage of Convenience

A teaming agreement among prime contractors and one or more subcontractors with complementing skills is a common strategy for winning competitive contracts. Teaming agreements can be beneficial to all parties, including the customer as long as the conditions warranting teaming prevail.

In this case study, a stable prime with good technical credentials and financial strength saw an opportunity to expand its business base although there would be need to venture into a new technology and marketplace. Penetrating a new market is not as easily done as one might envision. It is impossible to imagine the extent of the travail without having experienced such an undertaking.

The specific technology deemed crucial to winning the competition was not in the prime contractor's area of expertise. In addition, the prime contractor did not know the customer and the numerous organizational elements in the customer's shop well enough to submit a credible competitive proposal. Not the least of the manifold difficulties was raising $50 million to capitalize the venture and to buy certain intellectual properties that were key to a winning technical approach.

The solution to these problems appeared to lie in teaming with a company, or group of companies that had the complementing technology, experience, and established relationships with the customer's operatives, and moreover the willingness to share in the required financial investment of $50 million. Such an arrangement was affected in a climate that allowed all the team members to legitimately expect large future sales.

A honeymoonlike climate persisted through the initial phase of the program due, in no small measure, to the professional business interfaces which had existed prior to the teaming agreement, in particular the company chosen to be the major subcontractor. As in all marriages, however, the honeymoon persists only as long as the partners work hard at their relationship with candor and integrity at the personal level.

As time and program events progressed, however, it became evident that the major subcontractor had been somewhat less than candid about its production capability. The union that had served well in development was on the threshold of becoming a handicap in production. Nonetheless, 2 years elapsed before the critical mass of problems became visible to all including the customer.

A friendly divorce was arranged, and a replacement for the discarded partner was sought and found. Large amounts of time, energy, and money were consumed, however, in reorganizing and recovering from the setback.

Very simply, the problem was due to signing teaming agreements for the life of the program when the key subsystem provider had only great expectations for production capability. In essence, the groom did not truly know the bride.

EXERCISE Consider the following alternative courses of action that the prime contractor could have taken to penetrate the new market, and judge how effective they might have been. Were there other alternatives available to the prime?

1. The most obvious alternative would have been to team with another company that had the capability for both development and production and knew the customer. In this approach, however, be sure that the company's capability includes support services for the product while it is in use. Otherwise, the problem would simply be delayed for another year or so.

2. Another alternative could have been to limit the teaming agreement to the development phase of the program. There is little likelihood, however, that any potential subcontractor would not find it advantageous to enter into such an arrangement absent the prospect of production. Development in itself is not a large profit generator and is frequently subsidized because of the profit potential of follow-on production.

3. If the preceding alternative were selected, the prime could guarantee that a production bid from the subcontractor would be dealt with even-

handedly. This could be attractive because as a team member the subcontractor would have the strength of an incumbent.

4. Still another alternative could be to offer royalties to the original developer for the hardware produced by any other company that replaced the developer in production. This alternative could be appealing if other related development work would follow.

5. A more difficult alternative could be to train the developer to produce at the required rate. Some recent government contracts require the winner to train the eventual competitor for the production work. This strategy, called "leader–follower," was discussed in Section 5.4.2.

6. Still another alternative could be to attempt the acquisition of some company with needed technology and knowledge of the customer. However, there is always the possibility that the target firm might be larger than the suitor, and the only practical solution would be to acquire a specific division of this firm.

7. A longer-range alternative could be to grow the capability a brick at a time including technology and customer grass roots relationships.

Construct a table of alternative ideas. Try to mix and match these ideas for an optimum solution. Be sure to consider the issues of customer relations and credibility in the solution. Two or more people may find it beneficial to play the roles of prime contractor and subcontractors and replay these rolls in different scenarios generated from the table of alternative ideas.

REFERENCES

1. Defense Systems Management College, *Program Manager's Notebook Fact Sheet Number 6.14, Industrial Modernization Incentives Program*, 1985.
2. Deputy Secretary of Defense, *Initiative to Reduce Overhead*, 1984.
3. Martin Marietta Corporation, *Design to Cost/Affordability Manual*, 1986.
4. William M. Brueggemann, "Will Competition Reduce Cost? The Need for Common Business Sense in Decisions on Competition," *Program Manager*, March–April 1984.
5–8. Martin Marietta Corporation, *Design to Cost/Affordability Manual*, 1986.
9–12. Elwood S. Buffa, *Modern Production Management*, 4th ed., John Wiley & Sons, 1973.
13–17. Rodney D. Stewart and Richard M. Wyskida, *Cost Estimator's Reference Manual*, John Wiley & Sons, 1987.
18. Elwood S. Buffa, *Modern Production Management*, 4th ed., John Wiley & Sons, 1973.
19. N. Paul Loomba, *Linear Programming*, McGraw-Hill Book Company, 1964.
20–25. Elwood S. Buffa, *Modern Production Management*, 4th ed., John Wiley & Sons, 1973.

26. Robert H. Hayes and Steven C. Wheelright, *Restoring Our Competitive Edge, Competing through Manufacturing,* John Wiley & Sons, 1984.

27. Richard J. Schonberger, *Japanese Manufacturing Techniques, Nine Hidden Lessons in Simplicity.* The Free Press, 1982.

28. Robert H. Hayes and Steven C. Wheelright, *Restoring Our Competitive Edge, Competing through Manufacturing,* John Wiley & Sons, 1984.

29. Martin Marietta Corporation, *Design to Cost/Affordability Manual,* 1986.

30. Harry Press and Jack V. Michaels, "NIMBUS Spacecraft Development," *Astronautics and Aerospace Engineering,* April 1963.

31. Mark G. Matonek, *RE & VE Partners in Competition, Value World,* July/ August/September 1988.

32. U.S. Army Procurement Research Office, *APRO Report* 709-3, 1978.

6
ESTIMATING AND CONTROLLING COSTS

Cost estimating and subsequent control are key elements in design-to-cost programs. The success in design to cost is a direct function of how well costs were estimated initially from the viewpoint of realism and how well they are controlled during the course of the programs.

A cost estimate may be classed as a projection or prediction, but essentially it is an opinion based on a specific set of conditions. The usual ways of forming this opinion are estimating by expert opinion, estimating by analogy, parametric estimating, and industrial engineering estimating, which is often called "bottom-up estimating."

Wherever the estimate comes from, it is important to remember that it is the expected cost, provided there are no deviations from boundary conditions in the definition of the program. When the cost estimate varies because of deviations in these boundary conditions, cost must be estimated again and instituted as the revised program baseline.

The role of cost estimating in design-to-cost programs was first illuminated by the discussion of goal setting in Chapter 2. Next, organizational roles and responsibilities in the cost arena were delineated in Chapter 3. Chapters 4 and 5 addressed elements of design for inherently low cost and business strategies to further enhance affordability and profitability.

This chapter concentrates on those aspects of cost estimating that are key to realizing the full potential of these design approaches and business strategies, or in short, successful design to cost. The discussion is supplemented with references to contemporary literature containing extensive details on a wide range of estimating practices (1, 2), and begins with the enunciation of a recommended philosophy for design to cost. This is offered in the context of functional worth, could-cost, should-cost, and would-cost.

Insight is then given into cost element structures and the work-breakdown structure (WBS) that provide the framework for estimating costs for various phases of programs. The need for cost realism to ensure the viability of design-to-cost programs and how to communicate such realism are discussed next.

This is followed by the discussion of the methodologies for estimating cost that also vary as functions of program phases. The applicability of each of the four basic methods, and their relative advantages and disadvantages are presented.

The next section addresses learning curves and their use in cost estimating. Both their application and their probabilistic nature that contributes to risk are covered.

In the competitive world, it is essential that the confidence in cost estimates be established to ensure cogent decisions where alternatives are involved. Confidence is a function of many factors that include the amount of data (i.e., sample size) on which conclusions are based and the probability distributions governing the relationships depicted by the data.

Confidence is expressed in terms of limits or intervals, and confidence interval estimation is part of the greater subject of statistical inference and hypotheses testing. It is important for design-to-cost practitioners to be versed in the use of such techniques, and a brief introduction to this subject is provided along with regression and correlation analysis and Bayes's theorem in decision-making.

Expressions such as "then dollars," "now dollars," "constant-year dollars," "sinking fund," "capital recovery," and "internal rate of return" proliferate in design to cost, and they all relate to the concept of the time value of money. It is important that design-to-cost practitioners be proficient in these matters; therefore, the next section in this chapter is devoted to the subject.

Since much of the high-technology industrial sector is involved in contracts with the military, it is also important for design-to-cost practitioners to gain insight into the cost control required by the military, in particular the performance measurement requirements promulgated by the Department of Defense in DoD Instruction 7000.2.

The implementation rigor mandated by DoD Instruction 7000.2 is worthy of some emulation by the private sector of the economy. The use of Cost/Schedule Control Systems Criteria (C/SCSC) is explored, and a typical performance measurement system employed by defense contractors is described. A checklist for self audit for the adequacy of the cost and schedule control systems is provided.

Next, there are some observations on inflation, escalation, and price indexes used to come to grips with their impact on cost. The importance of disaggregate price indexes versus aggregate price indexes is discussed.

Following the summary of its contents, the chapter concludes with case studies and exercises that are intended to amplify key points in the chapter. The exercises allow the readers to relate the reported events to personal viewpoints and experiences.

6.1 PHILOSOPHY FOR DESIGN TO COST

Design to cost was described in Chapter 1 as a management approach that demands cost success along with the technical success of products or systems over their life cycles. This requires that organizations as a whole adopt a unique philosophy regarding the functionality and cost of products produced and sold.

6.1.1 Functional Worth

The functional worth of an item is the lowest cost means for fulfilling the requirement that the item is supposed to satisfy. As stated in Section 2.8, the functional worth of a picture hangar is the cost of a nail. In that context, the function of the nail is to mount a picture.

Functions of products, systems, and services fall into two classes: basic and secondary. The philosophy for design to cost is to provide only basic (i.e., primary) functions in the products, systems, and services unless secondary functions are explicitly requested by the customers.

A "basic function" denotes a performance feature that must be provided. It is the raison d'etre for the product, system, or service.

The basic function should not be confused with the provisioning implement. For example, the basic function provided by a screwdriver could be "transfer torque" to screws. However, the basic function could also be "open lids" of containers that could be provided by a pry bar as well as a screwdriver.

A "secondary function" denotes a performance feature that is optional and usually not a prerequisite for the performance feature that must be provided by the basic function. For example, if the basic function of paint were "protect surface," the secondary function would be "improve appearance."

Sometimes a secondary function supports a basic function, but then only because of the design approach for implementing the basic function. For example, the basic function of a radiator could be "provide heat." If an approach of hot water heating as opposed to radiant heating were selected, then a secondary function of the radiator could be "restrict flow." Initially, there should be no constraint in considering how these functions could be realized; restricting water flow could be provided by labyrinth design of the radiator or an external valve.

The following guidelines for identifying functions in the broadest possible terms ensure the greatest possible freedom for creatively developing alternative approaches and thus the greatest potential for improving value. The guidelines tend to suppress preconceived notions of the manner in which functions are to be performed.

Identify functions so as not to limit the ways they could be performed. Consider the simple operation of identifying a piece of equipment.

Instead of stating the function "install nameplate," which limits approaches to ways of mounting the nameplate, it would be preferable to state "label equipment," which allows alternatives to labels such as stencils and engraving to be considered.

Evaluate how items work rather than what they are. For example, a length of wire would be evaluated by "conduct current," rather than "made of copper" or "stranded construction."

Functions can then be fitted to items through the use of the functional analysis system technique (FAST) described in Section 2.8.2. Unnecessary functions with their corresponding provisioning implements can be eliminated.

6.1.2   Could-Cost, Should-Cost, and Would-Cost Concepts

Given that the functional worth of a particular product is understood, and the functionality of the product has been defined to exclude all except basic functions, the question then becomes how much will it cost to produce the product in the desired quantity. This is where the concepts of could-cost, should-cost, and would-cost enter the picture.

For years, the expression "should-cost" has connoted the most likely cost for developing and producing products or systems in accordance with the development and production specifications, with only a nominal amount of design changes resulting from maturation rather than requirements changes, and with only normal production allowances for scrap and rework. Should-cost is essentially the same as the concept of 50/50 cost introduced in the discussion of risk management in Section 2.9. The term "50/50 cost" connotes that there is a 50/50 chance that the particular cost would not be exceeded.

More recently, the term "could-cost" has been used to connote the cost which would result from eliminating all but essential requirements and most of the monitoring and control operatives encountered in the military marketplace. The current emphasis in the Department of Defense (DoD) on acquisition simplification is a major step in that direction as indicated by the pronouncement on could-cost by the Under Secretary of Defense for Acquisition (see Appendix 3).

Could-cost is somewhat akin to the concept of 20/80 cost also introduced in the aforementioned discussion of risk management. This is the cost that would result if none of the potential risk items were to materialize and if other non-value-adding costs were avoided. The term "20/80 cost" connotes there is only a 20 percent probability that the particular cost would not be exceeded.

At the other end of the spectrum, the term "would-cost" connotes the cost that would result were the risks to materialize and were other non-value-adding costs not avoided. Would-cost is also somewhat akin to the concept of 80/20 cost in the context of risk management. The term "80/20 cost" connotes that the probability is 80 percent that the particular cost would not be exceeded.

With this background, it is now possible to pronounce the following fundamental philosophy for design to cost:

> There should be an organization-wide commitment to the concept of could-cost.
>
> The functional worth of products, systems and services should be viewed as could-cost goals.
>
> Baseline designs should exclude all but basic functions.

6.2 COST ELEMENT STRUCTURES

It was pointed out in Sections 2.2 and 2.10 that requirements for design to cost need to be set in the context of program phases and are generally cited as goals for design to unit production cost (DTUPC), design to operation and support cost (DTOSC), and design to life-cycle cost (DTLCC).

Cost elements structures define the cost elements constituting these goals and, because the goals overlap programmatically, the definitions should be precise and unambiguous. In addition, cost traceability from early concept through final delivery, or through hardware retirement in the case of the customer, is an essential element of design to cost, and it is equally important to adopt cost structures that provide this function over the life cycle of programs.

Top-down and bottom-up estimating approaches are used progressively as programs mature. Figure 6.1 illustrates the salient differences between the

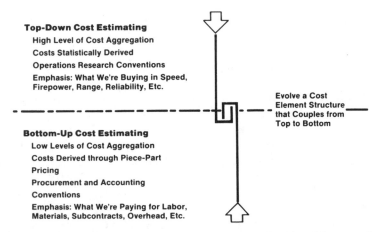

Figure 6.1 The cost-element structure challenge (3). (Reprinted by permission of the Martin Marietta Corporation.)

two approaches and the challenge of evolving a cost element structure that couples from top to bottom and preserves the integrity of both approaches.

The cost element structure should permit managers to avoid minutiae yet permit analysts to understand issues. The flow should relate from aggregate to disaggregate costs and maintain its integrity as programs mature. It should allow alternative design concepts, production philosophies, and business strategies to be assessed with confidence that nothing has been overlooked.

The following discussion is in the context of the defense establishment; however, it is basically applicable to the private sector dealing in high technology and is offered as a role model.

Life-cycle cost of weapon systems is divided into three major categories: research and development, investment, and operation and support. Time-phasing of these categories was shown in Figure 1.1 (in Chapter 1).

Cost element structures vary among the categories because the kinds of expenditure incurred vary as programs mature. The sections that follow first describe the salient differences in cost element structures, and then the use of work-breakdown structures (WBSs) to provide the media for cost aggregation over program life cycles.

6.2.1   Research-and-Development Phase

"Research-and-development (R&D) costs" refer to all customer and contractor costs associated with research, development, test, and evaluation of the system as illustrated in Figure 6.2. Specifically, R&D covers all costs during the concept initiation, validation, and full-scale development phases of the program. Research and development includes costs of feasibility stud-

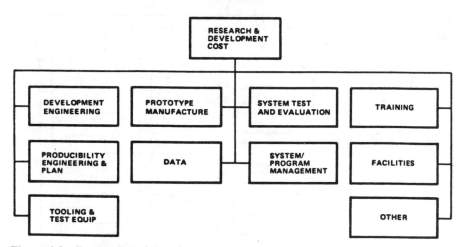

Figure 6.2   Research-and-development cost-element structure (4). (Source: Department of Army Pamphlet No. 11-2, *Research and Development Guide for Army Materiel Systems,* 1976.)

ies, engineering design, development, fabrication, assembly, test of engineering prototype models, initial system evaluation, and associated documentation.

Research-and-development costs normally terminate on satisfactory completion of testing and subsequent acceptance by the customer. However, in systems that have embedded computers, software development may continue throughout the hardware production phase and may be funded with R&D money.

Most R&D costs are nonrecurring; the exceptions being related to program management and data items. This is in contrast to the significant recurring as well as nonrecurring costs which are incurred in the investment phase.

6.2.2 Investment Phase

"Investment costs" refer to the expenditures required beyond the development phase to: introduce a new capability; procure initial, additional, or replacement equipment; or provide for major modification of an existing capability. Investment costs are also divided into nonrecurring and recurring as shown in Figure 6.3.

Nonrecurring investment costs are usually incurred only once during the investment phase. However, these costs can be incurred again if there is a change in the product design, manufacturing process, or contractor.

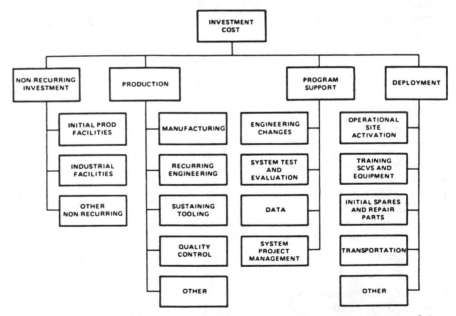

Figure 6.3 Investment cost-element structure (5). (Source: Department of Army Pamphlet No. 11-3, *Investment Cost Guide for Army Materiel Systems*, 1976.)

Recurring investment costs are incurred over the duration of the investment phase. They include both fixed and variable costs, with the variable
costs being generally subject to learning, implying a reduction in unit cost as
quantity increases.

Costs in this category terminate only when the total quantity of systems
ordered, including spares and ancillary equipment, is acquired and deployed, and trained personnel are operating the system.

6.2.3   Operation and Support Phase

Operation and support (O&S), shown in Figure 6.4, includes the costs of
personnel, material, facilities, training, and other direct and indirect costs
required to operate, maintain, and support the equipment or system during
the operational phase. Abbreviations used in the illustration are defined in
Appendix 2.

The category includes the costs of all parts consumed in operating and
maintaining the equipment as well as the cost of the supply system for parts,
components, equipment, and information. Costs are recurring with a few
exceptions such as the element "modification, materiel."

Operation and support usually constitutes the largest portion of the life-
cycle cost and thus represents a fertile area for cost saving through optimizing the operational aspects of system design. However, the contractor's
unilateral ability to impact O&S cost is limited, and without the active participation of the user in the design process, savings of only 15 percent or less
have been experienced.

6.2.4   Work-Breakdown Structure

The medium for depicting cost element structures is the work-breakdown
structure (WBS). The WBS serves to collect all costs associated with given
products or systems throughout their life cycle. The WBS should not be
confused with the generation breakdown (GB) that depicts the hierarchy of
component parts making up products and the way products are produced.

It is essential from both the contractual and the business viewpoints that
appropriate standards or guidelines be observed in preparing the WBS. This
function is provided for components of the Department of Defense by MIL-
STD-881A, and most other federal entities follow its guidelines (7). Similar
guidelines exist for the private sector, where the WBS is often called "work-
element structure" (WES) (8).

The WBS is mandatory in proposals and contracts for work with the
federal government in the R&D and investment phases. In the case of contracts, it is called the "contract work-breakdown structure" (CWBS).

For the purpose of both estimating and control, the WBS should be extended to the lowest level at which cost can be expended, although reporting
is generally to the third level. Table 6.1 is an example based on MIL-STD-
881A of a third-level WBS for the investment phase shown in Figure 6.3.

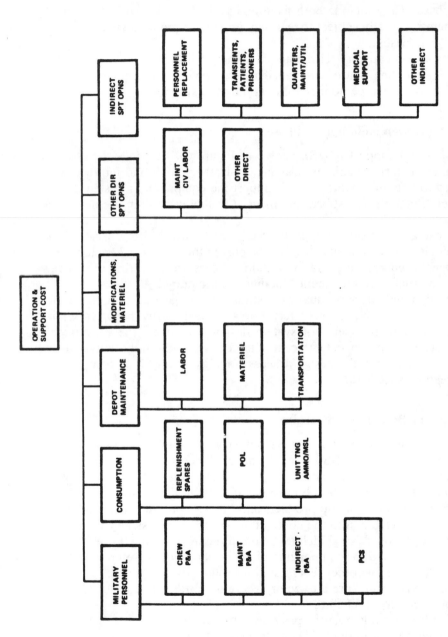

Figure 6.4 Operation-and-support cost-element structure (6). (Source: Department of Army Pamphlet No. 11-4, *Operating and Support Cost Guide for Army Materiel Systems*, 1976.)

TABLE 6.1 Summary Work-Breakdown Structure

Level 1	Level 2	Level 3
Electronic system		
	Prime mission equipment	
		Integration and assembly
		Sensors
		Communications
		Automatic data processing equipment
		Computer programs
		Data displays
		Auxiliary systems
	Training	
		Equipment
		Services
		Facilities
	Peculiar support equipment	
		Organizational/intermediate (including equipment common to depot)
		Depot (only)
	System test and evaluation	
		Development test and evaluation
		Operational test and evaluation
		Mock-ups
		Test and evaluation support
		Test facilities
	System–program management	
		System engineering
		Project management
	Data	
		Technical publications
		Engineering data
		Management data
		Support data
		Data depository
	Operational–site activation	

TABLE 6.1 (*Continued*)

Level 1	Level 2	Level 3
		Contractor technical support
		Site construction
		Site, ship, or vehicle conversion
		System assembly, instal- lation, and checkout on site
	Common support equip- ment	
		Organizational–interme- diate (including equip- ment common to depot)
		Depot (only)
	Industrial facilities	
		Construction, conver- sion, expansion
Acquisition or moderni- zation		
	Initial spares and initial repair parts	
		(Specify by allowance list, grouping, or hard- ware element)

6.3   ESTIMATING REALISM

The roots of cost realism in design to cost are valid ground rules and assumptions. The heart of the estimate is a sound, credible database consisting of historical and analytical data used to estimate costs and perform checks on the estimates. Beyond that, estimating realism is a function of the rigor applied in the estimating process and in documenting the estimate.

6.3.1 Ground Rules and Assumptions

"Ground rules" are defined as requirements specified by the customer, whereas "assumptions" are defined as boundary conditions selected by the contractor in the absence of pertinent ground rules. Therefore, ground rules and assumptions describe the scenario that the estimated cost reflects.

Table 6.2 lists some of the areas that must be defined explicitly. In the absence of specific ground rules in requests for proposal, explicit assumptions must be stated in the proposals.

TABLE 6.2   Ground Rules and Assumptions Checklist

Program plan
Product baseline
Cost element structures and relationships
Customer-furnished equipment, facilities, and services
Allowable costs
Periods of performance
Production quantities and rates
Learning and improvement curves
Shifts per day and days per week
Tooling and test equipment
Make-or-buy decisions
Strategic materials and precious metals
Procurement lead time
Inflation, escalation, and deescalation factors
Contractual relationships

TABLE 6.3   Cost Estimate Documentation Requirements

General

Describe product baseline
Identify cost elements included in estimates
Provide risk analysis for each estimate
Identify trade study effects on cost estimates
Present historical costs in constant-year dollars
Identify and justify learning and improvement curves

Expert Opinion, Analogy, and Parametric Cost Estimating

Identify and justify experts
Identify and justify analogous items
Identify and justify cost estimating relationships
Provide confidence intervals for each estimate

Industrial Engineering Estimating

Describe production philosophy, flow, and processes
Provide basis of estimate for each element
Cite labor standards and their derivation

Supplier Quotations

Present range and distribution of quotations
Distinguish estimates from quotations
Justify supplier selections
Quantify support costs added to quotations

It is imperative that every ground rule and assumption be given a critical examination for its validity in a real-world environment. Most questions regarding the validity of a product or its cost result from improper selection or inadequate documentation of assumptions and ground rules.

6.3.2 Database Credibility

The credibility of cost estimates is a direct function of the credibility of the database. In particular, care should be taken to adequately document ground rules and assumptions because of their pervasive effect in all program phases.

The term "baseline" in design-to-cost context connotes the point of departure for the performance and cost to be realized in the course of programs. It is essential that baselines are properly documented and controlled.

Table 6.3 summarizes requirements that should be imposed from the onset of programs in the interest of credible documentation. Documentation should be maintained strictly under configuration control as described in Section 3.6 to further ensure its credibility and to provide an audit trail of subsequent cost performance.

The alternative to reliable documentation is the inability to anticipate and prevent, or even rationalize cost growth due to causes other than inflation. Table 6.4 lists a number of factors that cause cost escalation.

TABLE 6.4 Cost-Escalation Factors

Immature, overstated, and understated requirements
Difference in perception of requirements
Inadequate specifications
Immature baseline definition
Inadequate up-front analysis
Complexity growth
Baseline changes
Redesign due to failures
Budget instability
Program stretchout
Lack of continuity
Supplier delinquency
Management changes
Rotation of personnel
Relocation of facilities
Union contract negotiations
Government regulation
Customer involvement
Customer's cost perception based on single estimate

6.4 ESTIMATING METHODOLOGY

The four classes of estimating methods are based on expert opinion, analogy, parametric relationships, and industrial engineering. Estimating methodology varies with program phases as a function of the maturity of the products or systems as shown in Figure 6.5.

The methods of cost-estimating relationships differ, but they all attempt to relate cost to product and programmatic variables. Table 6.5 summarizes techniques, applications, and tools by estimating method.

The cost of preparing estimates with extensive detail should be weighed against the value of the estimates; more detail does not necessarily ensure more accuracy. It should also be realized that most estimates are prepared with combinations of the various methods.

The key features, advantages, and disadvantages of the various methods are described in the following sections. Next, Pareto analysis is presented as a preferred approach to ranking cost drivers for investigation.

6.4.1 Expert Opinion

Sometimes, the only basis for a cost estimate is expert opinion. Although argumentative, it is often the only method available to the analyst because backup or historical data are sometimes scarce or nonexistent. In such instances, the analyst should be sure to include the assumptions and rationale that support the position.

The disadvantage of estimates based on expert opinion is that they are subject to bias, that increased program complexity can quickly degrade the

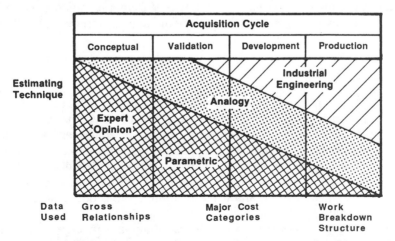

Figure 6.5 Time-phasing of cost-estimating methods (9). (Reprinted by permission of the Martin Marietta Corporation.)

TABLE 6.5   Cost Estimating Methods (10)

Method	Technique	Principal Acquisition Cycle Applications	Estimating Tools
Expert opinion	Use judgment of experts when supporting data, parametric CERs, or program definitions are insufficient	Conceptual	Delphi technique
	May be subject to bias and may not reflect growth in program complexity		
	Estimate cannot be quantified or substantiated		
Parametric	Cost-estimating relationships must be reasonable and have predictive value	Demonstration–validation	
	Use CERs that mathematically relate a parameter to cost	Conceptual	Cost models, cost databases
Analogy	Derive cost of a new program from data on past costs of similar programs	Demonstration–validation	Cost databases
	Limited to static technology and possibly to systems built by the same firm	FSED*a*	
	Requires expert opinion to determine similarities and differences	Production	
Industrial engineering	Derive detailed bottom-up estimates of all the operations required to develop and produce a specifically defined piece of equipment	FSED	Cost models, industrial engineering standards
	Use supplier quotes, worker-loading requirements by workstation, learning curves, and engineering standards built up from time-and-motion studies	Production	

Adapted by permission of the Martin Marietta Corporation (10).

a Full-scale engineering development.

estimates, and that the estimate cannot be substantiated or quantified. This can be offset to a some measure by the use of Delphi techniques as well as other techniques that quantify uncertainty in judgment rendered by experts (11).

6.4.2   Analogy

Analogy estimating derives costs of a new program from data on past costs of similar programs. This technique frequently involves estimating the incremental or marginal cost associated with program or equipment differences.

Analogy estimating is relatively simple and inexpensive to develop, and it has reasonable accuracy for similar or related systems. The disadvantage of analogy estimates is that it requires analogous products or systems. It is limited to static technology, and it may be limited to products and systems built by the same firm.

When using this approach, a considerable amount of expert opinion is required to determine the similarity and differences between the systems. Then cost adjusts are made for the differences. Cost adjustments can be based on known factors and rates, or on applicable estimating relationships.

Often, analogy estimates lack certain unknown but important details that, when eventually exposed, drive the cost estimates considerably higher.

6.4.3 Parametric Estimating

Parametric estimating is usually the only method that can be used to develop a detailed estimate from the limited data available during concept formulation, when only mission and performance envelopes are defined. Parametric estimating provides an inexpensive means of examining the cost impact of a variety of changes in system performance requirements.

Statistical techniques such as regression and correlation analysis are used to develop cost-estimating relationships contained in the parametric model. Statistical inference and hypotheses testing are used in estimating confidence in cost estimates derived parametrically. Section 6.6.1 provides details on the latter.

A typical relationship that can be developed is shown in Figure 6.6 where the squares indicate the known costs used in the predictive process. The technique for constructing such curves is called "regression" and is described in Section 6.6.2.

Cost-estimating relationships may assume numerous forms, varying from rule of thumb to the formally derived mathematical relationships that were shown in Figures 2.5 to 2.9. Generally, cost and related data are collected on

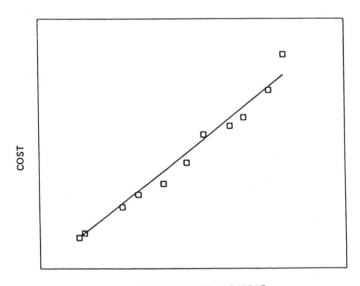

Figure 6.6 Typical parametric cost-estimating relationship (12). (Reprinted by permission of John Wiley & Sons, Inc.)

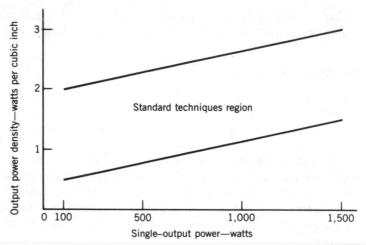

Figure 6.7   Volume as a function of output power (15). (Source: NAVMAT P3855-1, *Navy Power Supply Reliability,* 1982.)

existing systems, analyzed, converted to the form of some familiar relationship, and applied to a new system that is similar in form, fix, and function.

Weight and volume relationships, which equate to equipment density, are particularly meaningful in parametric estimating (13). For the power supply discussed in Section 4.8, power output would be added to the aforementioned for the relationships shown in Figures 6.7 and 6.8. Cost arguments would thus be expressed in terms of watts per cubic inch or watts per pound.

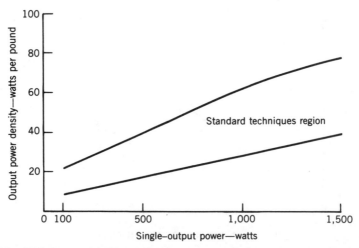

Figure 6.8   Weight as a function of output power (16). (Source: NAVMAT P3855-1, *Navy Power Supply Reliability,* 1982.)

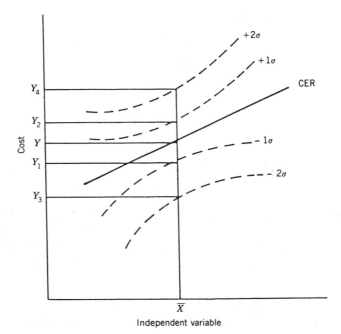

Figure 6.9 Parametric cost-estimating relationship confidence intervals (17). (Adapted by permission of John Wiley & Sons, Inc.)

Guidelines based on experience can be used to gauge the reasonableness of parametric estimates. Typically, the development cost of high-technology power supplies range from about 2.5 to 5 times the cost of the bill of material, and procured custom power supplies cost about 5 to 10 percent of total electronic systems production costs (14).

The disadvantage of parametric estimating is that available data may be insufficient to form valid cost conclusions on final products that may differ substantially from early conceptions. Parametric estimating is also sensitive to inconsistencies and irregularities in the data base. No mathematical technique can compensate for missing or inconsistent data.

However, parametric estimates have the advantage of being based on data that reflect the continuum of changes in high-technology programs. Use of parametric models takes into account statistical averages of such experiences.

As shown in Figure 6.9, this allows meaningful confidence intervals to be placed about cost-estimating relationships. The notation $\bar{X}$ in the illustration locates the mean value of the independent variable x. Note the increasing divergence in the confidence intervals for values of x less and greater than $\bar{X}$ and the increasing interval width from ± 1 standard deviation ($\pm 1\sigma$) to ± 2 standard deviations ($\pm 2\sigma$) and to ± 3 standard deviations ($\pm 3\sigma$). This subject is revisited in Section 6.5.2.

TABLE 6.6   Parametric Model Attributes

Structure

Replicates hardware generation breakdown
Starts characterizations no higher than subassembly level

Stacking

Replicates production flow
Compiles cost in accordance with make-or-buy decision criteria and build plan
 and with work-breakdown structure

An additional challenge in parametric modeling is to replicate the interaction between product designs and manufacturing processes. The model must satisfy the attributes listed in Table 6.6 to provide realistic estimates.

6.4.4   Industrial Engineering

The industrial engineering approach relies on detailed estimates of all the operations required to develop and produce a specifically defined product or system. It makes use of supplier quotations, worker-loading by work center and workstation, learning curves, and standards derived from time-and-motion studies. It is also referred to as "bottom-up estimating."

Product Area _____ WBS _____ Assy/Subassy # _____												
System/Subsystem _____ Title _____ Quantity_____												
							G/B Date _____					
							Need Date _____					
Item			Non Recurring				Total	Recurring				Total
GB Level	Part Number	Description	Labor $	Mtl $	S/C $	ODC $	$	Labor $	Mtl $	S/C $	ODC $	$

Figure 6.10   Industrial engineering estimate (18). (Reprinted by permission of the Martin Marietta Corporation.)

The advantage of the industrial engineering cost estimating is that it can provide accurate cost projections when detailed information is available. In addition, it can be applied independently to the various functional cost elements of products or systems. Thus, as more detailed information becomes available for specific elements, earlier estimates can be refined or replaced with the kind of detail given in Figure 6.10.

The disadvantage of industrial engineering estimating is that it cannot be used until detailed input data are available, by which time previous events may have precluded more attractive alternatives. In addition, the approach is usually more costly and time-consuming than the other methods.

6.5 LEARNING CURVES

Learning curves are essential elements in design to cost, wherein they are used to develop goals, prepare bids, and subsequently to plan and schedule manufacturing-related activities. Learning curves are used to project labor cost. Improvement curves are composites of a number of contributing learning curves for both labor and other cost elements such as parts and material.

6.5.1 Application

Learning curves allow expedient and accurate projection of future production cost given relevant historical data. They apply the principle of constant rate of improvement to unit progression in production. Thus, with an 80 percent curve, each time the quantity doubles, the cost is reduced by 20 percent.

There are two approaches to the application of learning curves, the *Wright* cumulative average system and the *Crawford* unit system. The Wright system, developed in the early 1930s, was used predominantly until recent years. Most organizations now use the Crawford system (19).

Learning curves typically range from 70 to 99 percent in high-technology applications, with assembly operations usually falling in the 70 to 89 percent

TABLE 6.7 Learning Curves Credibility Checklist

	Percentage Relative to Standards
Basic Product Concept	
Basic process concept	90–99
New process concept	85–95
New Product Concept	
Basic process concept	80–90
New process concept	75–85

TABLE 6.8   Learning Curve Factors

Proportion of manual to machine elements of work
Product and process technology
Product and process maturity
Personnel training and continuity
Design and manufacturing engineering support
Level of preproduction planning
Production quantity and rate
Period of performance
Quality criteria
Management effectiveness.

range and fabrication falling from 80 to 99 percent. Procurement learning curves range from 90 percent to 99 percent. Table 6.7 can serve as a credibility checklist for evaluating proposed learning curve values; the key discriminator is the maturity of products and processes.

6.5.2   Probabilistic Nature

The extent and rate of learning are influenced by many factors that should be understood and annotated in the form of ground rules or assumptions before learning curves are applied. Table 6.8 lists a number of the principal factors.

The attempt to capture the historical influence of these factors on learning curves in a high-technology program is shown in Figure 6.11. In simple terms, the illustration says that there is a 50/50 chance of achieving an 89 percent learning curve in the machine shop, 87 percent in chassis assembly and 85 percent in final assembly.

The more realistic 80/20 chance (i.e., 80 percent probability of occurrence) based on historical data was that only 95, 92, and 90 percent learning curves would be achieved. The increase in slope from the machine-shop curve to that of chassis assembly and of final assembly is reflective of the increased ratio of manual to automated processes.

6.6   ESTIMATING CONFIDENCE

It can be concluded from the preceding discussion of the probabilistic nature of learning curves that there is inherent uncertainty even in industrial engineering estimates that are based on well-known and well-documented relationships. It follows, therefore, that the uncertainty is still greater in the other forms of estimating that deal with the more conceptual relationships, and it is advisable to provide confidence intervals, especially for cost estimates by experts, by analogy or by parametric means.

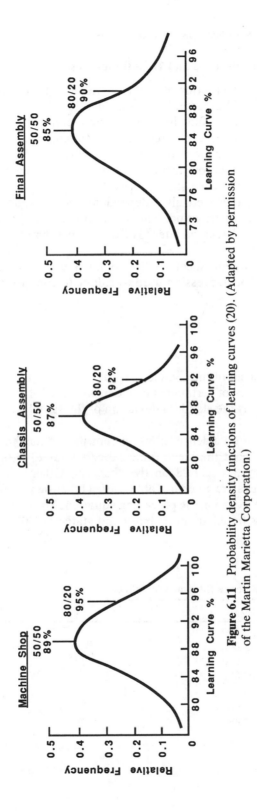

Figure 6.11 Probability density functions of learning curves (20). (Adapted by permission of the Martin Marietta Corporation.)

6.6.1 Statistical Inference and Hypotheses Testing

Confidence is stated in terms of expected value and the range of values the expected value could assume. The range of values is called the "confidence interval" and varies as a function of the desired confidence level at any given sample size. An example of a confidence statement is: "The 80 percent confidence interval for the expected cost saving of $720,694 is $693,217 to $748,171 on the basis of four independent estimates of the expected saving." Underlying this confidence statement is the assumption of normality. That is, that four estimates are truly independent and are thus governed by the normal probability distribution. This assumption is an hypothesis, and hypotheses testing is discussed later. The question at hand is how to calculate confidence interval.

Table 6.9 is the worksheet for the confidence interval given in the previous example. The expression used to calculate confidence interval CI is

$$CI = \bar{X} \pm z\left(\frac{s}{\sqrt{n}}\right) \qquad (6.1)$$

where $\bar{X}$ is the mean of the sample, z is the standard statistic used to determine the probability of certain areas under the curve of the normal probability distribution, s is the standard deviation of the sample, and n is the size of the sample.

For example, a confidence of 80 percent means that the area under the curve centered about the mean (i.e., expected value) is 0.80 and that this area is bound by $z = \pm 1.28$ on the abscissa. Other values of area as a function of z values are given in Table 6.10. The $\pm$ signs before the values of z account for the $\pm$ sign in the preceding equation. More extensive tables can be found in most books on probability and statistics (21).

TABLE 6.9   Confidence Interval Worksheet

Estimate, x_i ($)	$(x_i - X)^2$ ($)
750,000	38,688
725,000	352,688
700,000	1,916,688
800,000	3,160,688
Σx_i = $2,975,000	$\Sigma(x_i - X)^2$ = $5,468,752
Mean = X = $2,975,000/4	Variance = s^2 = 5,468,752/3
= $743,750	= 1,822,917
	Standard deviation = $\sqrt{s^2}$
	= 42,696

TABLE 6.10 z **Value as a Function of Area P under the Normal Curve**

P	z
.50	±0.0
.55	±0.06
.60	±0.84
.65	±0.94
.70	±1.04
.75	±1.15
.80	±1.28
.85	±1.44
.90	±1.64
.95	±1.96
.99	±2.58

The value of n to be used in Equation (6.1) is 4, and along with $z = 1.28$, $\bar{X} = \$743,740$, and $s = \$42,696$, yields

$$\text{CI} = \$743,740 \pm 1.28 \left(\frac{\$42,696}{\sqrt{4}}\right) \tag{6.2}$$

$$= \$716,415 \text{ to } \$771,065$$

at a confidence level of 80 percent.

The emphasis to this point has been on making inferences about a population from properties of a sample. The emphasis is turned around under hypotheses testing and starts by making an assumption, or hypothesis, about some population parameter, assigning a significance level to the hypothesis and then testing that hypothesis by analyzing a random sample of the population. Significance level is denoted by the Greek letter α (alpha) and is related to confidence level by $1 - \alpha$.

The hypothesis under test is called the "null hypothesis"; the term implying that there would be no deleterious effect in not rejecting the hypothesis. Note the use of the words "not rejecting the hypothesis" rather than "accepting the hypothesis" because the hypothesis might be rejected at a greater significance level. The notation H_0 is used to denote a null hypothesis. If H_0 were rejected on the basis of the sample, then an alternative hypothesis denoted by H_1 would, in fact, be accepted.

Decision rules are formulated in terms of significance level α. Alpha is the area under the normal probability curve residing in what is called the "rejection region." The remaining area, $1 - \alpha$, resides in what is called the "acceptance region." As shown in Figure 6.12, the rejection region can be either one or both tails depending on whether a one-tailed or two-tailed test is undertaken. In the case of the latter, the area in each tail is $\alpha/2$.

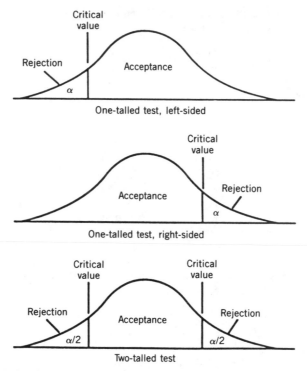

Figure 6.12   Rejection and acceptance regions (22). (Reprinted by permission of the Martin Marietta Corporation.)

Either the z statistic or the student's t statistic is used in testing hypotheses unless dealing with a small sample (less than 30) from a nonnormal population. In that case, nonparametric, or distribution-free methods are required (23).

The value of the test statistic at the boundary of the tail or tails contained in the rejection region is called the "critical value" and is determined from probability tables. The procedure is to calculate the test statistic for the random sample and reject H_0 when the calculated value is either less (more negative) than the critical value bounding the left tail or greater (more positive) than the critical value bounding the right tail. Otherwise, H_0 is not rejected.

The procedural steps for testing hypotheses are given below. It is convenient to follow these steps in a formal manner; however, the important thing is to observe the essence of each step:

1. State the null hypothesis indicating the value of the population parameter to be tested. For the example given above, this would be H_0: $\mu =$ \$743,740.

2. State the alternative hypothesis indicating a value of the population parameter other than that of the null hypothesis. For the example, this would be H_1: μ = \$743,740. The symbol $\neq$ denotes "not equal to."
3. Determine from the alternative hypothesis whether a one-tailed or two-tailed test is required, for example:

$$H_1: \quad \mu < \$743,740; \text{ one-tailed test, left-sided}$$

$$H_1: \quad \mu > \$743,740; \text{ one-tailed test, right-sided}$$

$$H_1: \quad \mu \neq \$743,740; \text{ two-tailed test}$$

4. Select the test statistic and determine the critical value for the significance level α.
5. Compute the value of the test statistic for the random sample.
6. Reject H_0 if the value of the test statistic falls beyond the critical value.

Hypotheses testing is conducted on means and proportion. The usual application in design to cost is on means, which is illustrated with two examples: one with a large-sized sample and the other with a small-sized sample. It is frequently required to validate manufacturers' claims for product life. What is done is to test the hypothesis that the mean product life is as stated on the basis of a random sample of the product.

Consider the claim of the manufacturer of highway lighting components that certain light sources have a mean life of 10,000 hr with a standard deviation of 400 hrs. A state highway department wishes to test 100 samples from a large shipment of these light sources and wishes to know what the minimum mean life value of the 100 samples tested should be to conclude with a significance level of α = 0.05 that the balance of the shipment is acceptable. The decision rules are stated as follows:

$$H_0: \quad \mu = 10,000 \text{ hr}$$

$$H_1: \quad \mu < 10,000 \text{ hr}$$

The inequality sign in the second equation signifies the need for a one-tailed test, left-sided.

The large sample size allows the assumption of normality and the use the z statistic for the test statistic. The z statistic is calculated with

$$z = \frac{X - \mu}{\sigma_{\bar{x}}} \tag{6.3}$$

where $\sigma_{\bar{x}}$ is called the "standard error of the mean" and is given by

$$\sigma_{\bar{x}} = \frac{\sigma}{\sqrt{n}} \tag{6.4}$$

The solution of Equation (6.4) yields $\sigma_{\bar{x}}$ = 40 hr.

The value of z in the first equation is called the "critical value" and is obtained from the table of areas under the normal curve that is given in most statistics books. The value of z is -1.645 when the area under the curve in the left tail of the distribution is 0.05. This value is substituted in Equation (6.3) along with $\sigma_{\bar{x}} = 40$ hr and the manufacturer's claim of $\mu = 10,000$ hr, obtaining $-1.645 = (\bar{X} - 10,000)/40$, or $\bar{X} = 9934.2$ hr.

It can be concluded, therefore, that the balance of the shipment should not be rejected if the mean life of the 100 samples tested is 9,934.2 hr or more.

It is now discerned that the light sources are extremely costly items and no more than 10 light sources are to be consumed in the acceptance test. Normality can still be assumed because of the large population. However, the approach is altered in this small-sample case, and the t statistic, instead of the z statistic, is used.

After the life test of the 10 light sources is completed, it is found that the sample mean is 9750 hr and the sample standard deviation is 350 hr. It is now necessary to test the hypothesis that the mean value of the entire shipment is 10,000 hr. The decision rules are unchanged from the previous example.

The t statistic is calculated with

$$t = \frac{\bar{X} - \mu}{s_{\bar{x}}} \tag{6.5}$$

where $s_{\bar{x}}$ is called the "standard error of the sample mean" and is given by

$$s_{\bar{x}} = \frac{s}{\sqrt{n}} \tag{6.6}$$

where s is the sample standard deviation.

Substituting $s = 350$ hr and $n = 10$ in the last equation yields $s_{\bar{x}} = 110.68$.

This value is substituted in Equation (6.5), along with $\bar{X} = 9,500$ hr, $\mu = 10,000$ hr, and $s_{\bar{x}} = 110.68$ hr, obtaining $t = -2.26$.

The table of critical values of the student's t distribution that is also given in most statistics books is entered with both significance level and degrees of freedom. Degrees of freedom equal $n - 1$, where n is the sample size, and for the example the value is $10 - 1$, or 9. The table indicates that for 9 degrees of freedom and $\alpha = 0.05$, the critical value for the left tail is $t = -1.83$.

The calculated value of $t = -2.26$ is smaller (more negative) than the critical value of $t = -1.83$ from the table. Therefore, for $\alpha = 0.05$, the null hypothesis that the mean life of the entire shipment is 10,000 hr should be rejected and, of course, the balance of the shipment should not be accepted.

6.6.2 Regression and Correlation

Much effort in design to cost is devoted to projecting budgets and costs, and it is appropriate that practitioners gain facility in regression and correlation analysis. Regression is used to determine the probable form of the relationships among variables. Correlation provides the quantitative means for measuring the strength of these relationships.

The work is usually limited to linear regression of two variables: one the independent and the other the dependent variable. The uppercase letters X and Y are used to denote the independent and dependent variables, respectively, whereas the lowercase letters x and y are used to denote specific values of the variables. The notations x_i and y_i signify the ith values of the variables.

Two variables X and Y are linearly related if their relationship is described by

$$Y = \alpha + \beta X + e \tag{6.7}$$

where the parameters α and β are called the "regression constant" and "regression coefficient," respectively. The parameter e, called the "residual error," represents the deviations of the individual values of Y about the mean of the values of Y.

Linear regression uses the method of least squares, which is based on the following postulate: *The sum of the squared deviations of observed values of y_i from the least-squares line derived from $y_i = \alpha + \beta x_i$ is smaller than the sum of the squared deviations of the observed values of y_i from any other straight line that can be drawn through the observed values of y_i.*

The linear regression model is thus a straight line that is given by

$$y_i = \alpha + \beta x_i \tag{6.8}$$

The values of α and β for any given set of X and Y data can be obtained by the simultaneous solution of the following normal equations:

$$\Sigma y_i = n\alpha + \beta \Sigma x_i \tag{6.9}$$

$$\Sigma x_i y_i = \alpha \Sigma x_i + \beta \Sigma x_i^2 \tag{6.10}$$

where n is the number of data points in the set.

Table 6.11 is an example of the worksheet used for calculating the regression of Y on X, where again X is the independent variable and Y is the dependent variable. Reversing the role of X and Y would alter the preceding equations.

The x_i values in the table are thousands of operations of a specific process in a production line. The y_i values are per-unit operation times in seconds and were observed in a methods–time–motion (MTM) study.

TABLE 6.11   Least-Squares-Method Worksheet

x_i	x_i^2	y_i	y_i^2	$x_i y_i$
1.5	2.25	14.5	210.25	21.75
2.0	4.0	15.0	225.0	30.0
2.5	6.25	11.5	132.25	28.75
3.0	9.0	13.0	169.0	39.0
3.5	12.25	9.5	90.25	33.25
4.0	16.0	11.0	121.0	44.0
4.5	20.25	8.5	72.25	38.25
5.0	25.0	10.0	100.0	50.0
5.5	30.25	9.0	81.0	49.5
6.0	36.0	7.0	49.0	42.0
37.5	161.25	109.0	1250.0	376.5

The first step in the procedure is to plot the scatter diagram shown in Figure 6.13. This allows one to judge the suitability of first-order (linear) versus higher-order curves for fitting the relationship between the independent and dependent variables. The illustration suggests that a linear (i.e., straight-line) fit may be suitable.

Values from Table 6.11 and $n = 10$ are substituted in Equations (6.9) and (6.10) to obtain the following normal equations:

$$109.0 = \alpha 10 + \beta 37.5 \tag{6.11}$$

$$376.5 = \alpha 37.5 + \beta 161.25 \tag{6.12}$$

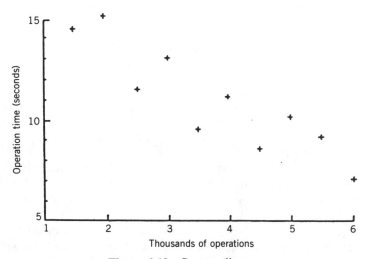

Figure 6.13   Scatter diagram.

Equations 6.11 and 6.12 are solved simultaneously, yielding $\alpha = 16.7636$ and $\beta = -1.5636$, which, when substituted in Equation (6.8), yield.

$$y_i = 16.7636 - 1.5636x_i \qquad (6.13)$$

Equation (6.13) is referred to as the "regression of Y on X" for the data in Table 6.11.

Equation (6.13) is now solved, first letting $x_i = 1$ and then for $x_i = 6$, obtaining $y_i = 15.2276$ and $y_i = 7.382$. The two sets of coordinates [(1, 15.2276) and 6, 7.382)] are located on the scatter diagram, and the least-squares line is drawn as shown in Figure 6.14.

The negative slope of the line in the illustration reflects the minus sign in the right-hand term of Equation (6.13). The relationship depicted for X and Y is called "inverse-linear" because increased values of X results in decreased values of Y at a constant rate.

The next question is what is the strength of the relationship between the variables X and Y as represented by the least-squares line in Figure 6.14. This answer is provided by what is called "correlation analysis" in the form of the coefficient of correlation, or the coefficient of determination, which is simply the square of the former.

The values of the coefficient of correlation range from -1 to $+1$. The closer the values are to either of these extremes, the greater the correlation between independent and dependent variables. These relationships are shown in Figure 6.15. Note that the relationship in part d resembles an exponential curve.

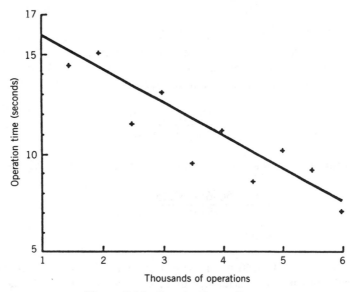

Figure 6.14   Least-squares line.

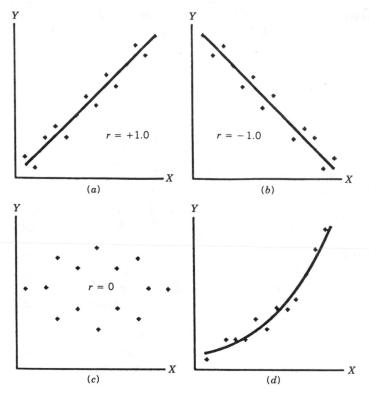

Figure 6.15   Correlation relationships: (*a*) direct-linear correlation; (*b*) inverse-linear correlation; (*c*) zero correlation; (*d*) second-order correlation.

The range of values of the coefficient of determination, which is the square of the coefficient of correlation, is 0 to 1. The equation for calculating the coefficient of determination, denoted by r^2, is

$$r^2 = \frac{b^2[\Sigma x_1^2 - (\Sigma x_1)^2/n]}{\Sigma y_1^2 - (\Sigma y_1)^2/n} \tag{6.14}$$

Substituting the values from Table 6.12 in Equation (6.14) yields

$$r^2 = \frac{(-1.5636)^2[161.25 - (37.5)^2/10]}{1250.0 - (109.0)^2/10} \tag{6.15}$$

$$= 0.8146$$

The value of $r^2 = 0.8146$ means that the regression of Y on X explains 81.46 percent of the total variability in Y. In other words, 81.46 percent of the variability in Y is a function of X, and 18.5 percent is due to other causes.

The value of the coefficient of correlation is the square root of 0.8146, or 0.9026. Because of the inverse relationship between Y and X, as shown in Figure 6.15, the coefficient of correlation is negative and r = −0.9026.

6.6.3 Confidence Limits

The next question concerns the confidence limits about the least-squares line as a function of the desired confidence level. The general form of the relationship is shown in Figure 6.16.

The parameters L_u and L_l denote the upper and lower limits of the confidence interval about the least-squares line for the regression of Y on X. Note that the interval is shortest at the mean of X ($\bar{X}$) and that the confidence interval grows wider as x moves away from the mean. The limits in the illustration are for a confidence of 95 percent. The spacing between the limits increases with increased values of confidence.

Note also the nonlinear (second-order) nature of the curves depicting the confidence limits. The nonlinearity is due to the following second-order relationship used to calculate confidence limits (CL).

$$CL = y_e \pm t_{1-\alpha/2} s_{Y|X} \sqrt{\frac{1}{n} + \frac{(x_e - \bar{X})^2}{\Sigma x_i^2 - (\Sigma x_1)^2/n}} \tag{6.16}$$

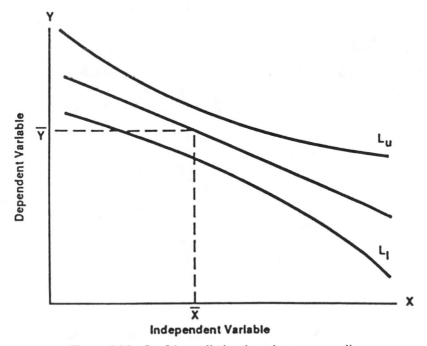

Figure 6.16   Confidence limits about least-squares line.

The notations y_e and x_e in Equation (6.16) denote the estimate of Y for a specific value of X. The appearance of the t statistic in the equation is necessitated by the small sample size.

The value of $t_{1-\alpha/2}$ is obtained from the table of the student's t distribution for the given significance level α and degrees of freedom (DF), which are given by $n - 1$. For a confidence of 95 percent or 0.95, $\alpha = 1 - 0.95$ or 0.05, $\alpha/2 = 0.025$, and $1 - \alpha/2 = 0.975$. The table would be entered in the 0.975 column and the row for DF = $10 - 1$ or 9, yielding the value of 0.3978 for the t statistic.

The notation $s_{Y|X}$ in Equation (6.16) is called the "unbiased estimate of the population standard deviation of Y given the standard deviation of X" and can be calculated with

$$s_{Y|X} = \sqrt{\frac{\Sigma y_1^2 - \alpha \Sigma y_1 - \beta \Sigma x_1 y_1}{n - 2}} \qquad (6.17)$$

The symbol $\bar{X}$ is the sample mean of the variable X and is given by

$$\bar{X} = \frac{\Sigma x_i}{n} \qquad (6.18)$$

For the data in Table 6.12, $\bar{X} = 37.5/10$ or 3.75.

6.6.4 Predictions

Regression and correlation are important tools for predicting future events from historical data. For example, an application could be to predict on the basis of the data in Table 6.11, the per-unit operation time when 70,000 operations are performed.

First, y_e is calculated using Equation (6.13):

$$y_e = 16.7636 - 1.5636(7) \qquad (6.19)$$

$$= 5.8184$$

Next, $s_{Y|X}$ is calculated using Equation (6.17):

$$s_{Y|X} = \sqrt{\frac{1250.0 - 16.7636(109.0) + 1.5636(376.5)}{10 - 2}} \qquad (6.20)$$

$$= 1.1970$$

Finally, the following variant of Equation 6.16 is used to calculate the 95 percent confidence limits for $y_e = 5.8184$ sec:

$$CL = y_e \pm t_{1-\alpha/2} s_{Y|X} \sqrt{1 + \frac{1}{n} + \frac{(x_e - \bar{X})^2}{\Sigma x_1^2 - (\Sigma x_1)^2}} \qquad (6.21)$$

$$= 5.8184 \pm 0.3978(1.1970) \sqrt{1 + \frac{1}{10} \pm \frac{(7.0 - 3.75)^2}{161.25 - (37.5)^2/10}}$$

$$= 5.8184 \pm 0.5875 \text{ sec}$$

Thus, it can be predicted with 95 percent confidence that when 70,000 operations are performed, the per-unit operation time will fall between 5.2309 and 6.4059 sec.

6.6.5 Bayes's Theorem in Decision Making

Bayes's theorem is at the heart of statistical decision theory and rational decisions are embodiments of Bayes's theorem. Most managers use Bayes's theorem involving a priori and a posteriori probabilities without realizing it.

Thomas Bayes (1702–1761), an English mathematician, developed the first precise, quantitative mathematical expression for inductive inference. His theorem on inverse probability, published posthumously in 1763, yields the probability that an event that has already occurred may have occurred in a particular way and provides a powerful tool for determining root causes of problems.

Applications of Bayes's theorem of inverse probability range from medicine, science, engineering, and manufacturing to economics and military strategy. Judicious use of Bayes's theorem greatly improves the quality of decisions, especially where root causes of discerned effects are to be deduced, or where associated risks of alternative approaches are to be evaluated.

Bayes's theorem employs both a priori probability and a posteriori probability to evaluate causal hypotheses. Its conclusions are both precise mathematically and tempered by empirical data. It is only controversial because of the subjective nature of assigning a priori probabilities to events yet to take place.

The essence of Bayes's theorem is that the probability of occurrence of one particular hypothesis is equal to its conditional probability divided by the sum of the conditional probabilities of all hypotheses. If a set of events is mutually exclusive and collectively exhaustive, Bayes's Theorem can be expressed as follows (24):

$$P(H_j|E) = \frac{P(H_j)P(E|H_j)}{\Sigma_{j=1}^{n} P(H_j)P(E|H_j)} \qquad (6.22)$$

where $P(H_{j|E})$ denotes the probability that hypothesis H_j caused the event E out of all possible hypothetical causes, given the event has occurred.

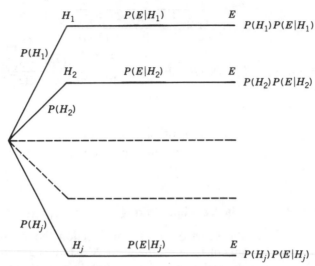

H_1 $P(E|H_1)$ E

$P(H_1)P(E|H_1)$

$P(H_1)$

H_2 $P(E|H_2)$ E

$P(H_2)P(E|H_2)$

$P(H_2)$

$P(H_j)$

H_j $P(E|H_j)$ E

$P(H_j)P(E|H_j)$

Figure 6.17 Bayes's theorem in tree form (25). (Reprinted by permission of the Martin Marietta Corporation.)

It is convenient to view Bayes's theorem in the probability tree form shown in Figure 6.17. The probability that event E was reached by the jth branch of the tree, given that it was reached through one of the n branches, is the ratio of the probability associated with the jth branch with all n branches of the tree.

Consider the example of an organization wishing to procure a new data processing facility that needs to know the most likely turnkey cost for budgeting. Data given in Table 6.12 relate cost hypotheses to their respective probabilities as estimated by the organization's staff and concluded from informal quotations by potential suppliers.

The concern is the likelihood that the facility might cost $5 million. The issue of staff conservatism and supplier optimism can be resolved by using Bayes's theorem. Applying Equation (6.22), the probability of the facility costing $5 million is

TABLE 6.12 Cost Estimating Data (26)

Cost Hypothesis, $	Staff Probability	Supplier Probability
5,000,000	0.60	0.40
4,500,000	0.25	0.30
4,000,000	0.10	0.20
3,500,000	0.05	0.10

Reprinted by permission of the Martin Marietta Corporation.

$$P(\$5 \text{ million} \mid Q_i) = \frac{(.60)(.40)}{(.60)(.40) + (.25)(.30) + (.10)(.20) + (.50)(.10)} \quad (6.23)$$

$$= .71$$

where $P(\$5 \text{ million} \mid Q_i)$ is the probability that the facility will cost $5 million given the supplier quotations.

6.7 TIME VALUE OF MONEY

Questions of technical feasibility, economic feasibility and financial feasibility are paramount in assessing alternative approaches and addressing issues of capital investment versus long-term return on investment (ROI). The essence of technical feasibility is that proposed products and processes perform their intended functions in the manner expected regarding performance and reliability. Economic feasibility requires that the total value of the ensuing benefits from pursuing these products and processes exceed the attendant costs with sufficient margin to warrant the investments.

There may or may not be a relationship between financial feasibility and economic feasibility depending on the magnitude of investments. Issues may range from the inability to obtain long-term financing to the competition for funding among various program areas in the companies.

The expression "planning horizon" is used to denote the period of time over which these issues of feasibility need be considered for both ongoing enterprises and new initiatives. Typically the planning horizon is at least 5 years, and sometimes 10 or more years.

In the case of 5 years or more, the resultant deliberations are documented in what is usually referred to as the "long-range operating plan" and govern all operational aspects of the particular organization from marketing through production. In the DoD, this document is called the "Five-Year Defense Program" (FYDP).

Plans for longer periods of time are more strategic in nature and are generally concerned with penetrating new marketplaces and attendant capital investments in technology and facilities. The state of the overall economy is as much a decision criterion in carrying out these plans as anything relating to the marketplaces of interest.

Irrespective of the extent of the planning horizon, expenditures and revenues addressed in these plans occur at different times, and it is necessary to consider the time value of money from a common time baseline in order to make meaningful trades and render cogent judgment. In essence, time is money.

The concept of "equivalence" is important in economic analysis and means simply that a dollar today is equivalent to something more than a dollar in the future if the dollar were invested today in an interest-bearing or profit-producing opportunity. Conversely, a dollar in the future is equivalent to something less than a dollar today under the same circumstances.

Table 6.13 defines a number of terms that are important in understanding the time value of money and in performing economic analysis. These terms are defined again in Appendix 1.

Most calculations of the time value of money are based on compound

TABLE 6.13   Economic Analysis Terms

Capital recovery. The point at which a loan or investment, adjusted for the time value of money, is recovered; usually expressed in terms of number of repayments, period of time, or number of units sold

Compound interest. Interest earned on interest earned on the principal

Constant-year dollars. A baseline or reference year, either prio. ⌐r future with respect to the present time, used for cost and earning comparisons; now and then dollars are converted to the baseline year using actual and projected inflation indices

Cost–benefit ratio. The ratio of the present value of benefits to the present value of costs

Discount rate. The factor, expressed as a percentage, used to calculate the present value of a sum of money in the future

Equivalence. The equivalent present value of a sum of money with a given value in the future

Future value. The value of a given sum of money at a future time equivalent to the value of the sum of money at the present time at a given interest rate

Interest rate. The ratio, expressed as a percentage, of interest earned or paid at the end of a given period of time to the money invested or borrowed at the beginning of the given period of time

Internal rate of return. The rate of return at which the present value of benefits equals the present value of costs

Now dollars. The value of a given sum of dollars at the current time

Opportunity cost. The return that would have been realized if the money had been invested in an alternative opportunity

Principal. The amount of money invested or borrowed

Present value. The value at the present time of a future payment of receipt at a given discount rate

Rate of Return. The ratio, expressed as a percentage, of profit to a given expense or investment adjusted for the time value of money

Simple interest. Interest earned on the principal

Sinking fund. Fund used to retire debt or acquire new equipment that is established by a series of deposits at fixed time intervals

Sunk cost. Previously expended or committed money that is not considered in future economic analysis

Then dollars. The value of future dollars adjusted from the value of a given sum of now dollars using projected inflation indices

Uniform series. Series of payments or receipts of fixed amounts, at fixed time intervals, and at fixed interest rate or discount rate interest. Depending on the number of time periods involved, many iterative calculations may be required. The task can be eased by using compound interest tables adapted specifically for time value of money or by applying the formulation described in this section.

Table 6.14 is an example of these compound-interest tables based on the rate of 10 percent compounded annually. The numbers in the table are factors used to multiply the principal amounts to arrive at the time-adjusted values. Published tables cover wide ranges of time periods and interest rates or discount rates (27). However, design-to-cost practioners are urged to become familiar with the formulation to facilitate the use of the tables and because occasionally certain combinations of rates and time periods that are of interest are not covered by the tables.

6.7.1 Single-Payments Formulation

The single-payments formulation allows the transformation of the time value of payment from one time frame to another. The relationships are (1) the future value of a single payment (or receipt) at the present time and (2) the present value of a single payment at a future time.

1. FUTURE VALUE OF A PRESENT SINGLE PAYMENT (FVPSP)

The most frequently encountered question is what a certain sum of money invested today at a certain interest rate will be worth several years from

TABLE 6.14   10 Percent Compound Interest Table

n	FVPSP	PVFSP	USPFV	FVUSP	USPPV	PVUSP
1	1.10000	0.90909	1.00000	1.00000	1.10000	0.90909
2	1.21000	0.82645	0.47619	2.10000	0.57619	1.73550
3	1.33100	0.75131	0.30211	3.31000	0.40211	2.48690
4	1.46410	0.68301	0.21547	4.64100	0.31547	3.16990
5	1.61051	0.62092	0.16380	6.10500	0.26380	3.79080
6	1.77160	0.56447	0.12961	7.71600	0.22961	4.35530
7	1.94870	0.51316	0.10541	9.48700	0.20541	4.86840
8	2.14360	0.46651	0.08744	11.43600	0.18744	5.33490
9	2.35790	0.42410	0.07364	13.57900	0.17364	5.75900
10	2.59370	0.38554	0.06275	15.93700	0.16275	6.14460

n: Number of periods
FVPSP: Future value of a present single payment
PVFSP: Present value of a future single payment
USPFV: Uniform series of payments for a future value
FVUSP: Future value of a uniform series of payments
USPPV: Uniform series of payments for a present value
PVUSP: Present value of a uniform series of payments

now. For example, an aerospace contractor, considering an investment of $5 million in tooling that could lead to profit of $500,000 in 5 years, might wish to know what the $5 million would be worth in 5 years if invested at 10 percent, compounded annually. The answer can be provided with the following equation:

$$FVPSP = PSP[(1 + 1)^n] \tag{6.24}$$

where PSP denotes the present single payment, i the interest rate expressed in decimal form, and n the number of time periods. In the example, PSP = $5 million, $i = 0.10$, and $n = 5$, and applying Equation (6.24) yields

$$FVPSP = \$5,000,000[(1 + .10)^5] \tag{6.25}$$
$$= \$8,052,550$$

The factor in the brackets in the right-hand side of Equation (6.24) is also given in the FVPSP column of Table 6.14. For $i = 10$ percent and $n = 5$, the value obtained from the table is 1.61051. Multiplying $5 million by this value yields $8,052,550, the same as the answer in Equation (6.24). The problem can also be addressed on the basis of interest being compounded daily. In this case, the value used for i in Equation (6.24) would be .10/365, or .0002739, the value of n would be five times 365, or 1825 (1826 if accounting for leap year), and the answer obtained would be $8,244,207. It would appear that investing the money is far more advantageous than acquiring the tooling when viewed from the aspect of the time value of money. However, as stated several times in this book, decisions to invest large sums of money on technology or facilities should be made on the basis of the overall growth strategy of the organization and not on just a single product line.

2. PRESENT VALUE OF A FUTURE SINGLE PAYMENT (PVFSP)

Another frequent question concerns the present value of a payment or receipt several years in the future at a certain discount rate. For example, a real estate developer obtains an option to buy a parcel of commercially zoned land 3 years from the present for the price of $500,000. The question is how much of the developer's current holdings should be sold and the proceeds invested at the present time to ensure that the $500,000 are available when needed. The current discount rate is 10 percent compounded annually. The answer can be provided by the following equation:

$$PVFSP = FSP/(1 + i)^n \tag{6.26}$$

where FSP denotes the future single payment, i the discount rate, and n the number of time periods. Substituting FSP = $500,000, $i = .10$, and $n = 3$ in Equation (6.26) yields

$$\text{PVFSP} = \frac{\$500,000}{(1 + .10)^3} \tag{6.27}$$

$$= \$375,657$$

The factor in the denominator in Equation (6.26) could be obtained from the PVFSP column in Table 6.14.

6.7.2 Uniform Series Formulation

A uniform series is defined as a "sequence of payments (or receipts) of a fixed amount, at periodic intervals of time, and at fixed interest or discount rates." The relationships allow the determination of either the amount of the periodic payments when future or present values are known or future or present values when the amounts of the individual periodic payments are known.

1. UNIFORM SERIES OF PAYMENTS FOR A FUTURE VALUE (USPFV)

This relationship applies to situations where the future value is known and the amount of the individual periodic payments needs to be determined. This is the case where sinking funds are to be established. For example, a manufacturer wishes to retire certain equipment at the end of 4 years from the present time. The cost will be $750,000 and the manufacturer needs to know the yearly contributions at an interest rate of 10 percent compounded annually. The answer can be provided with the following equation:

$$A = \frac{FVi}{(1 + i)^n - 1} \tag{6.28}$$

where A denotes the single payment value in the uniform series of payments, FV the future value of the sinking fund and i the interest rate. For the example, Equation (6.28) yields

$$A = \frac{\$750,000(0.10)}{(1 + .10)^4 - 1} \tag{6.29}$$

$$= \$161,603$$

The value of the factor $[i/(1 + i)^n - 1]$ can also be obtained from the USPFV column of Table 6.14.

2. FUTURE VALUE OF A UNIFORM SERIES OF PAYMENTS (FVUSP)

This relationship applies to situations where the amount of the individual periodic payment is known and there is need to determine the future value.

This is another case where sinking funds are to be established. For example, a turnpike authority has committed its net toll revenue to the redemption of bonds with a total value of $250 million in 10 years from the present time and has established a sinking fund. The net annual revenue is $23 million. At 10 percent interest compounded annually, will the value of the sinking fund in 10 years be sufficient to redeem the bonds? The answer can be provided with the following equation:

$$FV = A \frac{(1 + i)^n - 1}{i} \tag{6.30}$$

For the example, Equation (6.30) yields

$$FV = \$23,000,000 \frac{(1 + .10)^{10} - 1}{.10} \tag{6.31}$$

$$= \$366,560,072$$

The sinking fund will be sufficient to redeem the bonds. Again, the answer could have been obtained by applying the factor in the FVUSP column of Table 6.14.

3. UNIFORM SERIES OF PAYMENTS FOR A PRESENT VALUE (USPPV)

This relationship applies to situations where the present value is known and there is need to determine the amount of the individual periodic payments. This is the case of payments on a loan. For example, a contractor wishes to borrow $1 million for a period of 10 years and to know the amount of the individual periodic payments at an interest rate of 10 percent compounded annually. The answer can be obtained by applying the factor in the USPPV column of Table 6.14 or by the following equation:

$$A = PV \frac{i(1 + i)^n}{(1 + i)^n - 1} \tag{6.32}$$

For the example, Equation (6.32) yields:

$$A = \frac{\$1,000,000(.10)(1 + .10)^{10}}{(1 + .10)^{10} - 1} \tag{6.33}$$

$$= \$162,750$$

4. PRESENT VALUE FOR A UNIFORM SERIES OF PAYMENTS (PVUSP)

This relationship applies to situations where the amount of individual periodic payments is known and there is need to determine the present value. For example, the aforementioned contractor who needs to borrow $1 million and can afford to repay only $125,000 per year for 10 years. Within this limit, how much money can the contractor borrow at an interest rate of 10 percent compounded annually? The answer can be provided by the following equation:

$$PV = \text{USP} \frac{[(1 + i)^n - 1]}{i(1 + 1)^n} \tag{6.34}$$

where PV denotes the present value, or by applying the factor in the PVUSP column of Table 6.14.

For the example, applying Equation (6.34) yields

$$PV = \$125,000 \frac{(1 + .10)^{10} - 1}{(.10)(1 + .10)^{10}} \tag{6.35}$$

$$= \$768,075$$

The answer is appreciably less than what might have been expected.

6.7.3 Economic Analysis

The preceding calculations of time value of money are typical of those used in economic analysis of alternative approaches. The usual measures in economic analysis are (1) present value, (2) annual equivalent value; (3) benefit–cost ratio; and (4) internal rate of return.

1. PRESENT VALUE

Net present value is a popular criterion used to measure the cost-effectiveness of alternative approaches. The future values of the alternatives are determined first, and then discounted to the same baseline year using the same discount rate for all the future values. Consider, for example, two approaches that could realize production economies of $500,000 and $550,000 at the end of 2 and 3 years, respectively. Which approach is preferable? Applying Equation (6.26) with an assumed discount rate of 10 percent compounded annually for the two time periods yields

$$PV = \frac{\$500,000}{(1 + .10)^2} \tag{6.36}$$

$$= \$413,223$$

$$PV = \frac{\$550,000}{(1 + .10)^3} \tag{6.37}$$

$$= \$413,223$$

From a monetary viewpoint, either of the two approaches could be selected. From the viewpoint of shorter implementation time, however, the first approach would probably be selected.

2. ANNUAL EQUIVALENT VALUE

The measure of annual equivalent value extends the net present value to the lifetime of the alternative approaches under consideration This is referred to as an "annualized basis." For example, if the lifetimes of the two approaches in the previous example were both 5 years, the present value would be extended 2 + 5, or 7 years for the first approach and 3 + 5, or 8 years for the second. Applying Equation (6.32) with an interest rate of 10 percent yields for 7 years:

$$A = \frac{\$413{,}223(.10)(1 + .10)^7}{(1 + .10)^7 - 1} \tag{6.38}$$

$$= \$84{,}880$$

and for 8 years:

$$A = \frac{\$413{,}223(.10)(1 + .10)^8}{(1 + .10)^8 - 1} \tag{6.39}$$

$$= \$77{,}455$$

On an annualized basis, capital recovery is quicker with the first approach.

3. BENEFIT–COST RATIO

This measure is the ratio of the monetary value of benefits to costs. For example, if the implementation costs for the two approaches in the previous example were $125,000 and $100,000, the respective benefit cost ratios would be $413,223/$125,000, or 3.306, and $413,233/$100,000, or 4.132. On this basis, the second approach is preferable.

4. INTERNAL RATE OF RETURN

Internal rate of return (IRR) is defined as "the rate of return at which the present value of benefits equals the present value of costs." The approach in calculating IRR is to equate the annual benefit and the equivalent annual cost; the latter being derived by the expression for the present value of a uniform series of payments [Equation (6.34)]. Consider, for example, a shopping center estimated to cost $100 million with an estimated net annual return of $20 million for 10 years. The annual benefit and equivalent annual cost are equated as follows:

$$\$20,000,000 = \frac{\$100,000,000(i)(1 + i)^{10}}{(1 + i)^{10} - 1} \qquad (6.40)$$

Equation (6.40) can be solved by trial and error starting with a value for i that equals \$20,000,000/\$100,000,000, or .20. When $i = .20$, the value of the right-hand term in the equation is \$23,852,000, indicating that the IRR is less than 20 percent. Next, successively smaller values of i are tried until the value of the right-hand term of the equation equals \$20,000,000 or less. Using $i = .16$ yields the value of \$20,690,000 for the right-hand term and $i = .15$ yields the value of \$19,171,000. It usually suffices to say that the IRR is between 15 percent and 16 percent; however, a more precise value for IRR can be obtained by interpolation as follows:

$$i = .15 + (.01)(\$20,690,000 - \$20,000,000) \qquad (6.41)$$
$$\div (\$20,000,000 - \$19,171,000)$$
$$= .1583$$

The IRR for the example is therefore 15.83 percent.

6.8   ELEMENTS OF COST CONTROL

As stated earlier in this chapter, much of the high-technology industrial sector is involved in contracts with the military, and it is advantageous for design-to-cost practitioners to gain insight into the cost control required by the military. In particular, the cost–schedule control systems criteria promulgated by the Department of Defense (DoD) is worthy of consideration by the private sector of the economy because of the rigor they impart to cost control (28).

A typical performance measurement system employed by defense contractors in response to these criteria is offered as a role model. A checklist for self-audit is included.

Next some observations on the selection of price indices are offered because of their serious implications in fixed-price contracting with economic price adjustment (EPA) clauses. This is followed by the discussion of the concept of cost success as an organized activity patterned after the concept of mission success.

6.8.1   Cost–Schedule Control Systems Criteria

The DoD first issued DoD Instruction No. 7000.2, "Performance Measurement for Selected Acquisitions," in 1967. The instruction provided for the application of cost/schedule control system criteria (C/SCSC) on major system acquisitions under cost-reimbursable type contracts. The motivation was to stem the spiraling cost of developing new weapon systems, although the application of C/SCSC to major construction projects was also contemplated.

The C/SCSC introduced a number of new terms that were needed to convey the intent of the instruction. These terms are defined in Table 6.15. Review of the table will facilitate an understanding of the discussion that follows.

The overall objective of DoD Instruction 7000.2 is to provide an adequate basis for responsible decision-making by both contractor management and the management of DoD components. The specific objectives are to ensure that the contractor's management control system included policies, procedures, and methods relating to organization, planning and budgeting, accounting, and analysis that accomplished the maximum possible cost containment.

Toward this goal, specific criteria have been evolved for (1) organization, (2) planning and budgeting, (3) accounting, (4) analysis, and (5) revisions and access to data. The following brief dissertation on these criteria sets the stage for the extensive series of questions forming the self-audit checklist presented below.

1. ORGANIZATION

The contractor should define all authorized work and related resources to meet the requirements of the contract, using the contract work-breakdown structure (CWBS). The contractor should identify the internal organizational elements and the major subcontractors responsible for accomplishing the authorized work. The contractor should provide for the integration of the contractor's planning, scheduling, budgeting, work authorization, and cost accumulation systems with each other, the CWBS, and the organizational structure. The contractor should identify the managerial positions responsible for controlling overhead (indirect costs) and should provide for integration of the CWBS with the contractor's functional organizational structure in a manner that permits cost and schedule performance measurement for the CWBS and organizational elements.

2. PLANNING AND BUDGETING

The contractor should schedule the authorized work in a manner that describes the sequence of work and identifies the significant interdependencies required to meet development, production, and delivery requirements of the contract. The contractor should identify physical products, milestones, technical performance goals, or other indicators that will be used to measure output. The contractor should establish and maintain a time-phased budget baseline at the cost account level against which contract performance can be measured. Initial budgets established for this purpose will be based on the negotiated target cost. Any other amount used for performance measure-

◆ ment purposes must be formally recognized by both the contractor and the government. The contractor should establish budgets for all authorized work with separate identification of cost elements (e.g., labor and material). To the extent that the work can be identified in discrete, short-span work packages, the contractor should establish budgets for this work in terms of dollars, hours, or other measurable units. Where the entire cost account cannot be subdivided into detailed work packages, the contractor should identify the far-term effort in larger planning packages for budget and scheduling purposes. The contractor should provide that the sum of all work package budgets plus planning package budgets within a cost account equals the cost account budget and should identify relationships of budgets or standards in underlying work authorization systems to budgets for work packages. The contractor should identify and control level of effort activity by time-phased budgets established for this purpose. Only that effort that cannot be identified as discrete, short-span work packages or as apportioned effort should be classed as level of effort. The contractor should establish overhead budgets for the total costs of each significant organizational component whose expenses will become indirect costs and should reflect in the contract budgets at the appropriate level the amounts in overhead pools that will be allocated to the contract as indirect costs. The contractor should identify management reserves and undistributed budget and provide that the contract target cost plus the estimated cost of authorized but unpriced work is reconciled with the sum of all internal contract budgets and management reserves.

3. ACCOUNTING

The contractor should record direct costs on an applied or other acceptable basis in a formal system that is controlled by the general books of account and should summarize direct costs from cost accounts into the contract work breakdown structure (CWBS) without allocation of a single cost account to two or more CWBS elements. The contractor should summarize direct costs from the cost accounts into the contractor's functional organizational elements without allocation of a single cost account to two or more elements. The contractor should record all indirect costs that will be allocated to the contact, identify the bases for allocating the cost of apportioned effort, and identify unit costs, equivalent unit costs, or lot costs as applicable. The contractor's material accounting system should provide for (1) accurate cost accumulation and assignment of costs to cost accounts in a manner consistent with the budgets using recognized, acceptable costing techniques; (2) determination of price variances by comparing planned versus actual commitments; (3) cost performance measurement at the point in time most suitable for the category of material involved, but no earlier than the time of actual receipt of material; (4) determination of cost variances attributable to the excess usage of material; (5) determination of unit or lot costs when applicable; and (6) full accountability for all material purchased for the contract, including residual inventory.

TABLE 6.15   Cost–Schedule Control Systems Criteria Terminology

Actual cost of work performed. The costs actually incurred and recorded in accomplishing the work performed within a given time period

Actual direct costs. Those costs identified specifically with a contract, based on the contractor's cost identification and accumulation system as accepted by the cognizant government representatives (see "Direct costs")

Applied direct costs. The amounts recognized in the time period associated with the consumption of labor, material, and other direct resources, without regard to the date of commitment or the date of payment; these amounts are to be charged to work-in-process (WIP) in the time period that any one of the following takes place:

When labor, material, and other direct resources are actually consumed

When material resources are withdrawn from inventory for use

When material resources are received that are uniquely identified to the contract and scheduled for use within 60 days

When major components or assemblies are received on a line-flow basis that are specifically and uniquely identified to a single serially numbered end item

Apportioned effort. Effort that by itself is not readily divisible into short-span work packages but is related in direct proportion to measured effort

Authorized work. Effort that has been definitized and is on contract, plus that for which definitized contract costs have not been agreed to but for which written authorization has been received by the contractor

Budgeted cost for work performed. The sum of the budgets for completed work packages and completed portions of open work packages, plus the appropriate portion of the budgets for level of effort and apportioned effort

Budgeted cost for work scheduled. The sum of budgets for all work packages and planning packages scheduled to be accomplished (including in-process work packages), plus the amount of level of effort and apportioned effort scheduled to be accomplished within a given time period

Contract budget base. The negotiated contract cost plus the estimated cost of authorized, unpriced work

Cost account. Management control point at which actual costs can be accumulated and compared to budgeted costs for work performed; natural control point for cost–schedule planning and control, representing the work assigned to one responsible organizational element on one CWBS element

Cost account manager. The individual who has been assigned full responsibility for the scope of work of the cost account, including technical, schedule, and budget

Direct costs. Any costs that can be identified specifically with a particular final cost objective

Estimated cost at completion. Actual direct costs, plus indirect costs allocatable to the contract, plus the estimate of costs (direct and indirect) for authorized work remaining

Indirect costs. Costs that, because of their incurrence for common or joint objectives, are not readily subject to treatment as direct costs

Internal replanning. Replanning actions performed by the contractor for remaining effort within the recognized total allocated budget

Level of effort. Effort of a general or supportive nature that does not produce definite end products or results

Management reserve. An amount of the total allocated budget withheld for management control purposes rather than designated for the accomplishment of a specific task or set of tasks

Negotiated contract cost. The estimated cost negotiated in a cost-plus fixed-fee contract, or the negotiated target cost in either a fixed-price incentive contract or a cost-plus incentive-fee contract

Original budget. The budget established at or near the time the contract was signed

Performance measurement baseline. The time-phased budget plan against which contract performance is measured; formed by the budgets assigned to scheduled cost accounts and the applicable indirect budgets; for future effort, not planned to the cost account level, the performance measurement baseline also includes budgets assigned to higher level CWBS elements and undistributed budgets; it equals the total allocated budget less management reserve

Planning package. A logical aggregation of work within a cost account, normally the far-term effort, that can be identified and budgeted in early baseline planning but is not yet defined into work packages

Project summary work-breakdown structure. A summary WBS tailored to a specific defense materiel item by selecting applicable elements from one or more summary WBSs or by adding elements that are unique to the program

Significant variances. Differences between planned and actual performance that require further review, analysis, or action; appropriate thresholds should be established as to the magnitude of variances that will require variance analysis

Total allocated budget. The sum of all budgets allocated to the contract; consists of the performance measurement baseline and all management reserve; will reconcile directly to the contract budget base—any difference will be documented as to quantity and cause

Undistributed budget. Budget applicable to contract effort that has not yet been identified to CWBS elements at or below the lowest level of reporting to the government

Work package budgets. Resources that are formally assigned by the contractor to accomplish a work package and are expressed in dollars, hours, standards, or other definitive units

Work packages. Detailed short-span jobs or material items identified by the contractor for accomplishing work required to complete the contract; has the following characteristics:

Represents units of work at levels where work is performed

Is clearly distinguishable from all other work packages

Is assignable to a single organizational element

Has scheduled start and completion dates, and, as applicable, interim milestones that are representative of physical accomplishments

Has a budget or assigned values expressed in terms of dollars, hours, or other measurable units

Duration is limited to a relatively short span of time or it is subdivided by discrete-value milestones to facilitate the objective measurement of work performed

Is integrated with detailed engineering, manufacturing, or other schedules

4. ANALYSIS

The contractor should identify the following at the cost account level on a monthly basis using data from, or reconcilable with, the accounting system: (1) budgeted cost for work scheduled and budgeted cost for work performed; (2) budgeted cost for work performed and applied (actual where appropriate) direct costs for the same work; and (3) variances resulting from these comparisons classified in terms of labor, material, or other appropriate elements together with the reasons for significant variances. The contractor should identify on a monthly basis in the detail needed by management for effective control of budgeted indirect costs and actual indirect costs, and for dispositioning cost variances. The contractor should summarize the data elements and associated variances listed in the preceding items through the contractor organization and the CWBS to the reporting level specified in the contract. The contractor should identify significant differences on a monthly basis between planned and actual schedule accomplishment and the reasons, and identify management actions taken as a result of the above items. On the basis of performance to date and estimates of future conditions, the contractor should develop revised estimates of cost at completion for WBS elements identified in the contract and compare these with the contract budget base and the latest statement of funding requirements reported to the government.

5. REVISIONS AND ACCESS TO DATA

The contractor should incorporate contract changes in a timely manner, recording the effects of such changes in budgets and schedules. In the directed effort prior to negotiation of a change, such revisions should be based on the amount estimated and budgeted to the functional organizations. The contractor should reconcile original budgets for those elements of the CWBS identified as priced line items in the contract, and for those elements at the lowest level of the DoD Project Summary WBS, with current performance measurement budgets in terms of (1) changes to the authorized work and (2) internal replanning in the detail needed by management for effective control. The contractor should prohibit retroactive changes to records pertaining to work performed that will change previously reported amounts for direct costs, indirect costs, or budgets, except for correction of errors and routine accounting adjustments. The contractor should prevent revisions to the contract budget base except for government-directed changes to contractual effort. The contractor should internally document changes to the performance measurement baseline and on a timely basis notify the procuring activity through prescribed procedures. The contractor should provide the contracting officer and duly authorized representatives of the contracting officer access to all of the foregoing information and supporting documents.

6.8.2 Performance Measurement System

Figure 6.18 illustrates the integration of a typical performance measurement system into the control systems of a contractor. Although the DoD does not require a performance measurement system (PMS) in the fixed-price arena, its rigor is worthy of emulation by high-technology enterprises under all kinds of contracts and in all program phases.

The underlying rationale is to integrate the contractor's work authorization, planning, scheduling, budgeting, and cost accumulation systems with each other, the CWBS and the contractor's organizational structure. Therefore, the PMS consists of a subsystem for each these four aforementioned systems.

As shown in Figure 6.18, the CWBS is extended to lower-level elements and responsibility is established by organizational components who will do the work encompassed by the CWBS elements. The intersections of the CWBS and the organizational structure provide natural control points for the C/SCSC.

These control points provide the bases for allocating work to cost account managers and for the scheduling and budgeting of the associated tasks. The level in the CWBS at which functional responsibilities is established also establishes the cost account levels. Configuration control of the program baseline is imposed at the cost account level of the CWBS.

Progress is assessed as work is performed and cost is accumulated. The

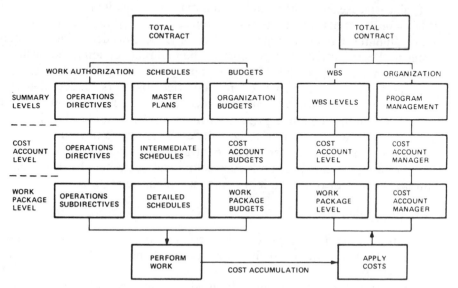

Figure 6.18 Integration of performance measurement system (29). (Reprinted by permission of the Martin Marietta Corporation.)

assessment of progress takes two forms: schedule status of work accomplished versus the work planned and the value of the work accomplished.

Schedule and cost variances, if any, are determined at the level of the tasks comprising the cost accounts. Corrective action evolves from the analyses of root causes of task variances. Summaries of the task variances at the cost account level, along with descriptions of the corrective actions taken, are reported to both management and the government (see Section 3.12.2).

Table 6.16 provides a checklist for self-audit of the adequacy of the contractor's approach to meeting the cost–schedule control systems criteria (C/SCSC). The table can provide an in-depth understanding of the intent of C/SCSC and a complete grasp of the essentials of effective cost control. Despite its length, design-to-cost practitioners are urged to review the table carefully and to use the table as a frequent reference.

The table consists of a series of action statements followed by reaction questions and is structured in the same fashion as the foregoing discussion: organization, planning and budgeting, accounting, analysis, and revisions and access to data.

6.8.3 Inflation, Escalation, and Price Indexes

One of the most difficult problems in cost estimating is dealing with inflation and escalation. Although they are often viewed as one, inflation and escalation are distinctly different, and the difference needs to be understood when attempting to estimate with realism.

Problems arise from either underestimating or overestimating future costs of labor or materials. In cost-plus fixed-fee contracts, additional costs due to underestimates may be recouped; however, the fee is eroded. Overestimates result in the reduction of target cost of the contract reducing the business base and increasing overhead in the company.

Similar effects are experienced in fixed-price contracts except additional costs due to underestimates are not recouped by contractors unless the contracts contain economic price adjustment (EPA) clauses. The implications of improper selection of price indexes for EPA are obvious.

In general, underestimates impact contractors at some future time. However, overestimates impact both contractors and customers by erroneously limiting the size of orders to less than what might be required.

1. INFLATION

Inflation is the time-oriented decrease in purchasing power of a nation's currency brought about by such factors as deficit spending and foreign trade imbalance. Inflation can be viewed as an extrinsic cost driver, induced by factors external to the program. The mode for dealing with inflation is primarily reactive, but certain steps can be taken to mitigate its effects. For example, the best countermeasure for inflationary pressure on raw materials

TABLE 6.16   Self-Audit Checklist (30)

Organization Criteria

1. Define all the authorized work and related resources to meet the requirements of the contract using the CWBS.

   Is only one CWBS used for the contract?

   Is all contract work included in the CWBS?

   Are the following items included in the CWBS?

   Contract line items and end items in consonance with MIL-STD-881A

   All CWBS elements specified for external reporting

   CWBS elements to be subcontracted with identification of subcontractors

   Cost account levels

2. Identify the internal organizational elements and the major subcontractors responsible for accomplishing the authorized work.

   Are all authorized tasks assigned to organizational elements at the cost account level as a minimum?

   Is subcontracted work defined and identified to the appropriate subcontractor within the proper CWBS element?

3. Provide for the integration of the contractor's planning, scheduling, budgeting, work authorization, and cost accumulation systems with each other; the CWBS; and the organizational structure.

   Are the contractor's management control systems listed above integrated with each other, the CWBS, and the organizational structure at the following levels?

   Total contract

   Cost account

4. Identify the managerial positions responsible for controlling overhead (indirect costs).

   Are the following organizational elements and managers identified clearly?

   Those responsible for establishing budgets and assigning resources for overhead performance

   Those responsible for overhead performance control of related costs

   Are the responsibilities and authorities of each of the above organizational elements or managers defined clearly?

5. Provide for the integration of the CWBS with the contractor's functional organizational structure in a manner that permits cost and schedule performance measurement for CWBS and organizational elements.

   Is each cost account assigned to a single organizational element directly responsible for the work and identifiable to a single element of the CWBS?

   Are the following elements for measuring performance available at the levels selected for analysis and control?

   Budgeted cost for work scheduled

   Budgeted cost for work performed

   Actual cost of work performed

TABLE 6.16 *(Continued)*

Planning and Budgeting Criteria

1. Schedule the authorized work in a manner that describes the sequence of work and identifies the significant task interdependencies required to meet the development, production, and delivery requirements of the contract.

    Does the scheduling system contain

    A master program schedule?

    Intermediate schedules as required that support cost account and work package start and completion dates?

    Are significant decision points, constraints, and interfaces identified as key milestones?

    Does the scheduling system provide for the identification of work progress against technical and other milestones and a for forecasts of completion dates of scheduled work?

    Are work packages formally scheduled in terms of physical accomplishment by calendar dates?

2. Identify physical products, milestones, technical performance goals, or other indicators that will be used to measure output.

    Are meaningful indicators identified for use in measuring the status of cost and schedule performance?

    Does the contractor's system identify work accomplishment against the schedule plan?

    Are current work performance indicators and goals relatable to original goals as modified by contractual changes, replanning, and reprogramming actions?

3. Establish and maintain a time-phased budget baseline at the cost account level against which contract performance can be measured. Initial budgets established for this purpose will be based on the negotiated target cost. Any other amount used for performance measurement purposes must be formally recognized both by the contractor and by the customer.

    Does the performance measurement baseline consist of the following?

    Time-phased cost account budgets

    Higher-level CWBS element budgets where not yet broken down into cost account budgets

    Undistributed budgets, if any

    Indirect budgets if not included in the above

    Is the entire contract planned in time-phased cost accounts to the extent practicable?

    In the event that future contract effort cannot be planned in sufficient detail to allow the establishment of cost accounts, is the remaining budget assigned to the lowest practicable CWBS elements for subsequent distribution to cost accounts?

    Does the contractor require sufficient detailed planning of cost accounts to constrain the application of budget initially allocated for future effort to current effort?

    Are cost accounts opened and closed based on the start and completion of work contained therein?

TABLE 6.16 (*Continued*)

Planning and Budgeting Criteria

4. Establish budgets for all authorized work with separate identification of cost elements.

    Does the budgeting system contain

    The total budget for the system, including estimates for authorized but unpriced work?

    Budgets assigned to major functional organizations?

    Budgets assigned to cost accounts?

    Are the budgets assigned to cost accounts planned and identified in terms of the following cost elements?

    Direct labor dollars and/or hours

    Material and/or subcontract dollars

    Other direct dollars

    Does the work authorization contain

    Authorization to proceed with all authorized work?

    Appropriate work authorization documents that subdivide the contractual effort and responsibilities within functional organizations?

5. To the extent that the authorized work can be identified in discrete, short-span work packages, establish budgets for this work in terms of dollars, hours, or other measurable units. Where the entire cost account cannot be subdivided into detailed work packages, identify the far-term effort in larger planning packages for budget and scheduling purposes.

    Do work packages reflect the actual way in which the work will be done, and are they a meaningful product or management-oriented subdivision of a higher-level element of work?

    Are detailed work packages planned as far in advance as practicable?

    Is work progressively subdivided into detailed work packages as requirements are defined?

    Is future work that cannot be planned in detail subdivided to the extent practicable for budgeting and scheduling purposes?

    Are work packages reasonably short in time duration, or do they have adequate objective indicators or milestones for in-process work evaluation?

    Do work packages consist of discrete tasks that are adequately defined?

    Can the contractor substantiate work package and planning package budgets?

    Are budgets or values assigned to work packages and planning packages in terms of dollars, hours, or other measurable units?

    Are work packages assigned to performing organizations?

6. Provide that the sum of all work package budgets plus planning package budgets within a cost account equals the cost account budget.

    Do the sums of all work package budgets plus planning package budgets within cost accounts equal the budgets assigned to those cost accounts?

7. Identify relationships of budgets or standards in underlying work authorization systems to budgets for work packages.

TABLE 6.16 *(Continued)*

Planning and Budgeting Criteria

Where engineered standards or other internal work measurement systems are used, is there a formal relationship between these values and work package budgets?

8. Identify and control level of effort activity by time-phased budgets established for this purpose. Only effort that cannot be identified as discrete, short-span work packages or as apportioned effort will be classed as level of effort.

Are time-phased budgets established for planning and control of level of effort activity by category of resource such as labor and/or material?

Is work properly classified as measured effort, level of effort, or apportioned effort and appropriately separated?

9. Establish overhead budgets for the total costs of each significant organizational component whose expenses will become indirect costs. Reflect in the contract budgets at the appropriate level the amounts in overhead pools that will be allocated to the contract as indirect costs.

Are overhead cost budgets or projections established on a facilitywide basis at least annually for the life of the contract?

Are overhead cost budgets established for each organization that has the authority to incur overhead costs?

Are all elements of expense identified to overhead cost budgets or projections?

Are overhead budgets and costs being handled according to the disclosure statement when applicable or otherwise classified properly?

Is the anticipated business base firm and potential) projected in a rational consistent manner?

Are overhead costs budgets established on a basis consistent with the anticipated direct business base?

Are the requirements for all items of overhead established by rational, traceable processes?

Are the overhead pools formally and adequately identified?

Are the organizations and items of cost assigned to each pool identified?

Are projected overhead costs in each pool and the associated direct costs used as the basis for establishing interim rates for allocating overhead to contracts?

Are projected overhead rates applied to the contract beyond the current year based on

Contractor financial periods such as annual?

The projected business base for each year?

Contemplated overhead expenditure for each period based on the best information currently available?

Are overhead projections adjusted in a timely manner to reflect

Changes in the current direct and projected base?

Changes in the nature of the overhead requirements?

TABLE 6.16 *(Continued)*

Planning and Budgeting Criteria

Changes in the overhead pool and/or organization structure?

Are the CWBS and organizational levels for application of the projected overhead costs identified?

10. Identify management reserves and undistributed budget.

Is all budget available as management reserve identified and excluded from the performance measurement baseline?

Are records maintained to show how management reserves are used?

Is undistributed budget limited to contract effort which cannot yet be planned to CWBS elements at or below the level specified for reporting to the customer?

Are records maintained to show how undistributed budgets are controlled?

11. Provide that the contract target cost plus the estimated cost of authorized but unpriced work is reconciled with the sum of all internal contract budgets and management reserves.

Does the contractor's system description or procedures require that the performance measurement baseline plus the management reserve equal the contract budget base?

Does the sum of the cost account budgets for higher-level CWBS elements, undistributed budgets, and management reserves reconcile with the contract target cost plus the estimated cost for authorized, unpriced work?

Accounting Criteria

1. Record direct costs on all applied or other acceptable basis in a formal system that is controlled by the general books of account.

Does the accounting system provide a basis for auditing records of direct costs chargeable to the contract?

Are elements of direct cost accumulated within cost accounts in a manner consistent with budgets using recognized, acceptable costing techniques and controlled by the general book of accounts?

2. Summarize direct costs from the cost accounts into the CWBS without allocation of a single cost account to two or more CWBS elements.

Is it possible to summarize direct costs from the cost account level through the CWBS to the total contract level without allocation of a lower-level CWBS element to two or more higher-level CWBS elements? This does not preclude the allocation of costs from a cost account containing common elements to appropriate using cost accounts.

3. Summarize direct costs from the cost accounts into the contractor's functional organizational elements without allocation of a single cost account to two or more organizational elements.

Is it possible to summarize direct costs from the cost account level to the highest functional organizational level without allocation of a lower-level organization's cost to two or more higher-level organizations?

TABLE 6.16 *(Continued)*

Accounting Criteria

4. Record all indirect costs that will be allocated to this contract.

    Does the cost accumulation system provide for summarization of indirect costs from the point of allocation to the contract total?

    Are indirect costs accumulated for comparison with corresponding budgets?

    Do the lines of authority for incurring indirect costs correspond to the lines of responsibility for management control of the same components of cost?

    Are indirect costs charged to the appropriate pools and incurring organizations?

    Are the bases and rates for allocating costs from each indirect pool consistently applied?

    Are the bases and rates for allocating costs from each indirect pool to commercial work consistent with those used to allocate such costs to government contracts?

    Are the rates for allocating costs from each indirect cost pool to contracts updated as necessary to assure a realistic monthly allocation of indirect costs without significant year-end adjustments?

    Are the procedures for identifying indirect costs to incurring organizations, indirect cost pools, and allocating the costs from the pools to the contracts formally documented?

5. Identify the bases for allocating the cost of apportioned effort.

    Is effort that is planned and controlled in direct relationship to cost accounts or work packages identified as apportioned effort?

    Are methods used for applying apportioned effort costs to cost accounts applied consistently and documented in an established procedure?

6. Identify unit costs, equivalent unit costs, or lot costs as applicable.

    Does the contractor's system provide unit costs, equivalent unit, or lot costs in terms of labor, material and other direct cost, and indirect costs?

    Does the contractor have procedures that permit identification of recurring and nonrecurring costs as necessary?

7. The contractor's material accounting system shall provide for (a) accurate cost accumulation and assignment of costs to cost accounts in a manner consistent with the budgets using recognized, acceptable costing techniques; (b) determination of price variances by comparing planned versus actual commitments; (c) cost performance measurement at the point in time most suitable for the category of material involved, but no later than the time of actual receipt of material; (d) determination of cost variances attributable to the excess usage of material; (e) determination of unit or lot costs when applicable; and (f) full accountability for all material purchased for the contract, including the residual inventory.

    Does the contractor's system provide for accurate cost accumulation and assignment to cost accounts in a manner consistent with the budgets using recognized, acceptable costing techniques?

    Does the contractor's system provide for determination of price variances by comparing planned versus actual commitments?

TABLE 6.16   (*Continued*)

Accounting Criteria

Is cost performance measured at a point in time suitable for the category of material involved, but no earlier than the actual receipt of material?

Does the contractor's system provide for determination of cost variances attributable to the use of more material than planned? Does the contractor's system provide for the determination of unit or lot costs when applicable?

Does the contractor's system provide for the accountability of all material including residual inventory?

Are material costs reported in the same period as that in which the budgeted cost for work performed is earned for that material?

Analysis Criteria

1. Identify the following at the cost account level on a monthly basis using data from, or reconcilable with, the accounting system: (a) budgeted cost for work scheduled and budgeted cost for work performed; (b) budgeted cost for work performed and applied direct costs for the same work; and (c) variances resulting from these comparisons classified in terms of labor, material, or other appropriate elements, together with the reasons for significant variances.

   Does the contractor's system include procedures for measuring performance of the lowest level of organization responsible for the cost account?

   Does the contractor's system include procedures for measuring the performance of critical subcontractors?

   Is cost and schedule performance measurement done in a consistent, systematic manner?

   Are the actual costs used for variance analysis reconcilable with data from the accounting system?

   Is budgeted cost for work performed calculated in a manner consistent with the way work is planned? For example, if work is planned on a measured basis, budgeted cost for work performed should be calculated on a measured basis.

   Does the contractor have variance analysis procedures and a demonstrated capability for identifying, at the cost account and other appropriate levels, cost and schedule variances as follows:

   Identifying and isolating problems causing unfavorable cost variances?

   Evaluating the impact of schedule changes and work arounds?

   Evaluating the performance of operating organizations?

   Identifying potential or actual overruns and underruns?

2. Identify on a monthly basis in the detail needed by management for effective control, budgeted indirect costs, actual indirect costs, and variances along with reasons.

   Are variances between budgeted and actual indirect costs identified and analyzed at the level of responsibility for their control?

   Does the contractor's cost control system provide for capability to identify the existence and causes of cost variances resulting from

TABLE 6.16   *(Continued)*

Analysis Criteria

Incurrence of actual indirect costs in excess of budgets by elements of expense?

Changes in the direct base to which overhead costs are allocated?

Are management actions taken to reduce indirect costs when there are significant adverse variances?

3. Summarize the data elements and associated variances listed in the preceding items through the contractor's organization and the CWBS to the reporting level specified in the contract.

Are data elements such as budgeted cost for work scheduled and for work performed and actual cost of work performed progressively summarized from the detail level to the contract level through the CWBS?

Are data elements summarized through the functional organizational structure for progressively higher levels of management?

Are data elements reconcilable between internal summary reports and reports forwarded to the government?

Are procedures for variance analysis documented and consistently applied at the cost account level, selected CWBS, and organizational levels at least monthly as a routine task?

4. Identify on a monthly basis significant differences between planned and actual schedule accomplishment together with the reasons.

Does the schedule system identify in a timely manner the status of work?

Does the contractor use objective results, design reviews, and tests to track schedule performance?

5. Identify managerial actions taken as a result of the preceding criteria items.

Are data disseminated to the contractor's managers in a timely, accurate, and usable manner?

Are data being used by managers in an effective manner to ascertain program or functional status, identify reasons for significant variances, and initiate appropriate corrective action?

Are there procedures for monitoring action items and corrective actions to the point of resolution, and are these procedures being followed?

6. On the basis of performance to date and estimates of future conditions, develop revised estimates of cost at completion for CWBS elements identified in the contract, and compare these with the contract budget base and the latest statement of funds requirements reported to the government.

Are estimates of costs at completion based on

Performance to date?

Actual costs to date?

Knowledgeable projections of future performance?

Estimates of the cost for contract work remaining to be accomplished considering economic escalation?

Are the overhead rates used to develop the contract cost estimate to completion based on

Historical experience?

TABLE 6.16   (*Continued*)

Analysis Criteria

Contemplated management improvements?

Projected economic escalation?

Anticipated business volume?

Are estimates of cost at completion generated with sufficient frequency to provide identification of future cost problems in time for possible corrective or preventive actions by both the contractor and the government program managers?

Are estimates of cost at completion generated by program personnel coordinated with those responsible for overall plant management to determine whether required resources will be available according to revised planning?

Are estimates of cost at completion generated by knowledgeable personnel for the following levels?

Cost accounts

Major functional areas of contract effort

Major subcontracts

CWBS elements contractually specified for reporting status to the government

Total contract (all authorized work)

Are the latest revised estimates of cost at completion compared with the established budgets at appropriate levels and causes of variances identified?

Are estimates of cost at completion generated in a rational, consistent manner?

Are there procedures established for appropriate aspects of generating estimates of cost at completion?

Are the contractor's estimates of cost at completion reconcilable with cost data reported to the government?

Revisions and Access to Data Criteria

1. Incorporate contractual changes in a timely manner, recording the effects of such changes in budgets and schedules. In the directed effort before negotiation of a change, base such revisions on the amount estimated and budgeted to the functional organizations.

   Are authorized changes being incorporated in a timely manner?

   Are all affected work authorizations, budgeting, and scheduling documents amended to properly reflect the effects of the authorized changes?

   Are internal budgets for authorized but unpriced changes based on the contractor's resource plan for accomplishing the work?

   If current budgets for authorized changes do not sum to the negotiated cost for the changes, does the contractor compensate for the differences by revising the undistributed budgets, management reserves, budgets established for work not yet started, or a combination of these?

2. Reconcile original budgets for those elements of the CWBS identified as price line items in the contract, and for those elements at the lowest level of the

TABLE 6.16 *(Continued)*

Revisions and Access to Data Criteria

DoD Project Summary WBS, with current performance measurement budgets in terms of changes to the authorized work and internal replanning in the detail needed by management for effective control.

Are current budgets resulting from changes to the authorized work and/or internal replanning reconcilable to original budgets for specified reporting items?

3. Prohibit retroactive changes to records pertaining to work performed that will change previously reported amounts for direct costs, indirect costs, or budgets, except for correction of errors and routine accounting adjustments.

Are retroactive changes to direct costs and indirect costs prohibited except for the correction of errors and routine accounting adjustments?

Are direct or indirect cost adjustments being accomplished according to acceptable accounting procedures?

Are retroactive changes to budgeted cost for work scheduled and budgeted cost for work performed prohibited, except for correction of errors and routine accounting adjustments?

4. Prevent revisions to the contract budget base, except for government directed changes to contractual effort.

Are procedures established to prevent changes to the contract budget base other than those authorized by contractual action?

Is authorization of budgets in excess of the contract budget base controlled formally and done with full knowledge and recognition of the procuring activity?

Are the procedures adequate?

5. Document internally changes to the performance measurement baseline, and on a timely basis notify the procuring activity through prescribed procedures.

Are changes to the performance measurement baseline made as a result of contractual redirection, formal reprogramming, internal replanning, application of undistributed budget, or the use of management reserve, properly documented and reflected in the cost performance report?

Are procedures in existence that restrict changes to budgets for open work packages, and are these procedures observed?

Are retroactive changes to budgets for completed work specifically prohibited in an established procedure, and is this procedure observed?

Are procedures in existence that control replanning of unopened work packages, and are these procedures observed?

6. Provide the contracting officer and duly authorized representatives of the contracting officer access to all the foregoing information and supporting documentation.

Does the contractor provide access to all pertinent records to the C/SCSC review team and surveillance personnel?

Source: DARCOM P715-4, AFSCP/AFLCP 173-5, NAVMAT P 5243. *Cost/Schedule Control Systems Critera Joint Implementation Guide.*

is to stockpile material in accordance with the relative need for the various materials. Anticipated labor cost increases should be addressed in terms of introducing robotics and automation and revising the make-or-buy posture for the particular products.

2. ESCALATION

Escalation is an intrinsic cost driver induced by factors that are essentially internal to the program, such as those given previously in Table 6.4 and repeated in Table 6.17. The mode for dealing with escalation should be proactive (31). The approach should be to undertake "what-if" exercises for each contingency listed in Table 6.17 and to develop alternate strategies to pursue in the event that the contingencies occur. The basic question is whether to implement the strategy at the present time or to wait until the contingency occurs. For example, should a certain supplier be delinquent in delivering a critical item, the alternate strategies could be to either seek other suppliers or to redesign the product to eliminate the dependency of the product on the particular item. In either case, decisions to implement the strategies and when to implement the strategies depends on perceptions of future costs. These perceptions depend in large measure on projections made from published price indexes.

3. PRICE INDEXES

The most commonly used indexes are the consumer price index and the producer price index. The primary sources of these data are monthly publi-

TABLE 6.17 Cost-Escalation Factors

Immature, overstated, and understated requirements
Difference in perception of requirements
Inadequate specifications
Immature baseline definition
Inadequate up-front analysis
Complexity growth
Baseline changes
Redesign due to failures
Budget instability
Program stretchout
Lack of continuity
Supplier delinquency
Management changes
Rotation of personnel
Relocation of facilities
Union contract negotiations
Government regulation
Customer involvement
Customer's cost perception based on single estimate

cations of the Bureau of Labor Statistics, U.S. Department of Commerce. The consumer price index (CPI) and its derivatives for wage and salary are integral to labor union contract negotiations and the nationwide competition for skilled workers. Design-to-cost practitioners should maintain their familiarity with the CPI. The *Statistical Abstract of the United States* is suggested as a readily available compendium (32). The producers price index (PPI), dating from 1890, is the oldest continuous statistical series published by the Bureau of Labor Statistics, and is now based on approximately 3400 commodity price series. It is also contained in the *Statistical Abstract of the United States*. The PPI and its derivatives are integral to contracting for future deliveries. The year 1960 with an index of 100 is the base year for the PPI, and an example is given in Table 6.18.

Figure 6.19 shows the behavior of the PPI from 1970 to 1986 by stage of processing by producers. It should he noted that from 1960 to 1970 the index increased by only about 30 percent, whereas it increased by about 200 percent from 1970 to 1980. Furthermore, it declined from 1985 to 1986. A great deal of deliberation is warranted in selecting price indexes as the contractual base for future deliveries irrespective of the type of contract that is being contemplated. Consider, for example, the need to project the price index for aluminum in the year 2000. Applying linear regression techniques from Section 6.6.2 to the crude material data in Table 6.18 yields the following least-squares equation:

$$y_i = -25,094.55 + 12.80906 x_i \qquad (6.42)$$

Substituting the year 2000 for x_i in the equation yields $y = 523.57$. This means that on the basis of the projection of crude material indexes, alumi-

TABLE 6.18   Producer Price Indexes (33)

Year	Crude Materials	Intermediate Material	Finished Goods
1970	112.3	109.9	110.3
1975	196.8	180.0	163.4
1977	209.2	201.5	181.7
1978	234.4	215.6	195.9
1979	274.3	243.2	217.7
1980	304.8	250.3	247.0
1981	329.0	306.0	269.8
1982	319.5	310.4	280.7
1983	323.6	312.3	285.2
1984	320.8	320.0	291.1
1985	306.1	316.7	293.7
1986	280.0	307.6	289.6

Source: U.S. Bureau of the Census, *Statistical Abstract of the United States: 1988.*

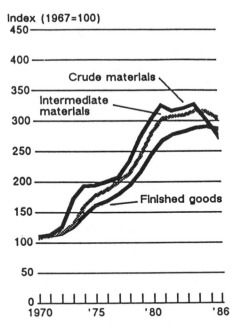

Index (1967=100)

Figure 6.19 Producer price indexes by stage of processing (35). (Source: U.S. Bureau of the Census, *Statistical Abstract of the United States: 1988*.)

num will cost 5.2357 times what it cost in 1960, the base year for the PPI. The PPI is referred to as an "aggregate index," meaning that it is a composite of many subindexes (approximately 3400). These are referred to as "disaggregate indexes." The objective in projections should be to use the most disaggregate index possible. A readily available compendium of such indexes is the *U.S. Industrial Outlook*, published annually by the U.S. Department of Commerce (34). Table 6.19 can be used as the first step toward disaggregate indexes and gives price indexes for nonferrous metals, which are still obtained from the *Statistical Abstract of the United States*. Applying linear regression to the data in this table yields the following least-squares equation:

$$y_i = -18,671.53 + 9.546776 x_i \qquad (6.43)$$

Substituting the year 2000 for x_i in the equation yields $y = 422.022$, compared to the value of 523.57 that was provided by the previous Equation (6.42). In Table 6.19 note the sharp decline in the price indexes for nonferrous metals in the years following 1980, which are not revealed by the producer price indexes in Table 6.18.

The next step in disaggregation are the price indexes for primary aluminum (i.e., virgin metal) given in Table 6.20. These data are from the *1987 U.S. Industrial Outlook*. Applying linear regression to the data in this table yields the following least-squares equation:

$$y_i = -11,651.39 + 5.928971 x_i \qquad (6.44)$$

TABLE 6.19   Producer Price Indexes for Nonferrous Metals (36)

Year	Index	Year	Index
1970	124.7	1982	263.6
1975	171.6	1983	276.1
1978	207.8	1984	277.1
1979	216.7	1985	262.5
1980	305.0	1986	259.7
1981	285.8		

Source: U.S. Bureau of the Census, *Statistical Abstract of the United States: 1988.*

Substituting the year 2000 for x_i in the equation yields $y = 206.55$. Note that the base year for the indexes in Table 6.20 is 1982 with an index of 100. Therefore, the projection now is that in the year 2000 aluminum will cost 2.0656 times what it cost in 1982. This is still less than what was projected both from the crude materials producer price indexes and from the nonferrous metals producer price indexes. It is also interesting to note the comments in the reference for Table 6.20 on the long-term prospects for aluminum, which are as follows: "The rate of growth in demand for primary aluminum has declined significantly because of increased secondary recovery, saturation of certain end-use markets, product improvements, and an increase in market share held by imported mill products. These developments, combined with low unstable prices, will force some U.S. smelters to close, either temporarily or permanently. Total aluminum shipments are expected to increase at a compound annual rate of about 3 percent throughout 1991" (38). Figure 6.20 compares the slopes of the least-squares lines given by Equations (6.42), (6.43), and (6.44). As is to be expected, the least-

TABLE 6.20   Producer Price Indexes for Primary Aluminum (37)

Year	Index	Year	Index
1972	33.5	1980	104.9
1973	36.2	1981	110.6
1974	56.1	1982	100.0
1975	56.3	1983	106.5
1976	61.7	1984	109.8
1977	71.3	1985	113.3
1978	75.3	1986	116.5
1979	88.3	1987	120.0

Source: U.S. Department of Commerce, *1987 U.S. Industrial Outlook.*

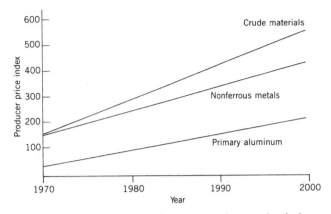

Figure 6.20   Least-squares lines for producer price indexes.

squares line for the primary aluminum producer price indexes demonstrates the most shallow slope.

6.9 SUMMARY

This chapter concentrated on those aspects of cost estimating and cost control that are especially key to realizing the full potential of design to cost starting with the philosophy for design to cost that must pervade the organizations and people involved in the effort. The concepts of functional worth, could-cost, should-cost, and would-cost, and how they relate to design to cost were illuminated.

The next section addressed cost element structures and the work-breakdown structure (WBS) that provide the framework for estimating costs for various phases of programs. These are the R&D phase, the investment phase, and the operation and support phase, which in the aggregate make up the life cycle of products or programs.

The role of the WBS in cost estimating and cost control was explored. An example of a WRS used in weapon system acquisition was offered as a role model for other high-technology programs.

The next section addressed the estimating realism needed to ensure the viability of design-to-cost programs and how to communicate such realism. The use of ground rules and assumptions was discussed, along with what is necessary to do in order to ensure the credibility of the data on which cost estimates are based.

It was pointed out that the alternative to reliable data is runaway cost. Specific documentation requirements were given, along with insight into factors that cause costs to escalate.

The next section discussed the methodologies for estimating cost that also vary as functions of program phases. These are expert opinion, analogy, parametric and industrial engineering.

The applicability of each of the four basic methods and their relative advantages and disadvantages were presented. Extensive details were provided on cost-estimating relationships (CERs) that are used in parametric estimating.

Because cost estimating attempts to capitalize on learning curves, the next section in the chapter was devoted to this subject. The probabilistic nature of learning curves was discussed from the viewpoint of causing risk.

The issue of risk leads to the subject of confidence in cost estimates, which was addressed in the next section. Confidence is a function of many factors that include the amount of data (i.e., sample size) on which conclusions are based and the probability distributions governing the relationships depicted by the data.

The subjects covered were statistical inference and hypotheses testing; regression and correlation analysis; confidence limits, and Bayes's theorem in decision-making. Step-by-step procedures were given and supported by a number of examples.

The next section turned to the subject of the time value of money. Expressions such as "then dollars," "now dollars," "constant-year dollars," "sinking fund," "capital recovery," and "internal rate of return" proliferate in design to cost, and it is important that design-to-cost practitioners be proficient in these matters.

The time value of money is part of the broader subject of economic analysis, and it was presented in this context. Terminology was defined, and formulation was presented and illustrated with a number of examples.

At this juncture, it was appropriate to introduce the subject of cost control, which was done in the context of the performance measurement requirements and cost–schedule control systems criteria (C/SCSC) promulgated by the Department of Defense in DoD Instruction 7000.2. The implementation rigor mandated by DoD Instruction 7000.2 is worthy of some emulation by the private sector of the economy.

A multipage checklist for self-audit for the adequacy of the cost and schedule control systems was provided. Despite its length, design-to-cost practitioners are urged to carefully review this checklist, which is a primer on effective cost control.

This was followed by some observations on inflation, escalation, and the producer price indexes (PPIs) used to come to grips with their impact on cost. The importance of disaggregate price indexes versus aggregate price indexes was discussed. The latter concern was illustrated by attempting price predictions first by using PPIs for crude materials, then for nonferrous metals, and finally for primary aluminum. The differences in predictions obtained for the year 2000 are quite revealing.

6.10   CASE STUDIES AND EXERCISES

The case studies in this chapter are intended to amplify key points in the discussion of cost estimating and cost control. The exercises allow the readers to relate personal viewpoints and experiences to the events unfolded in the case studies.

The case studies in this chapter underscore the need for cost-estimating realism and timely cost control to minimize the consequences of forces external to the program. Some of the exercises provide practice in several of the techniques covered in this chapter.

6.10.1   Erosion of Resources

One of the most difficult problems in cost estimating is dealing with inflation and escalation. Although they are often viewed as one, inflation and escalation are distinctly different, and the difference needs to be understood when attempting to estimate with realism.

As stated in Section 6.8.3, inflation is the time-oriented decrease in purchasing power of a nation's money brought about by such factors as deficit spending and foreign trade imbalance. Inflation can be viewed as an extrinsic cost driver, induced by factors external to the program. The mode for dealing with inflation is primarily reactive, but certain steps can be taken to mitigate its effects.

In contrast, escalation is an intrinsic cost driver induced by factors that are essentially internal to the program, such as those given in Table 6.17. The mode for dealing with escalation should be proactive.

Consider the contract executed in 1976 by one of the armed services and a producer of high-technology products to develop a tactical communication system and, starting in 1981, to deliver 120 production versions of the system over a 3-year period. Funding for the production version was based on a two-shelter configuration and an average unit cost of $2.45 million, for a total production cost of $294 million in 1976 dollars.

Production was delayed until 1983 because of requirements changes that resulted in redesign to a one-shelter configuration. The average unit cost was estimated again at that time, and although about one-half of the original amount of equipment would be produced, the cost was determined to be $4.84 million in 1983 dollars.

The total production cost of $594 million exceeded the funds that had been budgeted. The customer was forced to significantly reduce the quantity of systems to be delivered even though this resulted in reduced capability.

EXERCISE   Obtain producer price index for the years 1976 through 1983 from the *Statistical Abstract of the United States*. Estimate how much of the production cost increase was due to inflation and how much was due to escalation.

Convert the customer's 1976 production budget of $294 million to 1983 dollars. Assume a 90 percent learning curve and, from the baseline of 120 systems at $4.85 million each, determine the quantity that could be ordered within the budget limit.

6.10.2 Antilearning Phenomenon

The customary approach to assessing loss of learning due to breaks in production assumes that the slope and vertical position of the learning curve do not change, but that the first unit produced after the disruption ceases regresses to an earlier position on the learning curve, and that the pattern established in the past is repeated. Production breaks are usually accompanied by changes in the factors given in Table 6.9, and it is more realistic to assume that the slope of the learning is also changed.

The usual form of the expression for cost improvement with learning is

$$y = ax^b \tag{6.45}$$

where y is the cost to produce unit number x, a is the cost to produce the first unit, and b is the slope of the learning curve.

The slope of the learning curve is given by

$$b = \frac{\log(\text{learning curve})}{\log 2} \tag{6.46}$$

For example, the slope of the 95 percent learning curve is

$$b = \frac{\log 0.95}{\log 2} = -.074 \tag{6.47}$$

Given a first unit cost of $250, from Equation (6.45) the cost of unit number 1000 would be

$$y = \$250(1000 - .074) = \$149.50 \tag{6.48}$$

The usual form of the expression for the average unit cost of the quantity x is

$$y = \frac{[a/(1 + b)][x^{(1+b)} - 1]}{x} \tag{6.49}$$

The average unit cost for the example would therefore be

$$y = \frac{[\$250/(1 - .074)][1000^{(1-.074)}]}{1000} \tag{6.50}$$

$$= \$161$$

EXERCISE   Consider the case of the manufacturer of high-technology products who experienced a prolonged labor strike. Prior to the strike, the average unit cost of a particular model was perceived to be $2200 when produced in a continuous run of 1000 units on a 90 percent learning curve. These were produced after the strike and the actual cost was discerned to be $4250 for the one-hundredth unit.

Using the expressions given above, calculate the loss in learning that caused the cost increase. Which of the factors given in Table 6.9 were the key contributors to the loss in learning?

6.10.3   Environmental Protection

It had been suggested that the pollution detection devices of the environmental protection agency of a certain state were insufficiently sensitive to detect offenders. The agency claimed that its devices could detect excessive amounts of pollutants emitted by factories with a probability of .90 and a probability of .20 that factories not exceeding limits would fail the test.

The issue was whether to procure devices with a detection probability of .99 to apprehend more violators of the state's statutes, even though the increased sensitivity would increase the false alarm probability to .22. A consumer group claimed that 30 percent of the factories in the state emitted excessive pollutants.

EXERCISE   Using Bayes's theorem in tree form and the data given in Figure 6.21, calculate the probability that a factory failing the test actually

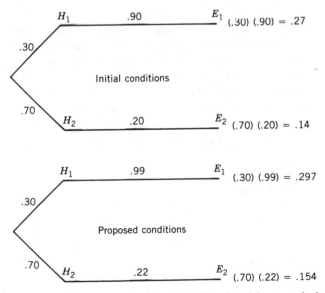

Figure 6.21   Environmental protection data (39). (Reprinted by permission of the Martin Marietta Corporation.)

emitted excessive pollutants under the initial conditions and under the proposed conditions. Recommend whether the agency should invest in more sensitive devices.

6.10.4   Deep in Space, Deeper in Debt

This case study exemplifies the cost implications of plunging into new frontiers. Although it concerns the National Aeronautics and Space Administration (NASA), there are parallels in industry when venturing into new technology and new marketplaces.

The General Accounting Office (GAO) is an arm of the Congress of the United States. The GAO recently reported to the U.S. Senate's Subcommittee on Science and Technology that several of NASA's deep-space programs were about to contribute to the national debt by dint of requiring additional funding that would exceed the original funding obligation by more than 70 percent.

Among the cited programs were: Galileo, a mission to the planet Jupiter; Magellan, a mission to the planet Venus; and Mars Observer. Table 6.21 lists some of the statistics provided to the Senate by the GAO.

It is NASA's contention that the Challenger tragedy in January 1986 was pivotal in the hardware redirection leading to the need for additional funding. For example, the Centaur upper-stage engine for the Space Shuttle was abandoned leaving the deep-space programs in search of a replacement booster engine. The GAO, however, contends that the overrun was ordained prior to the Challenger tragedy by inadequate upfront analysis accompanied by funding instability.

EXERCISE   This case study provides an opportunity for history to speak for itself. Using the methodology described in Section 6.6.2, derive the least-square equation for the regression of increased costs on the increased time from program inception to the anticipated launch dates.

Calculate the average time period from the date of inception to the anticipated date of launch. Use the student's t distribution to calculate the confidence limits for increased cost about the predicted increased cost for the average increased time period with a confidence level of 95 percent.

TABLE 6.21   Deep-Space Programs

Event	Galileo	Magellan	Mars Observer
Inception	1978	1984	1985
Original launch date	1989	1989	1992
Anticipated launch date	1996	1996	1994
Original cost estimate	$410 million	$295 million	$293 million
Current cost estimate	$1363 million	$514 million	$514 million

6.10.5 Money Is Power

A certain electric utility was challenged by the public service commission of that particular state for the utility's investment policy. The commission alleged that the utility had violated its charter by investing $725 million from a sinking fund in bonds yielding 7.5 percent interest compounded annually rather than retaining the fund for the acquisition of new power-generating equipment.

The utility countered that it decided to invest in bonds rather than in new equipment because of the anticipated low internal rate of return for the equipment investment, and that in the long run its customers would benefit from rate reductions. The utility had based its conclusion on the premise that the reduction in operating cost with the new equipment would average $50 million per year for the 25 years of the equipment lifetime.

EXERCISE   Using the relationships for the time value of money described in Section 6.7, calculate the internal rate of return on acquiring the new power generation equipment. Assume that the bonds would be held for the same period of time as the life of the new equipment.

What other criteria should be considered by public utilities in evolving investment policies? Public safety and the convenience of the public are good examples of these criteria. Among the foremost, however, is the public's perception of the basic integrity of utilities and their dedication to public service. List the criteria by their technical, economic, and societal significance.

REFERENCES

1. Rodney D. Stewart and Richard M. Wyska, *Cost Estimator's Reference Manual*, John Wiley & Sons, 1987.
2. Theodore Taylor, *Handbook of Electronics Industry Cost Estimating Data*, John Wiley & Sons, 1985.
3. Martin Marietta Corporation, *Design to Cost/Affordability Manual*, 1986.
4. Department of Army Pamphlet No. 11-2, *Research and Development Cost Guide for Army Materiel Systems*, 1976.
5. Department of Army Pamphlet No. 11-3, *Investment Cost Guide for Army Materiel Systems*, 1976.
6. Department of Army Pamphlet No. 11-4, *Operating and Support Guide for Army Materiel Systems*, 1976.
7. MIL-STD-881A, *Military Standard, Work Breakdown Structures for Defense Military Items*, 1975.
8. Rodney D. Stewart and Richard M. Wyska, *Cost Estimator's Reference Manual*, John Wiley & Sons, 1987.
9–10. Martin Marietta Corporation, *Ibid.*

11–12. Rodney D. Stewart and Richard M. Wyska, *Cost Estimator's Reference Manual,* John Wiley & Sons, 1987.

13. RCA Corporation, Morristown, NJ, *PRICE H Reference Manual,* 1985.

14–16. NAVMAT P3855-1, *Navy Power Supply Reliability* 1982.

17. Rodney D. Stewart and Richard M. Wyska, *Cost Estimator's Reference Manual,* John Wiley & Sons, 1987.

18. Martin Marietta Corporation, *Design to Cost Affordability Manual,* 1986.

19. Rodney D. Stewart and Richard M. Wyska, *Cost Estimator's Reference Manual,* John Wiley & Sons, 1987.

20. Martin Marietta Corporation, *Design to Cost Affordability Manual,* 1986.

21. Harold J. Larson, *Introduction to Probability Theory and Statistical Inference,* John Wiley & Sons, 1982.

22. Jack V. Michaels, "Probability and Statistics for Value Engineers, Tests of Hypotheses," *Value World,* April/May/June 1988. Copyright 1988, Martin Marietta Corporation.

23. Harold J. Larson, *Introduction to Probability Theory and Statistical Inference,* John Wiley & Sons, 1982.

24–26. Jack V. Michaels, *Bayes' Theorem in Decision Making, Reasoning from Effect to Cause,* 1987 International Conference of the Society of American Value Engineers. Copyright 1987, Martin Marietta Corporation.

27. Consolidated Capital Communications Group, Inc., *The Financial Desk Book,* 1985.

28. DoD Instruction No. 7000.2, *Performance Measurement for Selected Acquisitions.*

29. Martin Marietta Corporation, *Performance Measurement System,* 1979.

30. DARCOM P 715-4, AFSCP/AFLCP 173-5, NAVMAT P 5243. *Cost/Schedule Control Systems Criteria Joint Implementation Guide.*

31. Rodney D. Stewart and Richard M. Wyska, *Cost Estimator's Reference Manual,* John Wiley & Sons, 1987.

32–33. U.S. Bureau of the Census, *Statistical Abstract of the United States: 1988.*

34. U.S. Department of Commerce, *1987 U.S. Industrial Outlook.*

35–36. U.S. Bureau of the Census, *Statistical Abstract of the United States: 1988.*

37–39. U.S. Department of Commerce, *1987 U.S. Industrial Outlook.*

39. Jack V. Michaels, *Bayes' Theorem in Decision Making, Reasoning from Effect to Cause,* 1987 International Conference of the Society of American Value Engineers. Copyright 1987, Martin Marietta Corporation.

7
REMEMBERING HISTORY

By the year 2000, the high-technology industry will be dominated by those organizations that understand affordability and practice design to cost (1). This chapter coalesces many of the experiences, both favorable and unfavorable, of numerous organizations that ventured into high technology, into certain principles that are key to achieving and maintaining a competitive posture in the market place. These principles should be viewed as dictates for success in design to cost.

These dictates are enunciated in this chapter and are then summarized in a list of operational guidelines for design-to-cost practitioners. These dictates are also illuminated by two case studies, one revealing the consequences of inadequate cost trade studies at program inception and the other the importance of responding to market pressure even when well into an undertaking.

The most imperative need of all, however, is disciplined engineering. Its pervasiveness drives all aspects of development and production, and is the key to a successful transition from development to production. This observation is enforced with an overview of the recommendations of the Defense Science Board in regard to reducing risk in the transition from development to production. The guidance of the board also serves as an objectial summary of the book.

The chapter concludes with the four absolutes of design to cost. Adherence to these absolutes is mandatory.

7.1 DICTATES

Most problems are self-imposed and usually can be traced to lack of discipline. The foremost attribute of successful design-to-cost programs is discipline: discipline to evolve and proclaim realistic cost goals, discipline to forego appealing but nonessential features, discipline to minimize engineering changes, discipline to do thorough failure analyses, discipline to abide by test protocols, and discipline to persevere in the face of problems that will occur in even the best-managed programs.

This is stated eloquently by Norman R. Augustine in his classic work, *Revised and Enlarged Augustine's Laws*.

In the year 2054, the entire defense budget will purchase just one tactical aircraft. This aircraft will have to be shared by the Air Force and Navy 3½ days each per week except for leap year, when it will be made available to the Marines for the extra day.

(Law Number XI)

Augustine's Laws may be rooted in the defense establishment, but their dictates, summarized below, apply to all sectors of the economy (2).

Proposals to start new development programs should receive intense scrutiny, including verification that the need is valid, and that the cost of the proposed solution is commensurate with the benefits it offers. Without clear evidence of significant payoff, the program should not be started. The objective is to see how many good programs can be completed, not how many programs can be started.

The program approval and contractor selection process should be structured to reward realism, not optimism.

Once begun, absent truly substantive changes that affect in a very fundamental manner the basis for initiating an effort in the first place, the program should be left alone and maximum stability provided. Turbulence in funding and program guidance adds cost, wastes time, diverts management attention, deters capital investment, increases risk, and demotivates participants.

Debate regarding the need for a proposed program should be terminated when the point of diminishing returns has been reached. Prolonging the process beyond a reasonable point generally leads to only marginally better decisions and often sacrifices technological leadership. Compressing development to compensate for time lost to indecision is counterproductive.

Every requirement and imposed specification should add real value commensurate with its cost. The last few percent of capability costs a disproportionate amount.

Engineering development ordinarily should not be initiated until the technology it encompasses has been demonstrated.

Improving existing systems is often preferable to beginning new development. The already incurred cost and maturity of existing systems frequently permit reduction in future cost, schedule, and risk in satisfying new requirements.

Extreme capability incorporated in small quantities of hardware is frequently an inadequate substitute for larger quantities of less capable hardware.

Programs should be fully funded, and only those programs that enjoy a high enough priority to demand full funding throughout their existence should be initiated. Spreading limited funding over an excessive number of programs will in the long term produce less return on the funds invested.

Programs should plan for the unexpected and make provisions, on a probabilistic basis if necessary, for adequate resources to overcome unforeseen problems that do arise.

The progression of a program from development to production should not be keyed to the calendar, but rather keyed to specific milestones like successfully completed tests.

The extent of overlap permitted of successive phases in programs (concurrency) should be based on careful assessment of exposure in the event problems occur in predecessor phases. A moderate amount of concurrency generally goes a long way.

Rules, regulations, and reports are not substitutes for sound judgment. Managers should be given the latitude to manage as well as be held accountable for their actions.

Excessive layering of management levels is expensive, demotivating and generally counterproductive. Higher levels should focus on broader issues having greater potential consequences; lower levels should be permitted to focus on more detailed matters.

The sine qua non of successful program execution is the participation of

TABLE 7.1 Operational Guidelines (3)

Select a qualified, dedicated design-to-cost manager who reports directly to the program director, and collocate design-to-cost team members

Make cost an integral part of the review process, and route all cost-related actions through the design-to-cost manager for approval

Name the decision makers in design to cost, and give them unrestricted access to the program director; do not assign decision-making to committees

Allocate goals to individuals, not to organizations, and use goals as performance criteria for work appraisal

Establish a policy for awards and incentives, use performance as work appraisal criteria, and publicize cost performance at all levels

Use quantitative scoring techniques for evaluating alternative approaches

Flow down requirements and incentives to suppliers

Maintain configuration control of cost-related matters

Adapted with permission of the Martin Marietta Corporation.

competent and highly motivated people. Carefully selected but small groups of individuals can contribute far beyond their numbers and should be rewarded accordingly.

As in all endeavors, integrity and candor are paramount. Problems not surfaced remain problems not solved.

Table 7.1 is a list of some specific guidelines that were prepared by an aerospace contractor and pertain to the operational aspects of design-to-cost programs. They constitute a roadmap to success when observed in the framework of the aforementioned dictates.

7.2   LEARNING THE HARD WAY

The objective of the Main Battle Tank Program was to develop a more combat effective tank than was currently available yet one that would be sufficiently low in cost to be affordable in quantities needed to equip first-line armored forces in the 1980s. The evolution of the design started in the mid-1960s as a joint effort of the United States and West Germany.

The approach proved to be far too costly for either country, and a more austere version was pursued. The estimated production cost of the latter was still more than the Congress was willing to approve, and the program was terminated about 7 years after it had been started.

Several lessons had been learned that later proved invaluable in establishing requirements for a less complex and less costly tank, in particular the importance of cost versus performance trades at the inception of the program. The design of the predecessor had progressed too far to allow significant cost saving.

A typical problem was the inability to replace the complex and expensive automatic loader by adding a fourth crew member. The design had located the crew in the turret of the tank, and it could not be reconfigured for a four-person turret. Thus the automatic loader could not be eliminated.

Another lesson learned was that technology should be well in hand before engineering development is undertaken. The predecessor program was literally buried with problems in fire control, night vision, suspension, propulsion, and ammunition (4).

7.3   NOTABLE SUCCESS

By the end of the 1970s, the Ford Motor Company, which had already lost billions of dollars from having failed to respond to the motoring public's demand for performance, style, and quality, continued to face dim prospects. Today, however, Ford is hailed as number one in sales of U.S.-manufactured vehicles (5).

This dramatic turnaround started in 1980 when Ford recognized its failure in responding to the market pressure. Despite prior losses, the company invested billions of dollars in advanced technology, focusing on what the motoring public wanted.

The company listened to its own employees as well as expert automotive consultants. Innovative design was combined with affordable quality.

This has given Ford the image of design leader and, along with the emphasis on quality, has led to the domination of the automotive marketplace. Prior losses have been more than offset by current performance.

7.4 TRANSITION FROM DEVELOPMENT TO PRODUCTION

After all is said and done, the name of the game is "production." Production supplies the needs of both the public and private sectors. Production is where profits are reaped by contractors who strike the right combination of functionality, quality, and affordability.

Too often in the past, as a result of funding and schedule constraints, the technical integrity of programs has been compromised by deleting or deferring vital program elements that contribute to system performance, producibility, and supportability. This has added unintentionally to the life-cycle cost and postponed operational capability dates by pursuing development programs that did not yield producible designs and supportable configurations in a timely manner.

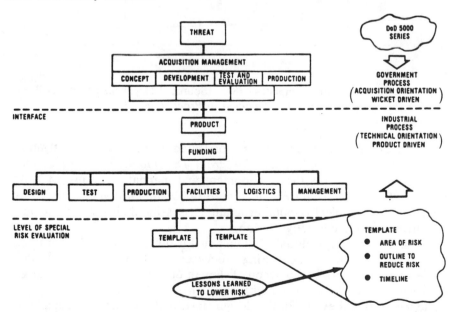

Figure 7.1 Transition problem perspective (7). (Source: Department of Defense DoD4245.7M, *Transition from Development to Production*, 1985.)

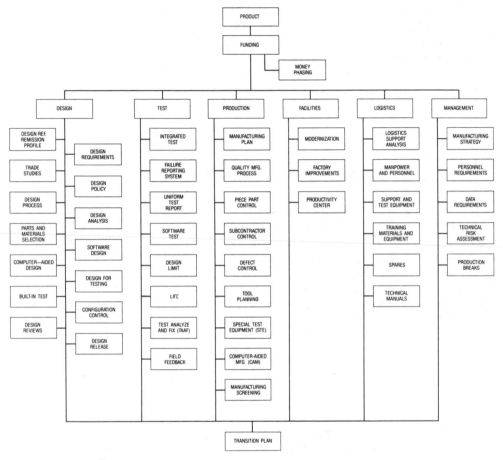

Figure 7.2 Critical-path templates (8). (Source: Department of Defense DoD4245.7M, *Transition from Development to Production,* 1985.)

This experience in the Department of Defense led to the promulgation of DoD Directive 4245.7, *Transition from Development to Production.* The directive authorizes the development and mandates the use of DoD 4245.7-M, *Transition from Development to Production Manual,* as the basis for structuring technically sound programs, assessing their risk, and identifying areas needing corrective action.

In essence, the major thrust of the manual is directed toward identifying and establishing critical engineering processes and their control methods. This leads to more organized accomplishment of these activities and places more significance and accountability on them.

The most critical events in the design, test, and production elements of the industrial process are transformed into what are referred to as "templates.'' Figure 7.1 illustrates the manual's perspective of the transition problem and the action level that must be reached in order to define understandable and achievable solutions to repetitive transition risks. Figure 7.2 identifies the critical-path templates for each major area—design, test, production, facilities, logistics, and management. These six areas constitute the critical-path hierarchy for funding, whose other critical path template is money-phasing (6).

1. FUNDING

Aside from the issue of the amount of money devoted to programs, the major risk stems from the time-phasing of the money. Risk is aggravated by authorizing development without attention to production. The development decision must be accomplished by adequate and timely development funding. In addition, the development decision is a commitment to production that must be supported by properly phased funding.

2. DESIGN

Accurate and complete specification of the design reference profile is required in order to support the acquisition process. The degree to which the specified mission profile corresponds to ultimate service use directly determines the degree of risk. Design requirements are translated from operational requirements and frequently are evolved or negotiated during the design process. They may include design requirements that can be verified only by postdevelopment test and as such are a common cause of risk. Trade studies are both essential and expected elements of acquisition programs. However, reducing production risk is not a usual subject of trade studies and in itself is a cause of risk. The existence or absence of documented corporate policies, backed up by controlled engineering practices manuals, has a direct bearing on risk in production. The design process should reflect a sound design policy and proper engineering disciplines and practices. Design analysis by specialty engineering is critical to low-risk design for production. Low-risk design should allow parts and materials to operate well below maximum allowable stress levels. Stress-derating policies must be in place at the start of hardware development. Failure to allocate system requirements clearly between hardware and software greatly increases the difficulty in isolating and correcting design problems. Experience shows that more than 60 percent of software errors are traceable to functional or logical design. Many modern design tools, such as computer-aided design (CAD), are not used to the proper extent because they are time-consuming and costly. This short-sightedness results in overall longer schedules and costs. In particular, design for testing is one of the many areas frequently neglected and the cost advantage of built-in test is often ignored. A common source of risk in the transition from development to production is the lack of adequate configuration control. The lack of specific direction and discipline in design reviews is another significant contributor to risk. The most critical area in design, however, is the issue of released engineering. The requirements for completely checked engineering drawings cannot be compromised for timely release to the factory without cost consequences.

3. TEST

The absence of a carefully integrated test plan is conducive to a high degree of risk. This is exacerbated by introducing production changes without recertification. The objective of failure reporting and corrective action is to prevent failure recurrence. Failure to flow down such requirements to suppliers is a major risk contributor, along with indiscriminate uses of non-uniform test reports. The cost for correcting software design errors after the design phase of programs multiplies at a much greater rate than for correcting hardware design errors. The relative relationship should be recognized in establishing design limits and requirements for life test. The practice of test, analyze, and fix (TAAF) should be employed as early as possible in development, and the use of field feedback should be maximized throughout the program lifetime.

4. PRODUCTION

Involvement of production and manufacturing engineering only after the design process has been completed is a fundamental error and a major risk in the transition from development to production. A similar observation applies to quality with the additional comment that failure to certify manufacturing processes as well as product designs is a frequent contributor to the risk profile. Piece-part control, subcontractor control, and defect control are other areas that are conducive to risk. Planning for tooling and special test equipment should be initiated early in development. Similarly, early implementation of computer-aided manufacturing (CAM) in conjunction with CAD will facilitate the development and debugging of the technical data package for production. Manufacturing screening, in particular environmental stress screening, can reduce field failure rates by as much as 90 percent and in-plant failure rates by as much as 75 percent. Electronic stress screening requirements should be established early in development.

5. FACILITIES

Current government contracting policy inhibits industry investment for modernization (see Section 5.2). However, many equipment failures in the field can be attributed to outmoded manufacturing processes. Motivation should be provided to adopt the productivity center approach, wherein technology and skilled workers are blended together.

6. LOGISTICS

Logistics support analysis (LSA) should be an integral part of the design process to minimize operation and support (O&S) costs of fielded systems. Systems should be designed with as complete an understanding as possible of workforce and personnel skill profiles. Support and test equipment should be developed in concert with prime mission equipment for both design efficiency and time-phasing. Training materials and equipment are in the same category as the foregoing, as are spare parts and technical manuals used for operations and repairs.

7. MANAGEMENT

The selection of manufacturing strategy should be supportive of the goals of both the customer and the contractor. Justifiable personnel requirements in both shops should be staffed with as little delay possible. An extensive amount of money is spent on data. The guideline should be to limit the data to what is necessary, but to always ensure its accuracy, completeness, and integrity. There can never be too much effort expended on technical risk assessment. The most devastating events from the viewpoint of schedule and cost are last-minute surprises. This is particularly critical in the domain of suppliers. Breaks in production impact costs in two fashions: (1) the effect of inflation and (2) the loss of learning. To a large measure, reductions in rate of production have the same deleterious effects.

7.5   WHAT IS PAST IS PROLOGUE

Without intervention, history will always repeat itself; even with intervention, many courses of events may remain essentially unaltered. One thing is certain, however. Those who do not remember the past are condemned to relive it.

Design to cost builds on memory of the past as the means for survival and growth in the high-technology marketplace, and this book has addressed the many principles and practices that are essential to successful design to cost. Above all, the following four absolutes are mandatory and serve as the epilogue of the book:

Elevate cost to at least the same level of concern as performance and schedule.

Emphasize design to cost from before the start to after the finish of the program. Product support is as important and as lucrative as product sales.

Set aside monetary reserve for risk management.

For every cost increase, cut something that does not add to the real value of the product.

REFERENCES

1. Peter G. Peterson, "The Morning After," *The Atlantic Monthly,* October 1987.
2. Norman R. Augustine, *Revised and Enlarged Augustine's Laws,* American Institute of Aeronautics and Astronautics, 1983.
3. Martin Marietta Corporation, *Design to Cost/Affordability Manual,* 1986.
4. Gerald T. Croskery and Cyril F. Horton, "XM-1 Main Battle Tank," *Defense Management Journal,* September 1974.
5. Motor Vehicle Manufacturers Association of the United States, Inc., *MMVA Motor Vehicle Facts and Figures,* 1987.
6–8. Department of Defense DoD 4245.7-M, *Transition from Development to Production,* 1985.

APPENDIX 1
DEFINITION OF TERMS

The following definitions of design-to-cost terms are consistent with those given in the Department of Defense (DoD) Instruction 5000.33, *Uniform Budget/Cost Terms and Definitions,* and DoD and armed services directives, instructions, and guides and other current sources. For comprehensive definitions of estimating terms, the reader is referred to the *National Estimating Society Dictionary,* National Estimating Society, 1001 Connecticut Avenue, NW, Washington, DC 20036.

Acquisition Cost. The cost of acquiring a new product or system and includes all elements of life-cycle cost except the cost of operation, support, and disposal.

Actual Cost of Work Performed. The costs actually incurred and recorded in accomplishing the work performed within a given time period.

Actual Direct Costs. Those costs identified specifically with a contract, based on the contractor's cost identification and accumulation system as accepted by the cognizant government representatives (see "Direct Costs").

Affordability. The characteristics of a product with a selling price that approaches its functional worth and is within the customer's ability to pay.

Applied Direct Costs. The amounts recognized in the time period associated with the consumption of labor, material, and other direct resources, without regard to the date of commitment or the date of payment. These amounts are to be charged to work-in-process in the time period that any one of the following takes place:

When labor, material, and other direct resources are actually consumed

When material resources are withdrawn from inventory for use

When material resources are received that are uniquely identified to the contract and scheduled for use within 60 days

When major components or assemblies are received on a line-flow basis that are specifically and uniquely identified to a single serially numbered end item

Apportioned Effort. Effort that by itself is not readily divisible into short-span work packages but is related in direct proportion to measured effort.

Authorized Work. Effort that has been definitized and is on contract, plus that for which definitized contract costs have not been agreed to but for which written authorization has been received by the contractor.

Budgeted Cost for Work Performed. The sum of the budgets for completed work packages and completed portions of open work packages, plus the appropriate portion of the budgets for level of effort and apportioned effort.

Budgeted Cost for Work Scheduled. The sum of budgets for all work packages and planning packages scheduled to be accomplished (including in-process work packages), plus the amount of level of effort and apportioned effort scheduled to be accomplished within a given time period.

Capital Recovery. The point at which a loan or investment, adjusted for the time value of money, is recovered. Usually expressed in terms of number of repayments, period of time, or number of units sold.

Compound Interest. Interest earned on interest earned on the principal.

Constant-Year Dollars. A baseline or reference year, either prior or future with respect to the present time, used for cost and earning comparisons. Now-dollars and then-dollars are converted to the baseline year using actual and projected inflation indices.

Contract Budget Base. The negotiated contract cost plus the estimated cost of authorized, unpriced work.

Contractual Design-to-Cost Target. A contractual design-to-cost is that portion of the program goal over which the contractor has control. Contractual design-to-cost targets for the production phase address only the system elements supplied by the contractor. Design-to-cost targets for O&S costs are structured to fit only the system elements covered by the contract such as spare parts and warranties, particularly the reliability improvement warranty (RIW).

Cost Account. Management control point at which actual costs can be accumulated and compared to budgeted costs for work performed. A cost account is natural control point for cost–schedule planning and control, since it represents the work assigned to one responsible organizational element on one CWBS element.

Cost Account Manager. The individual who has been assigned full responsibility for the scope of work of the cost account, including technical, schedule, and budget.

Cost–Benefit Ratio. The ratio of the present value of benefits to the present value of costs.

DD Form 1423. DoD forms used to document contract data requirements lists (CDRL).

Design to Cost. An acquisition management technique to achieve system designs that meet the stated cost parameters. Cost as a design parameter is addressed on a continuing basis as part of a system's development and production processes. The technique embodies early establishment of realistic but difficult cost objectives, goals, and thresholds and a well-managed effort to achieve them.

Design-to-Cost Goal. The design-to-cost goal is a specific cost number, in constant dollars, based on a specified production quantity and rate, established early during system development as a management objective and design parameter for subsequent phases of the acquisition cycle. Design-to-cost goals are estimates of selected cost elements of life-cycle cost (LCC) that are included in the design-to-cost parameters for major systems. Design-to-cost goals are usually expressed in terms of price to the customer.

Design to Life-Cycle Cost. Design to life-cycle cost is the totality of design to cost and goals are expressed in terms of overall acquisition, operation, and support costs. Design to life-cycle cost is synonymous with design to cost in its broadest context.

Design to Operation and Support Cost. Design to operation and support cost is an element of design to cost and is expressed in terms of operation and support costs.

Design to Unit Production Cost. Design to unit production cost is an element of design to cost, and goals are expressed in terms of the averge unit production cost for producing the specified hardware lot and generally include recurring materiel and labor costs, engineering change costs, program management costs, and production support costs.

Direct Costs. Any costs that can be identified specifically with a particular final cost objective.

Discount Rate. The factor, expressed as a percentage, used to calculate the present value of a sum of money in the future.

Equivalence. The equivalent present value of a sum of money with a given value in the future.

Estimated Cost at Completion. Actual direct costs, plus indirect costs allocatable to the contract, plus the estimate of costs (direct and indirect) for authorized work remaining.

Flyaway Cost. "Flyaway" is a generic term (similar to rollaway, sailaway, and driveaway), applied to an end item of hardware or software. Flyaway cost includes:

Work-breakdown structure (WBS) elements of:
> Major system equipment (MSE). Elements identified as end item(s). Includes basic units such as airframe, hull structure, propulsion, engine, electronics, ordnance, and installed GFE.
> System project management. All system project management effort is included, except effort that can be specifically associated with MSE hardware elements.

System test and evaluation. All system testing is included: development, component, and acceptance, except testing that can be specifically associated with MSE hardware elements.

Procurement funded costs (i.e., line item procurement program).

Production costs. Includes all engineering support to production, initial rate-sustaining tooling, manufacturing, purchased equipment, quality control, allowance for changes, warranties, first destination transportation, general and administrative (G&A), and profit associated with the cost occurring during the procurement phase of the life cycle.

Functional Worth. Least expensive way to perform a given function.

Future Value. The value of a given sum of money at a future time equivalent to the value of the sum of money at the present time at a given interest rate.

Generation Breakdown. Hierarchical structure of a product or system from the basic components through the final assembly.

Indirect Costs. Costs that, because of their incurrence for common or joint objectives, are not readily subject to treatment as direct costs.

Initial Production Facilities. Initial production facilities include all facilities, equipment, tooling, and associated planning and procedures required to accomplish the program objectives that are a direct charge to the contract.

Interest Rate. The ratio, expressed as a percentage, of interest earned or paid at the end of a given period of time to the money invested or borrowed at the beginning of the given period of time.

Internal Rate of Return. The rate of return at which the present value of benefits equals the present value of costs.

Internal Replanning. Replanning actions performed by the contractor for remaining effort within the recognized total allocated budget.

Investment Cost. "Investment cost" is defined as the sum of all costs resulting from the production and introduction of the materiel systems into the operational inventory. The term "investment cost" includes:

All costs to the government defined as contractor costs plus in-house costs, of products and services necessary to transform the results of R&D into a fully operational system consisting of the hardware, training, and support activities necessary to initiate operations

Costs of both a nonrecurring (i.e., costs to establish a production capability) and recurring nature (i.e., costs occurring repeatedly during production and delivery)

Costs of all production products and related services, no matter how such costs are funded

All costs resulting from production and introduction into operational inventory regardless of how the cost was allocated among unit equipment, maintenance, and training usage classifications

Just-in-Time. Material control strategy that schedules supplies as required for work without buffer stock or excess inventory.

Level of Effort. Effort of a general or supportive nature that does not produce definite end products or results.

Life-Cycle Cost. The life-cycle cost of a system is the total cost to the customer of acquisition and ownership of that system over its full life. It includes the cost of development, acquisition, operation, support, and disposal.

Management Reserve. An amount of the total allocated budget withheld for management control purposes rather than designated for the accomplishment of a specific task or set of tasks.

Mission Success. Technical oversight function having extremely broad scope and authority.

Negotiated Contract Cost. The estimated cost negotiated in a cost-plus-fixed-fee contract, or the negotiated target cost in either a fixed-price incentive contract or a cost-plus incentive fee contract.

Now Dollars. The value of a given sum of dollars at the current time.

Operation and Support Cost. "Operation and support" cost is defined as the sum of all costs of the operation, maintenance, and support (including personnel support) of the weapon system after it is accepted into the operational inventory. Operation and support cost buildup begins when the first production equipment becomes operational and continues throughout the service life and includes those costs associated with operating, modifying, maintaining, supplying, disposing, and supporting a support system in the inventory.

Opportunity Cost. The return that would have been realized had the money been invested in an alternative opportunity.

Original Budget. The budget established at, or near the time the contract was signed.

Performance Measurement Baseline. The time-phased budget plan against which contract performance is measured. It is formed by the budgets assigned to scheduled cost accounts and the applicable indirect budgets. For future effort, not planned to the cost account level, the performance measurement baseline also includes budgets assigned to higher-level CWBS elements and undistributed budgets. It equals the total allocated budget less management reserve.

Planning Package. A logical aggregation of work within a cost account, normally the far-term effort, that can be identified and budgeted in early baseline planning but is not yet defined into work packages.

Present Value. The value at the present time of a future payment or receipt at a given discount rate.

Principal. The amount of money invested or borrowed.

Price Indexes. Ratios indicating the relationships between prices at different time periods.

Producibility. The aggregate of characteristics that, when applied to equipment design and production planning, leads to the most effective and economic means of fabrication, assembly, inspection, test, installation, checkout, and acceptance.

Productivity. The ability to produce systems or equipment within the state of the production art and within the cost parameters established for the specified development effort.

Project Summary Work-Breakdown Structure. A summary work-breakdown structure (WBS) tailored to a specific defense materiel item by selecting applicable elements from one or more summary WBSs or by adding elements that are unique to the program.

Rate of Return. The ratio, expressed as a percentage, of profit to a given expense or investment adjusted for the time value of money.

Research-and-Development Cost. Research-and-development cost is the sum of all costs resulting from applied research, engineering design, analysis, development, test, evaluation, and management development efforts. The term "R&D cost" includes:

All costs to the customer (contractor costs plus in-house costs) of products and services necessary to bring a specific materiel system from concept to serial production

All costs to the customer of developing the specific capability, irrespective of how such costs are funded.

Significant Variances. Those differences between planned and actual performance that require further review, analysis or action. Appropriate thresholds should be established as to the magnitude of variances that will require variance analysis.

Sinking Fund. Fund used to retire debt or acquire new equipment that is established by series of deposits at fixed time intervals.

Sunk Cost. Previously expended or committed money that is not considered in future economic analysis.

Then Dollars. The value of future dollars adjusted from the value of a given sum of now dollars using projected inflation indices.

Total Allocated Budget. The sum of all budgets allocated to the contract. The total allocated budget consists of the performance measurement baseline and all management reserve. The total allocated budget will reconcile directly to the contract budget base. Any difference will be documented as to quantity and cause.

Undistributed Budget. Budget applicable to contract effort that has not yet been identified to CWBS elements at or below the lowest level of reporting to the government.

Uniform Series. Series of payments or receipts of fixed amounts, at fixed time intervals, and at fixed interest rate or discount rate.

Value Analysis. Value analysis is synonymous with value engineering.

Value Engineering. Value engineering is the formal technique to eliminate, without impairing essential functions or characteristics, anything that unnecessarily increases acquisition, operation, or support cost.

Value Engineering Change Proposal (VECP). A VECP is the formal means for implementing value engineering changes in ongoing contracts.

Value Engineering Incentive (VEI). A VEI clause in the contract allows the contractor voluntarily to suggest methods for performing more economically, and to share in any resulting savings.

Value Engineering Program Requirement (VEPR). A VEPR clause in the contract requires the contractor to establish a value engineering program that provides identification and submission to the government of methods for performing more economically. The contractor is paid but receives a smaller share of savings than under a VEI clause.

Variances. See "Significant Variances."

Wooden Round. Guided missile or smart weapon requiring zero maintenance after acceptance by the customer.

Work-Breakdown Structure. Hierarchical organization of hardware, software, service, and other tasks included in the overall program.

Work Packages. Detailed short-span jobs or material items identified by the contractor for accomplishing work required to complete the contract. A work package has the following characteristics:

It represents units of work at levels where work is performed.

It is clearly distinguishable from all other work packages.

It is assignable to a single organizational element.

It has scheduled start and completion dates, and, as applicable, interim milestones that are representative of physical accomplishments.

It has a budget or assigned values expressed in terms of dollars, hours, or other measurable units.

Its duration is limited to a relatively short span of time, or it is subdivided by discrete-value milestones to facilitate the objective measurement of work performed.

It is integrated with detailed engineering, manufacturing or other schedules.

Work Package Budgets. Resources that are formally assigned by the contractor to accomplish a work package and are expressed in dollars, hours, standards, or other definitive units.

Adapted with permission of the Martin Marietta Corporation.

APPENDIX 2
GLOSSARY OF ACRONYMS AND ABBREVIATIONS

ACI	Allocated configuration identification
AD	Advanced development
AFLC	Air Force Logistics Command
AFSC	Air Force System Command
AIAA	American Institute of Aeronautics and Astronautics
AMC	Army Materiel Command
AQL	Acceptable quality level
ARO	After receipt of order
ATE	Automatic test equipment
BAFO	Best and final offer
BITE	Built-in test equipment
BOM	Bill of Materials
CAB	Change Authorization Board
CAD	Computer-aided design
CAE	Computer-aided engineering
CAIG	Cost analysis improvement group
CAM	Computer-aided manufacturing
CCA	Circuit-card assembly
CCB	Change control board
CCOFM	Capital cost of facilities money
CDM	Configuration and Data Management
CDR	Critical design review
CDRL	Contract data requirements list
CER	Cost-estimating relationship
CES	Cost-element structure

CFE	Contractor-furnished equipment
CFSR	Contract fund status report
CI	Configuration item (also identification)
CIM	Computer-integrated manufacturing
CM	Configuration management
COEA	Cost–operation-effectiveness analysis
CPC	Computer program component
CPCI	Computer program configuration item
CPI	Consumer price index
CPM	Cost performance management; critical-path method
CPR	Cost performance report
CSC	Computer software component
CSCI	Computer software configuration item
C/SCSC	Contract–schedule control systems criteria
CTE	Commitment to excellence
CWBS	Contract work-breakdown structure
DAR	Defense acquisition regulation
DARCOM	Department of the Army Readiness Command
DARPA	Defense Advanced Research Projects Agency
DCAA	Defense Contract Audit Agency
DCAS	Defense Contract Administration Services
DCP	Decision-coordinating paper
DFA	Design for assembly
DID	Data item description
DoD	Department of Defense
DoE	Department of Energy
DoT	Department of Transportation
DSARC	Defense system acquisition review council
DT&E	Development test and evaluation
DTLCC	Design to life-cycle cost
DTOSC	Design to operation and support cost
DTUPC	Design to unit production cost
ECN	Engineering change notice
ECO	Engineering change order
ECP	Engineering change proposal
ED	Engineering development
EOQ	Economic order quantity
EPA	Economic price adjustment

FAA	Federal Aviation Agency
FAR	Federal Acquisition Regulation; false-alarm requirement
FAST	Functional analysis system technique
FCA	Functional configuration audit
FCI	Functional configuration identification
FDR	Fault detection requirement
FNR	Fault nondetection requirement
FOM	Figure of merit
FOT&E	Follow-on test and evaluation
FPI	Fixed-price incentive
FQR	Formal qualification review
FSED	Full-scale engineering development
FVPSP	Future value of a present single payment
FVUSP	Future value of a uniform series of payments
FY	Fiscal year
FYDP	Five-year defense program
G&A	General and administrative
GAO	General Accounting Office
GB	Generation breakdown
GBI	Generation-breakdown index
GFE	Government-furnished equipment
GFM	Government-furnished material
GFP	Government-furnished property
GNP	Gross National Product
GSE	Ground support equipment
HEW	Health, Education, and Welfare
ICAM	Integrated computer-aided manufacturing
ICD	Interface-control drawing
ICWG	Interface-control working group
IE	Industrial engineer
IG	Inspector General
ILS	Integrated logistics support
IMIP	Industrial modernization improvement (also incentives) program
IOC	Initial operational capability
IOT&E	Initial operating test and evaluation
IPF	Initial production facilities
IPS	Integrated program summary
IRR	Internal rate of return

JMNSS	Justification of major new system start
JIT	Just-in-time
LCC	Life-cycle cost
LET	Limited environmental test
LRE	Latest revised estimates
LRIP	Low-rate initial production
LRU	Line replaceable unit
LSA	Logistics support analysis
MAD	Magnetic anomaly detection
MICOM	Missile command
MIL SPEC	Military specification
MIL STD	Military Standard
MIMIC	Microwave–millimeter wave monolithic integrated circuits
MIS	Management information system
MOE	Measure of effectiveness
MPP	Manufacturing process plan
MPS	Master production scheduling
MRB	Material review board
MRP	Manufacturing resource planning
MSE	Major system equipment
MTBF	Mean time between failures
MTM	Methods–time measurements; methods–time–motion
MTTR	Mean time to repair
NASA	National Aeronautics and Space Administration
NAVMAT	Navy Material Command
NBS	National Bureau of Standards
NIB	Nickel boron
NOR	Notice of revision
NPA	Normal procurement allowance
O&M	Operation and maintenance
OMB	Office of Management and Budget
O&S	Operation and support
OSD	Office of the Secretary of Defense
PAT&E	Product Acceptance Testing and Evaluation
PCA	Physical configuration audit
PCI	Product configuration identification
PDM	Program decision memorandum
PDR	Preliminary design review
PEP	Production engineering and planning

PERT	Performance (also program) evaluation and review technique
PESO	Product Engineering Support Office
PIDS	Prime item development specifications
P³I	Preplanned product improvement program
PIP	Product improvement program
PME	Prime mission equipment
PMO	Program Management Office
PMS	Performance measurement system
PoDR	Point of diminishing returns
POL	Petroleum, oil, and lubricant
POM	Program-objective memorandum
PPI	Producer price index
PPL	Preliminary parts list
PRICE	Programmed review of information for costing and evaluation
PRR	Production readiness review
PWB	Printed wiring board
PVFSP	Present value of a future single payment
PVUSP	Present value of a uniform series of payments
QA	Quality assurance
QC	Quality control
R&D	Research and development
RDT&E	Research, development, test, and evaluation
RFD	Request for deviation
RFP	Request for proposal (also procurement)
RFQ	Request for quotation
RFW	Request for waiver
RIW	Reliability improvement warranty
R&M	Research and maintenance
ROI	Return on investment
ROTI	Return on tooling investment
RQL	Rejectable quality level
RSS	Root of the sum of squares
SAR	System acquisition review
SARC	System acquisition review council
SCN	Specification change notice
SDR	System design review
SECDEV	Secretary of Defense
SECNAV	Secretary of the Navy

SEMP	System engineering management plan
SFC	Shop Floor Control (Module)
SIC	Standard industrial code
SMM	Standard manufacturing method
SOW	Statement of work
SPI	Standard procedure instruction
SRR	System requirements review
ST	Special tools
STE	Special test equipment
TAAF	Test, analyze, and fix
TDP	Technical data package
TM	Technical manual
TMU	Time measurement unit
TPM	Technical performance measurement
TQC	Total quality control
TTO	Joint Tactical Communication Office
USPFV	Uniform series of payments for a future value
USPPV	Uniform series of payments for a present value
UUT	Unit under test
VECP	Value engineering change proposal
VEI	Value engineering incentive
VEP	Value engineering proposal
VEPR	Value engineering program requirement
VHSIC	Very high speed integrated circuit
VLSI	Very large scale integration
VSWR	Voltage standing-wave ratio
WBS	Work-breakdown structure
WES	Work-element structure
WIP	Work in process

Adapted with permission of the Martin Marietta Corporation.

APPENDIX 3
GOVERNMENT REQUIREMENTS

This appendix identifies and discusses requirements for design to cost and affordability established by the Department of Defense (DoD), armed services, and other government agencies. Copies of documents may be obtained from the Superintendent of Documents, Washington, DC 20402 and the Public Information Office of the various components of the DoD.

This appendix also contains the text of Office of Management and Budget (OMB) Circular A-131 on the subject of value engineering. Such circulars are published in the Federal Digest as the primary means of distribution.

1 DEPARTMENT OF DEFENSE

The DoD has traditionally operated under the assumption that defense systems and equipment must give the best performance that technology can provide, as cost is, at best, a secondary consideration. This practice has frequently resulted in reduction of the originally planned production quantities purchased, and the advanced technology has frequently had a lower field reliability than desired. Extensive and costly modifications and delays in upgrading the operational capability were not infrequent.

Because of the emphasis on high performance, the subsequent costs of production, operation, and support were not emphasized in the design and development of defense systems and equipment. Consequently, cost information obtained during the design phase was seldom fed back to development managers and design engineers.

As a consequence, there was little motivation for designers to consider future production, operation costs, and support costs. Yet, the original requirements and the subsequent engineering design are the most important factors driving such costs.

Department of Defense Directives 4245.3, 5000.1, and 5000.2 and related policy documents apply design-to-cost principles and concepts to all major defense system programs as well as to smaller programs and subsystems. Table 1 lists applicable DoD documents.

Instructions given by DoD in Directive 4245.3 are keyed to the activities shown in Figure 1 and establish the following policies:

1. Design to cost will be a parameter equal in importance to technical agreements and schedules.
2. Life-cycle-cost objectives will be established for each acquisition and separated into cost elements within the broad categories of development, production, operation, and support.
3. Cost requirements and the achievement of cost goals will be evaluated during design and development. Practical trade-offs between system capability, cost, and schedules will be continually examined.

TABLE 1   List of DoD Directives, Instructions, and Guides

Defense System Management College, *System Engineering Management Guide*, 1982.
DoD Directive 4005.1, *DoD Industrial Preparedness Production Planning*
DoD Directive 4120.3, *Defense Standardization and Specification Program*
DoD Directive 4120.3-M, *Defense Standardization Manual*
DoD Directive 4120.21, *Application of Specification, Standards, and Related Documents in the Acquisition Process*
DoD Directive 4245.3, *Design to Cost*
DoD Directive 4245.7, *Transition from Development to Production*
DoD Directive 4245.8, *DoD Value Engineering Program*
DoD Directive 5000.1, *Major System Acquisitions*
DoD Directive 5000.2, *Major System Acquisition Process*
DoD Directive 5000.3, *Test and Evaluation*
DoD Directive 5000.4, *OSD Cost Analysis Improvement Group*
DoD Directive 5000.34, *Defense Production Management*
DoD Directive 5000.39, *Acquisition and Management of Integrated Logistic Support*
DoD Directive 5000.43, *Acquisition Simplification*
DoD Directive 5010.19, *Configuration Management*
DoD Handbook 4245.8-H, *Value Engineering*
DoD Instruction 4200.15, *Manufacturing Technology Program*
DoD Instruction 4400.1, *Priorities and Allocations*
DoD Instruction 5000.33, *Uniform Budget/Cost Terms and Definitions*
DoD Instruction 7000.2, *Performance Measurement for Selected Acquisition*
DoD Guide LC-1, *Life-Cycle Costing*
DoD Guide LCC-2, *Life-Cycle Costing Casebook*
DoD Guide LCC-3, *Life-Cycle Cost for Systems*
DoD Manual 4120.3-M, *Defense Standardization Manual*
DoD Manual 4245.7-M, *Transition from Development to Production Manual*

4. The cost goals established in the development phase will be extended into subsequent phases of the system life cycle. Production cost will be rigorously controlled to the production goals.

5. As the system is introduced, operation and support (O&S) cost goals will be used to control initial outfitting cost, personnel, spares, rework, and other such items. In the operational feedback process, change requests generated by operational usage and feedback to design engineering will reflect the use of design-to-cost principles and trade-offs necessary to ensure that the lowest cost is obtained to achieve acceptable performance.

Department of Defense Directive 4245.3 requires the establishment of design-to-cost goals before beginning full-scale development. For any development program, design-to-cost concepts must be applied before the establishment of firm designs. Labor introduction is less effective, as the design cannot be changed to accommodate costs or because the change would be uneconomical because of cost or schedule impact.

The government's perspective of decisions affecting life-cycle cost is shown in Figure 2.2 of Chapter 2. Table 2 builds from this perspective and summarizes decision milestones, again from the government's perspective, which are amplified in the following paragraphs and must be clearly understood in a competitive environment.

1.1 Program Initiation

Cost considerations can have the greatest impact during this phase. Uncertainty surrounding cost estimates at this stage is large; therefore, cost considerations need to be in terms of cost differentials between competing concepts.

During the conceptual stage of this phase, there is no formal requirement for a program design-to-cost target. In some cases, however, the contractor is provided guidance as to the anticipated acceptable cost level as well as other design guidance.

The DoD requires as one of the outputs of the conceptual stage sufficient information to establish the system design-to-cost goals and targets with a reasonable level of confidence. The estimate needs to be in as much detail as possible and with substantiating data consistent with the degree of design definition.

For high-technology programs where state of the art is fluid or where performance to meet the threat is more important than cost, the cost should be refined with each major concept or design event. Firm goals are not established at these points but represent objectives to be validated during subsequent phases.

TABLE 2 Decision Milestones

Program Initiation		Demonstration and Validation		Full-Scale Engineering Development		Production and Deployment
• Alternative solutions		• Hardware demonstration of alternatives		• Prototype development		• Production
• Develop LCC[a] estimates of alternatives		• Refine LCC estimates of alternatives		• Trade-off process within system		• Deploy system
• Compare with affordability limits		• Identification of specific requirements in light of LCC impact		• Continuous refinement update of LCC estimate		
(DCP[b]) — ◊		(DCP) — ◊		(DCP) — ◊		
◊ Milestone 0 Sec Def Decision	◊ Milestone I Sec Def Decision		◊ Milestone II Sec Def Decision		◊ Milestone III Sec Def Decision	
• Mission element needs identified and prioritized	Selection of major system alternatives based on		• Tentative decision to produce and deploy		• Firm decision to produce and deploy	
• Affordability bounds and ceiling identified	• Life-cycle cost		• Major system alternative selected		• Revised LCC estimate compared with previous	
	• Operational effectiveness		• LCC estimate established			
	• Schedule		• Affordability decision			
			• DTC established			

Reprinted by permission of the Martin Marietta Corporation.

[a] Life-cycle cost.
[b] Decision-coordinating paper.

375

TIMES IN YEARS	(0-2)		(2-3)		(3-6)		(3-6)		(15-40)	
SYSTEM ACQUISITION PHASES	PROGRAM INITIATED	CONCEPT EXPLORATION	PROGRAM REFINED	DEMONSTRATION VALIDATION	TENTATIVE DECISION TO PRODUCE AND DEPLOY	FULL SCALE DEVELOPMENT	FINAL DECISION TO PRODUCE AND DEPLOY	PRODUCTION	DEPLOYMENT/ INITIAL OPERATING CAPABILITY	OPERATION AND SUPPORT	DISPOSAL
PURPOSE OF PHASE		CONCEPTUAL STUDIES INVESTIGATION OF ALTERNATIVE SOLUTIONS •DESIGN •PRODUCTION •LOGISTICS •TEST		IDENTIFICATION AND ANALYSIS OF MAJOR SYSTEM ALTERNATIVES •COMPETITIVE DEMONSTRATIONS		DESIGN AND TEST OF THE SELECTED SYSTEM ALTERNATIVE •DESIGN TRADEOFFS		RATE PRODUCTION OF SYSTEM		USER SUPPORT MODIFICATIONS/PRODUCT IMPROVEMENTS	
DECISION POINTS	POM/PDM		MS I (DISARC)		MS II (DISARC)		MS III (DISARC)				

REQUIRE-MENTS FORM-ULATION

THE COMMON THREAD IS PRODUCT DEFINITION

OPERATIONAL REQUIREMENT — REQUIREMENTS SCRUB — SRR — REQUIREMENT REVALIDATED — REQUIREMENT REVALIDATED

GAIN THOROUGH FAMILIARITY WITH THREAT AND OF RQMTS — REASSESS THREAT

TYPE A SYSTEM SPECIFICATION — TYPE B DEVELOPMENT SPECIFICATION — TYPE C, D, E PRODUCT/PROCESS/MATERIAL SPECIFICATION

BASELINES	FUNCTIONAL		ALLOCATED			PRODUCT					
	RFP SOW CDRL → CONTRACT		RFP SOW CDRL → CONTRACT		RFP SOW CDRL → CONTRACT		RFP SOW CDRL → CONTRACT				
SYSTEM ENGINEERING HARDWARE	SRD	SEMP		SDR	PDR		CDR	FCA	PCA	DESIGN DOCUMENTATION NECESSARY FOR PRODUCTION COMPLETE	DESIGN OF MODS/PIP
COMPUTER SOFTWARE PECULIAR SYSTEM ENGINEERING ACTIVITIES		POLICY (HOL, STANDARIZATION) TECHNOLOGY ASSESSMENT (VHSIC VLSI) SOFTWARE SYSTEM SYNTHESIS		CPCI SELECTION CPDP (CONTRACTOR) CRIPS/CRIMP/CRLCMP QA IV&V SOFTWARE ROMTS GENERATION SOFTWARE SYSTEM GENERATION		•SOFTWARE DESIGN •SOFTWARE CODING		•SOFTWARE TESTING REPRODUCED SOFTWARE ISSUE		POST DEPLOYMENT SOFTWARE SUPPORT (SOFTWARE MAINTENANCE)	

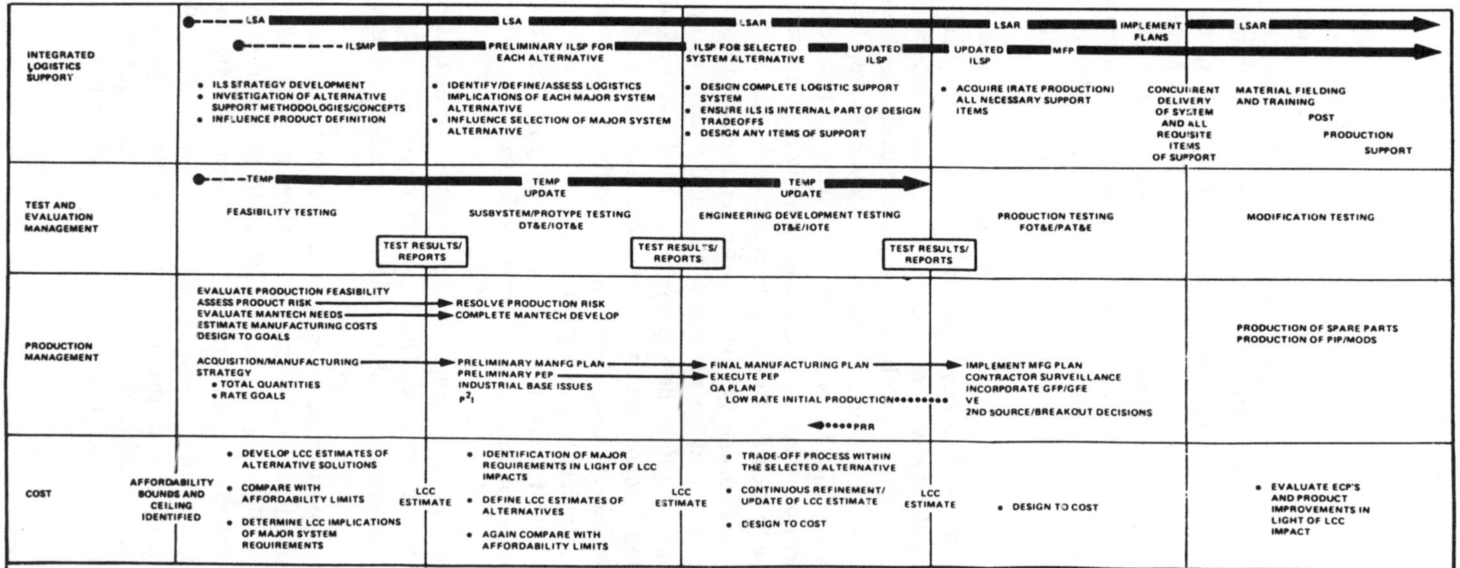

	●----- LSA	●----- LSA	ILSP FOR SELECTED SYSTEM ALTERNATIVE ━━ LSAR ━━ UPDATED ILSP	LSAR ━━ UPDATED ILSP ━━ MFP	IMPLEMENT PLANS ━━ LSAR
	●----- ILSMP	PRELIMINARY ILSP FOR EACH ALTERNATIVE			
INTEGRATED LOGISTICS SUPPORT	• ILS STRATEGY DEVELOPMENT • INVESTIGATION OF ALTERNATIVE SUPPORT METHODOLOGIES/CONCEPTS • INFLUENCE PRODUCT DEFINITION	• IDENTIFY/DEFINE/ASSESS LOGISTICS IMPLICATIONS OF EACH MAJOR SYSTEM ALTERNATIVE • INFLUENCE SELECTION OF MAJOR SYSTEM ALTERNATIVE	• DESIGN COMPLETE LOGISTIC SUPPORT SYSTEM • ENSURE ILS IS INTERNAL PART OF DESIGN • TRADEOFFS • DESIGN ANY ITEMS OF SUPPORT	• ACQUIRE (RATE PRODUCTION) ALL NECESSARY SUPPORT ITEMS	• CONCURRENT DELIVERY OF SYSTEM AND ALL REQUISITE ITEMS OF SUPPORT MATERIAL FIELDING AND TRAINING POST PRODUCTION SUPPORT
	●---- TEMP	TEMP UPDATE	TEMP UPDATE		
TEST AND EVALUATION MANAGEMENT	FEASIBILITY TESTING	SUBSYSTEM/PROTOTYPE TESTING DT&E/IOT&E TEST RESULTS/REPORTS	ENGINEERING DEVELOPMENT TESTING DT&E/IOTE TEST RESULTS/REPORTS	PRODUCTION TESTING FOT&E/PAT&E TEST RESULTS/REPORTS	MODIFICATION TESTING
PRODUCTION MANAGEMENT	EVALUATE PRODUCTION FEASIBILITY ASSESS PRODUCT RISK EVALUATE MANTECH NEEDS ESTIMATE MANUFACTURING COSTS DESIGN TO GOALS ACQUISITION/MANUFACTURING STRATEGY • TOTAL QUANTITIES • RATE GOALS	RESOLVE PRODUCTION RISK COMPLETE MANTECH DEVELOP PRELIMINARY MANFG PLAN PRELIMINARY PEP INDUSTRIAL BASE ISSUES PRR	FINAL MANUFACTURING PLAN EXECUTE PEP QA PLAN LOW RATE INITIAL PRODUCTION•••••••• •••••PRR	IMPLEMENT MFG PLAN CONTRACTOR SURVEILLANCE INCORPORATE GFP/GFE VE 2ND SOURCE/BREAKOUT DECISIONS	PRODUCTION OF SPARE PARTS PRODUCTION OF PIP/MODS
COST	AFFORDABILITY BOUNDS AND CEILING IDENTIFIED • DEVELOP LCC ESTIMATES OF ALTERNATIVE SOLUTIONS • COMPARE WITH AFFORDABILITY LIMITS • DETERMINE LCC IMPLICATIONS OF MAJOR SYSTEM REQUIREMENTS LCC ESTIMATE	• IDENTIFICATION OF MAJOR REQUIREMENTS IN LIGHT OF LCC IMPACTS • DEFINE LCC ESTIMATES OF ALTERNATIVES • AGAIN COMPARE WITH AFFORDABILITY LIMITS LCC ESTIMATE	• TRADE OFF PROCESS WITHIN THE SELECTED ALTERNATIVE • CONTINUOUS REFINEMENT/ UPDATE OF LCC ESTIMATE • DESIGN TO COST LCC ESTIMATE	• DESIGN TO COST LCC ESTIMATE	• EVALUATE ECP'S AND PRODUCT IMPROVEMENTS IN LIGHT OF LCC IMPACT

Figure 1 Acquisition life-cycle technical activities.

Faculty of Technical Management Department, School of Systems Acquisition Education, Defense Systems Management College, Fort Belvoir, Virginia, _Program Manager,_ January–February 1984.

1.2 Demonstration and Validation Phase

Life-cycle-cost estimates are required for the entrance into this phase that may involve prototype design, fabrication, and test. Often there is competition among contractors when funding considerations permit. This is normally the first phase in which design-to-cost targets are contractually specified. In this phase, the RFP specifies design-to-cost targets or affordability ceilings and the minimum acceptable performance and schedule constraints.

During the demonstration and validation phase, cost goals are targets against which the cost consequences of alternative design features can be measured for effectiveness. The best affordable mix of system performance and costs should be arrived at during the validation phase. The ultimate purpose of design to cost during the validation phase is to establish firm cost goals for the alternatives no later than the decision to enter full-scale engineering development.

Since this phase focuses on alternative system solutions, there is a large amount of life-cycle-cost activity. The key tasks are developing life-cycle-cost estimates of the system alternatives, comparing system scenarios with affordability limits, and challenging affordability bounds and ceilings. Trade study activities are performed including emphasis on system-level cost driver analysis and cost sensitivities. A preliminary assessment of the cost database required to support upcoming design-to-cost activity is performed.

It is necessary at this time to identify potential database areas that may be weak and to start collecting data and performing the required regression analyses. Trade studies are allocated against the system and individual end items, and the cost performance against these items is recorded and tracked.

Frequently during this phase, hardware and software demonstrations for alternatives take place. Prior life-cycle-cost estimates are refined and revalidated and more emphasis is placed on the specific requirements cost impacts. Cost goals are determined early in this phase. Early goals serve to identify cost drivers and to start outlining a program for effective cost reduction.

Design-to-cost techniques and value engineering methods are evaluated and the appropriate tasks are determined. Once the early goals are determined, the key program requirements are allocated against each end item or major subsystem.

"What-if" analysis is then performed on each requirement to determine its impact on the end items' unit production cost and life-cycle cost. As this phase nears its completion, design-to-cost goals and their documentation are finalized in preparation for full-scale engineering development. A design-to-cost profile is drawn for each end item showing its design-to-cost history and outlining the trades and analyses that prove a cost-effective design is in hand. This activity is necessary to allow the project to focus more tightly on business strategy when design-to-cost goals are submitted early in full-scale engineering development.

1.3   Full-Scale Engineering Development Phase

Formal design-to-cost goals are usually required to be submitted with proposals for this phase. These goals are then negotiated and updated or reallocated after contract award, and the formal design-to-cost program is under way. The goals are now allocated to the subsystems and disciplines and the tracking and reporting system is set into motion.

1.4   Production and Deployment Phase

It is necessary to ensure that design-to-cost goals properly reflect the production configuration. Any modification from the full-scale engineering development (FSED) prototype must be identified and the goal adjusted accordingly. It is now time to "produce to cost." Any modifications to program functions should have been made in FSED, so the focus is now on bringing the system in on schedule at cost. Design-to-cost and value engineering techniques are applied for that purpose.

The design concept is frozen in the production stage. The costs incurred in prototype fabrication provide a useful, but not conclusive, indication of the production unit costs. Trades between acquisition and life-cycle costs are still necessary; however, any trade-off decision affecting system level, configuration, performance, and life-cycle costs is likely to involve significant reorientation of the program and must be made by the DoD program manager or at higher levels.

In the production phase, the government rewards the contractor for cost performance that is better than the unit production design-to-cost target. Provisions are included in contracts to provide for measurement of actual costs and to prevent assignment of production-related costs to costs not covered by the design-to-cost target. Department of Defense Directive 4245.3 requires that production cost be rigorously controlled to the design-to-cost production unit cost goals. Factors such as engineering fixes, mission changes, and performance increases may increase costs during production. Techniques have been suggested by the government to counter such increases; these suggestions include value engineering and cost reduction oriented contractual product improvement programs.

1.5   Acquisition Simplification

The more recent DoD Directive 5000.43, *Acquisition Simplification,* reflects DoD's determination to reduce acquisition costs, expedite acquisition lead time, and field hardware of improved quality and technology. The directive became mandatory for new programs started in Fiscal Year 1987.

Streamlining considerations will be addressed in all proposal evaluations and source selections for systems acquisitions. It will be an agenda item for all DSARC reviews and incorporated into the acquisition plan for all systems. Program managers will be challenged to pursue this initiative as a management objective in the presolicitation phase, prototyping, FSED, and in production.

All solicitations will be "zero-based" insofar as specifications, standards, data, and management reporting are involved. Only first-tier specifications will be mandated; second-tier specifications, unless otherwise provided, are for guidance only. In initial development, all specifications are rigorously controlled to the design-to-cost production unit cost goals. Factors such as engineering fixes, mission changes, and performance increases may increase costs during production. Techniques have been suggested by the government to counter such increases; these suggestions include value engineering and cost-reduction-oriented contractual product improvement programs.

At the same time, the DoD has promulgated DoD Directive 4245.7, *Transition from Development to Production,* to ensure elements of program risk are identified and rectified throughout the acquisition cycle. Again producibility (i.e., cost) is a principal argument on a level with performance.

The new priority-to-cost philosophy attempts to recognize these economic and motivational realities. It recognizes that the "best" system design is not necessarily achieved by maximizing individual unit performance only, but is a function of need, performance, life-cycle cost, and quantities needed to address the threat. It recognizes that action in the engineering budget area significantly affects budgets in other areas, and that all of these tradeoffs must be made within realistic total resource constraints.

1.6 Could-Cost

The position of Undersecretary of Defense for Acquisition was first created in 1987 for someone to spearhead the drive for acquisition simplification and to be the czar of all major weapon systems procured by the DoD or its components. Recently, the newly appointed Undersecretary made the following pronouncement on the subject of "could-cost":

> Could-cost is a new approach for the DoD and its contractors aimed at substantial reduction in the cost of developing and producing weapon systems and other military products. Its implementation can be effective only through fundamental cultural changes in the way both the DoD and industry do business in equipping the military forces. These changes cut across the spectrum of the acquisition process, from the development of military requirements to the production and fielding of weapon systems. Most of these new directions require no new policy directives, no new legislation; in fact, existing directives, regulations and legislation not only permit these initiatives, they recommend them as the way to do business. The basis of could-cost is government and industry working together as a team to negotiate the elimination of non-value added effort in return for savings. This negotiation process is a two-way street in which both the government and industry give up the old, comfortable ways of doing business for the challenge of new ideas and new methods.

Could-cost means a thorough scrub of requirements and specifications at the very outset of a system's concept formulation and development. It means saying no to added capabilities, saying no to added sophistication not needed to meet essential mission requirements. This scrubbing of requirements has been done before, most notably on the D-5 missile program, but it must be extended and must include more cooperative acquisition efforts. Specifications need to take advantage of off-the-shelf and standard parts and use non-developmental acquisition wherever possible.

Could-cost means streamlining the contracting process. It means short RFPs based on performance requirements, devoid of detailed specifications, burdensome data deliverables, and "boiler-plate" language. It has been done successfully before; the lightweight fighters of the early 1970s, and the more recent transport prototype program sponsored by DARPA are examples of such innovative acquisitions.

Could-cost means drastically reducing both government and industry overhead. It means streamlined staffs, with few, if any personnel involved in non-value added activities such as public affairs, advertising, lobbying, bid preparation and marketing. It means drastic reductions in engineers charged to a program once it enters the production phase. It means reducing the number, frequency and scope of audits, and the amount of testing required.

Could-cost means tight configuration control, foregoing expensive upgrades beyond safety and reliability-driven modifications. It means minimizing engineering changes planning for which large engineering staffs are kept on the rolls. It means reducing the need for waivers and rework beyond the assembly line with the attendant need for inspection and reinspection.

Could-cost means revolutionary changes in manufacturing methods and facilities. It means the introduction of statistical process control to increase quality. It means the use of CAD/CAM techniques. It means increasing manufacturing yields through reduction in scrap and rework and through increase in productivity. It means more efficient office and plant space layout and utilization. It means being open to try new manufacturing techniques, materials and equipment.

Could-cost means stable development and production planning and implementation. It means stable funding and scheduling for both development and procurement phases of systems. It means using innovative stable contracting approaches such as multiyear procurements. It means tooling and hiring workforces for realistic and economic production rates and schedules; not "pie-in-the sky" projections made at the outset of major defense programs nor less than minimum sustaining rates in order to just get by.

Could-cost means all these things, but primarily could-cost means government and industry working together, not against each other, to give the best product at the lowest cost for the benefit of the military forces.
— Source: Undersecretary of Defense for Acquisition, U.S. Department of Defense, 1987.

2   ARMED SERVICES

The Joint Armed Services policy is that projected defense budget levels and rising costs of acquiring, operating, and supporting defense systems and equipment have made cost an essential design parameter. A list of pertinent documents of the Armed Services is given in Table 3.

TABLE 3   List of Armed Services Guides, Specifications, Standards, Policies, and Regulations

AF Regulation 800-11, *Life Cycle Cost Management*
AFCLM/AFSCM, *Repair Level Analysis*
AFLC Regulation 173-10, *AFLC Cost and Planning Factors*
AF Regulation 173-13, *Air Force Cost and Planning Factors*
AFSCFM 84-3, *Production Management*
AFLC/AFSCP 800-19, *Life Cycle Cost as a Design Parameter*
AFLCP/AFSCP 800-34, *Acquisition Logistics Management*
AFLCR 400-1, *Logistics Management Policy*
AFSC *Life Cycle Cost Implementation Techniques*
AFSC Pamphlet 800-3, *Acquisition Management: A Guide for Program Managers*
AFSC Pamphlet 800-7, *Configuration Management*
AFSCR 84-2, *Production Readiness Review*
ARA 70-64, *Design to Cost*
AR 700-127, *Integrated Logistic System*
AR 1000-1, *Basic Policies for Systems Acquisition*
DA 750-21, *Logistic Support Modeling*
DA, *Manufacturing Technology Handbook*
DAP 11-3, *Investment Cost Guide for Army Materiel Systems*
DAP 11-4, *Operating and Support Cost Guide for Army Materiel Systems*
DAP 11-5, *Standard for Presentation and Documentation of Life Cycle Cost*
DARCOM P715-4, AFSCP/AFLCP 173-5, NAVMAT P5243, *Cost/Schedule Systems Criteria Joint Implementation Guide.*
DARCOM P700-6, NAVMAT P5242, AFLCP/AFSCP 800-19, *Joint Design-to-Cost Guide*
DARCOM-P 750-16, *DARCOM Guide to Logistics Support Analysis Research and Development Cost Guide for Army Materiel Systems*
DARCOM REG 700-15, *ILS Implementation*
DOD-D-1000B, *Military Specification, Drawings, Engineering and Associate Lists*
MICOM P715-4H, *Design to Cost Handbook*
MIL-HDBK-248, *Tailoring Guide for Application of Specifications and Standards in Naval Weapons Systems Acquisitions*
MIL-HDBK-727, *Design Guidance for Producibility*
MIL-Q-9858, *Quality Program Requirements*
MIL-S-52779, *Software Quality Assurance Program Requirements*
MIL-S-83490, *Specifications, Types and Forms*
MIL-STD-480A, *Configuration Control-Engineering Changes, Deviations and Waivers*
MIL-STD-481A, *Configuration Control-Engineering Changes, Deviations and Waivers (short form)*

TABLE 3 (*Continued*)

MIL-STD-482, *Configuration Status Accounting Data Elements and Related Features*

MIL-STD-483, *Configuration Management Practices for Systems, Equipment, Munitions, and Computer Programs*

MIL-STD-490, *Specification Practices*

MIL-STD-499A, *Engineering Management*

MIL-STD-881A, *Work Breakdown Structure for Defense Materiel Items*

MIL-STD-1388-1,-2, *Logistics Support Analysis*

MIL-STD-1456, *Contractor Configuration Management Plans*

MIL-STD-1521A, *Technical Reviews and Audits for Systems, Equipments, and Computer Programs*

MIL-STD-1528, *Production Management*

MIL-STD-1567A, *Work Measurement*

MIL-STD-1662, *Equipment and Computer Programs*

MIL-STD-1679, *Weapon System Software Development*

MIL-STD-2165, *Testability Program for Electronic Systems and Equipments*

NAVGAC P-422, *Economic Analysis Handbook*

NAVMAT, *Life Cycle Cost Guide for Major Weapon Systems*

NAVMAT, *Life Cycle Cost Guide for Equipment Analysis*

SECNAV 4200.32, *Design to Cost*

TTO-ORT-037-76B-V3, *Life Cycle Costing, Joint Tactical Communication Office*

2.1 Army

The Army's basic policy is to include design-to-cost provisions in all development contracts and product improvement programs where anticipated production is expected to exceed $10 million. It is optional in smaller programs. Minimum essential performance characteristics are not to be compromised. Technically feasible alternatives are to be analyzed and cost performance trades are to be made for lowest life-cycle-cost solution. Cost goals must be validated before the start of successive phases.

Cost targets are equal in importance to performance requirements. Waivers of cost-related contractual provisions must be approved by the Director of Procurement and Production, Headquarters U.S. Army Materiel Development and Readiness Command.

2.2 Air Force

The Air Force requires that the technical performance measurement (TPM) be related to cost and schedule performance measurement. Cost, schedule, and technical performance measurements are made against common elements of the contract work-breakdown structure. The Air Force also requires a continuing system cost-effectiveness analysis be conducted to ensure that engineering decisions resulting from the review of alternatives are made only after considering the impact on system effectiveness and cost of acquisition and ownership.

2.3 Navy

The Navy has promulgated the *Joint Design-to-Cost Guide* under NAVMAT P5242 to all naval commands. Navy Material Command P5242 provides guidance for a design-to-cost effort and describes what design-to-cost goals should be established, incorporated into contracts, managed, and tracked.

3 OTHER GOVERNMENT AGENCIES

The replacement of the Defense Acquisition Regulation (DAR) by the Federal Acquisition Regulation (FAR) in 1984 has extended the emphasis on cost-consciousness from the military to other agencies in the federal government. For example, FAR Parts 7.103(F)(1), 48, and 52.248 establish design-to-cost and value engineering policies and procedures for all agencies. Table 4 lists some pertinent documents.

Nonmilitary agencies will probably evolve more specific policies and procedures as time progresses. It can be expected that the documents will initially be patterned after the military and will ultimately be tailored for the specific agency charters.

4 OFFICE OF MANAGEMENT AND BUDGET

The following is the text of OMB Circular A-131, with the effective date of February 3, 1988.

TO THE HEADS OF EXECUTIVE DEPARTMENTS AND ESTABLISH-MENTS

SUBJECT: Value Engineering

1. *Purpose*. The purpose of this Circular is to emphasize Value Engineering, as appropriate, by Federal Departments and agencies to identify and re-

TABLE 4 List of Non-military Cost-Related Documents

Federal Supply Service, *Life Cycle Costing Workbook*
HEW Publication HRP-0015880, *Life Cycle Budgeting and Costing*
NBS Publication 544, *Energy Design Economics*
OMB Circular A-76, Supplement 1, *Cost Comparison Handbook*
OMB Circular A-109, *Major System Acquisition*

duce nonessential procurement and program costs. The Circular requires agency heads to establish and improve Value Engineering programs.

2. *Background.* Value engineering in the Federal Government is a means for some Federal contractors and Government entities to change the plans, designs and specifications for Federal programs and projects. These changes are intended to lower the Government's cost for the goods and services and maintain necessary quality levels.

a. *Prior Reports.* Over the last several years, reports issued by the General Accounting Office (GAO) and many Inspectors General (IGs) have consistently concluded that wider use of Value Engineering would result in substantial savings to the Government. While some agencies have some Value Engineering programs, other agencies have not utilized Value Engineering fully. Even for agencies with established programs, the GAO and IG reports conclude that much more can and should be done to realize the benefits of Value Engineering.

b. *Identified Impediments.* The impediments that are frequently noted in these reports and that have prevented a greater use of Value Engineering include:

(1) Failure of senior management to allocate the necessary resources, both in effort and in funds, to establish and run Value Engineering programs;

(2) Absence of good criteria for selecting projects and programs for Value Engineering studies;

(3) Failure to properly perform Value Engineering studies;

(4) Inadequate attention by agency management to reviewing and implementing the recommendations made in Value Engineering studies.

c. *Other Problems.* Many of the problems noted in the GAO and IG reports are attitudinal. A common observation in many of the reports is that there are few incentives to use Value Engineering or other cost cutting techniques to save money on fully funded Federal programs and projects.

Obviously programs should be developed, critically reviewed and administered in the most cost effective manner possible. Value Engineering and other management techniques must ensure realistic project budgets and identify and remove nonessential capital and operating costs.

3. *Definitions.*

a. *Agency.* As used in this Circular, agency means any executive department, military department, government corporation, government controlled corporation or other establishment of the executive branch of the Federal government.

b. *Value Engineering.* An organized effort directed by a person trained in Value Engineering techniques to analyze the functions of systems, equipment, facilities, services and supplies for the purpose of achieving the essential functions at the lowest life cycle cost consistent with required performance and reliability, quality and safety.

c. *Value Engineering Change Proposal (VECP).* A change proposal that is submitted by a contractor under a Value Engineering incentive or program requirement clause included in a Federal contract.

d. *Value Engineering Proposal (VEP)*. A change proposal developed by employees of the Federal Government or contractor Value Engineering personnel employed by the agency to provide Value Engineering services for the contract or program.

4. *Policy*. Agencies shall establish Value Engineering programs and use Value Engineering, where appropriate, to reduce nonessential costs and improve productivity. Value engineering programs of agencies shall, at a minimum, provide for the following management and procurement practices.

a. *Management Practices*. Value Engineering programs must be tailored to the mission and organizational structure of each agency. For example, the cost and program/project size usually indicate the potential for Value Engineering. In most agencies, a relatively few programs or projects comprise the majority of costs and Value Engineering efforts should be concentrated on these programs and projects. Therefore, agencies shall:

(1) Emphasize, through training, evaluation and other programs, the potential of Value Engineering to reduce unnecessary costs.

(2) Establish a single entity within the agency to manage and monitor Value Engineering efforts, encourage the use of Value Engineering and maintain data on the program. This function shall achieve the purposes of this Circular. Value Engineering training shall be provided to the person responsible for the Value Engineering function and to other personnel responsible for developing, reviewing and analyzing Value Engineering actions.

(3) Report and update the name, address and telephone number of the person responsible for each agency's Value Engineering program to the Office of Federal Procurement Policy, Office of Management and Budget.

(4) Ensure that funds necessary for operating agency Value Engineering programs are included in annual budget requests, and provide annual summary Value Engineering program information to the Office of Management and Budget as requested.

(5) Establish criteria and guidelines to identify those programs and projects that are most appropriate for Value Engineering studies. The criteria and guidelines should recognize that the potential savings are generally greatest during the planning, design and other early phases of project/program development.

(6) Require that files be documented to explain why Value Engineering studies were not performed or required for any programs/projects meeting agency criteria.

(7) Establish guidelines to evaluate and process Value Engineering proposals.

b. *Procurement Practices*. Present procurement policies and practices for the use of Value Engineering are set forth in Parts 48 and 52 of the Federal Acquisition Regulation (FAR). Part 48 provides two basic incentive approaches for using Value Engineering. The first approach uses a Value Engineering Incentive (VEI) clause. In this approach the contractor's participation is voluntary and the contractor uses its resources to develop and submit VECPs. A contract clause provides that when a VECP is accepted any resulting savings are shared with the contractor on a preestablished—usually a percentage—basis set forth in the contract.

The second approach uses a Value Engineering Program Requirement (VEPR) clause and requires the contractor to conduct a specific Value Engineering effort within the contract, i.e., an effort to identify and submit to the Government methods for performing more economically. In this second approach, the contractor also shares in any savings resulting from the VECP, but at a lower percentage rate than under the voluntary approach. This effort generally is directed at the major cost items of a system or project.

The FAR presently permits agency heads to exempt their agencies from using Value Engineering provisions in contracts. The authority to totally exempt agencies from using Value Engineering provisions will be rescinded and the FAR will be modified to require that contracting activities include Value Engineering provisions in contracts except where exemptions are granted on a case-by-case basis or for specific classes of contracts. one time agency-wide exemptions will no longer be permitted. In addition, agency contracting activities will:

(1) Actively elicit VECPs from contractors.

(2) Promote Value Engineering through contractor meetings and the dissemination of promotional and informational literature regarding the Value Engineering provisions of contracts.

(3) Establish guidelines for processing Value Engineering Change Proposals and require that contract files list all change proposals requiring more than 45 days to accept or reject.

(4) Document all contract files to explain the rationale for accepting or rejecting Value Engineering Change Proposals.

(5) Use the Value Engineering clauses provided in the FAR for appropriate supply, service, architect–engineer and construction contracts.

(6) Use the Value Engineering program requirement clause (FAR 52.248-1 alternatives I or II) in initial production contracts for major systems programs and for contracts for research and development except where the controlling contracting officer determines and documents the file to reflect that such use is not appropriate (see Section 4 of Public Law 93-400, as amended (41 U.S.C. 403) for definitions of major systems).

5. *Sunset Review*. The policies contained in this Circular will be reviewed by the Office of Management and Budget three years from the date of issuance.

6. *Inquiries*. Further information about this Circular may be obtained by contacting the Office of Federal Procurement Policy, 726 Jackson Place, NW, Washington, DC 20503, Telephone (202) 395-6803.

James C. Miller III
Director
— Source: James C. Miller III, Office of Management and Budget, OMB
Circular A-131, February 3, 1988.

APPENDIX 4
SOLUTIONS TO NUMERICAL EXERCISES

SECTION 2.12.1 VALUE ENGINEERING IN DEFENSE

The exercise for this case study requires the projection of expenditures, or outlays, of the federal government over the next 5 years with and without the benefit of value engineering. The data in the 1988 edition of the *Statistical Abstract of the United States* are used for this solution. Outlays of the federal government for the years 1978 to 1987 are given in Table 1 and are used to project federal outlays for the years 1989 to 1983.

Linear regression, described in Section 6.6.2, is applied to derive the equation of the least-squares line fitting these data. With the use of Equations (6.9) and (6.10), the equation obtained from the data in Table 1 is

$$y = -\$12,8723.6012 + \$65.3127x \tag{1}$$

where y is the annual outlay in billions of dollars and x denotes the respective year.

Substituting the years 1989 through 1993 in Equation (1) yields the values given in Table 2 in the column titled "Without Value Engineering." The values in the column titled "With Value Engineering" assume annual savings of 20 percent. The consequence of across the board application of value engineering in the federal government could be a saving of \$1314 billion over the 5-year period.

SECTION 2.12.7 THE SUN SHINES BRIGHT

The exercise for this case study calls for the construction of trend lines (i.e., least-squares lines) for both the number of solar collector manufacturers and the amount of imported crude oil, and to predict the state of the solar

TABLE 1   Outlays of the Federal Government, Billions of Dollars

1978	458.7	1983	808.3
1979	503.5	1984	851.8
1980	590.9	1985	946.3
1981	678.2	1986	989.8
1982	745.7	1987	1015.6

Source: U.S. Bureau of the Census, *Statistical Abstract of the United States: 1988.*

collector industry in the year 2000. First, Equations (6.9) and (6.10) are applied to the data in Table 2.22, yielding the following equation of the least-squares line for the data:

$$y = 603.8016 - 0.1978x \tag{2}$$

where y is the number of manufacturers in business and x denotes the respective year. Plotting Equation (2) yields one of the trend lines called for in the exercise.

Substituting the value of 2000 for x in Equation (2) yields approximately 208 as the number of manufacturers who will be in business in the year 2000.

This number can be tested by the correlation between the number of manufacturers in business and the amount of crude oil imported annually. First, Equations (6.9) and (6.10) are applied to the data in Table 2.23 and yield the following equation of the least-squares line fitting these data:

$$y = 217616.6286 - 107.6132x \tag{3}$$

where y is the amount of crude oil imported annually in thousands of barrels per day and x denotes the respective year. Plotting Equation (3) yields the other trend line called for in the exercise.

TABLE 2   Projected Outlays of the Federal Government (Billions of Dollars)

Year	Without Value Engineering	With Value Engineering
1989	1183.4	946.7
1990	1248.7	999.0
1991	1314.0	1051.2
1992	1379.3	1103.4
1993	1444.6	1155.7
	6570.0	5256.0

Substituting the value of 2000 for x in Equation (3) yields approximately 2390 thousand barrels per day as the amount of crude oil that will be imported in the year 2000.

Next, Equations (6.9) and (6.10) are applied to the data in both Tables 2.22 and 2.23, this time letting x equal the amount of crude oil imported annually and y, the number of manufacturers in business. The resultant equation of the least-squares line fitting the data is:

$$y = -28.7944 + 0.0534x \qquad (4)$$

Substituting the value of 2390 for x in Equation (4) yields $y = 98.8316$; that is, approximately 99 manufacturers will be in business in the year 2000 as opposed to the 208 derived from Equation (1).

Reconciliation of the difference is attempted by looking at the coefficient of correlation or rather its square, the coefficient of determination r^2, of the amount of crude oil imported annually and the number of manufacturers in business. This is calculated by applying Equation (6.14) to the data in Tables 2.22 and 2.33, yielding $r^2 = .4641$. The interpretation of this value is that about 46 percent of the variability of the number of manufacturers in business annually is a function of the amount of crude oil imported. Therefore, it might be expected that in the year 2000, the number could be 99/.4641, or approximately 213, which is closer to the number obtained with Equation (1) than with Equation (4).

SECTION 2.12.8 CONCEPT OF PROPORTIONALITY

The exercise for this case study calls for the preparation a profile of outlays by the customer for the years 1979 to 1986 and, then, the determination of which of two procurement approaches would have been less costly to the customer in the long run. The profiles of outlays for the two approaches are given in Tables 3 and 4. The average unit cost in both cases is $1.768 million in 1978 dollars.

TABLE 3   Profile of Outlays under Original Schedule

Year	Quantity	Cost ($) without EPA	Cost ($) with EPA
1979	24	42,432,000	46,283,551
1980	24	42,432,000	51,887,777
1981	24	42,432,000	56,972,693
1982	24	42,432,000	60,326,573
1983	24	42,432,000	61,971,057
			277,441,651

TABLE 4   Profile of Outlays under Revised Schedule

Year	Quantity	Cost ($) without EPA	Cost ($) with EPA
1979	12	21,216,000	23,141,774
1980	12	21,216,000	25,943,887
1981	12	21,216,000	28,486,345
1982	21	37,128,035	52,785,803
1983	21	37,128,035	54,224,727
1984	21	37,128,035	55,493,253
1985	21	37,128,035	56,591,379
			296,667,168

The cost with economic price adjustment (EPA) is derived from multiplying the cost without EPA by the ratio of the producer price index (PPI) for machinery and equipment, given in Table 2.25, for the respective year to the PPI for 1978, which is the base year for the exercise. For the years 1979 to 1985, these ratios are 213.9/196.1, 239.8/196.1, 263.3/196.1, 278.8/196.1, 286.4/196.1, 293.1/196.1, and 298.9/196.1.

Next, Equation (6.26) is applied to calculate the present value in base year 1978 of the annual outlays in Tables 3 and 4. A discount rate of 10 percent compounded annually (see Table 6.15) is assumed. The results of the calculations are given in Table 5.

It would appear from Tables 3 and 4 that the revised schedule approach is $296,667,168 minus $277,441,651, or $19,225,517 more costly than the original schedule approach. However, from the viewpoint of the time value of money as given in Table 5, the original schedule approach is $207,445,439 minus $193,971,511, or $13,473,928 more costly than the revised schedule approach, and the latter approach may be justifiable on a financial basis.

TABLE 5   Present-Value ($) Calculations for Base Year 1978

Year	Original Schedule	Revised Schedule
1979	42,075,913	21,037,955
	42,882,653	21,444,325
	42,804,153	21,402,075
	41,203,652	36,053,231
	38,479,068	33,669,217
	—	31,324,27
	—	29,040,4
	207,445,439	193,97

TABLE 6 Percent Change in Annual Producer Price Indexes

1981	9.2	1984	2.1
1982	4.0	1985	0.9
1983	1.6	1986	−1.4

SECTION 3.14.1 MANUFACTURING TO COMPETE

The exercise for this case study requires the comparison of the average annual percentage increase in operating income per employee for the five companies given in Table 3.24 to the average percent change in the annual producer price indexes (PPIs) for the years 1981 through 1986. The latter data are obtained from the 1988 edition of the *Statistical Abstract of the United States* and are given in Table 6.

The average percentage increase in operating income per employee given in Table 3.24 is 26.62 percent. The average percent change in PPIs given in Table 6 is 2.73 percent.

In essence, the operating efficiency for the five cited companies has increased almost an order of magnitude more than the increase in the PPI over the years 1981 to 1986. It is reasonable to expect the trend for efficiency increasing at a greater rate than the increase in PPI to continue over the next decade.

SECTION 3.14.2 ORGANIZING FOR PROFIT

The exercise for this case study requires an estimate of the reduction in the cost of goods sold that resulted from the reduction in the procurement and material handling labor. The ratio of the number of boxes in Figures 3.16 and 3.17, which describe the before-and-after reorganization cycle in this partic-ular company, is used as the measure of labor reduction.

There are 12 boxes in Figure 3.16 and 8 boxes in Figure 3.17. Therefore, labor reduction factor is 12/8, or 1.5. The original cost of goods sold was million, of which 60 percent was expended on labor for procurement handling, or $270 million. The new labor expenditure is $270 mil-or $180 million, and represents a saving of $90 million to the

.5 CONFIGURATIONAL FAUX PAS

's case study requires the application of tim determine the loss of leverage resulti

TABLE 4   Profile of Outlays under Revised Schedule

Year	Quantity	Cost ($) without EPA	Cost ($) with EPA
1979	12	21,216,000	23,141,774
1980	12	21,216,000	25,943,887
1981	12	21,216,000	28,486,345
1982	21	37,128,035	52,785,803
1983	21	37,128,035	54,224,727
1984	21	37,128,035	55,493,253
1985	21	37,128,035	56,591,379
			296,667,168

The cost with economic price adjustment (EPA) is derived from multiplying the cost without EPA by the ratio of the producer price index (PPI) for machinery and equipment, given in Table 2.25, for the respective year to the PPI for 1978, which is the base year for the exercise. For the years 1979 to 1985, these ratios are 213.9/196.1, 239.8/196.1, 263.3/196.1, 278.8/196.1, 286.4/196.1, 293.1/196.1, and 298.9/196.1.

Next, Equation (6.26) is applied to calculate the present value in base year 1978 of the annual outlays in Tables 3 and 4. A discount rate of 10 percent compounded annually (see Table 6.15) is assumed. The results of the calculations are given in Table 5.

It would appear from Tables 3 and 4 that the revised schedule approach is $296,667,168 minus $277,441,651, or $19,225,517 more costly than the original schedule approach. However, from the viewpoint of the time value of money as given in Table 5, the original schedule approach is $207,445,439 minus $193,971,511, or $13,473,928 more costly than the revised schedule approach, and the latter approach may be justifiable on a financial basis.

TABLE 5   Present-Value ($) Calculations for Base Year 1978

Year	Original Schedule	Revised Schedule
1979	42,075,913	21,037,955
1980	42,882,653	21,444,325
1981	42,804,153	21,402,075
1982	41,203,652	36,053,231
1983	38,479,068	33,669,217
1984	—	31,324,276
1985	—	29,040,432
	207,445,439	193,971,511

TABLE 6   Percent Change in Annual Producer Price Indexes

1981	9.2	1984	2.1
1982	4.0	1985	0.9
1983	1.6	1986	−1.4

SECTION 3.14.1   MANUFACTURING TO COMPETE

The exercise for this case study requires the comparison of the average annual percentage increase in operating income per employee for the five companies given in Table 3.24 to the average percent change in the annual producer price indexes (PPIs) for the years 1981 through 1986. The latter data are obtained from the 1988 edition of the *Statistical Abstract of the United States* and are given in Table 6.

The average percentage increase in operating income per employee given in Table 3.24 is 26.62 percent. The average percent change in PPIs given in Table 6 is 2.73 percent.

In essence, the operating efficiency for the five cited companies has increased almost an order of magnitude more than the increase in the PPI over the years 1981 to 1986. It is reasonable to expect the trend for efficiency increasing at a greater rate than the increase in PPI to continue over the next decade.

SECTION 3.14.2   ORGANIZING FOR PROFIT

The exercise for this case study requires an estimate of the reduction in the cost of goods sold that resulted from the reduction in the procurement and material handling labor. The ratio of the number of boxes in Figures 3.16 and 3.17, which describe the before-and-after reorganization cycle in this particular company, is used as the measure of labor reduction.

There are 12 boxes in Figure 3.16 and 8 boxes in Figure 3.17. Therefore, the labor reduction factor is 12/8, or 1.5. The original cost of goods sold was $450 million, of which 60 percent was expended on labor for procurement material handling, or $270 million. The new labor expenditure is $270 million/1.5, or $180 million, and represents a saving of $90 million to the company.

SECTION 3.14.5   CONFIGURATIONAL FAUX PAS

The exercise for this case study requires the application of time value of money relationships to determine the loss of leverage resulting from inade-

TABLE 7 Percent Change in Annual Producer Price Indexes

1977	6.5	1981	9.2
1978	7.8	1982	4.0
1979	11.1	1983	1.6
1980	13.5		

quate emphasis on configuration control. It is given that the original production cost estimate prepared in 1976 was $294 million in then-year dollars, and that the estimate had grown to $594 million in 1983 dollars 7 years later. The data in Table 7, obtained from the 1988 edition of the *Statistical Abstract of the United States,* are used to convert the later estimate to 1976 dollars.

First the annual percent changes in the PPI are compounded as follows:

$$(1.065)(1.078)(1.111)(1.135)(1.092)(1.04)(1.016) = 1.6704 \qquad (5)$$

The later production cost estimate expressed in 1976 dollars is therefore $594,000,000/1.6704, or $355,603,448. The difference between the later and the original estimates is $355,603,448 minus $294,000,000, or $61,603,448. Twenty-five percent of this difference is attributed to inadequate configuration control and is $15,400,862 in 1976 dollars.

It is also given in the exercise that over the 7-year period an additional expenditure of $5 million would have provided sufficiently adequate configuration management to have prevented the aforementioned expenditure of $15,400,862. The sum of $5 million divided by 7 yields a uniform series of annual payments of $714,286 each.

Next, Equation (6.34) is applied for the present value (i.e., in 1976) of a uniform series of seven annual payments of $714,286 at a discount rate of 10 percent compounded annually, yielding a present value of $3,477,430. The loss in leverage resulting from inadequate emphasis on configuration control is thus $15,400,862/3,477,430, or 4.4288 : 1.

SECTION 4.12.5 ALL FOR ONE AND ONE FOR ALL

The exercise for this case study requires trades among the various casting processes to replace forging as the means for fabricating components for 500 navigation pods and the calculation of the attendant saving.

The baseline average unit structural cost is $64,000. The total structural cost for 500 navigation pods is 500 times $64,000, or 32 million.

Each pod will use eight castings, replacing four forgings with an average unit recurring cost of $2000. Thus, the average unit cost of each casting should be less than four times $2000, or $8000 in quantities of 500. Similarly, the average unit structural cost of each navigation pod should be eight times $8000, or $64,000 in quantities of 500.

Two assumptions are needed to complete this exercise. First, it is assumed that the castings will be made of nonferrous metal alloys. On this basis, permanent mold casting would be the preferred approach for the quantity involved (see Table 4.7).

Next, it is assumed that the relative cost relationships in Figure 4.19 are applicable to these forgings and their replacement castings. The illustration shows that the ratio of the relative cost of permanent mold castings to the relative cost of forgings in quantities of 500 is about 1.2:3.4, or about 0.35:1.

This ratio is applied to the baseline average unit structural cost and multiplied by 500 as follows:

$$(0.35)(\$64,000)(500) = \$11.2 \text{ million} \tag{6}$$

This cost from using castings represents a saving of $20.8 million from the baseline cost of 32 million from the use of forgings.

SECTION 4.12.7   HOPE SPRINGS ETERNALLY

The exercise for this case study requires the calculation of the sample mean and standard deviation for the data given in Table 4.49, the construction of the steel coil tolerance centering distribution similar to the one shown in Figure 4.28, and the designation of the applicable process control state in accordance with the criteria given in Table 4.23.

An intermediate step is the preparation of a frequency table as given in Table 8. Next, the sample mean of the data $\bar{X}$ and the standard deviation are computed to be

$$\bar{X} = 52.62 \tag{7}$$

$$s = 4.84 \tag{8}$$

Next, the tolerance centering distribution for the steel coils is constructed as shown in Figure 1. It can be seen that the lot distribution mean falls within

TABLE 8   Frequency Table

Cell Interval	Frequency	Cell Interval	Frequency
41–42	2	51–52	8
43–44	1	53–54	9
45–46	2	55–56	5
47–48	4	57–58	4
49–50	7	59–60	8

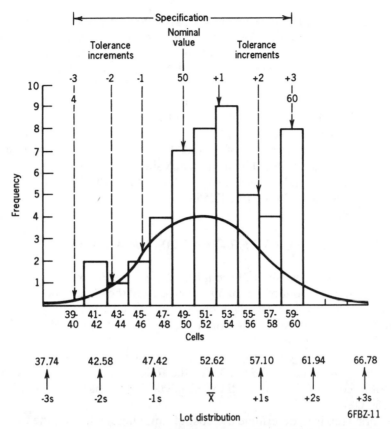

Figure 1   Steel coils tolerance centering distribution (Reprinted by permission of the Martin Marietta Corporation. From Jack V. Michaels, *Tolerance Centering: The Quality Control Alternative,* Proceedings of the 1988 International Conference, The Society of American Value Engineers.)

the nominal value and the plus 1 tolerance increment value of the specification; however, the ±3-sigma values of the distribution fall beyond the ±3 tolerance increment values. Since no out-of-specification items were found by inspection, Process Control State III is designated.

SECTION 5.12.1   BEST BUT NOT FINAL

The exercise for this case study requires the repeated application of time value of money relationships to determine the present value of the additional cost imposed by a 12-month delay in the successful launch of a particular missile. Three successive prior failures were experienced at 3-month intervals. The additional costs are due to the range days consumed at each failure and additional administration by the customer and the contractor.

Five additional range days at a cost of $100,000 per day were consumed at each of the three failures for a per-failure cost of $100,000 times 5, or $500,000. Equation (6.34) is applied to determine the present value of a uniform series of three payments of $500,000, at a discount rate of 10 percent compounded annually, yielding a present value of $1,243,450.

The additional administrative costs to the customer and contractor are $50,000 and $250,000, or 300,000 per month.

Again, Equation (6.43) is applied to determine the present value of a uniform series of 12 payments of $300,000, at a discount rate of 10 percent compounded annually, yielding a present value of $2,044,108. The present value of the total additional cost of the 12-month delay is therefore $1,243,450 + $2,044,108, or $3,287,558.

SECTION 5.12.2 LEADER–FOLLOWER AT WORK

The exercise for this case study requires the estimation of the average unit cost of the first buy (out of six) of 5000 rounds and the estimation of what the six buys of 30,000 rounds might have cost the customer under a prime-subcontractor relationship rather than one of leader–follower if a 90 percent learning curve were applicable.

The average unit costs for buy 6 are given as $26,000 for the leader producing 3750 rounds and $27,000 for the follower producing 1250 rounds. The total cost of buy 6 is thus $26,000(3750) plus $27,000(1250), or $131,250,000.

The first step is to determine the cost of unit number 1 given the total cost of the buy of the rounds between two specific cumulative unit quantities; in this exercise, numbers 25,001 and 30,000. The cost of unit number 1 is found by dividing the total cost of buy 6 (i.e., $131,250,000) by the difference between the cumulative average factor at the end of the buy (i.e., at number 30,000) and the cumulative average factor at the round just prior to the first number in the buy (i.e., 25,000).

Cumulative average factors are measures of cost improvement as a function of quantity and are available from a number of sources such as U.S.

TABLE 9   Cumulative Average Factors for 90 Percent Learning Curve

Quantity	Cumulative Average Factor
5,000	1615.022
10,000	2907.449
15,000	4100.717
20,000	5233.831
25,000	6324.831
30,000	7381.721

Army Missile Command, *Experience Curve Tables,* Defense Documentation Center AD-612803 and AD-612804, 1962. Table 9 gives values of cumulative total factors needed for this exercise.

The calculations proceed as follows:

Cumulative average factor at round 30,000:   7381.721
Less: Cumulative average factor at round 25,000:   6324.218

Cumulative average factor difference: 1057.503
Divide Buy 6 cost by cumulative average factor difference:
$$\frac{\$131,250,000}{1057.503} = \$124,113$$
∴ First round cost = $124,113

The next step is to determine the cumulative average cost per round for the six buys given the cost of the first round. The cumulative average unit cost, or simply, average unit cost is found by multiplying the cost of round 1 by the cumulative average factor at round 30,000, yielding the total of the 30,000 rounds with a 90 percent learning curve, and by dividing the total cost by 30,000 for the average unit cost, as follows:

$$\frac{\$124,113(7381.721)}{30,000} = \$30,539 \tag{9}$$

It can be seen that the average unit cost is more than 10 percent greater without the pressure of leader–follower.

SECTION 5.12.5 COMPETITIVE BALANCE

The exercise for this case study requires the calculation of the sample mean and standard deviation for the two sets of data in Table 4.14 and, then, modification of these data so as to reduce the relative inconsistency between the two in terms of the ratio of their respective mean and standard deviation.

First, the sample mean $\bar{X}$ and standard deviation s of the saving percentage data are calculated as $\bar{X} = 10.8125$ and $s = 19.3988$. The ratio of $\bar{X}$ to s is 10.8125/16.7348, or 0.6461.

Next, the sample mean $\bar{X}$ and standard deviation s of saving \$ million data are calculated as $\bar{X} = 19.3988$ and $s = 39.2888$. The ratio of $\bar{X}$ to s is 19.3988/39.2888, or 0.49375, indicating significantly more dispersion than in the other set of data.

Negative values are eliminated from Table 5.14 in an attempt to reduce the inconsistency. The resultant changes in the saving percentage data are $\bar{X} = 18.0818$ and $s = 15.0258$, for a ratio of 1.2034. The resultant changes in the saving \$ million data are $\bar{X} = 37.1317$ and $s = 34.9040$, for a ratio of 1.0638.

The dispersion in both sets of data and the relative inconsistency between the two sets of data have been reduced appreciably.

SECTION 6.10.1   EROSION OF RESOURCES

The exercise for this case study requires the application both of producer price indexes (PPI) and of the learning-curve phenomenon. The PPI is used to assess how much of the cost growth in a certain production budget is due to inflation and how much to escalation. The learning curve is used to explore alternative quantities that could be produced.

The production budget estimate of $294 million in 1976 dollars grew to $594 million in 1983 dollars for a quantity of 120 systems. The compounded annual percent changes in the PPI from 1976 through 1983 serve as the measure of cost growth due to inflation. The PPI values in Table 10 are from the 1988 edition of the *Statistical Abstract of the United States* and are compounded as follows:

$$(1.044)(1.065)(1.078)(1.111)(1.135)(1.092)(1.04)(1.016) = 1.7439 \quad (10)$$

The original production budget converted from 1976 dollars to 1983 dollars is $294 million (1.7439), or $512.7 million, and can be attributed to inflation. The balance of $594 million minus $512.7 million, or $81.3 million, is due to escalation.

The average unit cost of 120 systems with a total cost of $512.7 million is $512.7 million/120, or $4.2725 million. Little learning, that is, a 99 percent learning curve, is the basis for the average unit cost of $4.2725 million. The question now is how many systems could be procured with a total cost of $512.7 million were a 90 percent learning curve assumed.

The solution requires the use of the cumulative average factor for a 90 percent learning curve in a fashion that is somewhat similar to the solution of the exercise in Section 5.12.2. The problem is that the quantity that is used to look up the value of the cumulative average factor is unknown, although it is known that it is less than 120.

Therefore, a trial-and-error approach is followed after the cost of the first system is determined with a learning curve of 90 percent. This is done by

TABLE 10   Percent Change in Annual Producer Price Indexes

1976	4.4	1980	13.5
1977	6.5	1981	9.2
1978	7.8	1982	4.0
1979	11.1	1983	1.6

dividing the total cost by the cumulative average factor at the quantity of 120 and a learning curve of 90 percent as follows:

$$\frac{\$594 \text{ million}}{67.925} = \$8.7449 \text{ million} \tag{11}$$

The challenge now is to determine the next smaller quantity whose respective cumulative average factor when multiplied by $8.7448 million most closely equals the total cost of $512.7 million. This happens at a quantity of 101 whose respective cumulative average factor is 58.637 for

$$(58.637)\$8.7448 \text{ million} = \$512.7747 \text{ million} \tag{12}$$

SECTION 6.10.2   ANTILEARNING PHENOMENON

The exercise for this case study requires the application of Equations (6.45), (6.46), and (6.49) to determine the loss of learning resulting from a prolonged labor strike. Prior to the strike, the average unit cost of a particular model was perceived to be $2200 when produced in a continuous run of 1000 units on a learning curve of 85 percent. Production was resumed after the strike, but the actual cost of the one-hundredth unit produced was discerned to be $4250.

It is first necessary to derive the first unit cost under the baseline condition of an average unit cost of $2200 for a quantity of 1000 and a learning curve of 85 percent. Equation (6.49) is applied, yielding a first unit cost of $8510.

Next, Equation (6.45) is applied to derive the slope b of the learning curve that provides the cost improvement $8510 for the first unit cost to $4250 for the one-hundredth unit. A value of $b = -.1520$ is obtained.

Then, Equation (6.46) is applied with $b = -.1520$, yielding a learning curve value of 0.90, or 90 percent. The loss of learning that resulted from the strike is therefore 90 percent minus 85 percent, or 5 percent. It should be noted this seemingly small percentage change increased cost significantly.

SECTION 6.10.3   ENVIRONMENTAL PROTECTION

The exercise for this case study requires the repeated application of Equation (6.22) to the data shown in Figure 6.21 to conclude whether to invest in more sensitive pollution detection equipment.

The equation is first applied to the data under the initial conditions, yielding $P = .66$ as the probability that a factory failing the test actually emits excessive pollutants. The equation is then applied to the data under proposed conditions, yielding $P = .66$ as the probability that a factory failing the test actually emits excessive pollutants.

The same answers result from both applications of Equation (6.22). The conclusion should be not to invest in more sensitive devices.

SECTION 6.10.4   DEEP IN SPACE, DEEPER IN DEBT

The exercise for this case study requires the application of Equations (6.8), (6.9), and (6.10) to estimate the expected cost for the average increase in program duration and then the application of Equation (6.1) to derive the 95 percent confidence limits, or interval, for the expected cost. Because of the small sample size, the student's t statistic is used in Equation (6.1) rather than the normal z statistic.

First, the data given in Table 6.21 are converted to the format given in Table 11 to illuminate the magnitude of the increases in program duration and cost. Then, Equations (6.8) to (6.10) are applied to these data yielding the following equation of the least-squares line fitting the data:

$$y = \$75 + \$73x \tag{13}$$

where y denotes the increased cost in millions of dollars and x, the associated increased time.

The average value of the increased times given in Table 11 is $(7 + 7 + 2)/3$, or 5.3333. Substituting 5.3333 for x in Equation (13) yields:

$$y = [\$75 + \$73(5.3333)]\text{million} = \$464.3309 \text{ million} \tag{14}$$

Next, Equation (6.1) is applied using the t statistic to derive the confidence interval CI about the expected increased cost of \$464.33 million as follows:

$$CI = \frac{\$464.3309 \pm \$(4.3030)(423.1989)}{\sqrt{3}} \text{ million} \tag{15}$$

$$= -\$587.0382 \text{ million to } +\$1515.70 \text{ million}$$

TABLE 11   Increased Cost as a Function of Increased Time

Increased Time (Years)	Increased Cost (Millions $)
7	953
7	219
2	221

The value of 4.3030 in Equation (15) is the t statistic for $n - 1$, or 2 degrees of freedom, and for the area under the curve of .95. The value 423.1989 is the sample standard deviation for cost, and the value 3 is the sample size n for cost.

The answers to the Equation (15), which range from a negative value of $587.0382 million to a positive value of $1515.70 million, are measures of the reliability of any conclusion based on the limited data available. It can be stated, however, that the average delay in the aforementioned three programs was 5.3333 years, and also stated with 95 percent confidence that a delay of 5.3333 years in a comparable program could cost up to $1515.70 million more.

SECTION 6.10.5   MONEY IS POWER

The exercise for this case study requires the calculation of the internal rate of return (IRR) for acquiring equipment and the comparison of the IRR to investing in bonds. The approach in Section 6.7.3 is followed.

It is stated that an investment of $725 million in new equipment would reduce annual operating cost by $50 million over the 25-year life of the equipment, whereas investing the money in bonds would yield annual payments of 7.5 percent, or $54.375 million. This statement, however, does not consider the time value of money, which is a consideration in the calculation of the IRR.

Trial and error is used in calculating IRR; the approach is to equate the annual benefit (i.e., saving of $50 million) and the equivalent annual cost (i.e., amortization of $725 million. The latter is derived by the expression for the present values of a uniform series of payments given by Equation (6.3).

The task is simplified, however, since the interest lies in knowing only whether the IRR is greater or less than 7.5 percent. The amount of the future series of payments is calculated as follows:

$$\frac{\$725 \text{ million}(0.075)(1.075)^{25}}{(1.075)^{25} - 1} = \$65.04 \text{ million} \tag{16}$$

The IRR of investing in new equipment would need to be less than 7.5 percent for the answer to Equation (16) to be $50 million. This indicates that the utility did not err in its judgment.

INDEX